Sadlier

We Believe™

Jesus Shares God's Life

WITH PROJECT DISCIPLE

Pray
Learn
Celebrate
Share
Choose
Live

Parish Edition Catechist Guide
Grade Two

Sadlier

Nihil Obstat
Monsignor Michael F. Hull, S.T.D.
Censor Librorum

Imprimatur
✠ Most Reverend Dennis J. Sullivan, D.D.
Vicar General of the Archdiocese of New York
January 27, 2010

The *Nihil Obstat* and *Imprimatur* are official declaration that these books are free of doctrinal or moral error. No implications contained therein that those who have granted the *Nihil Obstat* and *Imprimatur* agree with the content, opinion or statements expressed.

The Subcommittee on the Catechism, United States Conference of Catholic Bishops, has found the doctrinal content of this manual, copyright 2011, to be in conformity with the *Catechism of the Catholic Church*.

Printed in the United States of America.

S® is a registered trademark of William H. Sadlier, Inc.
WeBelieve™ is a registered trademark of William H. Sadlier, Inc.

William H. Sadlier, Inc.
9 Pine Street
New York, NY 10005-1002

ISBN: 978-0-8215-6412-7
123456789 WEBC 14 13 12 11 10

Sadlier

WE BELIEVE Drawn from the wisdom of the community, this program was developed by nationally recognized experts in catechesis, curriculum, and child development. These teachers of the faith and practitioners helped to frame these age-appropriate and appealing lessons. In addition, a team including respected catechetical, liturgical, pastoral, and theological experts shared their insights and inspired the development of the program.

Catechetical and Liturgical Consultants

Dr. Gerard F. Baumbach
Director, Center for Catechetical Initiatives
Concurrent Professor of Theology
University of Notre Dame
Notre Dame, Indiana

Carole M. Eipers, D.Min.
Vice President, Executive Director of Catechetics
William H. Sadlier, Inc.

Patricia Andrews
Director of Religious Education
Our Lady of Lourdes Church
Slidell, LA

Reverend Monsignor John F. Barry, P.A.
Pastor, American Martyrs Parish
Manhattan Beach, CA

Sister Maureen Shaughnessy, SC
Sisters of Charity of Saint Elizabeth
Convent Station, NJ

Mary Jo Tully
Chancellor, Archdiocese of Portland

Reverend Monsignor John M. Unger
Deputy Superintendent for Catechesis and Evangelization
Archdiocese of St. Louis

Curriculum and Child Development Consultants

Brother Robert R. Bimonte, FSC
Executive Director
NCEA Department of Elementary Schools

Sr. Carol Cimino, SSJ, Ed.D.
National Consultant
William H. Sadlier, Inc.

Gini Shimabukuro, Ed.D.
Associate Professor
Catholic Educational Leadership Program
School of Education, University of San Francisco

Catholic Social Teaching Consultants

John Carr
Executive Director
Director of Justice, Peace, and Human Development
United States Conference of Catholic Bishops
Washington, D.C.

Joan Rosenhauer
Associate Director
Department of Justice, Peace, and Human Development
United States Conference of Catholic Bishops
Washington, D.C.

Mariology Consultant

Sister M. Jean Frisk, ISSM, S.T.L.
International Marian Research Institute
Dayton, OH

Inculturation Consultants

Allan Figueroa Deck, S.J., Ph.D., S.T.D.
Executive Director
Secretariat of Cultural Diversity in the Church
United States Conference of Catholic Bishops
Washington, D.C.

Kirk P. Gaddy, Ed.D.
Educational Consultant
Baltimore, MD

Reverend Nguyễn Việt Hưng
Vietnamese Catechetical Committee

Scriptural Consultant

Reverend Donald Senior, CP, Ph.D., S.T.D.
Member, Pontifical Biblical Commission
President, The Catholic Theological Union
Chicago, IL

Theological Consultants

Most Reverend Edward K. Braxton, Ph.D., S.T.D.
Official Theological Consultant
Bishop of Belleville

Norman F. Josaitis, S.T.D.
Theological Consultant

Reverend Joseph A. Komonchak, Ph.D.
Professor, School of Theology and Religious Studies
The Catholic University of America

Most Reverend Richard J. Malone, Th.D.
Bishop of Portland, ME

Sister Maureen Sullivan, OP, Ph.D.
Associate Professor
St. Anselm College, Manchester, NH

Media/Technology Consultants

Sister Judith Dieterle, SSL
Past President, National Association of
Catechetical Media Professionals

Sister Jane Keegan, RDC
Technology Consultant

Educational Advisors

Grade K Noelle Deinken, Thousand Oaks, CA
Bernadette Miller, Wantagh, NY

Grade 1 Gerry Mayes, Vero Beach, FL
Nancy McGuirk, Staten Island, NY

Grade 2 Joan Fraher, Altamonte Springs, FL
Dr. Jeannette Holmes, Stockton, CA

Grade 3 Robin Keough, Boston, MA
Mary Olson, Buffalo Grove, IL

Grade 4 Michaele Durant, San Diego, CA
Sarah Pollard, Covington, KY

Grade 5 Rose Heinrichs, Grosse Pointe, MI
Anne Kreitsch, Howard Beach, NY

Grade 6 Barbara Connors, Seekonk, MA
Sue MacPherson, Ballwin, MO

Contents

UNIT 1 Jesus Christ Is With Us Always 17

1 Jesus Is the Son of God

• God the Father sent his Son, Jesus, to be with us. • Jesus is human like us. • Jesus did things only God can do. • Jesus, the Son of God, taught us about God the Father and God the Holy Spirit.

Matthew 8:14–15

As Catholics . . . . Parables

PROJECT DISCIPLE *featuring* The Sign of the Cross

Take Home Respecting all people

Chapter Test

2 Jesus Christ Gives Us the Church

• Jesus gathered many followers to be his disciples. • Jesus died and rose to new life. • Jesus promised to send the Holy Spirit. • The Holy Spirit helps the Church to grow.

Matthew 4:18–22; 28:1–5;
Acts of the Apostles 2:1–4

As Catholics . . . . .Celebrating the Resurrection

PROJECT DISCIPLE *featuring* Disciple Pledge

Take Home Talking about Apostles and disciples

Chapter Test

3 We Celebrate God's Love

• We Belong to the Catholic Church. • Catholics celebrate God's love by praying and worshiping. • Our Church celebrates with seven special signs called sacraments. • Jesus is present with us in the sacraments.

Psalm 100:1–5

As Catholics . . . . Our Parish

PROJECT DISCIPLE *featuring* The Seven Sacraments

Take Home Sharing ways to worship God

Chapter Test

4 We Celebrate Baptism

• At Baptism we become children of God and members of the Church. • At Baptism we receive grace, a share in God's life. • We celebrate the Sacrament of Baptism with special words and actions. • We can show that we are children of God by what we say and do.

Rite of Baptism

As Catholics . . . . Godparents

PROJECT DISCIPLE *featuring* Welcoming Church Members

Take Home Talking about family Baptisms

Chapter Test

5 We Celebrate Confirmation

• We celebrate the Gift of the Holy Spirit in the Sacrament of Confirmation. • Confirmation seals us with the Gift of the Holy Spirit and strengthens us. • We celebrate the Sacrament of Confirmation with special words and actions. • The Holy Spirit helps baptized Catholics and confirmed Catholics.

Rite of Confirmation

As Catholics . . . . Sacred Chrism

PROJECT DISCIPLE *featuring* The Holy Spirit as Helper

Take Home Working to spread the Gospel

Chapter Test

SEASONAL CHAPTERS

6 The Church Year

• The Church year helps us to follow Jesus.

Mark 2:14

7 Ordinary Time

• In Ordinary Time we celebrate Jesus Christ and learn to follow him.

Psalm 145:2; Matthew 6:9; 19:14

Unit 1 Jesus Christ Is With Us Always

Unit 2 Jesus Calls Us to Penance and Reconciliation

FAITH STATEMENTS FOR EACH CHAPTER

1 God the Father sent his Son, Jesus, to be with us. • Jesus is human like us. • Jesus did things only God can do. • Jesus, the Son of God, taught us about God the Father and God the Holy Spirit.

2 Jesus gathered many followers to be his disciples. • Jesus died and rose to new life. • Jesus promised to send the Holy Spirit. • The Holy Spirit helps the Church to grow.

3 We belong to the Catholic Church. • Catholics celebrate God's love by praying and worshiping. • Our Church celebrates with seven special signs called sacraments. • Jesus is present with us in the sacraments.

4 At Baptism we become children of God and members of the Church. • At Baptism we receive grace, a share in God's life. • We celebrate the Sacrament of Baptism with special words and actions. • We can show that we are children of God by what we say and do.

5 We celebrate the Gift of the Holy Spirit in the Sacrament of Confirmation. • Confirmation seals us with the Gift of the Holy Spirit and strengthens us. • We celebrate the Sacrament of Confirmation with special words and actions. • The Holy Spirit helps baptized Catholics and confirmed Catholics.

6 The Church year helps us to follow Jesus.

7 In Ordinary Time, we celebrate Jesus Christ and learn to follow him.

8 The Bible is the book of God's Word. • The Old Testament is the first part of the Bible. • The New Testament is the second part of the Bible. • Jesus wants us to listen to his teachings.

9 Jesus taught us the Great Commandment. • The Ten Commandments help us to live as God's children. • God wants us to show him our love and respect. • God wants us to show that we love others as we love ourselves.

10 Jesus wants us to follow the commandments. • God gives each person free will. • Friendship with God is hurt by sin. • Jesus taught us about God's forgiveness.

11 Jesus invites us to celebrate God's forgiveness. • Jesus shares God's forgiveness and peace in the Sacrament of Penance and Reconciliation. • We examine our conscience. • We tell God we are sorry for our sins.

12 We ask for God's forgiveness in the Sacrament of Penance and Reconciliation. • We celebrate God's forgiveness in the Sacrament of Penance. • We celebrate the Sacrament of Penance with our parish community. • Jesus wants us to forgive others.

13 Advent is a season of waiting and preparing.

14 Christmas is a season to give glory to God.

CATECHISM OF THE CATHOLIC CHURCH

Paragraphs: 422, 470, 548, 243–244, 787, 638, 729, 737, 1267–69, 1119, 1123, 1127, 1213, 1267, 1250, 1234–1243, 1265–66, 1285, 1295–96, 1299–1300, 1303, 1168, 1173

Paragraphs: 104, 121, 124, 127, 2055, 2059, 2067, 2069, 2074, 1730, 1850, 981, 1441, 1446, 1454, 1451, 1455, 1468, 1469, 1425, 524, 526

SCRIPTURE AND THE RITES OF THE CHURCH

Matthew 8:14–15; 4:18–22; 28:1–5; 6:9; 19:14
Luke 8:22–25
Acts of the Apostles 2:1–4, 38–41
Psalms 100:1–5; 145:2
Mark 11:1, 8–10; 2:14
Rite of Baptism Rite of Confirmation
John 10:14

Isaiah 48:17; 9:1
Samuel 7:22
Luke 4:42–43; 15:4–6, 11–24; 1: 2:1–20
Matthew 7:24–27; 22:35–39; 18:21–23
Psalm 113:3; 119:64
Rite of Penance
John 15:9–10

SAINTS AND CATHOLIC PROFILES; FEASTS AND DEVOTIONS

Our Lady of the Rosary
The Holy Family

Feast of Pentecost
Sacred Chrism – Blessed Oil
The Church Year
Ordinary Time
The Rosary

Saint Francis of Assisi
Saint Philip Neri

Aspirations
The Bible
An Act of Contrition
Advent and the Advent Wreath
Christmas

15 Jesus brings us life. • Jesus celebrated a special meal with his disciples. • In the Eucharist we remember and celebrate what Jesus did at the Last Supper. • The Mass is a meal and a sacrifice.

16 We are united with Jesus Christ and to one another. • The Church celebrates the Mass. • The parish gathers for the celebration of Mass. • When Mass begins, we praise God and ask for his forgiveness.

17 We listen to God's Word during the Liturgy of the Word. • We listen and respond to readings from the Old Testament and the New Testament. • We listen as the Gospel is proclaimed. • Together we pray the Creed and the Prayer of the Faithful.

18 We bring forward the gifts of bread and wine. • The Eucharistic Prayer is the great prayer of thanks and praise. • We pray the Our Father and ask God for forgiveness and peace. • We receive Jesus Christ in Holy Communion.

19 We are sent to share God's love with others. • Jesus is present in the Blessed Sacrament. • Jesus is with the Church as we share God's love. • Jesus is with us as we share his peace with others.

20 Lent is a season of preparing.

21 The Three Days celebrate the Death and Resurrection of Jesus.

22 We are called by God. • Married people and single people are called by God. • Priests are called by God. • Religious sisters and brothers are called by God.

23 Catholics belong to parish communities. • Bishops lead and serve the Church. • The pope is the leader of the Church. • The Church is in every part of the world.

24 Prayer keeps us close to God. • Jesus prayed to God his Father. • Jesus teaches us to pray. • We pray as Jesus did.

25 The Church honors the saints. • The Church honors Mary. • We honor Mary with special prayers. • We honor Mary on special days.

26 We live in God's love. • Jesus taught us to love others. • We love and respect others. • We respect God's creation.

27 Easter is a season to celebrate the Resurrection of Jesus.

Paragraphs: 1406, 1339, 1341, 1382, 1348, 1368, 1389, 2643, 1349, 197, 1350, 1353, 1355, 1386, 1332, 1418, 1397, 1416, 628, 540

Paragraphs: 30, 1604, 1658, 1578, 1618, 2179, 886, 882, 831, 2560, 2599, 2759, 2767, 957, 963, 2676, 971, 1694, 1823, 1825, 307, 641

John 6:2–14,51; 15:5; 14:27; 13:34–35
Mark 14: 22–24
Luke 22:19; 8:1; 15:8–10
Matthew 18:20
The Roman Missal
Galatians 3:26–28

Isaiah 43:1
Philippians 4:4–5
Luke 11:1; 1:28–30,38–42; 24:1–9; 22:19
1 Corinthians 13:4,5,8,13
John 13:34–35; 15:12
Colossians 3:13

Saint Paul

The Blessed Sacrament
Grace Before Meals
Celebration of the Mass
Holy Days of Obligation
Lent
Ash Wednesday
The Three Days

Saint Frances of Rome
Saint Elizabeth Ann Seton
Saints Peter and Paul
Saint Brigid
Saint Catherine of Siena
Saint Rose of Lima
Saint Martin de Porres
Saint John Bosco
Saint Frances Cabrini
Mary

Morning Prayer
Evening Prayer
Processions
The Rosary
The Hail Mary
Feast Days of the Blessed Mother

Go to **www.webelieveweb.com** for the Scope and Sequence of the *We Believe with Project Disciple* Program, K–6.

Sadlier **We Believe** Scope and Sequence

Welcome to...

Sadlier
We Believe
with PROJECT DISCIPLE

This Program is...

* Rooted in Scripture
* Faithful to the Tradition of the Catholic Church
* Spirited by the General and National Directories for Catechesis
* **Christocentric,** centering on the Person of Jesus Christ
* **Trinitarian,** inviting relationship with God the Father, God the Son, and God the Holy Spirit
* **Ecclesial,** supporting faith that is lived in the domestic church and the universal Church.

New to the program is **PROJECT DISCIPLE**, an exciting and integral feature of every chapter. Built on the Six Tasks of Catechesis, **PROJECT DISCIPLE** pages contain **hundreds and hundreds** of new activities, so disciples at every grade level:

1. **LEARN** about their faith
2. **CELEBRATE** the Mass and sacraments
3. **CHOOSE** to show love and respect
4. **PRAY** every day
5. **SHARE** faith with others
6. **LIVE** out their faith

Six Tasks of Catechesis

"These six tasks of catechesis constitute a unified whole by which catechesis seeks to achieve its objective: the formation of disciples of Jesus Christ."

(National Directory for Catechesis, #20, p.63)

	Tasks of Catechesis	Disciples . . .	In Grade 2 . . .
Learn	Catechesis promotes knowledge of the faith.	**learn** about Jesus Christ and their Catholic faith through Scripture and Tradition.	Children will learn how Jesus shares God's life with us.
Celebrate	Catechesis promotes a knowledge of the meaning of the liturgy and the sacraments.	**celebrate** their faith by learning about and participating in the liturgy and the sacraments.	Children will focus on participation in the Mass and the reception of the Sacraments of Eucharist and Penance.
Choose	Catechesis promotes moral formation in Jesus Christ.	**choose** to follow Jesus' example and his teachings, to live the commandments and the spirit of the Beatitudes.	Children will reflect on their choices in light of the Gospel and prepare for the Sacrament of Penance and Reconciliation.
Pray	Catechesis teaches the Christian how to pray with Christ.	**pray** to God—Father, Son, and Holy Spirit—every day and in many different ways.	Children will pray as Jesus did, both as individuals and as a community of faith.
Share	Catechesis prepares the Christian to live in community and to participate actively in the life and mission of the Church.	**share** in the lives of their families, parish, and school, and participate in the mission of the Church to share the Good News of Jesus Christ.	Children will learn about their own parish and about the Church around the world. They will learn about Mary and the saints and about each person's call from God to serve others.
Live	Catechesis promotes a missionary spirit that prepares the faithful to be present as Christians in society.	**live** their faith by giving witness to the life and teachings of Jesus Christ through their words and deeds.	Children will spread the Good News of Jesus Christ in their neighborhoods and in the world by living their Catholic faith.

FAQ's

Here are some questions that we have been asked about *We Believe* with **PROJECT DISCIPLE**.

I try to highlight any Scripture content that appears in a chapter. Are you offering even more Scripture content?

Yes! Our program is based on Scripture. Check out the Scope & Sequence. But we've added even more! Look for *What's the Word?* activities in **Project Disciple** as well as many *Pray Today* activities. In addition, your guide contains a new Scripture reproducible master for every chapter!

What do you have for family?

Lots! The popular *Sharing Faith with My Family* page is now a reproducible master. An informative Parent's page starts each unit and is filled with exciting doable family activities. And don't forget the **Project Disciple** *Take Home* activity offered in each chapter. Plus, you can always go to **www.webelieveweb.com**.

I love your website. Are you updating it?

Always! **www.webelieveweb.com** is a tremendous success. Keep visiting to see new resources for you, the children, and their families that are interactive and downloadable.

Our class is "going green." Are you?

Definitely! Look at pages T22–T23 in this guide to find exciting ways that *We Believe with Project Disciple* can help your class go green. And congratulations!

Is assessment an important part of the program?

Absolutely! Each core chapter ends with a full page chapter test, and we provide unit tests as well. Plus, we offer both standard and alternative forms of assessment to meet your teaching needs. Lots of users supplement all this with the *We Believe Assessment* books and/or *Test Generators*—which feature online testing and reporting!

What exactly will Project Disciple do for me as a catechist?

Evaluate! Grounded in the Six Tasks of Catechesis, the hundreds of new **Project Disciple** activities, while informative and fun, will serve the serious goal of ascertaining whether the children are truly growing in and living out their faith. So **Project Disciple** enables you to monitor the faith formation of your children.

Your primary downloads in *Lives of the Saints* are great! Each saint really comes alive for my group. Please keep them coming!

Thanks! We receive loads of e-mails praising our saint bios/downloads at **www.webelieveweb.com**. We'll keep them coming! And we've added more saints to each text in **Project Disciple** (*see Saint Stories*).

I really like the way you reference each chapter's content to paragraphs from the Catechism. Are there other references to correlations?

Many! Chapter correlations to the Six Tasks of Catechesis, to Catholic Social Teaching, and to Catechetical Formation in Chaste Living are all available on **www.webelieveweb.com**.

Wow. It sounds like there's a lot of great new material in *We Believe with Project Disciple*. I've used *We Believe* for 5 years now. Please keep the "good stuff." We've been very successful.

Terrific! Don't worry. What has made you successful will continue to do so. The music, the prayers, the sound catechetical formation built on Scripture and the doctrine of the Church—it's all still there. But now with all the added advantages of **Project Disciple**! So have another great year!

See **www.webelieveweb.com** for study guides, games and activities and more...

The Profile of a Second Grade DISCIPLE

Knowing the characteristics of second graders
will help you to implement
Grade 2 *We Believe* with **PROJECT DISCIPLE**.

Characteristics of Second Graders	Guiding Their Growth as Disciples of Jesus Christ
Second Graders are moving from an egocentric stage to a more concrete operational one. Thus, they are starting to make larger connections that go beyond their own immediate concerns.	Enlarge their worldview by connecting children's experiences with those of others. Invite children to imagine themselves in a biblical story or a scenario in which they have to make a choice. Ask questions about how they might feel, react, or respond.
Second graders have an average attention span of seven minutes. They are lively, curious, and easily distracted.	Keep presentations brief, and engage children in activities with a level of simplicity and "do-ability" that sparks their curiosity and retains their interest.
Second graders are growing in their ability to work cooperatively with others.	When engaging children in group or partnering activities, stress the importance of love and mutual respect in the community of faith and beyond.*
Second graders have a great capacity for wonder. It forms a natural foundation for developing a lifelong appreciation for the awesome mysteries of God.	Allow time for children to be silent and reflective. Set aside a prayer space where children can be quiet and listen to God. Foster their sense of wonder about all of God's creation.

* *Catechetical Formation in Chaste Living*, United States Catholic Conference of Bishops, #1

The Child's pages

Each chapter follows a proven **3-step** catechetical process: *We Gather, We Believe, We Respond.*

1 WE GATHER

Children gather in prayer at the beginning of every chapter. They gather to pray and focus on their life as they begin each day's lesson. They respond to God's call and his grace through prayer and reflection on their experience. They pray, sing, and explore the ways the faith speaks to their lives.

2 WE BELIEVE

Each chapter presents the truths of the Catholic faith found in Sacred Scripture and Tradition, and in accordance with the Magisterium of the Church. The main faith statements of each chapter are highlighted. The content of faith is presented in ways that are age-appropriate, culturally sensitive, and varied.

3 WE RESPOND

Throughout each chapter children are encouraged to respond in prayer, faith, and life. They are invited to respond to the message of the lesson. Through prayer, song, and actions that express their beliefs, children are called to live out their discipleship among their peers, their families, and their school and parish communities.

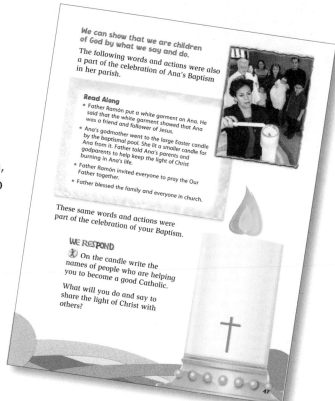

We can show that we are children of God by what we say and do.

The following words and actions were also a part of the celebration of Ana's Baptism in her parish.

Read Along
• Father Ramón put a white garment on Ana. He said that the white garment showed that Ana was a friend and follower of Jesus.
• Ana's godmother went to the large Easter candle by the baptismal pool. She lit a smaller candle for Ana from it. Father told Ana's parents and godparents to help keep the light of Christ burning in Ana's life.
• Father Ramón invited everyone to pray the Our Father together.
• Father blessed the family and everyone in church.

These same words and actions were part of the celebration of your Baptism.

WE RESPOND
On the candle write the names of people who are helping you to become a good Catholic.

What will you do and say to share the light of Christ with others?

47

Plus   **PROJECT DISCIPLE** activities sharpen discipleship skills. Children learn, celebrate, choose, pray, share, and live out their faith.

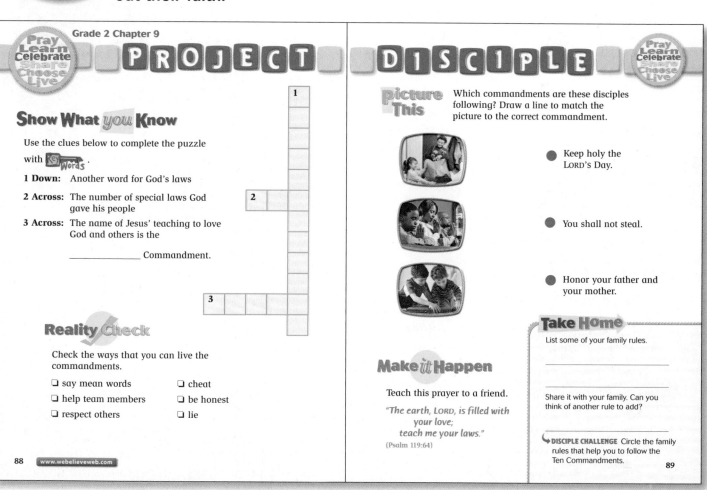

Grade 2 Chapter 9

Pray Learn Celebrate Share Choose Live

PROJECT   DISCIPLE

Show What you Know

Use the clues below to complete the puzzle with  Key Words.

1 Down: Another word for God's laws

2 Across: The number of special laws God gave his people

3 Across: The name of Jesus' teaching to love God and others is the

_____ Commandment.

Reality Check

Check the ways that you can live the commandments.

❏ say mean words   ❏ cheat
❏ help team members   ❏ be honest
❏ respect others   ❏ lie

Picture This

Which commandments are these disciples following? Draw a line to match the picture to the correct commandment.

● Keep holy the LORD's Day.

● You shall not steal.

● Honor your father and your mother.

Make it Happen

Teach this prayer to a friend.

"The earth, LORD, is filled with your love; teach me your laws."
(Psalm 119:64)

Take Home

List some of your family rules.

_____

_____

Share it with your family. Can you think of another rule to add?

_____

↪ **DISCIPLE CHALLENGE** Circle the family rules that help you to follow the Ten Commandments.

Assessment

In the *We Believe* with **Project Disciple** program:

For each chapter a chapter test is provided. A suggestion for an alternative-assessment activity is provided in the guide.

For each unit standard assessment is provided in the text and alternative assessment in the guide.

Assessment Resources
Assessment Book of **Reproducible Masters**, with chapter, unit, semester, and final tests

CD-ROM *Test Generator and Resource* (for MAC or WIN) You can:

- assign/score/report tests online
- customize tests, edit/add questions
- print tests from a question bank
- allow students to take tests on their Local Area Network (LAN)
- plan schedules in calendar format
- access and print chapter resources

Seasonal Chapters

The *We Believe* program integrates liturgy and catechesis through culturally-rich and diverse prayer experiences and ritual celebrations. It also provides special seasonal chapters that help children to understand and celebrate the different seasons and feasts of the Church.

For the Family

In each unit a *Dear Family* page in the child's text is designed specifically for the family. It provides content overview, additional activities, faith formation for parents, and applications for family life.

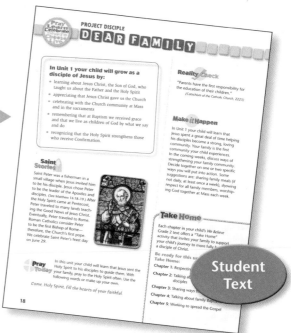

Student Text

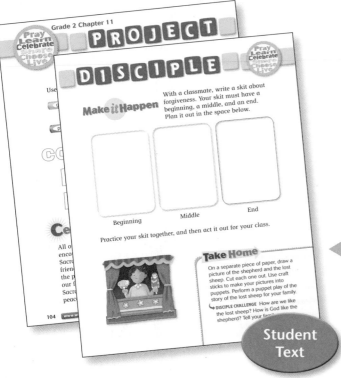

In each chapter a *Take Home* activity in the child's text provides another opportunity to share faith at home. Ways are suggested for all family members to live as disciples.

Student Text

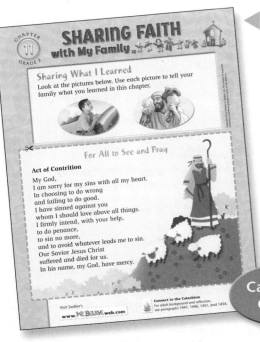

For each chapter A *Sharing Faith with My Family* reproducible master is provided. Activities and discussions are student-initiated, inviting the child to be the evangelizer. Be sure to send this page home.

Catechist Guide

On the Web Families can visit **www.webelieveweb.com** for study guides, games, safe activities for their children, and great information and enrichment for themselves.

The Catechist's Pages

Your guide provides you with everything you need!

Overview and Lesson Planning Guide

- Goal of the chapter
- References to the *Catechism of the Catholic Church*
- *Key Words*
- References for correlations to The Six Tasks of Catechesis, Catholic Social Teaching, and Catechetical Formation in Chaste Living
- Background for catechists

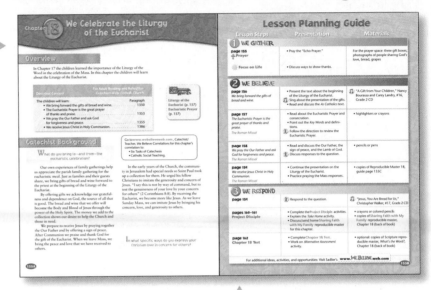

- All the plans you need for a successful lesson
- Resources and materials for clear presentation

Enrichment and Additional Resources

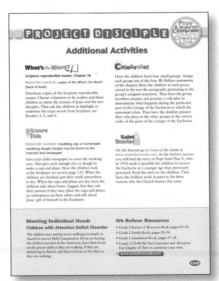

- Directions for using the chapter's *What's the Word?* reproducible master (in the back of the book)
- Even more activities directly related to the six tasks of catechesis
- Strategies for meeting the individual needs of the children
- Program resources for the chapter

- A *Chapter Story* for use in your lesson presentation
- *Faith and Media* that provides creative ways to connect lesson content to the electronic world

- A *Chapter Project* that gives you the opportunity to further involve the children and extend the chapter

Reproducible Masters

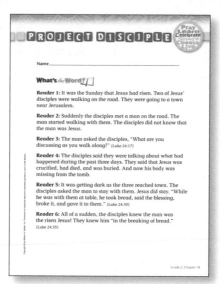

Family

- The children become the evangelizers as they share what they have learned in the chapter.
- The children share activities and prayer with their families. (See back of guide.)

Scripture

- A Scripture activity gives you the opportunity to deepen the children's understanding of God's Word.
- Skits, interactive activities, and more... (See back of guide.)

Chapter Content

- Additional fun activities reinforce and enrich the material taught in the chapter.
- Options for alternative assessment or family use

Lesson Plan Pages

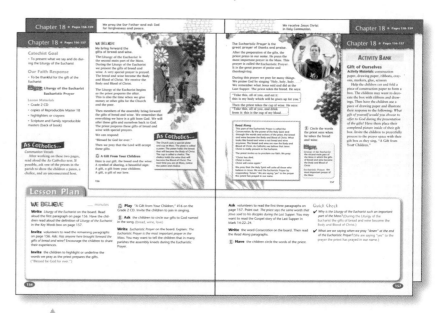

- Ideas on how to enhance the Prayer Space from week to week
- An online link to the week's liturgy
- A *Family Connection Update* that invites volunteers to share the outcome of the *Take Home* activity from the previous lesson

- Clear goals for the lesson
- Key vocabulary words
- Helpful *Teaching Tips*
- A "recipe" for clear presentation of the lesson
- An *Activity Bank* with additional and varied activities

Lesson Plan Pages continued

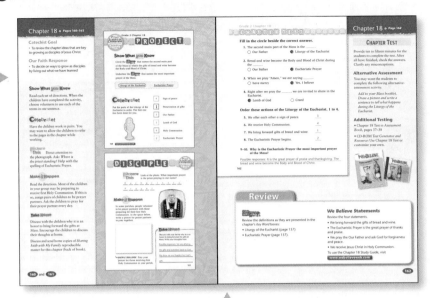

- Clear, concise directions for the activities from the child's pages that relate to the six tasks of catechesis

- Suggestions to encourage children to use the *Take Home* activity with their family

- End–of–chapter test with annotations
- Opportunities for alternative assessment
- Review of key words and faith content statements
- Reference to the chapter online study guide and to ancillary *Assessment Books* and CD-ROM *Test Generators*

Just look at the variety of PROJECT DISCIPLE activities!

Show What you Know . . . Check what's been learned

picture This . . . . See and show disciple skills

Reality Check . . . . "Check-off" ideas and choices

Make it Happen . . . . Live out what's been learned

What's the Word? . . . . . . All about Scripture

Question Corner . . . . Take a quiz or answer a question

Fast Facts . . . . Learn even more

What Would you do? . . . Make the right choices

Pray Today . . . . Talk and listen to God

Celebrate! . . . . All about worshiping God

Saint Stories . . . . Find great role models

More to Explore . . . . Get information from the Internet and library

Take Home . . . . Share faith at home

Now, pass it on! . . . . Evangelize!

➥ **DISCIPLE CHALLENGE** . . . . . Go a step further!

Sadlier also offers these *We Believe* resources:

- *Review & Resource Book*
  Even more engaging activities

- *Family Book*
  Home Lesson Plans for teaching and/or reviewing

- **Music CD and Program Songbook**
  Program songs and lyrics and arrangements

www.webelieveweb.com

your 24/7 Teaching Assistant

* **In Your Classroom** Study Guides for every grade; Vocations—Letters from Africa; downloadable and whiteboard activities; Project Disciple; Online games—and much more!

* **In Your Office** This week's liturgy with reflection/discussion and activities based on Sunday readings; catechist development; teaching tips and resources —always relevant to your needs!

* **In Your Students' Homes** Study Guides; Catechetical Development for families; Project Disciple; Sharing Faith as a Family; From My Home to Yours—always being updated!

"We are with you when you need us!"

This Year
Go Green!

Focus On

The sunflower is a vibrant sign of God's creation. Its bright yellow hue reflects the sun's warmth and radiates joy. Who would want to live in a world devoid of such beauty? When we litter our landscapes through careless practices, we take away from the earth's natural beauty. Throughout the year, focus attention on ways to protect the environment by encouraging the children to dispose of trash through the practice of the three R's: reduce, reuse, recycle.

Take Action

Talk to the children about reducing the use of disposal items and reusing items rather than throwing them in the trash. Brainstorm a list of ways to reduce and reuse materials in the classroom and at home. Keep a running list of ways the children have utilized this practice over the course of the year.

Invite the children to decorate recycling receptacles. Use bright colors to paint sunflowers, faces, slogans, and other catchy ideas for promoting the practice of recycling. Place these in the classroom, or seek permission to place them on the playground or other places in the school or parish.

Class Action

Arrange to take the children to a recycling center. Make up a list of questions to ask about the use of recycled materials.

Reflect and Pray

At the beginning of the year, invite the children to study the art on the cover of their *We Believe* books. Talk about how the picture is free from clutter and litter. Use this as a way to introduce a green theme for the year that focuses on ways to protect the environment through the practice of the three R's.

Compose a class litany, thanking God for the beauty of creation. Invite each child to contribute one "item" for the litany. Afterwards talk about the importance of respecting God's creation through proper disposal of trash.

Visit **www.webelieveweb.com** to find a Green Event for your parish or school.

Grade 2 Greenprint!

Focus on

This year I protected the environment.

I reduced _____

I reused _____

I recycled _____

Take Action

This year, here are some ways we reduced and reused materials in our classroom.

1. _____   3. _____

2. _____   4. _____

Class Action

We visited a recycling center. I learned…

_____

_____

Reflect and Pray

Thank you, God, for _____

_____   _____
Signed   Date

WE☩BELIEVE

The *We Believe* program will help us to

learn

celebrate

share

and

live our Catholic faith.

Throughout the year we will hear about many saints and holy people.

Saint Brigid

Saint Catherine of Siena

Saint Elizabeth Ann Seton

Saint Frances Cabrini

Saint Frances of Rome

Saint Francis of Assisi

Saint John Bosco

Saint Joseph

Saint Martin de Porres

Mary, Mother of God

Saint Peter

Saint Paul

Saint Philip Neri

Saint Rose of Lima

Together, let us grow as a community of faith.

Welcome!

WE GATHER

✝ **Leader:** Welcome everyone to Grade 2 *We Believe*.
As we begin each chapter, we gather in prayer.
We pray to God together.

Let us sing the *We Believe* song!

♫ **We Believe, We Believe in God**

We believe in God;
We believe, we believe in Jesus;
We believe in the Spirit
who gives us life.

We believe, we believe
in God.

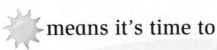 means it's time to

think about
talk about
write about
draw about
act out

Life

at home
in our neighborhood
at school
in our parish
in our world

Talk about your life right now.

What groups do you belong to?

Why do you like to be a member of these groups?

Each day we learn more about God.

WE BELIEVE

We learn about

- God the Father, God the Son, and God the Holy Spirit
- Jesus, the Son of God who became one of us
- the Church and its teachings.

We find out about the different ways Catholics live their faith and celebrate God's love.

 is an open Bible . When we see it, or something like this (John 13:34), we hear the Word of God.

Each of these signs points out something special that we are going to do.

means that we will make the Sign of the Cross and pray .

Key Word means it is time to review the important words we have learned.

means we have an activity . We might

talk   **write**   **act**
    draw
        sing
work together   **imagine**

There are all kinds of activities! We might see in many parts of our lesson. Be on the lookout!

♫ means it's time to sing ! We sing songs we know, make up our own songs, and sing along with those in our *We Believe* music program.

As Catholics...

Here we discover something special about our faith. Don't forget to read it!

13

WE RESPOND

We can respond by

- thinking about ways our faith affects the things we say and do

- sharing our thoughts and feelings

- praying to God.

Then in our homes, neighborhood, school, parish, and world, we can say and do the things that show love for God and others.

When we see **We Respond** we think about and act on what we have learned about God and our Catholic faith.

In this space, draw yourself as a *We Believe* second grader.

We are so happy you are with us!

14

Show What you Know

We "show what we know" about each chapter's content. A disciple is always learning more about his or her faith.

We sharpen our disciple skills with each chapter's Project Disciple pages!

Picture This Pictures are a great way for us to see and show our disciple skills.

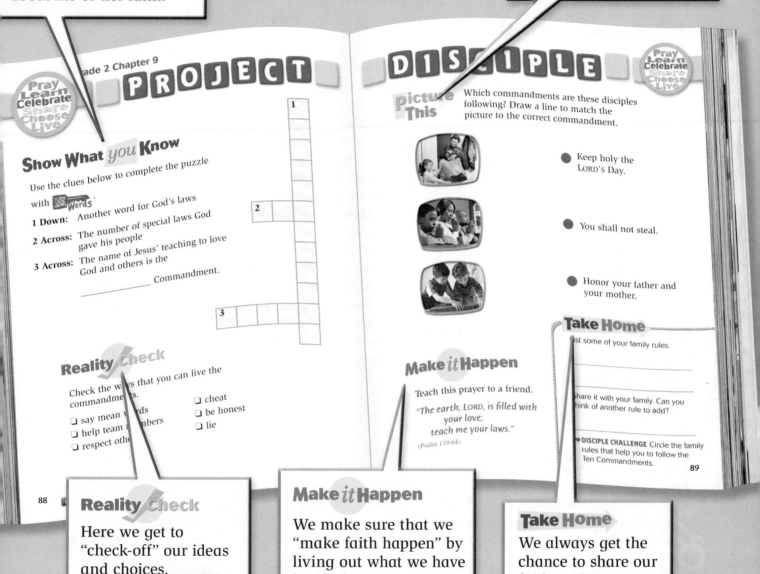

(Left page — PROJECT)

Grade 2 Chapter 9

PROJECT

Pray Learn Celebrate Share Choose Live

Show What you Know

Use the clues below to complete the puzzle with **Key Words**.

1 Down: Another word for God's laws

2 Across: The number of special laws God gave his people

3 Across: The name of Jesus' teaching to love God and others is the _____ Commandment.

Reality Check

Check the ways that you can live the commandments.

- ☐ say mean words
- ☐ help team members
- ☐ respect others
- ☐ cheat
- ☐ be honest
- ☐ lie

88

(Right page — DISCIPLE)

DISCIPLE

Pray Learn Celebrate Share Choose Live

Picture This Which commandments are these disciples following? Draw a line to match the picture to the correct commandment.

- ● Keep holy the LORD's Day.
- ● You shall not steal.
- ● Honor your father and your mother.

Make it Happen

Teach this prayer to a friend.

"The earth, LORD, is filled with your love; teach me your laws."

(Psalm 119:64)

Take Home

List some of your family rules.

Share it with your family. Can you think of another rule to add?

➤ **DISCIPLE CHALLENGE** Circle the family rules that help you to follow the Ten Commandments.

89

(Callout boxes)

Reality Check Here we get to "check-off" our ideas and choices.

Make it Happen We make sure that we "make faith happen" by living out what we have learned.

Take Home We always get the chance to share our faith "at home."

There are **LOADS of ACTIVITIES** that make us better disciples! Just look at this additional list.

What's the Word?—all about Scripture
Question Corner—take a quiz
Fast Facts—learn even more about our faith
What Would You Do?—making the right choices
Pray Today—talking and listening to God

Celebrate!—all about worshiping God
Saint Stories—finding great role models
More to Explore—getting information from the Internet and library
Now, Pass It On—invites us to witness to our faith
Don't forget to look for the **Disciple Challenge**—count how many you can do this year!

And every chapter ends with a Chapter Test!

PROJECT DISCIPLE

You are on a journey this year to become a disciple of Jesus Christ.

This year you will:

- **learn** about the ways Jesus shares his life with us.

- **pray** as Jesus did.

- **celebrate** God's love, especially in the Sacrament of the Eucharist.

- **choose** to follow God's law by loving God and others.

- **share** God's gifts with family and friends.

- **live out** the gift of faith by serving the needs of others.

Have a great year!

WE BELIEVE

GRADE 2 DISCIPLE CONTRACT

As a disciple of Jesus, this year I promise to

_____

_____

Name

_____

Date

Pray
Learn
Celebrate
Share
Choose
Live

And remember, you can always visit

www.webelieveweb.com

for all kinds of activities, games, study guides, and resources.

Jesus Christ Is With Us Always

Seasonal Chapters

17

Unit 1

C...

Rea...
cha...
What a...
learning about...
a few volunteers to...
explain to the children t...
be learning about Jesus Christ,...
sacraments, and the beginning of th...
Church. Also have a class discussion
about the photographs and
illustrations on this page.

HOME CONNECTION

Project Disciple
Dear Family

Sadlier *We Believe* calls on families
to become involved in:

• learning the faith

• prayer and worship

• living their faith.

Highlighting of these unit family
pages and the opportunities they
offer will strengthen the partnership
of the Church and the home.

For additional information and
activities, encourage families to
visit Sadlier's

www.WeBelieveweb.com

Pray Learn Celebrate Share Choose Live

PROJECT DISCIPLE
DEAR FAMILY

In Unit 1 your child will grow as a disciple of Jesus by:

• learning about Jesus Christ, the Son of God, who taught us about the Father and the Holy Spirit

• appreciating that Jesus Christ gave us the Church

• celebrating with the Church community at Mass and in the sacraments

• remembering that at Baptism we received grace and that we live as children of God by what we say and do

• recognizing that the Holy Spirit strengthens those who receive Confirmation.

Reality Check

"Parents have the first responsibility for the education of their children."

(Catechism of the Catholic Church, 2223)

Make *it* Happen

In Unit 1 your child will learn that Jesus spent a great deal of time helping his disciples become a strong, loving community. Your family is the first community your child experiences. In the coming weeks, discuss ways of strengthening your family community. Decide together on one or two specific ways you will put into action. Some suggestions are: sharing family meals (if not daily, at least once a week), showing respect for all family members, worshiping God together at Mass each week.

Saint Stories

Saint Peter was a fisherman in a small village when Jesus invited him to be his disciple. Jesus chose Peter to be the leader of the Apostles and disciples. (See Matthew 16:18-19.) After the Holy Spirit came at Pentecost, Peter traveled to many lands teaching the Good News of Jesus Christ. Eventually, Peter traveled to Rome. Roman Catholics consider Peter to be the first Bishop of Rome— therefore, the Church's first pope. We celebrate Saint Peter's feast day on June 29.

Take Home

Each chapter in your child's *We Believe* Grade 2 text offers a "Take Home" activity that invites your family to support your child's journey to more fully become a disciple of Christ.

Be ready for this unit's Take Home:

Chapter 1: Respecting all people

Chapter 2: Talking about Apostles and disciples

Chapter 3: Sharing ways to worship God

Chapter 4: Talking about family Baptisms

Chapter 5: Working to spread the Gospel

Pray Today

In this unit your child will learn that Jesus sent the Holy Spirit to his disciples to guide them. With your family, pray to the Holy Spirit often. Use the following words or make up your own.

Come, Holy Spirit, fill the hearts of your faithful.

Overview

In this chapter the children will learn that God the Father sent his Son, Jesus, to be with us. Jesus is God's greatest gift.

Doctrinal Content	For Adult Reading and Reflection *Catechism of the Catholic Church*
The children will learn:	Paragraph
• God the Father sent his Son, Jesus, to be with us.	422
• Jesus is human like us.	470
• Jesus did things only God can do.	548
• Jesus, the Son of God, taught us about God the Father and God the Holy Spirit.	243–244

Key Words

Holy Family (p. 20)
divine (p. 23)
Blessed Trinity (p. 23)

Go to **www.webelieveweb.com**, Catechist/Teacher, We Believe Correlations for this chapter's correlation to:
- Six Tasks of Catechesis
- Catholic Social Teaching
- *Catechetical Formation in Chaste Living.*

Catechist Background

What amazes you?

Sometimes we read or hear of an event that is so amazing that we need time to comprehend its meaning. The birth of Jesus is a most amazing event. Out of love God the Father sends his only begotten Son to us. The honor of becoming the Mother of God's Son is offered to a humble young woman. Mary's remarkable faith is evident in her response to God's invitation, "May it be done to me according to your word" (Luke 1:38).

Jesus is true God and true man, but for thirty years Jesus' divinity was concealed in his ordinary life with Mary and Joseph. God, through his Son, entered fully into our humanity. Picture Jesus learning, loving, growing, praying.

It was only when Jesus left home and began preaching that his divine power gradually became evident. In Jesus the poor, the sick, the hungry, and even the sinner experienced God's love and healing touch. Jesus reached out to all people to reveal God's love for all people.

Jesus taught his followers about God the Father. He promised that God the Holy Spirit would come to help them. The mystery of this Triune God who is Father, Son, and Holy Spirit can overwhelm us. Yet, like Mary, we can make our own act of faith. We can do so each time we pray the Sign of the Cross.

How will you show your faith in God's love?

Lesson Planning Guide

Lesson Steps	Presentation	Materials

① WE GATHER

Lesson Steps	Presentation	Materials
page 19 ✝ **Prayer**	• Praise and thank God.	For the prayer space: small table; Bible; picture of Jesus; fresh or paper sunflowers
☀ **Focus on Life**	• Name favorite gifts from God.	• chart paper

② WE BELIEVE

Lesson Steps	Presentation	Materials
page 20 *God the Father sent his Son, Jesus, to be with us.*	• Present and discuss the text about the Holy Family. • Point out the *Key Word* and definition. ⟨𝑋⟩ Discuss together Jesus' childhood activities.	
page 21 *Jesus is human like us.*	• Read and discuss the teachings of Jesus. ⟨𝑋⟩ Complete the activity. • Read and discuss *As Catholics*.	• colored pencils or markers
page 22 *Jesus did things only God can do.* 📖 *Matthew 8:14–15*	• Read and discuss the text and the Scripture story. • Point out the *Key Word* and definition. ⟨𝑋⟩ Reflect on responses to question.	• copies of Reproducible Master 1, guide page 19C 🎵 "The Storm at Sea," #2, Grade 2 CD
page 23 *Jesus, the Son of God, taught us about God the Father and God the Holy Spirit.*	• Read and discuss the text about the Blessed Trinity. • Point out the *Key Word* and definition.	• pencils

③ WE RESPOND

Lesson Steps	Presentation	Materials
page 23	⟨𝑋⟩ Complete the activity about showing love for the Persons of the Trinity.	
pages 24–25 **Project Disciple**	• Complete the **Project Disciple** activities. • Explain the *Take Home* activity. • Discuss/send home **Sharing Faith with My Family** reproducible master for this chapter.	• colored pencils or crayons • copies of **Sharing Faith with My Family** reproducible master, Chapter 1 (back of book)
page 26 **Chapter 1 Test**	• Complete **Chapter 1 Test**. • Work on *Alternative Assessment* activity.	• optional: copies of Scripture reproducible master, *What's the Word?*, Chapter 1 (back of book)

For additional ideas, activities, and opportunities: Visit Sadlier's **www.WeBelieveweb.com**

19B

Sing the song together.

Draw pictures to show what Jesus did.

 Luke 8:22–25

The Storm at Sea
("Twinkle, Twinkle")

One night on a boat at sea,
Jesus slept so peacefully.
Suddenly a great storm came,
Wind and waves and driving
        rain.
Water poured into the boat.
It could no longer stay afloat!

Jesus' friends let out a cry,
"Jesus, help or we will die!"
Jesus spoke to winds and sea,
To the waves, "Be still," said he.
The friends of Jesus were
        amazed
Because the wind and waves
        obeyed.

PROJECT DISCIPLE

Additional Activities

What's *the* Word?

Scripture reproducible master, Chapter 1

Materials needed: copies of *What's the Word?* (back of book); optional—props and costumes for dramatization

Distribute copies of the Scripture reproducible master. Choose three volunteers to be readers and other volunteers to mime the actions of the characters as the script is being read. Then help the children write what they would have said to Jesus.

Reality Check

In this chapter the children learned to pray the Sign of the Cross. Ask the children: *When do you pray the Sign of the Cross?* Write the following on the board. Have children copy the list on a separate piece of paper and put checks before their responses.

• in the morning at home

• before religion class

• at Mass on Sunday

• before night time prayers

Then invite the children to share other times when they pray the Sign of the Cross.

More *to* Explore

Materials needed: a map of Israel

Display a map of Israel. Point out on the map the town of Nazareth in the northern part of the country. As you do so, explain this is where Jesus grew up. Then point to the town of Bethlehem in the south. Explain that this is where Jesus was born. Then point to the city of Jerusalem, which is also in the south. Explain that Jesus traveled there with his family. They went to pray to God in the Temple there.

Pray Today

Materials needed: small paper plates, crayons, yellow construction paper, glue sticks, scissors

Give each child a paper plate. Have each child print *Jesus* in the center of the plate. Then on the construction paper help the children trace their hands with fingers together four times and cut them out. Then help the children glue the hands around the plates to make sunflower petals.

Have the students hold up their flowers as you pray, *Jesus, help us grow in your love.* Display the flowers in the prayer space.

Meeting Individual Needs
Welcoming Children to the Group

Some children may have problems adjusting to social situations because they are shy, are from different backgrounds, or are new to the group. Be sensitive to these children. Make the time to help them meet others with whom they can identify and feel comfortable. This individual attention will help the children gain self-confidence.

We Believe Resources

• Grade 2 *Review & Resource Book*, pages 4–6

• Grade 2 *Family Book*, pages 5–7

• Grade 2 *Assessment Book*, pages 3–4

• Grade 2 CD-ROM *Test Generator and Resource*: Use Chapter 1 Test or customize your own.

• **www.webelieveweb.com**

Enrichment Ideas

Chapter Story

Charles could not wait to see his friends. He and his sister had just returned home to Space Station GAR. They had spent summer vacation with their Aunt Roxanne and her family who lived on Earth.

Charles went to see his friend Raul. Raul had never been to Earth. He wanted to hear all about it.

Charles said, "Raul, I had so much fun. Aunt Roxanne and my cousins live near the ocean. We went to the beach a lot. We made sand castles and watched the waves wash them away. We gathered seashells. We watched gulls fly over the water and crabs crawl in the sand.

"At night we sat outside on the front steps. Bugs called fireflies flew all around us. I could hear the ocean waves and other bugs making creaking sounds. My cousin told me they were crickets."

Raul said, "Wow, you spent a lot of time outside."

Charles answered, "Well, we stayed inside when it rained. My cousin couldn't believe I got excited about the storms. I wasn't afraid at all when I heard thunder booming. After one storm, I looked up at the sky and saw a rainbow like the ones we learned about last year. We took trips to many different places. I saw alligators in a marsh. I saw sheep, cows, and horses on a ranch."

Then Charles's mother called him to tell him to come home. Raul said, "I can't wait until you tell me more about your trip, Charles. I'll see you tomorrow morning. Don't forget that it's the first day of school."

▶ *Name some of God's gifts Charles saw on his visit to Earth.*

FAITH and MEDIA

▶ To begin to give the children an awareness and an understanding of media, consider building on an example in this week's lesson: Jesus using stories to teach. This is an example of the use of what we call *media*; that is, it is a way of sending a message or telling people something. Jesus walked from town to town to tell people stories about God's love; today writers and photographers place news stories and pictures on the Internet to enable people to read and see the latest news without delay. Let the children know that the many different things we use to send messages, or tell people something, or show people something are *all* media: videos, Web sites, magazines, text messages.

CHAPTER PROJECT: MANY GIFTS

Use construction paper to make an outline of a gift-wrapped box on one of your bulletin boards or walls. The outline should be large enough so that many half-sheets of 8½" × 11" paper can eventually be placed within it. Label the box *Gifts from God* and place a bow on top. Place a sheet of paper at the center of the box with the words *Jesus is God's greatest gift to us*. Set aside a few minutes for the children to think about the many gifts that they have received from God. These gifts may include personal qualities, such as a sense of humor or the gift of patience, or they might include family members, pets, and friends. Have the children describe or draw pictures of their gifts on the sheets of paper, and place these within the box outline. Refer to the box periodically to reinforce the idea that God has given us many gifts.

Jesus Is the Son of God

(1)

WE GATHER

✝**Leader:** Let us stand and pray.

Child 1: Glory to the Father,
All: Glory to the Father,

Child 2: and to the Son,
All: and to the Son,

Child 3: and to the Holy Spirit:
All: and to the Holy Spirit:

All: as it was in the beginning, is now, and will be for ever. Amen.

God has filled our world with wonderful gifts. Name your favorite.

19

PREPARING TO PRAY

In this gathering prayer, the children will praise the Three Persons of the Blessed Trinity.

• Choose a prayer leader and three other children to do the readings. Prepare them for their roles in the gathering prayer.

♫ For words and music to all the songs on the Grade 2 CD, see Sadlier's *We Believe Program Songbook*.

The Prayer Space
• Designate an area of the room as your prayer space. Place a small table in the prayer space. On the table place a Bible, a picture or statue of Jesus, and a vase containing fresh or paper sunflowers (optional).

📖 **This Week's Liturgy**
Visit **www.webelieveweb.com** for this week's liturgical readings and other seasonal material.

Lesson Plan

WE GATHER ___ minutes

✝ Pray

• Invite the children to gather in the prayer space. Remind the children that God is with us as we pray. Pray the Sign of the Cross together.

• Ask the children to pretend they are sunflowers. Have them raise their arms to praise God. Then invite the prayer leader to begin.

☀ Focus on Life

• Have each child name his or her favorite gift from God. Write the children's responses on chart paper. Display the chart paper in the prayer space.

• Share the *Chapter Story* on guide page 19E.

Family Connection Update

Encourage the children to share special times they spent with their families during the summer.

Catechist Goal

• To present that God the Father sent his Son, Jesus, to be with us and that Jesus is God's greatest gift

Our Faith Response

• To show love for God the Father, God the Son, and God the Holy Spirit

 **Key Words** Holy Family

divine

Blessed Trinity

Materials

• colored pencils
• copies of Reproducible Master 1
• Grade 2 CD
• Scripture and Family reproducible masters (back of book)

As Catholics...

To Teach As Jesus Did—Parables

   After working on these two pages, read the *As Catholics* text. Have volunteers name parables that they may have heard. Explain that the story of the good neighbor, or good Samaritan (Luke 10:29–37), is a parable.

WE BELIEVE

God the Father sent his Son, Jesus, to be with us.

God the Father loves us very much. He gives us many gifts. Jesus is God's greatest gift to us. Jesus is the Son of God.

Mary was a young Jewish girl. God the Father sent an angel to Mary. The angel told her that God chose her to be the Mother of his Son. Mary agreed to God's plan. The angel also told her to name the child Jesus. The name Jesus has a special meaning. It means "God saves."

After Jesus was born, he lived with his mother, Mary, and his foster father, Joseph. We call Jesus, Mary, and Joseph the **Holy Family**.

The Holy Family lived in the town of Nazareth. As Jesus grew, he learned from his family members and teachers about the Jewish faith. He learned and obeyed God's laws. He prayed and celebrated religious holidays.

🧒 Talk about what Jesus did when he was your age.

Key Word
Holy Family the family of Jesus, Mary, and Joseph

20

Lesson Plan

WE BELIEVE _____ minutes

Point out the sentence in blue type at the top of page 20. Explain that this is a *We Believe* statement and that this statement tells us what the page is about. Read the statement aloud together. Then invite volunteers to read the first two paragraphs. Stress the following points:

• *Jesus is God's greatest gift to us.*
• *Jesus is the Son of God.*

Ask: *What do you remember about Jesus' family?* Have the children share what they have learned in previous years. Then write *Holy Family* on the board and explain: *We call Jesus, Mary, and Joseph the Holy Family.* Ask the children to read silently while you read aloud the last two paragraphs on page 20.

🧒 **Ask** the children to identify things Jesus may have done when he was their age. Write the responses on the board or on chart paper. Ask volunteers to circle the activities that we do today.

Jesus is human like us.

When Jesus was about thirty years old, he began to teach in many places. Jesus wanted everyone to know that they could share in God's great love. That was the Good News Jesus gave to God's people.

Jesus was God's Son but he was also human. People could see Jesus and talk to him. They could touch him and hear him. Jesus told them:

• God loves all people.

• God wants all people to love God, themselves, and others.

• God is their Father.

• God should be the most important one in their lives.

Jesus also taught people by his actions. He fed the hungry. Jesus comforted those who were sad or lonely. He cared for the poor.

Jesus wanted people to know that God always cares for them. Jesus helped people to know that they could always pray to God his Father. Jesus taught the people a prayer that we still pray today.

Find the name of the prayer Jesus taught. Unscramble the sets of letters.

U R O   H R A F E T

Our Father

21

As Catholics...

When Jesus taught, he used parables. Parables are short stories. In these stories, Jesus talked about things from everyday life. Some of the things he talked about were flowers, seeds, birds, sheep, and families. The crowds listened carefully to these stories. Jesus used these parables to tell everyone about God's love.

Have you ever heard one of Jesus' parables?

ACTIVITY BANK

Multiple Intelligences
Spatial, Interpersonal
Activity Materials: chart paper, crayons, and markers

Have the children work in groups. Give each group a sheet of chart paper that tells one way Jesus may have acted when he was young. (Jesus helped his mother; Jesus helped Joseph; Jesus played games with his friends; Jesus shared meals with his family; Jesus prayed to God.)

Have the groups draw a picture to illustrate the assigned action and to write sentences to tell what Jesus is doing. Display all the groups' work.

The Church
Cultural Practices

Explain that people in many cultures name their sons and daughters in honor of Jesus, Mary, and Joseph. Explain that some people of Spanish descent name their sons Jesús as a way of honoring Jesus. Discuss other cultural practices such as naming children in honor of certain saints or relatives.

Explain that Jesus traveled to many towns and villages to tell people about God the Father. Then have volunteers read the first two paragraphs on page 21. Stress: *Many people came to see and listen to Jesus.*

Read aloud together the list of what Jesus taught by his words. Explain: *Jesus also taught by his actions.* Then have a volunteer read the last two paragraphs.

Read the activity directions. Then help the children complete the activity.

Quick Check

✔ *Who belonged to the Holy Family?* (Jesus, Mary, and Joseph belonged to the Holy Family.)

✔ *What was the Good News Jesus gave to God's people?* (We can share in God's great love.)

✔ *What are some things Jesus did for people?* (He fed the hungry, comforted the sad or lonely, cared for the poor.)

Jesus did things only God can do.

Jesus is the Son of God. He did amazing things for people. He showed people that he was divine. **Divine** is a word we use to describe God. This means that Jesus is God and could do things only God can do.

Matthew 8:14–15

One day Jesus visited the family of Peter, one of Jesus' closest friends. "Jesus entered the house of Peter, and saw his mother-in-law lying in bed with a fever. He touched her hand, the fever left her, and she rose and waited on him." (Matthew 8:14–15)

Jesus healed many other people, too. He brought people back to life. He even forgave people their sins.

What would you like to say to Jesus about the wonderful things he did?

22

Teaching Tip

Wait Time

When you ask a question, pause briefly to allow children time to think about their responses. Some children need more time to process the question you have asked. Then repeat the question before calling on volunteers to share their responses. This helps to refocus children who may have already lost their concentration.

Lesson Plan

WE BELIEVE (continued)

Ask the children to read aloud the *We Believe* statement at the top of page 22. On the board write the word *divine*. Ask the children to read silently as you read aloud the first paragraph.

Introduce the word *miracle* by saying it, but not writing it. Explain: *Because Jesus was God he had the power to heal people. We call Jesus' healings miracles.*

Direct the children's attention to the picture of Jesus. Read the Scripture story aloud. Then ask: *What do you think Peter's family said to Jesus and to each other after the woman was healed?*

Explain that Jesus did other things only God can do. Ask a volunteer to read the paragraph following the Scripture story.

Read the question. Pause briefly to allow children time to reflect on their responses. Invite volunteers to share what they would like to say.

Distribute copies of Reproducible Master 1. Together read aloud the words to "The Storm at Sea." Play the song, #2 on the Grade 2 CD. Replay the recording, having the children sing along. Have the children illustrate the lyrics. Encourage the children to share the song with their families.

Jesus, the Son of God, taught us about God the Father and God the Holy Spirit.

On the night before Jesus died, he shared a very special meal with his close friends. Jesus told them about God the Father. Then Jesus said that he would ask his Father to send the Holy Spirit. God the Holy Spirit would help them to remember everything that Jesus taught them.

Jesus taught us that there is only one God. But there are Three Persons in One God.

The Father is God.
The Son is God.
The Holy Spirit is God.
We call the Three Persons in One God the **Blessed Trinity.**

WE RESPOND

 How can you show your love for God the Father, God the Son, and God the Holy Spirit? Write one way here.

_____

_____

Remember the Blessed Trinity.

✝ Pray the Sign of the Cross.

In the name of the Father,
and of the Son,
and of the Holy Spirit.
Amen.

Key Words

divine a word used to describe God

Blessed Trinity the Three Persons in One God

23

ACTIVITY BANK

Multiple Intelligences
Bodily-Kinesthetic

Have the children work in groups. Ask the members of each group to use their own words and actions to dramatize one of the lesson's Scripture stories.

Parish
Praying for the Sick

Together write a prayer to Jesus asking him to help the members of the children's families and parish who are sick. Write the prayer on a sheet of poster board. Display the prayer poster in the prayer space. Remember to pray it often during the coming week.

Ask volunteers to share what Jesus told people about God the Father. Then read aloud the first paragraph on page 23.

Write *Blessed Trinity* on the board or on chart paper. Explain that the word *blessed* means "holy." Circle the letters *tri-* in Trinity. Explain that these letters mean "three." Stress: *There is only one God, but there are Three Persons in One God.* Have the children highlight or underline in their texts: *The Father is God; the Son is God; the Holy Spirit is God.*

WE RESPOND   ___ minutes

Connect to Life Read the *We Respond* question. Have the children write their responses. (Possible responses: pray, say their names respectfully.) Ask volunteers to share what they have written. Then encourage the children to choose one thing they will each do this week to show their love.

Pray Review the hand gestures for praying the Sign of the Cross. Have the children pray together the Sign of the Cross.

Catechist Goal
- To review the chapter ideas that are key to growing as disciples of Jesus Christ

Our Faith Response
- To decide on ways to grow as disciples by living out what we have learned

Lesson Materials
- crayons or colored pencils

Show What you Know

Read each direction line. Pause after each to allow the children to find the correct *Key Word* and complete the task. Check the children's work.

Picture This
Read each set of directions. For the picture on the left, refer the children to pages 20–21 of the student text. For the one on the right, refer them to pages 22–23.

Pray Today
Read aloud the directions. When all are finished, check the correct ordering. For *Disciple Challenge*, encourage the children to share the prayer with a friend. The Sign of the Cross is taught in Grade 1 *We Believe*. This is a review.

Make it Happen

Discuss together the meaning of the word *amazing*. Read the directions. When all have finished writing, ask volunteers to share their responses with the group.

Take Home

Read the activity suggestion. Encourage the children to discuss with their families ways of respecting others.

Discuss and send home copies of *Sharing Faith with My Family* reproducible master for this chapter (back of book).

Grade 2 Chapter 1
PROJECT

Show What you Know

Use the Key Words in the box to complete the activities below.

- Underline the word that means the family of Jesus, Mary, and Joseph.
- Circle the word used to describe God.
- Check the word that is the Three Persons in One God.

> (divine)
> ✓ Blessed Trinity
> Holy Family

Picture This

Jesus is human like us. Draw something Jesus did that you can do.

> Possible responses: tell people about God; feed the hungry; care for the poor; comfort the sad and lonely; pray

Jesus is divine. He did things only God can do. Draw something Jesus did that only God can do.

> Possible responses: healed the sick; brought the dead back to life; forgave sins; calmed the storm at sea

24 www.webelieveweb.com

DISCIPLE

Pray Today
Put the parts of the prayer in order. Number the pictures from 1 to 5.

Amen.	and of the Son,	Spirit.	In the name of the Father,	and of the Holy
5	2	4	1	3

↳ DISCIPLE CHALLENGE Say this prayer with a friend.

Make it Happen

What is an amazing thing that Jesus did?

Possible responses: healed the sick; forgave sins; calmed the storm at sea

Now, pass it on!

Take Home

God wants us to respect every person on earth. He wants us to respect people who are older than us. He wants us to respect people who are our age, or younger than us. He wants us to respect people who are different from us. As a family, think about some ways you can show respect to people you know.

25

CHAPTER TEST

Fill in the circle beside the correct answer.

1. The members of the Holy Family are Jesus, Mary, and _____.
   ○ Peter   ● Joseph

2. The name _____ means "God saves."
   ● Jesus   ○ Trinity

3. _____ told Mary God wanted her to be the Mother of his Son.
   ● An angel   ○ Joseph

4. Because Jesus is _____, he did things only God can do.
   ○ human   ● divine

5. The prayer we say to remember the Blessed Trinity is the _____.
   ○ Our Father   ● Sign of the Cross

Circle the correct answer.

6. Did Jesus teach people only by things he said?   Yes   (No)

7. Did Jesus teach that God always cares for us?   (Yes)   No

8. Are there Three Persons in One God?   (Yes)   No

9–10. Write two things Jesus did to help people.

Possible responses: taught the Good News; fed the hungry; comforted the sad and lonely; cared for the poor; taught the Our Father; healed the sick; forgave sins

CHAPTER TEST

Provide ten to fifteen minutes for the students to complete the test. After all have finished, check the answers. Clarify any misconceptions.

Alternative Assessment

You may want the students to complete the following alternative-assessment activity.

Write sentences or draw pictures to tell some ways that Jesus showed God's love.

Additional Testing

• Chapter 1 Test in *Assessment Book*, pages 3–4

• CD-ROM *Test Generator and Resource*: Use Chapter 1 Test or customize your own.

Review

Review the definitions as they are presented in the chapter's *Key Word* boxes:

• Holy Family (page 20)

• divine (page 23)

• Blessed Trinity (page 23).

We Believe Statements

Review the four statements.

• God the Father sent his Son, Jesus, to be with us.

• Jesus is human like us.

• Jesus did things only God can do.

• Jesus, the Son of God, taught us about God the Father and God the Holy Spirit.

To use the Chapter 1 Study Guide, visit

www.webelieveweb.com

Chapter 2 Jesus Christ Gives Us the Church

Overview

In Chapter 1 the children learned that God the Father sent his Son, Jesus, to be with us. In this chapter the children will continue to learn about the work of Jesus and the beginning of the Church.

Doctrinal Content	For Adult Reading and Reflection *Catechism of the Catholic Church*
The children will learn:	Paragraph
• Jesus gathered many followers to be his disciples.	787
• Jesus died and rose to new life.	638
• Jesus promised to send the Holy Spirit.	729
• The Holy Spirit helps the Church to grow.	737

disciples (p. 29)
Apostles (p. 29)
Resurrection (p. 29)
Church (p. 31)

Catechist Background

What inspires you to follow Jesus?

From the moment of your Baptism, you have been called by name to follow Jesus' way to the Father. What moves you to know, love, and serve God is the power and presence of the Holy Spirit. The Holy Spirit moves you to respond to your vocation as a catechist.

In the Gospel of Saint Luke, we read about the beginning of Jesus' ministry. He stood up to read and was handed a scroll of the prophet Isaiah. He unrolled the scroll and found the following passage:

"The Spirit of the Lord is upon me,
because he has anointed me
to bring glad tidings to the poor."
(Luke 4:16–18)

The same Spirit is with us today.

To teach as Jesus did takes courage. The first followers of Jesus needed this same courage as they began to speak about Jesus in public. Before he

Go to **www.webelieveweb.com**, Catechist/Teacher, We Believe Correlations for this chapter's correlation to:
• Six Tasks of Catechesis
• Catholic Social Teaching
• *Catechetical Formation in Chaste Living.*

faced Death on the cross, Jesus promised to send the Holy Spirit to help all his followers and to encourage them to continue his mission. Even after Jesus rose from the dead, his Apostles and disciples needed such encouragement.

As he was about to return to his Father, Jesus told his followers, "You will receive power when the holy Spirit comes upon you" (Acts of the Apostles 1:8). The Holy Spirit did come upon the disciples and inspired them to go out and spread the Good News. The Holy Spirit continues to be present in the Church today. Each time we enter a classroom and have the courage to teach the faith, we experience the presence of the Holy Spirit.

How do you acknowledge the presence of the Holy Spirit in your life's work?

Lesson Planning Guide

Lesson Steps	Presentation	Materials

① WE GATHER

Lesson Steps	Presentation	Materials
page 27 ✝ **Prayer** 📖 *Matthew 4:18–22* ☀ **Focus on Life**	• Gather at the prayer table. • Listen to the Scripture reading. • Respond in word and action. • Discuss the question.	For the prayer space: items that remind children of the seashore 🎵 "Come Follow Me," #3, Grade 2 CD

② WE BELIEVE

Lesson Steps	Presentation	Materials
page 28 *Jesus gathered many followers to be his disciples.*	• Present who the first disciples of Jesus were. 🏃 Complete the activity about being Jesus' disciples.	• crayons or colored pencils
page 29 *Jesus died and rose to new life.* 📖 *Matthew 28:1–5*	• Read and discuss the text and Scripture reading. • Point out the *Key Words* and definitions. 🎵 Sing Alleluia. • Read and discuss *As Catholics*.	🎵 "Sing for Joy" by Bernadette Farrell, #4, Grade 2 CD (option)
page 30 *Jesus promised to send the Holy Spirit.* 📖 *Acts of the Apostles 2:1–4*	• Read and discuss the text and Scripture reading. 🏃 Complete the puzzle activity.	
page 31 *The Holy Spirit helps the Church to grow.*	• Present and discuss the ways the Holy Spirit helps the Church. • Point out the *Key Word* and definition.	• large sheet of paper • copies of Reproducible Master 2, guide page 27C

③ WE RESPOND

Lesson Steps	Presentation	Materials
page 31	🏃 Discuss and act out what members of the Church do.	
pages 32–33 **Project Disciple**	• Complete the **Project Disciple** activities. • Explain the *Take Home* activity. • Discuss/send home **Sharing Faith with My Family** reproducible master for this chapter.	• crayons or colored pencils • copies of **Sharing Faith with My Family** reproducible master, Chapter 2 (back of book)
page 34 **Chapter 2 Test**	• Complete **Chapter 2 Test**. • Work on *Alternative Assessment* activity.	• optional: copies of Scripture reproducible master, *What's the Word?*, Chapter 2 (back of book)

For additional ideas, activities, and opportunities: Visit Sadlier's **www.WeBelieveweb.com**

Name

Use one color to fill in all the X spaces.
Use another color to fill in the O spaces.

PROJECT DISCIPLE

Pray
Learn
Celebrate
Share
Choose
Live

Additional Activities

What's the Word?

Scripture reproducible master, Chapter 2

Materials needed: copies of *What's the Word?* (back of book); optional—props and costumes for dramatization

Distribute copies of the Scripture reproducible master. Choose two volunteers to take the parts of Readers 1 and 2. Choose two volunteers to take the parts of the blind men. Have the other children take the part of the crowd. Then provide about five minutes for the children to write their reports on the lines provided on the reproducible master.

Make it Happen

Materials needed: half sheets of 8 ½ x 11 in. drawing paper, crayons or colored pencils

Have the children work in pairs. Give each pair a half sheet of paper. On the drawing paper, ask each pair to write a text message about Jesus.

When the children have completed their messages, ask each pair to exchange their messages with another pair of children.

Picture This

Materials needed: tag board sheets (1 for each group of children) with the outline of a church drawn on each sheet, magazines, construction paper strips, glue sticks, and empty paper spools

Introduce the activity at the end of the chapter. Have the children work in small groups. Give each group a sheet of tag board. Have someone in each group cut out the church. Have the group members cut out faces of people from the magazines and glue them in the church. Help the children glue the churches to empty spools so the churches stand.

Give each group a small piece of construction paper on which to draw and cut out a small cross to place at the top of the church. Stress the definition of *Church* given on pupil page 31.

Show What you Know

Assign each child to one of two teams. Then ask the members of each team to write five questions about the concepts they have learned in the chapter. Explain that they can use their texts.

Then have the teams challenge each other by asking their questions. Score 20 points for each correct answer. Make sure to congratulate all the children.

Meeting Individual Needs
English Language Learners

Children who are learning English may have difficulty reading pages with extensive text. Whenever possible, use visual aids to increase comprehension. Have the children list or underline key information.

We Believe Resources

- Grade 2 *Review & Resource Book*, pages 7–9
- Grade 2 *Family Book*, pages 8–10
- Grade 2 *Assessment Book*, pages 5–6
- Grade 2 CD-ROM *Test Generator and Resource*: Use Chapter 2 Test or customize your own.

- **www.webelieveweb.com**

Enrichment Ideas

*Chapter Story

With great excitement Ron opened the envelope and quickly reached inside. There was a letter from Mrs. Smith, who had been his first grade teacher last year. "How odd," he thought, "to get a letter from Mrs. Smith during summer vacation."

"What does it say?" Ron's mom asked as Ron handed her the page that came with the letter. Ron began to read aloud,

> *Dear Ronald,*
> *Do you remember the activity that we did on the last day of school? I gave each student a list of people in the class. I asked you to write next to each name something about the person that you liked or admired.*
> *Well, here is the list of all the good things that people said about you! I hope you enjoy reading about what a wonderful person you are! I agree with them all!*
> *Mrs. Smith*

Ron looked up at his mother as she read the words on the page she was holding. Ron was surprised to see small tears coming from her eyes. "This is really something," his mother said softly, handing the page to her son.

Ron glanced at the list of things that his classmates had said about him. He read about what a good friend he was, how he was always willing to help, how much fun he was to be with, and how smart he was. The words *like*, *admire*, *great*, and *good friend* appeared more than once on the list.

As Ron finished reading, he felt something really wonderful inside. It was the good feeling of being proud of himself.

"Mom," Ron said, "do you think Mrs. Smith could be my second grade teacher?"

▶ *What did this kind teacher do for her students?*

FAITH and MEDIA

▶ Look for examples on television and in children's movies of people who follow a leader. Explore with the children what qualities a particular leader has that moves people to follow him or her. Jesus was a leader, too. How similar to Jesus are the other leaders that you have discussed? Reflect as an adult on the kinds of heroes that are presented to children in the media. Invite the children to reflect on times when they act as leaders— for example, on the playground. How can they lead others in the ways that Jesus did?

▶ If a parish Web site exists, have the children find out more about their parish community and its leaders.

CHAPTER PROJECT: SEQUENCE LINE

Have the children work in groups to study the order of events in the chapter, starting with the call of the disciples and ending with the beginning of the Church. They might use words and drawings on paper plates to show each of the events described in the chapter: calling of disciples, ministry of Jesus, his Crucifixion and Death and Resurrection, Pentecost, and the Holy Spirit present in the Church today. Have them decorate a paper plate in a way appropriate for the particular event. Then, using a long ribbon or string, have them hang the paper plates in the order in which the events took place in the life of Jesus and the first disciples. Hang this sequence line in a prominent place. You might use this as a way of reviewing at the end of the chapter.

WE GATHER

✝ **Leader**: Let us take a quiet moment to listen carefully to a story about Jesus.

📖 Matthew 4:18–22

One day Jesus was walking by the sea. He saw Peter and Andrew catching fish with a net. Jesus called them, and asked them to come follow him. "At once they left their nets and followed him."

(Matthew 4:20)

All: (Clap twice after each line of this response.)

Jesus says to all of us, "Come, follow me."
Come and learn how very happy you can be.
Loving God and loving others
We are sisters now and brothers.
Jesus says to all of us,
"Come, follow me."

 Name some of your teachers and helpers. How do you follow their example?

27

PREPARING TO PRAY

For this gathering prayer the children will listen to God's Word and respond in word and action.

• Choose a prayer leader. Point out what the leader should read. Give the leader a few minutes to prepare.

• The words for the response may be sung to the tune of "If You're Happy." Play "Come Follow Me," #3, on the Grade 2 CD. Have the children practice singing.

The Prayer Space

• In the prayer space, place items that will bring to mind Jesus' calling of his first disciples by the Sea of Galilee: sand, shells, pebbles, model boat.

📖 **This Week's Liturgy**
Visit **www.webelieveweb.com** for this week's liturgical readings and other seasonal material.

Lesson Plan

WE GATHER _____ minutes

✝ Pray

• Invite the children to pray the Sign of the Cross together. Then ask them to listen carefully as the prayer leader begins.

• Read the Scripture passage aloud. Then pause briefly. Explain: *Followers of Jesus can be happy doing as he asks.*

• Ask the children to clap twice after reading or singing each line of the prayer response. Then pray the response together.

Focus on Life

• Have the children name some of their teachers and helpers.

• Have the children share ways in which they follow their teachers' and helpers' example.

• Share the *Chapter Story* on guide page 27E.

Family Connection Update

Invite the children to share their family discussions about ways of respect.

Catechist Goal

• To explain that as Jesus' disciples we are guided by the Holy Spirit to be active members of the Church

Our Faith Response

• To identify oneself as a disciple of Jesus and to live as a member of the Church

 **disciples**   **Apostles**
           Resurrection   **Church**

Materials

• colored pencils or crayons
• large sheet of paper
• copies of Reproducible Master 2
• Option: Grade 2 CD
• Scripture and Family reproducible masters (back of book)

Celebrating the Resurrection

    After working on these two pages, read the *As Catholics* text. Discuss the importance of the celebration of the Resurrection to all of us.

WE BELIEVE

Jesus gathered many followers to be his disciples.

Jesus taught people about God the Father's love. He cared for those who were sick and poor.

Many people began to follow Jesus. Those who followed Jesus were called his **disciples**.

Jesus taught the disciples to love and to help one another. Jesus helped them to become a community of people who believed in him.

From this community, Jesus chose twelve disciples to become its leaders. We call these twelve men the **Apostles**.

 Jesus invites you to follow him, too!

Write your name on the line.

_____

is a disciple of Jesus.

What is one thing you can do as Jesus' disciple?

28

Lesson Plan

WE BELIEVE   _____ minutes

Invite the children to look at the picture of Jesus with the people. Ask: *What do you think Jesus is saying?*

Read the *We Believe* statement below the picture. Point out to the children:

• *Jesus taught people through his words and actions.*
• *He was kind, good, and fair to everyone.*

Write the word *disciples* on the board or on chart paper. Pronounce the word and explain: *Followers of Jesus are called disciples.*

Choose volunteers to read the text on page 28. Stress: *Every baptized person is called to be a follower or disciple of Jesus.*

Invite the children to complete the activity on page 28 by writing their names on the line provided.

Point out that Jesus chose twelve disciples to be the leaders of all the disciples. These leaders are the Apostles.

Brainstorm things we can do as Jesus' disciples. Write the suggestions on a large sheet of paper. Encourage the children to choose one thing they can do this week.

Ask a volunteer to read the *We Believe* statement at the top of page 29 and the two paragraphs that follow. Ask: *How do you think Jesus' disciples felt when Jesus died?*

Jesus died and rose to new life.

Jesus tried to share his Good News with everyone. Some of the people did not want to follow Jesus. They did not believe in the amazing things Jesus said and did in God's name. There were people who wanted to put Jesus to death.

Jesus was put to death on a cross. Then his body was placed in a tomb.

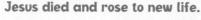 Matthew 28:1–5

Early on Sunday morning, some women disciples of Jesus went to visit the tomb. An angel was sitting in front of the tomb. The angel said that Jesus had risen from the dead.

Jesus died and rose to save us from sin. Jesus' rising from the dead is called the **Resurrection**. We celebrate Jesus' Resurrection on Easter.

♪ Let us sing Alleluia to show our joy in Jesus' Resurrection.

Key Words

disciples those who follow Jesus

Apostles the twelve men chosen by Jesus to be the leaders of his disciples

Resurrection Jesus' rising from the dead

As Catholics...

We celebrate the Resurrection of Jesus Christ at Easter and on every Sunday of the year. At every Mass we remember that Jesus died and rose to new life. Remember this at Mass this week.

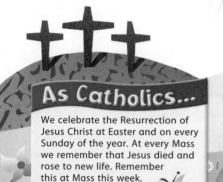  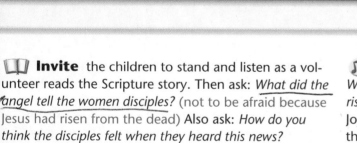

ACTIVITY BANK

Multiple Intelligences
Musical-Rhythmic
Activity Materials: rhythm-band instruments, Grade 2 CD

Encourage the children to express joy through music. They can play rhythm instruments, clap their hands, wave their arms, or dance as you sing an Alleluia song.

Teach the children the following words to "Sing for Joy," #4 on the Grade 2 CD.

Sing and shout for joy, Alleluia!
Sing and shout for joy, Alleluia!
Sing and shout for joy, Alleluia!
Alleluia! Alleluia!

📖 **Invite** the children to stand and listen as a volunteer reads the Scripture story. Then ask: *What did the angel tell the women disciples?* (not to be afraid because Jesus had risen from the dead) Also ask: *How do you think the disciples felt when they heard this news?* Encourage the children to conclude that they were happy and excited.

Ask the children to be seated. Write the word *Resurrection* on the board. Say the word and ask the children to repeat it. Then read aloud together the paragraph about Jesus' Resurrection.

♪ **Explain:** *Alleluia is a word we use to praise God. We sing Alleluia to express our happiness that Jesus has risen.* You may want to play the Alleluia song "Sing for Joy." It is #4 on the Grade 2 CD. Play it twice, inviting the children to join in singing the second time.

Quick Check

✔ *What is a disciple of Jesus?* (A disciple is someone who follows Jesus.)

✔ *What do we call Jesus' rising from the dead?* (We call Jesus' rising from the dead the Resurrection.)

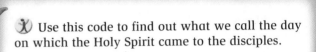

Jesus promised to send the Holy Spirit.

The risen Jesus visited his disciples before he returned to Heaven. He promised to send the Holy Spirit to help them.

Acts of the Apostles 2:1–4

One morning, the disciples were all together. Mary, the mother of Jesus, and some women were among them.

Suddenly, they heard a noise like a strong wind. Then they saw what looked like flames of fire over each of them. "And they were all filled with the holy Spirit." (Acts of the Apostles 2:4)

Use this code to find out what we call the day on which the Holy Spirit came to the disciples.

E	P	T	C	O	S	N
1	2	3	4	5	6	7

P E N T E C O S T
2 1 7 3 1 4 5 6 3

On Pentecost, a large crowd had gathered. The disciples wanted to tell the people about Jesus.

Peter spoke to the crowd. He asked them to be baptized and receive the Gift of the Holy Spirit. Many people were baptized that day.

30

Lesson Plan

WE BELIEVE (continued)

Remind the children that the Holy Spirit is the Third Person of the Blessed Trinity. Read together the *We Believe* statement on page 30. Then ask a volunteer to read the first paragraph.

Ask a volunteer to read the Scripture story.

Have everyone imagine that they were with the disciples when the Holy Spirit came. Ask: *What would you have said and done?*

Read the activity directions. Have the children work in pairs to solve the puzzle.

Continue the account of Pentecost by reading aloud the last two paragraphs on page 30. Explain that just as some of the early followers of Jesus heard about him from Peter, so do we hear about Jesus from other people. Ask: *Who are some of the people who have told you about Jesus?*

Read together the *We Believe* statement on page 31. Write the word *Church* on the board. Point to the definition in the *Key Word* box and encourage the children to memorize this definition. Have the children point to themselves and say: *We are the Church.*

The Holy Spirit helps the Church to grow.

On Pentecost, the Church began. The **Church** is all the people who are baptized in Jesus Christ and follow his teachings.

The first members of the Church were helped by the Holy Spirit to
- believe in Jesus and pray
- be brave in following Jesus
- love one another and be a community
- teach and help people as Jesus did.

The Holy Spirit helps us in these ways, too.

The Holy Spirit helps us to live as Jesus wants us to live. The Holy Spirit helps us to tell others about Jesus Christ.

WE RESPOND

Talk about some things members of the Church do.

Act out one thing you would like to do as a member of the Church.

Key Word

Church all the people who are baptized in Jesus Christ and follow his teachings

HOLY SPIRIT PARISH
HELPING

31

ACTIVITY BANK

Multicultural Connection
Catholic Celebrations
Activity Materials: pictures of Catholic celebrations from various cultures

Show the children pictures of Catholic celebrations from a variety of cultures. Check Catholic magazines and newspapers. Make sure the people in the pictures are celebrating something special, such as Pentecost or a feast of Mary or the saints. Encourage the children to share details of any cultural celebrations in which they have participated.

Multiple Intelligences
Bodily-Kinesthetic
Invite the children to act out the events described on page 30. Ask for volunteers to take the parts of Jesus, his disciples, and the wind. Read or paraphrase the Scripture story of Pentecost, while the children act out their parts.

Ask a volunteer to read the list of ways the Holy Spirit helped the first members of the Church. Have the children look at the list and ask them to suggest similar ways in which we are helped by the Holy Spirit. Stress: *The Holy Spirit helps us each day to be disciples of Jesus.*

WE RESPOND ___ minutes

Connect to Life Direct attention to the photo on page 31. Ask: *What are the people doing?* Brainstorm with the children about other things members of the Church do. List the suggestions on a large sheet of paper. Invite the children to select something they would like to do. Then have each child act it out. Praise the children's good intentions. Encourage them to put into practice what they have acted out for the group.

Distribute Reproducible Master 2. (See guide page 27C.) Have the children do the activity now or work on it at home. Stress the message that the children find in the puzzle (We are the Church).

Catechist Goal

● To review the chapter ideas that are key to growing as disciples of Jesus Christ

Our Faith Response

● To decide on ways to grow as disciples by living out what we have learned

Show What *you* Know

Help the children complete the sentences. Then have them work with partners to complete the word-search puzzle.

What's *the* Word?

Read the directions. Refer the children to page 28 to find the answer.

Make *it* Happen

Have the student's work on the pledge quietly. Ask the children to respect each other's privacy as they are working.

What Would *you* do?

Have the children look at the illustration as you read the situation. Ask the students to complete the activity.

Take Home

Ask volunteers to share what they have learned about the Apostles and disciples. Make a chart on the board, listing similarities and differences between the two groups. Encourage the children to do the activity with their families.

Discuss and send home copies of *Sharing Faith with My Family* reproducible master for this chapter (back of book).

Pray Learn Celebrate Share Choose Live

Grade 2 Chapter 2

PROJECT

Show What *you* Know

Solve the clues below. Then find the **Key Words** hidden in the word search.

1. Those who follow Jesus are _____disciples_____.

2. The twelve men chosen by Jesus to be the leaders of his disciples are the _____Apostles_____.

3. Jesus' rising from the dead is called the _____Resurrection_____.

```
L E S C Y T M N W D Y P
U R E R J E S L H F E E
F U L M S O H I T O N N
Y A P O S T L E S O C O
O D I I E N A M I H E I
H X C C D C A E C A B A
R E S U R R E C T I O N
N I I I R T H Q L H V R
V L D N C H I S M T Y A
```

What's *the* Word?

In the Bible there is a book that tells stories about the twelve men Jesus chose to be the leaders of his disciples. Guess the name of this book.

Acts of the A p o s t l e s

32 www.webelieveweb.com

DISCIPLE

Pray Learn Celebrate Share Choose Live

Make *it* Happen   Finish this disciple pledge.

> I will be a disciple of Jesus.
>
> I will be kind to _____.
>
> I will pray for _____.
>
> I will teach _____ how I follow Jesus.
>
> I will show _____ how I love God and others.

Possible responses: names of childrens' family members, friends, or loved ones

What Would *you* do?

At recess, you see your friend Jen fall down and hurt her hand. She is crying. Draw or write what you could do as a disciple of Jesus.

Possible responses: give Jen a hug; tell a teacher or supervisor; walk with Jen to the nurse

Take Home

Talk as a family about ways Apostles and disciples are alike and different.

↳ **DISCIPLE CHALLENGE** Quiz your family members. Do they know how many Apostles Jesus chose? He chose 12. After Jesus died, the Apostles were the leaders of Jesus' disciples. **33**

CHAPTER TEST

Circle the correct answer.

1. Do we celebrate Jesus' Resurrection on Easter? **(Yes)** No

2. Were Peter, Andrew, Mary, and Martha the only disciples of Jesus? Yes **(No)**

3. Did the Church end on Pentecost? Yes **(No)**

4. Did Jesus die and rise to new life to save us? **(Yes)** No

Use the words in the box to complete the sentences.

5. The twelve men Jesus chose to be the leaders

   of his disciples are the ___Apostles___.

6. The ___Church___ is all the people who are baptized in Jesus Christ and follow his teachings.

7. Jesus' rising from the dead is called

   the ___Resurrection___.

8. The day the Holy Spirit came to help the disciples

   is ___Pentecost___.

Church

Apostles

Pentecost

Resurrection

9–10. Write two ways that the Holy Spirit helps the Church.

Possible responses: helps the Church to live as Jesus wants; helps the Church to tell others about Jesus

Chapter 2 • Page 34

CHAPTER TEST

Provide ten to fifteen minutes for the students to complete the test. After all have finished, check the answers. Clarify any misconceptions.

Alternative Assessment

You may want the students to complete the following alternative-assessment activity.

Imagine you were in the crowd on the first Pentecost. What did you hear Peter or another disciple say? Write about what you heard.

Additional Testing

• Chapter 2 Test in *Assessment Book*, pages 5–6

• CD-ROM *Test Generator and Resource*: Use Chapter 2 Test or customize your own.

Review

Review the definitions as they are presented in the chapter's *Key Word* boxes:

• disciples (page 29)
• Apostles (page 29)
• Resurrection (page 29)
• Church (page 31).

We Believe Statements

Review the four statements.

• Jesus gathered many followers to be his disciples.
• Jesus died and rose to new life.
• Jesus promised to send the Holy Spirit.
• The Holy Spirit helps the Church to grow.

To use the Chapter 2 Study Guide, visit

www.webelieveweb.com

Chapter 3 · We Celebrate God's Love

Overview

In Chapter 2 the children learned about the work of Jesus and the beginning of the Church. In this chapter the children will learn more about Jesus, the sacraments, and ways we worship God.

Doctrinal Content	For Adult Reading and Reflection *Catechism of the Catholic Church*
The children will learn:	Paragraph
• We belong to the Catholic Church.	1267–1269
• Catholics celebrate God's love by praying and worshiping.	1119
• Our Church celebrates with seven special signs called sacraments.	1123
• Jesus is present with us in the sacraments.	1127

Key Words

Catholics (p. 37)
parishes (p. 37)
faith (p. 37)
worship (p. 37)
sacrament (p. 39)

Catechist Background

How do you find Jesus in the sacraments?

Of the four Gospel writers, Saint John perhaps best highlights for us the sacramental quality of the deeds that Jesus performed during his earthly ministry. John tells us that Jesus fed the hungry crowds with bread from heaven (John 6:1–15, 22–58). He tells us that Christ raised Lazarus to life and so promised believers a share in a life that will never die (John 11:1–20). He tells us that on the night before he died Jesus washed his disciples' feet and told them that this act was a model for them to follow (John 13:1–20). Jesus touched and healed peoples' bodies and souls. His physical actions had a spiritual effect.

Pope Saint Leo the Great once observed that our Redeemer's visible deeds have passed over into the sacraments. These words offer us a helpful way of understanding what we do every time we gather to celebrate the sacraments—the seven special actions of the Church that we receive from Christ.

In Baptism Christ gives us God's life, that we might never die. He washes us clean as he makes us his disciples. In the Eucharist, Christ feeds us with his heaven-sent Bread of Life.

In the sacraments of the Church, Christ continues his ministry. He is feeding us, healing us, forgiving our sins, and making us whole. Every time we gather in his name to celebrate the sacraments, Jesus is truly with us.

What do you need from Jesus today?

Go to **www.webelieveweb.com**, Catechist/Teacher, We Believe Correlations for this chapter's correlation to:
- Six Tasks of Catechesis
- Catholic Social Teaching.

Lesson Planning Guide

Lesson Steps	Presentation	Materials

 ① WE GATHER

page 35 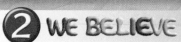 **Prayer** 📖 *Psalm 100:1–3, 4–5* ☀ **Focus on Life**	• Gather in the prayer space. • Pray psalm verses. • Discuss the directive and respond to the question.	• percussion instruments: drum, maracas, tambourine, cymbals For the prayer space: Alleluia banner, pictures or statue of Jesus

② WE BELIEVE

page 36 *We belong to the Catholic Church.*	• Read and discuss the text and photographs about the Church community. 🧍 Complete the activity.	• pen or pencil
page 37 *Catholics celebrate God's love by praying and worshiping.* 📖 *Psalm 100:1–3*	• Read and discuss the text. • Praise God with words from Scripture. • Point out the *Key Words* and definitions. 🧍 Do the activity. • Pray Alleluia together.	• crayons or highlighters
page 38 *Our Church celebrates with seven special signs called sacraments.*	• Discuss signs used for celebrations. • Present the text. 🧍 Complete the activity.	• pens or pencils
page 39 *Jesus is present with us in the sacraments.*	• Present the Seven Sacraments. • Read and discuss *As Catholics.*	• crayons or highlighters • copies of Reproducible Master 3, guide page 35C

 **③ WE RESPOND**

page 39	🧍 Discuss the *We Respond* question. • Spend time in silent prayer.	
pages 40–41 **Project Disciple**	• Complete the **Project Disciple** activities. • Explain the *Take Home* activity. • Discuss/send home **Sharing Faith with My Family** reproducible master for this chapter.	• pencils • copies of **Sharing Faith with My Family** reproducible master, Chapter 3 (back of book)
page 42 **Chapter 3 Test**	• Complete **Chapter 3 Test**. • Work on *Alternative Assessment* activity.	• optional: copies of Scripture reproducible master, *What's the Word?*, Chapter 3 (back of book)

For additional ideas, activities, and opportunities: Visit Sadlier's **www.WeBelieveweb.com**

35B

Name _____

Use this code to find the words to complete each sentence below. The sentences tell something important about our Church.

A	C	E	G	I	J	M	N	R	S	T	U
1	2	3	4	5	6	7	8	9	10	11	12

Our Church celebrates Seven

___ ___ ___ ___ ___ ___ ___ ___ ___ ___ .
10   1   2   9   1   7   3   8   11 10

They are special ___ ___ ___ ___ ___
                  10   5   4   8   10

given to us by ___ ___ ___ ___ ___ .
                6   3   10 12 10

Additional Activities

What's the Word?

Scripture reproducible master, Chapter 3

Materials needed: copies of *What's the Word?* (back of book); optional—props and costumes for dramatization

Distribute copies of the Scripture reproducible master. Choose four volunteers to be readers. Explain that the other children in the group will be people in the crowd. Go over the words in the script. Stress that the words of the crowd are ones of praise and thanks to Jesus Christ, the Son of God.

Show What you Know

Materials needed: poster board or chart paper; markers

Help the children do an acrostic for the word *Catholic*. Print the letters vertically on the poster board or chart paper. Have volunteers use each letter to begin words or phrases that explain the meaning of the word.

Example: **C** hurch community

When you are finished using the letters, have volunteers add illustrations.

Celebrate!

After you have presented the charts of the Seven Sacraments, explain that we celebrate the sacraments most often in our parish church. Have the students turn to the diagram of the parish church on pages 238 and 239 of their books. Help the children locate the numbered items in the illustration. Read the brief description given for each on the guide pages. If you have time, take a tour of your parish church and point out the location of the items in your church, particularly the baptismal font or pool, the reconciliation room or confessionals, and the altar.

Question Corner

After you have presented *We Believe*, on page 37, ask the students to identify events that they have celebrated or continue to celebrate with their parish community. Also ask: *Why is it special to pray, work, and share God's love with our parish communities?*

Meeting Individual Needs
Children with Attention-Deficit Disorder

Children who have attention-deficit disorder (ADD) may need special facilitating techniques to keep them on track. One effective technique is to make a performance chart that lists daily goals. Each day the child with ADD records whether these goals were met. Affirm the children when they have accomplished their goals and encourage the children even when they have not met their goals.

We Believe Resources

- Grade 2 *Review & Resource Book*, pages 10–12
- Grade 2 *Family Book*, pages 27–29
- Grade 2 *Assessment Book*, pages 17–18
- Grade 2 CD-ROM *Test Generator and Resource*: Use Chapter 3 Test or customize your own.
- **www.webelieveweb.com**

Enrichment Ideas

Chapter Story

The Kowalski family had just become members of Saint Rose of Lima parish. Last Sunday after Mass, Father Dave asked Carla and her dad, "Are you coming to the parish's fiftieth anniversary celebration?"

Carla answered, "Father, we don't know many people."

Father Dave said, "Well, come and you'll meet more people. You'll also learn more about our parish."

The next Sunday Carla and her parents went to the celebration. First they celebrated Mass with the parish community. Then they joined the people of the parish in the hall for a special lunch.

The walls of the hall were covered with photographs. Some showed people celebrating the Sacraments of Baptism and Confirmation. Some showed groups of children on their First Holy Communion day. There was a large photo of the first couple who were married in the parish. This couple were at the lunch with their children and their grandchildren. Carla and her parents met them all.

When the Kowalskis sat down to eat, Carla was surprised. Her new friend Tamara and her family were at the same table. Then Father Dave came over to say hello. He invited Carla and Tamara to join the other children in the front of the hall. "Come and get your picture taken. We need more photos for our parish's next special anniversary celebration."

When the Kowalskis were on their way home, Carla's mom said, "What a special parish community we belong to! I hope we can do our part to make other people feel as welcome as I do right now."

▶ *Would you like to belong to Saint Rose of Lima parish? Tell why or why not.*

FAITH and MEDIA

▶ On page 38, after reading *As Catholics*, tell the children about two kinds of media parishes use to tell the parish community about parish events and to tell others about the parish community: the parish bulletin (bring one to class) and the parish Web site (if your parish has one, visit the site with the children).

▶ Remind the children that when we sing and play instruments at Mass, we are using our voices and instruments to send a message of praise to God. We are also showing our love for God to everyone who can hear us singing and playing. Our music is another example of media.

CHAPTER PROJECT: PARISH GUESTS

Invite different parish leaders (pastor, director of religious education, a member of the liturgy committee, a member of the social justice committee) to talk to the children for a brief time.

Ask each speaker to stress with the children that they are all important members of the parish community. Allow time for questions and answers about this person's role in the parish.

Help the children make thank-you cards to send to each speaker.

We Celebrate God's Love

WE GATHER

✞ Let us stand to pray.

Group 1:

"Shout joyfully to the LORD, all you lands;
worship the LORD with cries of gladness;
come before him with joyful song."

Group 2:

"Know that the LORD is God,
our maker to whom we belong,
whose people we are."

Groups 1 and 2:

"Give thanks to God, bless his name;
good indeed is the LORD,
Whose love endures forever."

Psalm 100:1–3, 4–5

Name communities to which you belong. What do you do together in these groups?

35

PREPARING TO PRAY

Children will pray a psalm of praise. Explain: *Jesus may have prayed these words when he joined others in worshiping God the Father.*

• Form two groups. Ask the children to read over their group's verses. Explain that the word *endures* in the third verse means "lasts."

• Have available a few percussion instruments: drum, maracas, tambourine, and cymbals. Choose a volunteer to play each instrument at the beginning and end of the psalm. Give them a pattern of beats to follow and have them practice a few times together.

The Prayer Space

• Have volunteers help you to make an Alleluia banner. Display the banner in your prayer space. On the prayer table, place a picture or statue of Jesus.

📖 **This Week's Liturgy**

Visit **www.webelieveweb.com** for this week's liturgical readings and other seasonal material.

Lesson Plan

WE GATHER ____ minutes

✞ Pray

• Have the children open their books to the *We Gather* prayer on page 35. Ask Group 1 to stand on one side of the prayer space and Group 2 to stand on the other side. Remind the group: *Jesus is with us.* Have the musicians play. Then nod to indicate that Group 1 should begin reading.

• Pause briefly after Group 1 has finished. Then nod to indicate that Group 2 should begin. Then nod to both groups to read the third verse. Ask the musicians to play.

☀ Focus on Life

• Remind the children that communities work together for the good of others. Then ask the children to name some of the communities they belong to, and discuss what they do together in these groups. Point out that their families are the first communities to which they belong.

• Read the *Chapter Story* on guide page 35E.

Family Connection Update

Invite the children to share their families' discussions about Apostles and disciples.

Catechist Goal

• To teach that we belong to the Catholic Church and that the Church celebrates with seven special signs called sacraments

Our Faith Response

• To name ways we will prepare for the sacraments

 **Catholics** **parishes**
faith **worship**
sacrament

Materials

• colored pencils or crayons
• copies of Reproducible Master 3
• Scripture and Family reproducible masters (back of book)

Teaching Note

Learning About the Church

This lesson gives the children a brief introduction to the Church today. The children will learn more about the Church and its leadership in Chapter 23, "The Church Lives Today."

WE BELIEVE

We belong to the Catholic Church.

We belong to the Church community that is called the Catholic Church. We are **Catholics**. We become members of the Church when we are baptized. We are led and guided by the pope and bishops.

Some of the things that Catholics throughout the world share and celebrate are:

• the belief that Jesus is the Son of God
• the belief that Jesus suffered, died, and rose again to save us
• God's life and love
• a call to help and serve others as Jesus did.

We worship and work together in communities called **parishes**. Our parish communities are led and guided by priests. They work with men and women of the parish. The whole parish serves the needs of others, especially the poor, sick, and lonely.

🧑 Complete the sentence by writing the name of your parish.

I belong to

_____

parish.

36

Lesson Plan

WE BELIEVE _____ minutes

Write on the board *Catholic Church*. Stress: *The Catholic Church is a community that has millions of members throughout the world.* Then ask a volunteer to read the first paragraph on page 36.

Emphasize: *There are many members of the Catholic Church, and we all share and celebrate certain things.* Read aloud the things listed in the second paragraph.

Explain: *Catholics worship and work together in parish communities.* Then ask the children to read silently as you read the third paragraph aloud. Point out to the children that they are important members of the parish. Have the children take turns standing while the other children say: *(child's name) is a very important member of the Church.*

🧑 **Write** the name of your parish on the board or on chart paper. Ask the children to write the name in their texts.

Catholics celebrate God's love by praying and worshiping.

Jesus and his disciples often shared and celebrated their faith in God. **Faith** is a gift from God. It helps us to trust God and believe all that he tells us.

Catholics, too, gather to celebrate their faith in God and his love. We **worship** God. This means we give him thanks and praise. When we gather to worship, God is with us. We often praise God with words from Scripture:

"Shout joyfully to the LORD, all you lands;
   worship the LORD with cries of gladness;
   come before him with joyful song." (Psalm 100:1–2)

Key Words

Catholics baptized members of the Church, led and guided by the pope and bishops

parishes communities that worship and work together

faith a gift from God that helps us to trust God and believe in him

worship to give God thanks and praise

We gather as a parish community each week at Mass. We celebrate all that Jesus has done for us through his life, his Death, and his Resurrection. We celebrate that Jesus is with us always. We praise God the Father, through his Son, Jesus Christ, together with the Holy Spirit. God gives us the strength to go out and share his great love.

Color this word we use in worship.

37

ACTIVITY BANK

Parish
Invitational Signs
Activity materials: poster board, crayons, markers, and other art supplies

Have the children work in groups. Explain that each group is going to make a poster to invite others to be active members of the parish. Write the following sentences on the board.

- *Come worship with us.*
- *Come celebrate God's love with us.*
- *Come help us to help others.*

Have each group choose one of these sentences to print on their posters. Then help the groups make and decorate their signs. Ask the pastor to display these posters in the church vestibule or parish hall.

Invite the children to look at the pictures on pages 36–37. Ask: *How do the pictures show what Catholics do in their parish communities?*

Write the word *worship* on the board. Explain: *We worship God just as the people did in Jesus' time.* Have volunteers read aloud the first two paragraphs on page 37.

Invite all the children to read together the verse from Psalm 100.

Explain: *We gather with our parish community to worship God.* Read aloud the third paragraph. Have the children highlight or underline the first three sentences of the paragraph.

Invite the children to color the letters of the word *Alleluia.* Ask: *What other words can we say to worship God?* (Possible responses: Amen; Glory; We praise you; We thank you.)

Quick Check

✔ *When do we become members of the Catholic Church?* (We become members when we are baptized.)

✔ *How do Catholics celebrate God's love?* (We gather together and worship him.)

As Catholics...

Our Parish

After working on these two pages, read aloud the *As Catholics* text. Remind the children that our parish community gathers together to celebrate the sacraments.

Teaching Note

Read Along

When you see **Read Along** either read the material to the children or ask a proficient reader to do so. The **Read Along** feature is used to make the children feel confortable with the material. It is also used since many children enjoy having information read to them.

Our Church celebrates with seven special signs called sacraments.

The Church celebrates with signs. But the signs the Church uses are different from ordinary signs.

The special signs the Church celebrates are the Seven Sacraments. A **sacrament** is a special sign given to us by Jesus. God makes us holy through the sacraments. Jesus gave us these sacraments so that we can share in God's own life.

We gather as a Church community to celebrate these sacraments. We become stronger in faith. We grow as followers of Jesus.

As Catholics...

In the Catholic Church, our parish is like our home. Millions of Catholics all around the world gather in their parish communities. In their parishes, Catholics praise and worship God. They celebrate the sacraments. They learn more about their faith. Together they do good works for the people in their communities and in the world.

Tell what happens when we celebrate the sacraments. Put these words in correct sentence order.

share   life   own   God's   in   We

We share in God's own life.

38

Lesson Plan

WE BELIEVE (continued)

List on the board or chart paper the following celebrations: Valentine's Day, Fourth of July, birthday. Ask the children what might be a sign of each celebration. Write each sign beside the celebration listed. (Possible responses: Valentine's Day, heart; Fourth of July, flag; birthday, balloons)

Write the word *sacrament* on the board. Explain: *A sacrament is a special sign that Jesus has given us.* Then have volunteers read aloud the three paragraphs on page 38.

Emphasize that we gather as a Church community to celebrate the Seven Sacraments. Ask the children to share the names of the sacraments they know or have learned about. (Note: The Grade 1 *We Believe* text presents the Sacraments of Baptism, Eucharist, and Penance and Reconciliation.)

Read aloud the activity directions. Have the children write the words of the sentence in correct order.

Jesus is present with us in the sacraments.

Through God's gift of faith, we believe Jesus is with us. Every time we celebrate the sacraments, Jesus is with us through the power of the Holy Spirit. The sacraments help us to live as friends of Jesus.

Key Word
sacrament a special sign given to us by Jesus

The Seven Sacraments
Read Along

Baptism We become children of God and members of the Church. We receive the Holy Spirit for the first time.

Confirmation This sacrament seals us with the Gift of the Holy Spirit and strengthens us. Confirmation makes us stronger followers of Jesus.

Eucharist This is the sacrament of the Body and Blood of Christ. We receive Jesus himself in Holy Communion.

Penance and Reconciliation In this sacrament, God forgives our sins. We tell our sins to the priest. We are given God's forgiveness and peace.

Anointing of the Sick This is the sacrament for those who are sick or are in danger of death. The priest prays that they may be healed in body, mind, and spirit.

Matrimony In this sacrament, a man and a woman become husband and wife. They promise to love and be faithful to each other always.

Holy Orders In this sacrament, a man becomes a deacon, a priest, or a bishop. He then serves the Church by leading and guiding God's people.

WE RESPOND

Which of the Seven Sacraments are you looking forward to celebrating this year?

Talk to Jesus about ways you are getting ready to celebrate these sacraments with your parish community.

39

ACTIVITY BANK

Multiple Intelligences
Spatial
Activity Materials: hangers, paper plates (3 for each child), lengths of yarn or string, hole punch

Help the children make sacrament mobiles. Give each child three paper plates. On one of their paper plates, have the children write *Baptism, Confirmation,* and *Eucharist.* On another plate have them write *Penance and Reconciliation* and *Anointing of the Sick.* On the third plate have them write *Matrimony* and *Holy Orders.* Help the children punch a hole at the top of each plate and use a piece of string or yarn to attach each plate to the hanger. Suggest that the children show their mobiles to their families and share with them what they have learned about these sacraments.

Ask the children to read aloud the *We Believe* statement and the first paragraph on page 39. Then ask the children to highlight or underline the paragraph's second sentence.

Read the explanation of each sacrament. (See *Teaching Note* on page 38.) Have the children highlight or underline the sacrament's name.

Encourage the children to memorize the names of the Seven Sacraments, but do not require that they memorize the entire explanation of each sacrament. Throughout the *We Believe* program the children will learn about the meaning and celebration of each of the Seven Sacraments.

Distribute copies of Reproducible Master 3. Have the children work on the activity now or at home. (first sentence, sacraments; second sentence, signs and Jesus)

WE RESPOND ____ minutes

Connect to Life Explain to the children that their families and the parish community help them to prepare to celebrate certain sacraments for the first time. Ask volunteers to share what these sacraments are.

Pray Have the children close their eyes and quietly pray to Jesus to thank him for the sacraments. Then pray together: *Jesus, help us to remember that you are with us always.*

Catechist Goal
- To review the chapter ideas that are key to growing as disciples of Jesus Christ

Our Faith Response
- To decide on ways to grow as disciples by living out what we have learned

Show What you Know

You may want the children to work in pairs to decode the *Key Words*. Then have each of the partners use each word in a sentence.

Celebrate!

Write the name of the parish on the board. Help the students fill out the membership card.

Make it Happen

Read the riddle. Have the children refer to the chart on page 39. Ask a volunteer to name the sacrament.

Then have the students refer to these charts to write their riddles. Allow about five minutes of time for solving the riddles.

Reality Check

Read the directions and list of sacraments. You may want to share with the children the sacraments you have celebrated.

Take Home

Encourage the children to do the activity at home.

Discuss and send home copies of *Sharing Faith with My Family* reproducible master for this chapter (back of book).

Grade 2 Chapter 3

Pray Learn Celebrate Share Choose Live

PROJECT

Show What you Know

Use the code to find the Key Words.
Tell what each word means.

A	C	E	F	H	I	L	M	N	O	P	R	S	T	W
1	2	3	4	5	6	7	8	9	10	11	12	13	14	15

F	A	I	T	H		C	A	T	H	O	L	I	C	S
4	1	6	14	5		2	1	14	5	10	7	6	2	13

W	O	R	S	H	I	P		P	A	R	I	S	H	E	S
15	10	12	13	5	6	11		11	1	12	6	13	5	3	13

S	A	C	R	A	M	E	N	T
13	1	2	12	1	8	3	9	14

Celebrate! Complete this membership card.

_____
(your name)

belongs to the Catholic Church.

_____
(your name)

is a member of _____ parish.

DISCIPLE

Pray Learn Celebrate Share Choose Live

Make it Happen Solve this riddle.

I am a sacrament that is celebrated by a man and a woman.
I make them husband and wife.
What sacrament am I?

Matrimony

Now write your own riddle about one of the sacraments. Ask a friend to guess it.

See page 39.

What sacrament am I?

Reality Check

Which sacraments have your family members celebrated?

- ☑ Baptism
- ❑ Confirmation
- ❑ Eucharist
- ❑ Penance and Reconciliation
- ❑ Anointing of the Sick
- ❑ Matrimony
- ❑ Holy Orders

Take Home

Finish the sentence using words from the box.

| pray | sing | go to Mass | act like Jesus |

My favorite way to worship God is to

_____

Ask your family members to share their favorite ways to worship God.

CHAPTER TEST

Fill in the circle beside the correct answer.

1. Jesus and his disciples _____ shared and celebrated their faith in God.
   - ● often
   - ○ never

2. Faith is a gift from God that helps us to trust in God and believe _____ that he tells us.
   - ○ some things
   - ● all

3. The Church celebrates _____ Sacraments.
   - ○ Twelve
   - ● Seven

4. _____ gave us the sacraments.
   - ○ The disciples
   - ● Jesus

5. When we celebrate the sacraments, we become _____ in faith.
   - ● stronger
   - ○ weaker

Circle the correct answer.

6. Are the sacraments the same as ordinary signs? **Yes** (**No**)

7. Do we worship God when we praise him? (**Yes**) **No**

8. Are parishes communities that worship and work together? (**Yes**) **No**

9–10. Write two things that all Catholics share and celebrate.

Possible responses: the belief that Jesus is the Son of God; that Jesus suffered, died, and rose again to save us; God's life and love; a call to
42 help and serve others as Jesus did

CHAPTER TEST

Provide ten to fifteen minutes for the children to complete the test. After all have finished, check the answers. Clarify any misconceptions.

Alternative Assessment

You may want the students to complete the following alternative-assessment activity.

Pretend a friend from school was absent this week. Write a few sentences to tell the friend what you learned about sacraments.

Additional Testing

• Chapter 3 Test in *Assessment Book*, pages 7–8

• CD-ROM *Test Generator and Resource*: Use Chapter 3 Test or customize your own.

Review

Review the definitions as they are presented in the chapter's *Key Word* boxes:

- Catholics (page 37)
- parishes (page 37)
- faith (page 37)
- worship (page 37)
- sacrament (page 39).

We Believe Statements

Review the four statements.

• We belong to the Catholic Church.

• Catholics celebrate God's love by praying and worshiping.

• Our Church celebrates with seven special signs called sacraments.

• Jesus is present with us in the sacraments.

To use the Chapter 3 Study Guide, visit

www.webelieveweb.com

Overview

In Chapter 3 the children discovered more about Jesus, the sacraments, and the ways we worship God. In this chapter the children will learn about the Sacrament of Baptism.

Doctrinal Content	For Adult Reading and Reflection *Catechism of the Catholic Church*
The children will learn:	Paragraph
• At Baptism we become children of God and members of the Church.	1213, 1267
• At Baptism we receive grace, a share in God's life.	1250
• We celebrate the Sacrament of Baptism with special words and actions.	1234–1243
• We can show that we are children of God by what we say and do.	1265–66

Key Words

grace (p. 45)
Original Sin (p. 45)
Baptism (p. 45)

Go to **www.webelieveweb.com**, Catechist/ Teacher, We Believe Correlations for this chapter's correlation to:
• Six Tasks of Catechesis
• Catholic Social Teaching
• *Catechetical Formation in Chaste Living.*

Catechist Background

If asked, why would you become a godparent?

In Hispanic families it is a very great honor to be asked to become a godparent. The person chosen becomes a *compadre* to the parents of the child to be baptized into the faith. An indestructible bond of love and support is created between the parents and the *compadre*. It is renewed and intensified by constant sharing and working together.

In a similar way, we are bound to one another when we renew our baptismal promises each Sunday. Yes, the moment we bless ourselves with the holy water we recall the love the Father, Son, and Holy Spirit have for us. Each time we recite the Creed as a faith community, we renew our baptismal promises to believe in God and his Church as our sacramental means to salvation. Again,

when we pray the Our Father, "truly the summary of the whole gospel, the most perfect of prayers" (*CCC* 2774), we affirm our baptismal vows to grow in the image and likeness of God in Christ Jesus.

By remembering our own baptismal promises at Mass, we can positively answer the question, will our children have faith? Yes, they will share with us "one Lord, one faith, one baptism" (Ephesians 4:5).

How can you renew your baptismal promise to grow in Christ?

Lesson Planning Guide

Lesson Steps	Presentation	Materials

 WE GATHER

Lesson Steps	Presentation	Materials
page 43 ✛ We Gather in Prayer ☀ Focus on Life	• Profess our faith. • Share responses to the question.	For the prayer space: pictures of water scenes, white tablecloth, a small glass bowl, holy water, cross, a white baptismal garment and candle • Grade 2 CD (option)

② WE BELIEVE

Lesson Steps	Presentation	Materials
page 44 *At Baptism we become children of God and members of the Church.*	• Read about becoming a member of the Church. 🯄 Fill out the membership card.	• colored pencils or pens
page 45 *At Baptism we receive grace, a share in God's life.*	• Discuss water and Baptism. • Present the *Key Words* and definitions. 🯄 Follow the directive for the activity. • Thank God for the gift of grace.	
page 46 *We celebrate the Sacrament of Baptism with special words and actions.* *Rite of Baptism*	• Present the text about the celebration of Baptism. 🯄 Share responses to the question.	• video of a baby's Baptism (option)
page 47 *We can show that we are children of God by what we say and do.* *Rite of Baptism*	• Continue discussing the celebration of Baptism. • Read and discuss *As Catholics*.	• white baptismal garment, white candle (option) • copies of Reproducible Master 4, guide page 43C

③ WE RESPOND

Lesson Steps	Presentation	Materials
page 47	🯄 Do the activity and share responses to the question.	• crayons or colored pencils
pages 48–49 **Project Disciple**	• Complete the Project Disciple activities. • Explain the *Take Home* activity. • Discuss/send home **Sharing Faith with My Family** reproducible master for this chapter.	• colored pencils or markers, paper • copies of **Sharing Faith with My Family** reproducible master, Chapter 4 (back of book)
page 50 **Chapter 4 Test**	• Complete Chapter 4 Test. • Work on *Alternative Assessment* activity.	• optional: copies of Scripture reproducible master, *What's the Word?*, Chapter 4 (back of book)

For additional ideas, activities, and opportunities: Visit Sadlier's 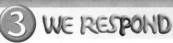**web.com**

Name _____

My Baptism

Fill in the missing information.
Ask your family to help you.

My Baptism

The date of my Baptism was _____

My godparents are _____

_____

The priest who baptized me was

_____

The church where I was baptized was

_____

Some people who celebrated with me were

_____

_____

_____

PROJECT DISCIPLE

Pray
Learn
Celebrate
Share
Choose
Live

Additional Activities

What's *the* Word?

Scripture reproducible master, Chapter 4

Materials needed: copies of *What's the Word?* (back of book); optional—costumes and props

Distribute copies of the Scripture reproducible master. Choose three volunteers to take the parts of the three readers. Choose other volunteers to mime the actions of the story as they listen to the readers.

Invite the children to circle the names of the Three Persons of the Blessed Trinity.

Picture This

Materials needed: drawing paper, crayons or colored pencils

After you have finished reading the story of Jesus' baptism on the Scripture reproducible master, have the children illustrate the story.

When the drawings are finished, display them in the prayer space.

Make *it* Happen

Explain that the water used in the celebration of the Sacrament of Baptism comes from the bodies of water that surround us. Stress that it is everyone's responsibility to use water wisely and to enjoy this life-giving gift of God.

Brainstorm with the children ways that they can conserve water at home. On the board or chart paper, list the ways. Display the chart in the prayer space.

Celebrate!

If possible, take the children into the church to show them the baptismal pool or font and the Easter candle. When you return from your visit, have the children look at the diagram of the church on pages 238–239 of the texts. Discuss the similarities and differences of the placement and look of the baptismal pools or fonts in the book and in the church.

Meeting Individual Needs
Children with Auditory Needs

Children with auditory needs may have a difficult time with a shift in activities. Use cues to alert these children when it is time to change focus. Designate a special hand gesture or give the children directions face-to-face.

We Believe Resources

- Grade 2 *Review & Resource Book*, pages 13–15
- Grade 2 *Family Book*, pages 14–16
- Grade 2 *Assessment Book*, pages 9–10
- Grade 2 CD-ROM *Test Generator and Resource*: Use Chapter 4 Test or customize your own.

www.webelieveweb.com

Chapter Story

Last night at supper William's mom asked, "What happened at school today?"

William explained that Maria Santos's mother talked to the class about Junior Rangers. He said, "Mrs. Santos told us that if we wanted to join, we should come to the first meeting on Monday. She told us that sometimes the rangers went on trips, sometimes they helped people in the neighborhood, and sometimes they did arts and crafts."

William asked his mom if he could join. On the way to the first meeting he said, "I hope the older rangers are nice to new members."

When William walked in, Maria and her older brother Marcos came over to shake William's hand. Marcos said, "I'm your ranger partner. I'll help you learn the rangers' pledge and work with you on a few projects. Today we'll sit together during the welcome ceremony. Then I'll introduce you to the other rangers."

William's mom picked him up after the meeting. As soon as he got in the car he said, "I really like Junior Rangers! I can hardly wait for the meeting next week. We are going to plant a tree in the park and then play soccer. And Mom, could you make cookies for me to bring for snack time?"

▶ *What did Marcos do to welcome William to the Junior Rangers?*

FAITH and MEDIA

▶ On page 46, if you have the children act out the celebration of Ana's Baptism, consider videotaping the role-play. If you have done the *Chapter Project*, consider taping the children's *Children of God* celebration.

▶ After the children have read and talked about Ana's Baptism, remind them that Ana's family might use media to share this special celebration with family and friends who cannot be at the celebration, and with Ana herself when she is older. (You might want to do this in connection with the showing of a video-taped Baptism; see *Teaching Tip,* p. 44.) Explain that Ana's family might videotape Ana's Baptism or post pictures of the celebration on a family Web site for family and friends to visit.

CHAPTER PROJECT: CHILDREN OF GOD CELEBRATION

Explain to the children that you want to celebrate that they are children of God and members of the Church. Have the children help you plan the celebration. Together decide on decorations, activities, music, and prayer. Have the children work on preparations for the event. Choose a day and time for the "Children of God" celebration.

We Celebrate Baptism

WE GATHER

✟ The word Amen is a prayer. When we pray this word, we are saying "Yes, we believe!" Let us respond Amen together after each of these prayers.

Child 1: God the Father, we believe in you.

Child 2: God the Son, we believe in you.

Child 3: God the Holy Spirit, we believe in you.

All: We are baptized. We are children of God. We live out the Good News of Jesus every day.

☀ What would you do to welcome a new baby to your family?

43

PREPARING TO PRAY

In this gathering prayer the children profess their belief in the Three Persons of the Blessed Trinity.

• Ask for three volunteers to read the three parts of the prayer. Help them prepare for the prayer.

• You may want the children to sing "We Believe, We Believe in God," #1 on the Grade 2 CD. Have the children practice the song. The words are on page 11 of the text.

The Prayer Space

• In the prayer space display pictures of water scenes. Place on the prayer table a white tablecloth, a small glass bowl filled with holy water, and a cross. On the table also place a white garment and a white candle, which are given to a child at Baptism.

📖 **This Week's Liturgy**
Visit **www.webelieveweb.com** for this week's liturgical readings and other seasonal material.

Lesson Plan

WE GATHER _____ minutes

✟ Pray

• Invite the children to gather in the prayer space with their books. Have them take turns dipping their fingers in the bowl of holy water and making the sign of the cross.

• Read aloud the introductory paragraph on page 43. Then invite the first volunteer to say his or her part of the prayer. After all three children have prayed and all have responded, ask the children to put down their books. Have them join hands and pray: *Amen. Yes, we believe.*

• Sing together "We Believe, We Believe in God." (optional)

☀ Focus on Life

• Read and discuss the question. Ask: *What would you do at a "welcome celebration"?* Invite volunteers to share their responses.

• Read the *Chapter Story* on guide page 43E.

Family Connection Update

Ask volunteers to share their families' favorite ways to worship God.

Catechist Goal

• To explain that at Baptism we become children of God and members of the Church and that we celebrate the sacrament with special words and actions

Our Faith Response

• To pray for all those who help us to live and grow as good Catholics

 **grace**   **Original Sin**
Baptism

Materials

• crayons or colored pencils

• copies of Reproducible Master 4

• Scripture and Family reproducible masters (back of book)

Teaching Tip

Audiovisual Aids

Contact the children's parents before presenting this chapter about Baptism. Ask whether anyone has a video of a family baptismal celebration that you can show to the group.

WE BELIEVE

At Baptism we become children of God and members of the Church.

The López family is very happy! They have just welcomed a new baby into their family. The baby's name is Ana.

Soon Ana will belong to another family, the Catholic Church. In Baptism Ana will become a child of God and a member of the Church. When we were baptized, we became children of God and members of the Church, too.

Everyone in Ana's family is looking forward to bringing the newest member of their family to the parish church for Baptism. The whole parish will celebrate her Baptism.

Ⓧ Many things happened for you at your Baptism. Write your name on each line on the membership card to remember two important things.

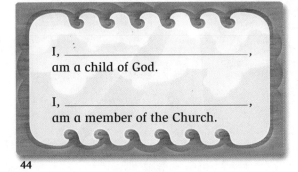

I, _____,
am a child of God.

I, _____,
am a member of the Church.

44

Lesson Plan

WE BELIEVE

_____ minutes

Read aloud the *We Believe* statement on page 44. Have volunteers read the three paragraphs. Then ask:

• *Why is the Lopez family happy?* (They have a new baby.)

• *What is everyone in the family looking forward to?* (Ana's Baptism)

• *What will Ana become when she is baptized?* (a child of God and member of the Church)

Ⓧ **Stress:** *Baptism is the first sacrament everyone receives.* Then read the activity directions. Have the children write their names to complete the membership card.

Brainstorm with the children reasons why water is important in our lives. Remind the group: *Water is one of God's gifts of creation.*

Ask volunteers to describe other gifts God has given to us. Write the word *grace* on the board. Explain: *Grace is a special gift from God given to us at Baptism. Grace is God's life in us.* Have the children read the *We Believe* statement on page 45. Then ask a volunteer to read the first paragraph.

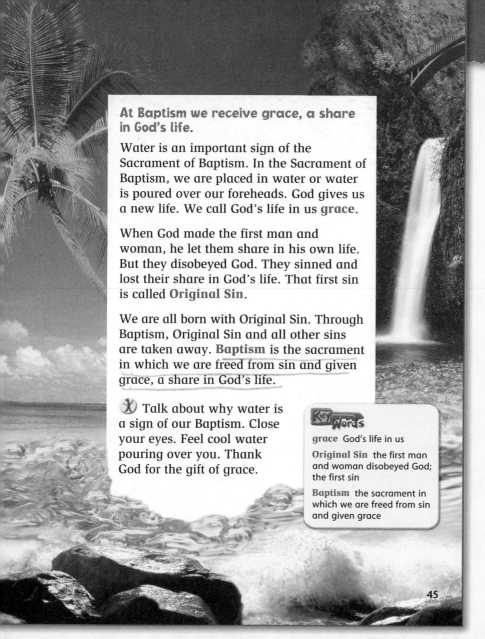

At Baptism we receive grace, a share in God's life.

Water is an important sign of the Sacrament of Baptism. In the Sacrament of Baptism, we are placed in water or water is poured over our foreheads. God gives us a new life. We call God's life in us **grace**.

When God made the first man and woman, he let them share in his own life. But they disobeyed God. They sinned and lost their share in God's life. That first sin is called **Original Sin**.

We are all born with Original Sin. Through Baptism, Original Sin and all other sins are taken away. **Baptism** is the sacrament in which we are freed from sin and given grace, a share in God's life.

Talk about why water is a sign of our Baptism. Close your eyes. Feel cool water pouring over you. Thank God for the gift of grace.

Key Words

grace God's life in us

Original Sin the first man and woman disobeyed God; the first sin

Baptism the sacrament in which we are freed from sin and given grace

45

ACTIVITY BANK

Curriculum Connection
Science
Activity Materials: flower seeds, cups, potting soil, watering cans

Help the children understand why water and light are necessary for life and growth. Give each child a paper cup filled with potting soil and one or two flower seeds. (Marigold seeds are good for this purpose.) Have the children write their names on the cups. Ask the children to plant the seeds in the soil. Have the children take the plants home. Tell them to place the cups on the window sill or in another place that has light. Point out that they should make sure the plants have enough water. Tell the children that when their plants start to flower, they can give them to their parents or godparents.

Keep your explanation of Original Sin as simple as the one presented in the second paragraph. Read aloud the second paragraph. Explain: *All human beings are born with Original Sin. We are not perfect. Through Baptism Original Sin and all other sins are removed.*

Read aloud the third paragraph. Ask the children to highlight or underline the definition of *Baptism* in the last sentence of the paragraph.

Discuss why water is a sign of our Baptism. Help the children to conclude that when we are baptized with water, we receive God's life within us. Water is the sign of grace.

Invite the children to close their eyes and imagine water being poured on them. Encourage them to thank God for the gift of water.

Quick Check

✔ *What do we become at Baptism?* (We become children of God and members of the Church.)

✔ *What is grace?* (Grace is God's life in us.)

As Catholics...

Godparents

After working on these two pages, read aloud the *As Catholics* text. Explain that godparents should give their godchildren an example of living the Christian life. Discuss ways the children can thank their godparents.

We celebrate the Sacrament of Baptism with special words and actions.

This is what happened when the López family and their friends celebrated Ana's Baptism.

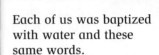

Read Along

- Father Ramón and the parish community greeted the family.

- Father told Ana's parents and godparents that they should help Ana to keep growing in faith.

- Father traced the sign of the cross on Ana's forehead. Ana's parents and godparents did this also. This action showed that Ana now belonged to Jesus in a special way.

- Father Ramón read a story about Jesus. Father talked about the story.

- Father blessed the water in the baptismal pool.

- Father asked Ana's parents and godparents whether they reject sin and believe in God.

- Father placed Ana in the water of the baptismal pool three times. He said the words of Baptism. It was with water and these words that Ana was baptized:

    Ana, I baptize you in the name
      of the Father,
    and of the Son,
    and of the Holy Spirit.

Each of us was baptized with water and these same words.

 Who do you think was at your Baptism?

As Catholics...

Godmothers and godfathers are very special people. They are chosen by the parents of the child being baptized. They have a special role in this sacrament. They agree to help the parents teach the child about their Catholic faith. The godparents help the child to live as a friend of Jesus. They help the child to love God and others.

46

Lesson Plan

WE BELIEVE (continued)

Invite the children to think about a favorite kind of celebration. Ask: *What are some things you say during the celebration? What are some things you do?* Have volunteers share their responses. Then explain: *We use both words and actions in the celebration of Baptism.*

Ask the children to share what they know about Baptism. (In the *We Believe* program, Baptism is first introduced in the Kindergarten text and further developed in the Grade 1 text.) Tell the children they are now going to read about the special words and actions used in Baptism. Invite them to listen as you read aloud the text on page 46.

Invite the children to act out the steps of Baptism described on page 46. Assign the roles of Father Ramón, the members of the parish, Ana's parents, and Ana's godparents. Invite those playing roles of individuals to come to the front of the group. Explain that as you read the text, the children should act out what is happening.

Begin the discussion of the question by sharing who was at your Baptism. If a video of an infant's Baptism is available, show it now.

We can show that we are children of God by what we say and do.

The following words and actions were also a part of the celebration of Ana's Baptism in her parish.

Read Along

- Father Ramón put a white garment on Ana. He said that the white garment showed that Ana was a friend and follower of Jesus.

- Ana's godmother went to the large Easter candle by the baptismal pool. She lit a smaller candle for Ana from it. Father told Ana's parents and godparents to help keep the light of Christ burning in Ana's life.

- Father Ramón invited everyone to pray the Our Father together.

- Father blessed the family and everyone in church.

These same words and actions were part of the celebration of your Baptism.

WE RESPOND

On the candle write the names of people who are helping you to become a good Catholic.

What will you do and say to share the light of Christ with others?

ACTIVITY BANK

Liturgy
Baptism in the Parish

If possible, take the children into the church to show them the baptismal font and the Easter candle. If possible, invite the pastor or a member of the parish staff to explain how Baptism is celebrated in your parish. Tell families when the next parish celebration of the sacrament will take place and invite them to be present.

Family
Thank-You Notes

Activity Materials: writing paper or blank note cards

Invite the children to write to their godparents to thank them for being an important part of their faith life. Ask them to tell their godparents what they are learning in religion class. Encourage the children to ask their parents for help in writing and sending their notes.

Continue the reading about Ana's Baptism on page 47. Emphasize: *These words and actions were part of our celebrations of Baptism.* Have the children look at the photographs on pages 46–47 and tell what is happening in each one.

Show the group the candle and the white garment that are on the prayer table. Explain: *These objects are reminders of our Baptism.*

Distribute copies of Reproducible Master 4. (See guide page 43C.) Encourage the children to take the sheet home and complete the activity with their families' help.

WE RESPOND ___ minutes

Connect to Life Point out the large candle on page 47. Allow the children time to write on the candle the names of people who are helping them to live and grow as Catholics.

Help the children think of ways that they can share the light of Christ with others. Write the responses on the board. Then have children choose one thing that they will actually do.

Catechist Goal

- To review the chapter ideas that are key to growing as disciples of Jesus Christ

Our Faith Response

- To decide on ways to grow as disciples by living out what we have learned

Lesson Materials

- colored pencils or crayons

Show What you Know

Help the children complete the crossword puzzle.

Picture This

Refer the children to pages 46 and 47 to help them complete the activity. Help the children conclude that the third photo shows the family praying the "Our Father" with the priest.

Make it Happen

While the children are designing their cards, you may want to play "We Believe, We Believe in God," #1 on the Grade 2 CD.

Fast Facts

Read aloud or ask a volunteer to read aloud the *Fast Fact*.

Take Home

Read the directions. Allow a few minutes for the children to write two questions. Encourage all to ask their family members these questions.

Discuss and send home copies of *Sharing Faith with My Family* reproducible master for this chapter (back of book).

Grade 2 Chapter 4

PROJECT

Show What you Know

Complete the crossword puzzle with Key Words.

1 Across: God's life in us

2 Down: The sacrament in which we are freed from sin and given grace

3 Across: The first sin is called

_____ Original _____ Sin.

Crossword solution:
- 1 Across: g r a c e
- 2 Down: B a p t i s m
- 3 Across: O r i g i n a l

Picture This

Write what is happening in each photo from Ana's Baptism.

Father is placing Ana in the water of the baptismal pool three times.

Ana's godmother is lighting a candle for Ana from the Easter candle.

Everyone is praying the Our Father.

48 www.webelieveweb.com

DISCIPLE

Make it Happen

Design a card for someone who has just been baptized. Use words and pictures.

Possible responses: (words) Baptism; welcome; grace; light of Christ; children of God; member of the Church	Possible responses: (pictures) water; cross; Easter candle; family; baptismal font or pool

Fast Facts

God's life in us is called grace. Because God's grace is so important to us, many people name their babies Grace. More than 92,000 baby girls have been named Grace in the past ten years.

(Social Security Administration, 2008)

Take Home

Interview your parents or godparents about your Baptism. Write the questions you will ask them.

_____

_____

_____

49

CHAPTER TEST

Check the sentences that tell what happens at Baptism.

1. ✔ We become children of God.

2. ____ We become grandparents.

3. ✔ We receive grace, a share in God's life.

4. ✔ We become members of the Church.

Fill in the circle beside the correct answer.

5. When we are baptized, we are placed in _____ or it is poured on our foreheads three times.
   - ● water
   - ○ oil

6. When we are baptized, we are _____ Original Sin.
   - ○ given
   - ● freed from

7. The priest baptizes us in the name of the Father, and of the Son, and of _____.
   - ○ our godparents
   - ● the Holy Spirit

8. We show that we are children of God _____.
   - ● by what we say and do
   - ○ only by what we say

9–10. Write two reasons Baptism is a special celebration for us.

Possible responses: We become children of God and members of the Church. We are freed from sin and given grace.

50

CHAPTER TEST

Provide ten to fifteen minutes for the students to complete the test. After all have finished, check the answers. Clarify any misconceptions.

Alternative Assessment

You may want the students to complete the following alternative-assessment activity.

Make a Baptism picture dictionary. Draw a picture of a candle, cross, white garment, baptismal pool or font. Explain how each thing is used in Baptism.

Additional Testing

• Chapter 4 Test in *Assessment Book*, pages 9–10

• CD-ROM *Test Generator and Resource*: Use Chapter 4 Test or customize your own.

Review

KeyWords

Review the definitions as they are presented in the chapter's *Key Word* boxes:

• grace (page 45)
• Original Sin (page 45)
• Baptism (page 45).

We Believe Statements

Review the four statements.

• At Baptism we become children of God and members of the Church.

• At Baptism we receive grace, a share in God's life.

• We celebrate the Sacrament of Baptism with special words and actions.

• We can show that we are children of God by what we say and do.

To use the Chapter 4 Study Guide, visit

www.webelieveweb.com

Overview

In Chapter 4 the children learned that at Baptism we become children of God and members of the Church. In this chapter they will learn that the Holy Spirit comes to us in a special way in the Sacrament of Confirmation.

Doctrinal Content	For Adult Reading and Reflection *Catechism of the Catholic Church*
The children will learn:	Paragraph
• We celebrate the Gift of the Holy Spirit in the Sacrament of Confirmation.	1285
• Confirmation seals us with the Gift of the Holy Spirit and strengthens us.	1295–96
• We celebrate the Sacrament of Confirmation with special words and actions.	1299–1300
• The Holy Spirit helps baptized Catholics and confirmed Catholics.	1303

Key Word

Confirmation
(p. 53)

Catechist Background

What stands out in your memory about your own Confirmation?

Go to **www.webelieveweb.com**, Catechist/ Teacher, We Believe Correlations for this chapter's correlation to:
- Six Tasks of Catechesis
- Catholic Social Teaching
- *Catechetical Formation in Chaste Living.*

In Baptism, we receive the gift of faith as a gift outright. In Confirmation, that faith is "sealed with the promised holy Spirit, which is the first installment of our inheritance" (Ephesians 1:13–14). Led by the Spirit, baptized and confirmed Catholics are empowered to serve the Church and the world.

You could read it on their glowing young faces. You could hear it in their wild cheering and applause. Some say you could reach out and touch it. What was IT? *Enthusiasm* erupting at various World Youth Days in cities across the globe— Denver, Toronto, Sydney. The enthusiasm of the young people moved others to sing and pray with them.

However, the real force or dynamism motivating this outpouring was and is the Holy Spirit.

Without a doubt in Baptism we have been called by name and in the Sacrament of Confirmation we have been gifted by the Holy Spirit's "seven *gifts* . . . wisdom, understanding, counsel, fortitude, knowledge, piety, and fear of the Lord . . . the *fruits* are charity, joy, peace, patience, kindness, goodness, generosity, gentleness, faithfulness, modesty, self-control, chastity" (CCC 1831–1832). Surely, these gifts and fruits were overflowing at every gathering of the young people.

What gifts of the Holy Spirit help you in your teaching?

Lesson Planning Guide

Lesson Steps	Presentation	Materials

1 WE GATHER

Lesson Steps	Presentation	Materials
page 51 **We Gather in Prayer** **Focus on Life**	• Reflect on God's love. • Pray to the Holy Spirit. • Discuss what happened on Pentecost.	prayer space items: a yellow or orange tablecloth, a carafe of olive oil, pins, small paper flames (one for each child)

2 WE BELIEVE

Lesson Steps	Presentation	Materials
page 52 *We celebrate the Gift of the Holy Spirit in the Sacrament of Confirmation.*	• Read and discuss the text about the Gift of the Holy Spirit. Discuss ways the Holy Spirit helped the first disciples.	
page 53 *Confirmation seals us with the Gift of the Holy Spirit and strengthens us.*	• Present the text about Baptism and Confirmation connection. • Present the *Key Word* and definition. 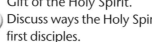 Complete the activity.	• red crayons
page 54 *We celebrate the Sacrament of Confirmation with special words and actions.* *Rite of Confirmation*	• Present the text about the celebration of Confirmation. • Present the *Key Word* and definition. Discuss ways the Holy Spirit helps us.	• cooking oil, bowl, cotton swabs, paper towels
page 55 *The Holy Spirit helps baptized Catholics and confirmed Catholics.*	• Read and discuss the way the Holy Spirit helps those confirmed.	• copies of Reproducible Master 5, guide page 51C

3 WE RESPOND

Lesson Steps	Presentation	Materials
page 55	🏃 Do the *We Respond* checklist activity. • Read and discuss *As Catholics*. 🎵 Pray to the Holy Spirit by singing.	🎵 "Make Us Strong," #5, Grade 2 CD
pages 56–57 **Project Disciple**	• Complete the Project Disciple activities. • Explain the *Take Home* activity. • Discuss/send home Sharing Faith with My Family reproducible master for this chapter.	• colored pencils or crayons • copies of Sharing Faith with My Family reproducible master, Chapter 5 (back of book)
page 58 **Chapter 5 Test**	• Complete Chapter 5 Test. • Work on *Alternative Assessment* activity.	• optional: copies of Scripture reproducible master, *What's the Word?*, Chapter 5 (back of book)

For additional ideas, activities, and opportunities: Visit Sadlier's **www.WeBelieveweb.com**

Name _____

Find Confirmation words in the puzzle. Circle them.
Then use the correct word to complete the sentence at
the bottom of the page.

anointing

seals

fire

strong

oil

bishop

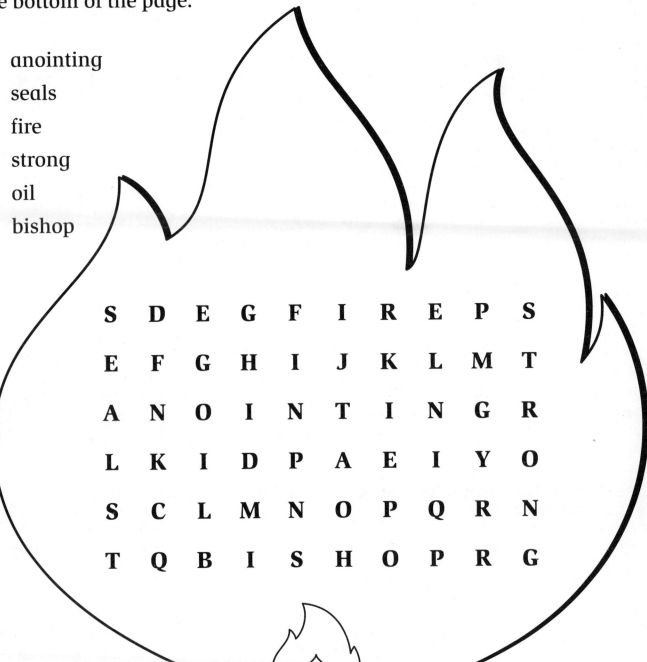

S D E G F I R E P S

E F G H I J K L M T

A N O I N T I N G R

L K I D P A E I Y O

S C L M N O P Q R N

T Q B I S H O P R G

 Confirmation is the sacrament that _____
us with the Gift of the Holy Spirit.

PROJECT DISCIPLE

Pray
Learn
Celebrate
Share
Choose
Live

Additional Activities

What's *the* Word?

Scripture reproducible master, Chapter 5

Materials needed: copies of *What's the Word?* (back of book); red colored pencil or crayon

Distribute copies of the Scripture reproducible master. Choose three volunteers to be readers. Ask the other children in the group to make the sounds of the wind and the crowd at the appropriate times.

Point out the words taken directly from the Bible: Acts of the Apostles 2:4 and 2:41. Have the students draw flames next to these quotations.

Pray Today

Materials needed: drawing paper (8 ½ in. x 11 in.); heart and flame patterns; colored pencils, crayons, or washable markers

Give each child a sheet of drawing paper to make a prayer plaque. Write the following prayer on the board: "Holy Spirit, fill our hearts with love." Have the children copy the prayer on the drawing paper. Then have the children trace a heart pattern or flame pattern or both on the drawing paper and color. Encourage the children to take their plaques home to share with family members.

Show What *you* Know

Materials needed: index cards (2 for each child); crayons or colored pencils

Review what the children learned about the Sacraments of Baptism and Confirmation. Have them draw waves of water and write Baptism on one card and draw a flame and write Confirmation on the other. Then read statements about what happens in these two sacraments, alternating between the two sacraments. After you read each statement, have each child identify the correct sacrament by holding up the appropriate card. Check the cards the children are holding up and clarify any misconceptions some children may have.

What Would *you* do?

Play a game of Charades. Have the children form two teams. Then refer the team members to the list of actions that the Holy Spirit helps us to do on student page 55. Have the teams take turns acting out a way to perform one of the actions listed while the other team tries to guess which action is being done.

Meeting Individual Needs
Children with Allergies

On page 54, the children are asked to dab some olive oil on the palm of one of their hands. Before the lesson, send a note home to ask parents or guardians about their children's allergies. Make a list and keep it in a convenient place. Consult the list before doing any activity that may cause an allergic reaction.

We Believe Resources

- Grade 2 *Review & Resource Book*, pages 16–17
- Grade 2 *Family Book*, pages 17–19
- Grade 2 *Assessment Book*, pages 11–12
- Grade 2 CD-ROM *Test Generator and Resource*: Use Chapter 5 Test or customize your own.

www.webelieveweb.com

Enrichment Ideas

Chapter Story

Paula was excited. She and her mother were going camping with their neighbors: the Morgans. Mr. and Mrs. Morgan were bringing their granddaughter Maya. Paula was happy because she and Maya were in the same grade.

It was late in the afternoon when the group arrived at the campgrounds. Paula and Maya helped Mr. Morgan gather wood for the campfire while Paula's mother and Mrs. Morgan put up the tent.

Maya said, "Paula, wait until you taste Grandpop's campfire chili. It is delicious."

Mr. Morgan answered, "That's right. Cooking it on the fire makes it taste extra good." Then he took out a special stand to go over the fire. He put the pot of chili on the stand to warm.

After dinner they cleaned up and gathered around the campfire again. Mr. Morgan helped Paula and Maya put marshmallows on long sticks. They held the sticks over the fire to toast the marshmallows while Mrs. Morgan told wonderful stories about people who lived long ago. She said, "Just think about ways fire helped people then."

Then Paula and Maya watched the grown-ups put out the fire. Paula said, "Our campfire time was really special. I can't wait until tomorrow night."

▶ *How did having a campfire help the Morgans, Paula, and her mother?*

FAITH and MEDIA

▶ On page 55, if you are going to use the *Activity Bank: Faith and Media* discussion activity, come prepared to suggest characters in books, movies, or television programs who show by their actions that the Holy Spirit is guiding them.

CHAPTER PROJECT: HOLY SPIRIT TORCHES

Help the children to make Holy Spirit torches. Give each child an empty paper towel roll to use as the base. Then have the children use aluminum foil to cover the roll. Next, give each child a sheet of yellow or orange construction paper to use to make the flame. Help the children attach the "flame" to the "torch" by using tape or glue. Have the children carry their torches in a procession. Play "Make Us Strong," #5, Grade 2 CD. The words are on page 55 of the children's books.

WE GATHER

✝ Close your eyes. Be very still.
  Breathe in. Breathe out.
  Try to feel God's love around you.

Join hands and form a prayer circle.
Pray the following words:

Come, Holy Spirit,
fill the hearts of your
faithful people
and kindle in us
the fire of your love.

 Use your own words to tell what
happened on the first Pentecost.

51

PREPARING TO PRAY

The children will reflect and pray about the ways the Holy Spirit is present in our lives.

• Have the children read the words of the prayer. Explain that the word *kindle* means "to start a fire burning."

• Give each child a paper flame you have made previously. Have the children write their initials on one side of their flames. On the other side of the flames, have them write what they would like the Holy Spirit to help them to do.

The Prayer Space

• On the prayer table place a tablecloth and a carafe filled with olive oil.

• Have straight pins available for attaching the children's flames to the tablecloth.

 This Week's Liturgy
Visit **www.webelieveweb.com** for this week's liturgical readings and other seasonal material.

Lesson Plan

WE GATHER ___ minutes

✝ Pray

• Have the children sit quietly at their desks. Read the directions for the introductory reflection slowly and prayerfully.

• Remind the children that a flame is a sign used to remind us of the Holy Spirit. Invite the children to stand and bring their flames to the prayer table. Help each child pin his or her flame to the tablecloth.

• Read each line of the prayer to the Holy Spirit. Pause at the end of each line for the children to echo the words.

☀ Focus on Life

• Share the *Chapter Story* on guide page 51E. Then, if necessary, read the Scripture story (Acts of the Apostles 2:1–4) and the explanatory paragraphs found in Chapter 2, page 30 of the children's text.

Family Connection Update

Invite volunteers to share what they learned about their Baptism celebrations.

Catechist Goal

• To emphasize that we celebrate the Gift of the Holy Spirit in the Sacrament of Confirmation

Our Faith Response

• To name ways in which the Holy Spirit can help us as baptized Catholics

 Confirmation

Lesson Materials

• red crayon
• Grade 2 CD
• copies of Reproducible Master 5
• Scripture and Family reproducible masters (back of book)

Teaching Note

Ages for Confirmation

The United States Conference of Catholic Bishops decreed in 2001 that the age for conferring the Sacrament of Confirmation in the dioceses of the United States is to be between the age of discretion (seven years old) and about sixteen years of age.

WE BELIEVE

We celebrate the Gift of the Holy Spirit in the Sacrament of Confirmation.

Jesus promised to send the Holy Spirit to the Apostles and other disciples to be their helper. The Holy Spirit helped the disciples to remember everything Jesus had said and done.

The Holy Spirit filled the disciples with courage and faith. They began to tell everyone about Jesus. The disciples told everyone Jesus died for us and rose to new life.

The Apostles baptized many people. They laid their hands on people so that they too might receive the Holy Spirit. They wanted them to be strong in faith and to care for one another's needs.

Talk about ways the Holy Spirit helped Jesus' first disciples.

The Holy Spirit is God, the Third Person of the Blessed Trinity. The Holy Spirit was sent by the Father and Jesus to help and guide the Church. The Holy Spirit is still with us today. We celebrate the Gift of the Holy Spirit in the Sacrament of Confirmation.

The Church often uses a picture of fire or a flame to remind us of the Holy Spirit. Like fire, the Holy Spirit gives us light, warmth, and energy.

52

Lesson Plan

WE BELIEVE _____ minutes

Invite volunteers to read the first three paragraphs.

Ask: *How did the Holy Spirit help the first disciples of Jesus?* (helped them to be strong and brave; helped them to remember what Jesus had said and done)

Write the word *Confirmation* on the board or chart paper. Pronounce it for the children. Ask volunteers to read the two paragraphs in the flame on page 52.

Ask: When did you first receive the Holy Spirit? (at Baptism) Direct attention to the graphic representation on page 53. Explain: Baptism and Confirmation are like partners. Then ask a volunteer to read aloud the first paragraph on this page.

Read the activity directions. Have the children trace over the circles. Discuss what the diagram illustrates.

Read aloud the last two paragraphs on page 53. Invite the children to pray for the people in the parish who are preparing for Confirmation.

Confirmation seals us with the Gift of the Holy Spirit and strengthens us.

The Sacraments of Baptism and Confirmation are like partners. Baptism makes us children of God and members of the Church. Each of us received the Holy Spirit when we were baptized. **Confirmation** is the sacrament that seals us with the Gift of the Holy Spirit and strengthens us.

Use a red crayon to trace over the circles. Talk about what the drawing shows.

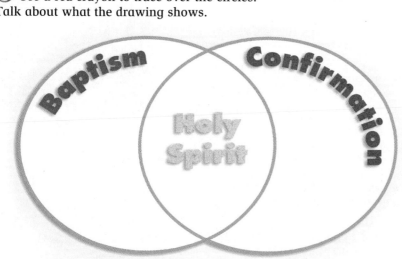

The parish community prays for the people about to be confirmed. The community gathers with them for the celebration of the sacrament.

Most often a bishop comes to the parish to confirm people. Sometimes the bishop appoints a priest to do the confirming.

53

Key Word

Confirmation the sacrament that seals us with the Gift of the Holy Spirit and strengthens us

ACTIVITY BANK

Multiple Intelligences
Intrapersonal
Activity Material: writing paper, basket

Write on the board the following prayer beginning:
Holy Spirit, please help me to . . .

Invite the children to copy these words on the writing paper and then complete the prayer in their own words. Have the children fold the papers and place them in a basket. Place the basket on the prayer table.

Curriculum Connection
Art
Activity Materials: magazines, glue, scissors, poster board or large sheets of construction paper

Work in groups. Give each group a large sheet of poster board or construction paper. Have the children look through magazines to find images that represent light and warmth. Invite the children to cut out these images and use them to make a collage. Encourage the children to label the collage, *The Holy Spirit, Giver of Light and Strength.*

Quick Check

✔ *Which sacrament seals us with the Gift of the Holy Spirit?* (Confirmation seals us with the Gift of the Holy Spirit.)

✔ *Why does the Church use fire as a symbol for the Holy Spirit?* (Fire helps us by giving us light, warmth, and energy. The Holy Spirit helps us share the light and warmth of God's love with others.)

Sacred Chrism—Blessed Oil

After working on these two pages, read aloud the *As Catholics* text. Remind the children that it is in the Sacrament of Holy Orders that a man can be ordained as a priest. Have a volunteer answer the question about being anointed. (at Baptism)

We celebrate the Sacrament of Confirmation with special words and actions.

At Confirmation we are anointed with oil called Sacred Chrism. This shows that we are set apart to do God's work. It shows that the Holy Spirit is with us. A person called a sponsor helps us as we get ready for Confirmation.

Celebrating Confirmation
Read Along

The bishop talks with the people about their faith. He calls them to serve others. Then the bishop and priests who are present stretch out their hands over those receiving the sacrament. The bishop prays that the Holy Spirit will strengthen these people with special gifts.

The bishop dips his right thumb in blessed oil, called Sacred Chrism. He traces a cross on each person's forehead with the Sacred Chrism.

We call tracing the cross with oil the anointing with Sacred Chrism.

The bishop prays,
"(Person's name), be sealed with the Gift of the Holy Spirit."
The person responds, "Amen."
Then the bishop says,
"Peace be with you."
Those who were confirmed say,
"And also with you."

Name one way the Holy Spirit helps you.

54

Lesson Plan

WE BELIEVE (continued)

Invite the children to gather near the prayer table. Let the children dip a cotton swab into the oil and smear a little on the palm of one of their hands. Explain that oil plays an important part in Confirmation. Then read aloud the first paragraph on page 54.

Read the words and actions used during the celebration of Confirmation.

Explain that you will read the prayers of the bishop. Ask the children to read the responses of those being confirmed.

Remind the children: *We received the Gift of the Holy Spirit at Baptism.* Have volunteers name ways the Holy Spirit helps them.

Invite the children to read with a partner the list of ways the Holy Spirit helps baptized Catholics and confirmed Catholics. (See page 55.) Ask the partners to name real-life examples or situations to match some of the listed items. Provide this example: *People who are happy with all God has given them take care of their things and share them with others.* Allow time for partners to share their examples with the whole group.

The Holy Spirit helps baptized Catholics and confirmed Catholics.

The Holy Spirit helps Catholics who have been baptized and Catholics who have been confirmed to do the following things.

- Love God and others as Jesus taught.
- Worship God and celebrate the sacraments.
- Treat others with respect.
- Care for those who are poor, hungry, or sick.
- Be fair.
- Be peacemakers.
- Be happy with all that God has given them.
- Live out their faith.
- Stand up for what they believe.

As Catholics...

The week before Easter is called Holy Week. Each year during Holy Week, the bishop blesses three oils of the Church. The oils are given to all the parishes that make up the diocese. One blessed oil is called *Sacred Chrism.* It is used for anointing in the Sacraments of Baptism, Confirmation, and Holy Orders.

When were you anointed with Sacred Chrism?

WE RESPOND

Check the actions on the list that are easy for you to do. Underline the difficult ones. Then decide to do one today.

Ask the Holy Spirit for help by singing this song.

🎵 **Make Us Strong**
(*"My Darling Clementine"*)

Holy Spirit, Holy Spirit,
Holy Spirit, make us strong,
So that we can follow Jesus
And bring God's love to everyone.

55

ACTIVITY BANK

Sacraments
Invite a Guest Speaker

To enrich the children's understanding of the Sacrament of Confirmation, invite a confirmed Catholic, either an adolescent or an adult to speak to the class. Ask the speaker to share with the children the difference the Holy Spirit makes in his or her life. Allow the children to ask appropriate questions.

Faith and the Media
The Holy Spirit's Help

Invite the children to read the list of ways the Holy Spirit helps baptized and confirmed Catholics. Ask the children to discuss characters in books, movies, or TV programs who show that the Holy Spirit is guiding them.

Distribute Reproducible Master 5. Explain to the children that they may see the words printed across or down. Have the children work on the puzzle now or have the children take the sheet home. Encourage them to ask their families to help them. (Across: fire, 1st row; anointing, 3rd row; bishop, 6th row; Down: seals, 1st row; oil, 3rd row; strong, 10th row. The word *seals* completes the sentence.)

WE RESPOND ____ minutes

Connect to Life Explain the activity directions: *I will pause after I read each action listed. Put a check beside the action if it is easy for you to do. Underline the action if it is difficult for you.*

🎵 **Play** "Make Us Strong," #5 on the Grade 2 CD and ask the children to sing along.

Catechist Goal

• To review the chapter ideas that are key to growing as disciples of Jesus Christ

Our Faith Response

• To decide on ways to grow as disciples by living out what we have learned

Lesson Materials

• colored pencils or crayons
• drawing paper or poster board

Show What you Know

Have the children complete the message by filling in the words. To check the children's work, have them read aloud the completed sentence.

What's the Word?

Have the children sit quietly and ask them to listen carefully as you read the Scripture passage. Refer them to pages 28, 30, and 31 in Chapter 2 to help them recall ways the Holy Spirit helped Jesus' disciples and helps us.

Make it Happen

Have the children design Confirmation posters. Then have them make their posters on drawing paper or poster board. Then put all the posters together to make one giant class poster.

Reality Check

Have a volunteer read aloud the directions and the items on the list.

Take Home

Read aloud the suggestion for the family activity. Encourage the children to talk about the work of the family members.

Discuss and send home copies of *Sharing Faith with My Family* reproducible master for this chapter (back of book).

56 and **57**

Pray Learn Celebrate Share Choose Live

Grade 2 Chapter 5

PROJECT

Show What you Know

Use the word bank to finish this important message.

Word bank: Confirmation • anointing with Sacred Chrism

The ___anointing___

___with___ ___Sacred Chrism___ shows that the

Holy Spirit is with us at ___Confirmation___.

Now, pass it on!

What's the Word?

At Pentecost, the disciples were "all filled with the holy Spirit" (Acts of the Apostles 2:4).

Remember the ways the Holy Spirit helped the disciples. Think about the ways the Holy Spirit helps us today, too.

The Holy Spirit helps disciples to follow Jesus Christ; to know and share God's love.

56   www.webelieveweb.com

DISCIPLE

Pray Learn Celebrate Share Choose Live

Make it Happen

Design a poster to teach others about Confirmation. Plan it here.

What words will be on your poster?
Possible responses: anointing with oil; Gift of the Holy Spirit; Sacred Chrism; faith; service; "Be sealed with the Gift of the Holy Spirit."

What pictures will be on your poster?
Possible responses: bishop; blessed oil; flame

When your poster is complete, display it in your classroom or home to share it with others.

Reality Check

Check the things the Holy Spirit helps baptized and confirmed Catholics to do.

❏ Be selfish
☑ Play fairly
☑ Love God and others
☑ Respect others
❏ Tell lies
☑ Teach others about Jesus

Take Home

The Church teaches that we should appreciate the work every person does. Talk about the kind of work the members of your family do.

↳ **DISCIPLE CHALLENGE** Talk about the ways each family member's work can spread the message of God's love.

57

Fill in the circle beside the correct answer.

1. The Sacrament of Confirmation seals us with the Gift of _____.
   - ○ fire
   - ● the Holy Spirit

2. At Confirmation the bishop or priest traces a _____ with Sacred Chrism on a person's forehead.
   - ● cross
   - ○ flame

3. The Church uses _____ to remind us of the Holy Spirit.
   - ○ a cross
   - ● fire

4. At Confirmation the _____ shows that we are set apart to do God's work.
   - ● anointing with Sacred Chrism
   - ○ clapping of hands

Check the sentences that tell what the bishop does at Confirmation.

5. ____ He pours water on a person's forehead.

6. ✔ He talks with the people about their faith.

7. ✔ He traces a cross on a person's forehead with Sacred Chrism.

8. ✔ He prays special prayers.

9–10. Write two ways the Holy Spirit helps confirmed Catholics.

Accept ways listed on page 55.

58

CHAPTER TEST

Provide ten to fifteen minutes for the students to complete the test. After all have finished, check the answers. Clarify any misconceptions.

Alternative Assessment

You may want the students to complete the following alternative-assessment activity.

With a partner act out what happens at Confirmation. Then write sentences about what happens.

Additional Testing

• Chapter 5 Test in *Assessment Book*, pages 11–12

• CD-ROM *Test Generator and Resource*: Use Chapter 5 Test or customize your own.

Review

Review the definitions as they are presented in the chapter's *Key Word* boxes:

• Confirmation (page 53).

We Believe Statements

• We celebrate the Gift of the Holy Spirit in the Sacrament of Confirmation.

• Confirmation seals us with the Gift of the Holy Spirit and strengthens us.

• We celebrate the Sacrament of Confirmation with special words and actions.

• The Holy Spirit helps baptized Catholics and confirmed Catholics.

To use the Chapter 5 Study Guide, visit

www.webelieveweb.com

The Church Year

By means of the yearly cycle the Church celebrates the whole mystery of Christ, from his incarnation until the day of Pentecost and the expectation of his coming again.

(Norms Governing Liturgical Calendars, 17)

Overview

In this chapter the children will learn that we celebrate the different seasons of the Church year.

For Adult Reading and Reflection
You may want to refer to paragraph 1168 of the *Catechism of the Catholic Church.*

Catechist Background

Go to **www.webelieveweb.com**, Catechist/ Teacher, We Believe Correlations for this chapter's correlation to the Six Tasks of Catechesis.

What seasons of the Church year do you celebrate in a special way?

The annual cycle of liturgical seasons makes present to us the mysteries of redemption that we celebrate. By opening "up to the faithful the riches of her Lord's powers and merits," the Church encourages us to take hold of these riches in our own lives and to be "filled with saving grace" (CCC 1163).

The Triduum is at the heart of the liturgical year. On these days, we celebrate the Passion, Death, and Resurrection of Jesus Christ. On Easter itself, the greatest feast, the Church rejoices in the Lord's victory over death and his gift of new life to all believers. The joyful celebration of the Easter season extends until Pentecost Sunday.

During all the liturgical seasons, each Sunday is a celebration of the Lord's Resurrection, a "little Easter." Every week we gather in liturgical assembly

to celebrate the Liturgy of the Word and the Liturgy of the Eucharist. Here we meet the risen Lord who strengthens us to be his disciples in our world today.

In each liturgical season, the liturgy empowers us to move beyond the limits of historical time and place and enter into God's time of salvation. We are present to Jesus' Death and Resurrection, present to his mercy and compassion, present to his challenges and his call to us in the here and now. In the liturgy we learn to know and love Jesus. We find that "Jesus Christ is the same yesterday, today, and forever" (Hebrews 13:8).

In what way will you enter into the celebration of the Church year?

Lesson Planning Guide

Lesson Steps	Presentation	Materials
① WE GATHER		
page 59 **Introduce the Season**	• Read the *Chapter Story*. • Introduce the Church year. • Proclaim words on a banner.	
page 60	• Share responses to the question and directive.	
② WE BELIEVE		
pages 60–62 *The Church year helps us to follow Jesus.*	• Present the text and chart about the seasons of the Church year. • Play a Church season game.	
③ WE RESPOND		
page 62	🏃 Complete a Church year time line.	• crayons or colored markers
Text page 63 **Guide page 63–64** **We Respond in Prayer**	• Together follow Jesus through the Church year in prayer.	🎵 "Come Follow Me," #3, Grade 2 CD • prayer space items: Bible and picture or statue of Jesus • purple, gold or white, and green party streamers
Text page 64 **Guide pages 63–64, 64A** **Project Disciple**	• Complete the Project Disciple activities. Discuss the *Take Home* activity. • Complete the Reproducible Master 6 activity. See guide pages 64A and 59C. • Discuss/send home Sharing Faith with My Family, guide page 64B.	• pencils, colored pencils or crayons • construction paper (one sheet for each child) • scissors, glue stick, brad fasteners • copies of Reproducible Master 6, guide page 64A • copies of Sharing Faith with My Family, guide page 64B

For additional ideas, activities, and opportunities: Visit Sadlier's **www.WeBelieveweb.com**

Chapter Story

Keri's family was always very busy. They didn't take time to notice that nature's appearance changed from season to season. They didn't take time to see the flowers blooming in spring or the puffy white clouds floating in the summer skies. The family didn't wonder at the colorful autumn leaves falling from the trees in the park or the snow-lined trees in winter.

But one Sunday morning last winter it was snowing so hard Keri's family had a hard time getting home from church. "I guess we won't be going anywhere else today," said Dad.

Keri decided to sit and look out the window. Keri was surprised that she was having fun watching the snow covering the ground like a giant blanket. "Come and watch the snow with me," Keri called to her family.

Keri's dad, mom, and brother joined her at the window. "You know," said Keri's dad, "we all have been missing something by being so busy all the time. Let's make a promise that we are going to stop and enjoy the beauty of God's world throughout the seasons."

How can Keri help her family keep the promise?

PROJECT DISCIPLE
Additional Activities

picture This

Distribute copies of Reproducible Master 6, guide page 64A. Have the children color each season's section with the appropriate seasonal color.

Then read the directions for making the wheel. Give each child a sheet of construction paper on which to paste the wheel. The pointer can be attached with a brad fastener or a paper fastener. Then have the children move the pointer to the current Church season. Encourage the children to share the wheels with their families. Explain: *At the beginning of each season, move the pointer to that season.*

Make it Happen

At the beginning of each Church season, talk about and decide on doing one protect-the-environment project. For example, during the Advent season, try turning off lights to save energy. At Christmas, work on a project to help animals in shelters or to protect an endangered species.

Encourage the children to discuss their projects with their families and to invite family members to work on the projects with your class.

Jesus said, "Follow me."

Mark 2:14

SEASONAL
CHAPTER 6

This chapter presents an overview of the Church Year.

THE CHURCH YEAR

Catechist Goal

• To introduce the seasons of the Church year

Our Faith Response

• To appreciate the celebrations of the Church year

Gather In My Name
Whole Community Catechesis

An Online Resource

Celebrate the **Church year** *as a class, school, and/or a parish community.* Gather In My Name *events come complete with detailed leader's guides, preparation charts, handouts, promotional ideas, organizational materials, and much more. Go to:*

www.webelieveweb.com

59

Lesson Plan

Introduce the Season ___ minutes

• **Pray** the Sign of the Cross and the Our Father.

• **Read** aloud the *Chapter Story* on guide page 59C. Discuss God's gifts of creation for each season.

• **Write** the names of the seasons on the board. For each season have the children name God's gifts that they associate with that season. For example in the fall we think of colored leaves, pumpkins, and birds flying south for the winter.

• **Ask** the children to open their books to page 59. Explain that the Church has seasons that we celebrate as followers of Jesus. These seasons have different names. Explain that different gifts of creation are associated with different seasons of the Church year (Ordinary Time, green plants; Advent, evergreen branches).

• **Read** the words on the banner. Give the children time to pray quietly to Jesus about ways they will follow him.

Lesson Materials

- copies of Reproducible Master 6
- crayons or colored pencils
- Grade 2 CD
- scissors, glue, brad fasteners

Teaching Note

The Church Year Lessons

The purpose of this lesson is to introduce the children to the seasons of the Church year. The children will study each season in a coming chapter: Ordinary Time, Chapter 7; Advent, Chapter 13; Christmas, Chapter 14; Lent, Chapter 20; Three Days, Chapter 21; Easter, Chapter 27. Try to present each lesson as close to the beginning of the season as possible.

The Church year helps us to follow Jesus.

WE GATHER

What does it mean to follow Jesus? Name some ways you follow Jesus.

WE BELIEVE

All during the year, we gather with our parish to worship. Together we celebrate the Eucharist and the other sacraments.

The Church year is made up of special times called seasons. During the different seasons, we grow in love for Jesus. We grow as his followers.

60

Lesson Plan

WE GATHER ___ minutes

Focus on Life Read the *We Gather* question. Help the children to conclude that following Jesus means loving God, ourselves, and others as Jesus did. Then ask the children to name ways that they follow Jesus.

- **Remind** the children that we become followers of Jesus when we are baptized. Ask: *How are the children in the photos on page 59 showing that they are Jesus' followers?*

WE BELIEVE ___ minutes

- **Explain:** *Today we are going to learn about the seasons of the Church year. We will discover how celebrating these seasons helps us to be faithful followers of Jesus.*

- **Ask** volunteers to read the first two *We Believe* paragraphs. Direct attention to the photo of the assembly at Mass. Point out that we celebrate the Church seasons with our families, friends, and parish.

- **Direct** the children's attention to the Church calendar chart. Explain: *The chart shows the seasons of the Church year. Advent is the first season we celebrate.* Have the children find the Advent space.

- **Have** volunteers read the description of each season. After each paragraph is read, ask the children to point to the season on the chart. Explain: *There is a special color for each season. The priest wears this color when he celebrates Mass.* Have the children say aloud the color for each season.

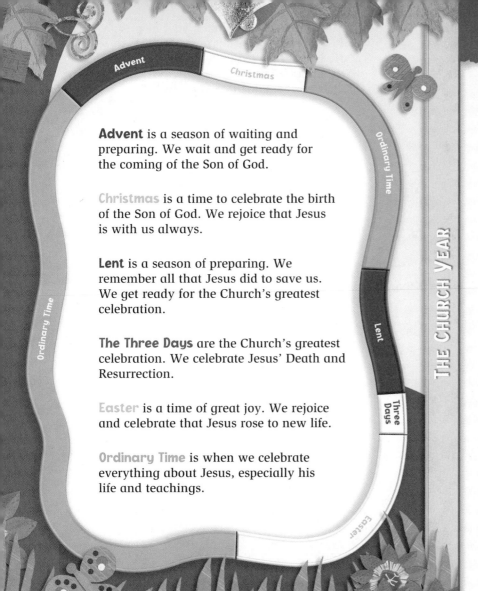

Advent is a season of waiting and preparing. We wait and get ready for the coming of the Son of God.

Christmas is a time to celebrate the birth of the Son of God. We rejoice that Jesus is with us always.

Lent is a season of preparing. We remember all that Jesus did to save us. We get ready for the Church's greatest celebration.

The Three Days are the Church's greatest celebration. We celebrate Jesus' Death and Resurrection.

Easter is a time of great joy. We rejoice and celebrate that Jesus rose to new life.

Ordinary Time is when we celebrate everything about Jesus, especially his life and teachings.

THE CHURCH YEAR

61

ACTIVITY BANK

Multiple Intelligences
Musical, Interpersonal

Teach the children to sing the following words to the tune of "If You're Happy."

O Jesus, we are happy following you.
Jesus, we are happy the whole year through.
We'll remember you're the reason why we celebrate each season.
O Jesus, we are happy following you.

Have the children stand in a circle and join hands. After you say the name of each season (begin with Advent), have the children move in a circle while singing the song.

• **Play** "Name That Season." Have the children work in pairs. Read the following clues. Ask each pair to write the name of the season you are describing.

◆ We celebrate Jesus' Death and Resurrection. (the Three Days)

◆ We celebrate everything about Jesus. (Ordinary Time)

◆ We remember all Jesus did to save us. (Lent)

◆ We celebrate the birth of the Son of God. (Christmas)

◆ We get ready for the coming of the Son of God. (Advent)

◆ We rejoice that Jesus rose to new life. (Easter)

Reread the clues and have the children read the correct answers.

• **Ask** the children to point to Advent on the calendar chart. Have them go in clockwise order, pointing to each season and reading the name of the season.

Quick Check

✔ *What happens during the different seasons of the Church year?* (We grow in love for Jesus, and we grow as his followers.)

✔ *Which season do we celebrate twice during the year?* (Ordinary Time)

CONNECTION

Catholic Social Teaching

Call to Family, Community, and Participation

During each of the liturgical seasons, our families gather with our parish to celebrate the sacraments, especially the celebration of Mass. Encourage the families to participate in the parish liturgical celebrations. For each season help the children to make seasonal symbols to share with their families. Also check your parish bulletin for announcements about parish service projects (Christmas toy collection, fish fry or soup suppers during Lent). Share this information with the children. Encourage them to ask their families to participate.

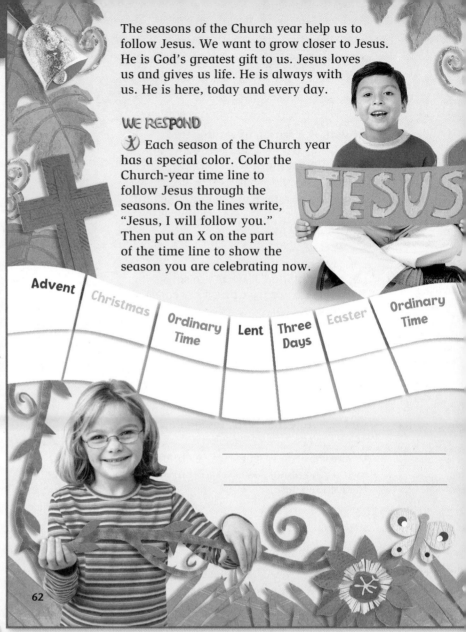

The seasons of the Church year help us to follow Jesus. We want to grow closer to Jesus. He is God's greatest gift to us. Jesus loves us and gives us life. He is always with us. He is here, today and every day.

WE RESPOND

Each season of the Church year has a special color. Color the Church-year time line to follow Jesus through the seasons. On the lines write, "Jesus, I will follow you." Then put an X on the part of the time line to show the season you are celebrating now.

Advent | Christmas | Ordinary Time | Lent | Three Days | Easter | Ordinary Time

62

Lesson Plan

WE BELIEVE (continued)

• **Invite** a volunteer to read aloud the *We Believe* paragraph. Have the children highlight or underline the last three sentences.

WE RESPOND ___ minutes

Connect to Life Read the *We Respond* activity directions. Have the children color the seasons' spaces on the time line. Then ask: *What season of the Church year are we celebrating now?* After the children have answered, ask them to find the season's space on the time line and mark it with an X. Then have them write: *Jesus, I will follow you.*

• **Take** the children on a tour of the parish church. Point out the seasonal color on banners, flowers, or other decorations that help us remember the current liturgical season. Also ask one of the priests to show the children the colored vestments he wears for Mass.

• **Read** aloud last Sunday's Gospel (It may be found in a missalette.) Ask the children: *What do we learn about Jesus in the reading?*

✝ We Respond in Prayer

Leader: We will follow Jesus through the Church year.

Reader 1: We pray in Advent:
All: Come, Lord Jesus!

Reader 2: We pray at Christmas:
All: Rejoice! Jesus is born!

Reader 3: We pray in Lent:
All: Lord, have mercy.

Reader 4: We pray during the Three Days:
All: Jesus, bring us to new life.

Reader 5: We pray at Easter:
All: Alleluia! Christ is risen!

Reader 6: We pray in Ordinary Time:
All: Jesus, we will follow you.

Leader: We remember that Jesus is with us always. May we always follow him!
All: Amen.

THE CHURCH YEAR

63

We Respond in Prayer (p. 63)

Get ready by placing a white cloth on the prayer table. You may want to display green, purple, and gold party streamers in the prayer space.

As the children gather in the prayer space, play "Come Follow Me," #3 on the Grade 2 CD. Then lead the children in prayer.

 This Week's Liturgy

Visit **www.webelieveweb.com** for this week's liturgical readings and other seasonal material.

Project Disciple (p. 64)

Celebrate!

Read the activity directions for drawing. Then read the directions for playing the game (see *Take Home* directions). Allow time for the children to play the game with partners.

Reality Check

Read aloud the directions. If children are having difficulty, suggest some of the possible responses marked on the student page.

Take Home

Encourage the children to play the matching game with their families.

Discuss and send home copies of *Sharing Faith with My Family*, guide page 64B.

Project Disciple Additional Activities
See the activities suggested on page 59C of the guide.

Pray Learn Celebrate Share Choose Live

Grade 2 The Church Year
PROJECT DISCIPLE

Celebrate!

Draw a picture in each space to tell about the Church season. Cover each space with a scrap of paper. Then play a memory game. See pages 61, 63.

The Three Days	Lent	Easter
Advent	Christmas	Ordinary Time
Easter	The Three Days	Lent
Christmas	Advent	Ordinary Time

Reality Check

Write three ways that you can follow Jesus through the Church year.

Possible responses: pray; go to Mass;

celebrate the sacraments

Take Home

Play your memory game with a family member. Take turns to find matching pairs of seasons.

▶ **DISCIPLE CHALLENGE**
When you find a matching pair, name something you do to celebrate that season.

Name _____

1. Color the spaces on the Church year wheel.

2. Cut out the wheel and glue it to a sheet of construction paper.

3. Cut out the pointer.

4. Use a paper fastener to attach the pointer to the wheel.

5. Move the pointer to the Church year season we are celebrating now.

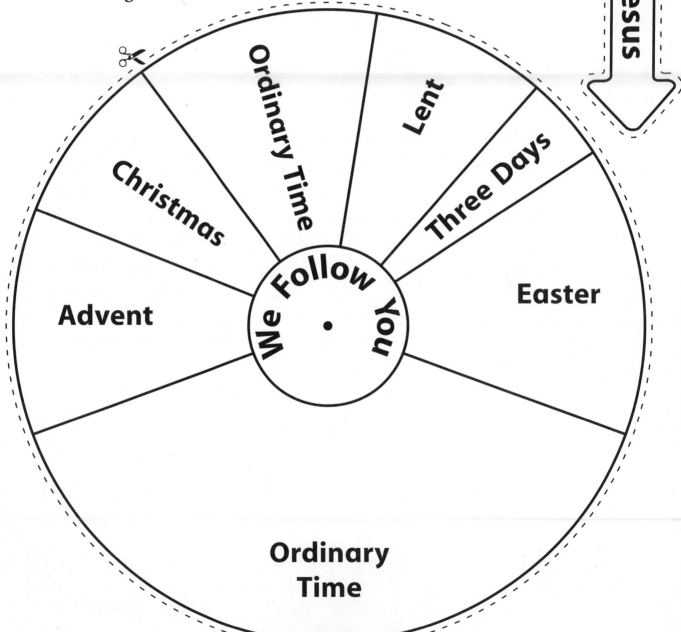

SHARING FAITH
with My Family

Sharing What I Learned

Look at the pictures below. Use them to tell your family what you learned in this chapter.

A Family Prayer to Follow Jesus

May the peace of Christ rule in our hearts, and may the Word of Christ in all its richness dwell in us, so that whatever we do in word and in work, we will do in the name of the Lord. Amen.

Around the Table

Show your family the Church year chart on page 61. Show them the season we are celebrating now. Tell what season comes next. Talk about what your family can do at home to celebrate this season or to prepare for the next one. How can you share this season with an elderly person or someone who lives alone?

Visit Sadlier's

www.WeBelieveweb.com

Connect to the Catechism
For adult background and reflection, see paragraph 1168.

64B

Ordinary Time

Apart from those seasons having their own distinctive character, thirty-three or thirty-four weeks remain in the yearly cycle that do not celebrate a specific aspect of the mystery of Christ. Rather, especially on the Sundays, they are devoted to the mystery of Christ in all its aspects. This period is known as Ordinary Time.

(Norms Governing Liturgical Calendars, 43)

Overview

In this chapter the children will learn that in Ordinary Time we celebrate Jesus Christ and learn to follow him.

For Adult Reading and Reflection
You may want to refer to paragraph 1173 of the *Catechism of the Catholic Church*.

Catechist Background

Go to **www.webelieveweb.com**, Catechist/ Teacher, We Believe Correlations for this chapter's correlation to the Six Tasks of Catechesis.

How do Sundays make a difference in your week?

During the season of Ordinary Time, we celebrate the life and teachings of Jesus Christ. Ordinary Time is the only season that we celebrate twice during the year. The season of Ordinary Time that comes after Pentecost and before Advent is the longest season of the year. There are also some weeks of Ordinary Time between the seasons of Christmas and Lent.

Ordinary Time is named for the ordinal numbers that mark its Sundays. In Ordinary Time, the Gospel for that year (Matthew, Mark, or Luke) is read in consecutive order. These Gospels proclaim the events of Christ's ministry as well as his teachings and parables.

The key days of every season are Sundays. This is because Sunday is the day of Christ's Resurrection. Sunday is the day when the community of believers "encounters the risen Lord who invites them to his banquet" (CCC 1166). As Pope John Paul II wrote, "Weekly attendance at the Sunday Eucharist and the cycle of the liturgical year make it possible to give a rhythm to Christian life and to sanctify time, which the risen Lord opens to the blessed eternity of the kingdom" ("On the Pastoral Care of the Liturgy," March 8, 1997). Each Sunday we gather as disciples ready to hear the Word of the Lord, to be nourished by his Body and Blood, and to encourage one another to love and serve the Lord.

When we gather to celebrate the Eucharist, we give thanks for the saving Passion, Death, and Resurrection of the Lord Jesus. We join in the rhythm of the season and sanctify our days in time. We also rejoice in Jesus' promise of life, now and forever.

How does participating in Sunday's celebration of the Eucharist give rhythm to your life?

Lesson Planning Guide

Lesson Steps	Presentation	Materials

① WE GATHER

Lesson Steps	Presentation	Materials
page 65 **Introduce the Season**	• Read the *Chapter Story*. • Introduce Ordinary Time. • Pray a psalm verse.	
page 66	• Share responses to the questions.	

② WE BELIEVE

Lesson Steps	Presentation	Materials
pages 66–68 *In Ordinary Time, we celebrate Jesus Christ and learn to follow him.*	• Present the text and chart about Ordinary Time. 🏃 Do the picture-study activity about Jesus and his teachings.	

③ WE RESPOND

Lesson Steps	Presentation	Materials
page 68	🏃 Do the drawing activity.	• crayons or colored pencils
Text page 69 **Guide page 69–70** **We Respond in Prayer**	• Honor Mary and the Blessed Trinity. 🎵 Honor Mary in song.	🎵 "Yes, We Will Do What Jesus Says," Paule Freeburg and Christopher Walker, #6, Grade 2 CD • prayer space: green tablecloth, house plant
Text page 70 **Guide pages 69–70, 70A** **Project Disciple**	• Complete the Project Disciple activities. Discuss the *Take Home* activity. • Complete the Reproducible Master 7 activity. See guide pages 70A and 65C. • Discuss/send home Sharing Faith with My Family, guide page 70B.	• pencils, crayons or colored pencils • large index cards • scissors, glue • green construction paper • copies of Reproducible Master 7, guide page 70A • copies of Sharing Faith with My Family, guide page 70B

For additional ideas, activities, and opportunities: Visit Sadlier's **www.WeBelieveweb.com**

Chapter Story

At the dinner table on Friday night, José said, "I guess Sunday will be another boring day."

Everyone at the table looked surprised. They thought about what they had done last Sunday. José's mother and sister had gone shopping. His dad had gone fishing with friends. José had stayed home with his grandmother.

The family decided that they wanted to do something this Sunday to make it a special family day. José's grandmother suggested, "Let's call Aunt Teresa and invite her and your cousins over."

José's sister said, "That's a great idea. Let's get together and have a picnic in the park."

José's mom said, "I have to work, but I'll join you in the park when I'm finished."

When everyone left the table that night, they were excited, especially José. He told everyone, "I can hardly wait until Sunday comes."

What would you like to do on Sunday to make it a special day for your family?

PROJECT DISCIPLE
Additional Activities

Celebrate!

Distribute copies of Reproducible Master 7, guide page 70A. Read aloud the activity directions. Have the children work in pairs. Explain: *When you find a letter, write it on the back of your activity sheet. There are nine letters hidden in the picture.*

When most of the pairs have finished finding the letters, have volunteers show where the letters are in the drawing. Ask the children what word the letters spell. Write *celebrate* on the board and ask the children to write the word to complete the prayer on the activity sheet.

Provide time for the children to color the scene. Encourage them to take their prayer posters home and pray the prayer often with their families.

Make it Happen

Ask the children to think about the stories about Jesus and his disciples that they have read in Unit 1. With the children choose one that they would like to dramatize for a younger group of children.

Invite a younger group of children to participate in an Ordinary Time celebration with your class. Prepare the dramatization of the Scripture story. If possible have a treat prepared to share.

ORDINARY TIME

"Every day I will bless you;
I will praise your name forever."
Psalm 145:2

SEASONAL

CHAPTER 7

This chapter helps us to understand
the season of Ordinary Time.

65

Catechist Goal

• To explain ways we celebrate
Ordinary Time

Our Faith Response

• To appreciate Sunday as the most
special day of the week

Gather In My Name
Whole Community Catechesis

An Online Resource

Celebrate **Ordinary Time** *as a class,
school, and/or a parish community.*
Gather In My Name *events come
complete with detailed leader's guides,
preparation charts, handouts, promotional ideas, organizational materials,
and much more. Go to:*

www.webelieveweb.com

Lesson Plan

Introduce the Season ___ minutes

• **Pray** the Sign of the Cross and the words *Jesus, be
with us.*

• **Read** aloud the *Chapter Story* on guide page 65C.
Discuss some of the special things that José's family
wanted to do on Sunday. Have volunteers share what
they can do to help make Sunday a special day.

• **Stress:** *We should be happy followers of Jesus every
day of the week.* Have the children open their books
to page 65.

Read aloud the chapter title. Explain: *Ordinary Time is
special because we learn a lot about Jesus in this season.*

• **Invite** the children to look at the photo on the page.
Ask: *What are the children doing to show that they are
happy?* Discuss the responses.

• **Pray** together the psalm verse below the
photograph.

Lesson Materials

- copies of Reproducible Master 7
- crayons or colored pencils
- large index cards
- Grade 2 CD
- scissors, glue
- green construction paper

Teaching Tip

Children Who Are Logical-Mathematical Learners

Invite the children who are logical-mathematical learners to participate in the *We Gather* activities. Have these children lead the discussion of the *We Gather* questions.

> In Ordinary Time, we celebrate Jesus Christ and learn to follow him.

WE GATHER

What are some things that you put in order? How do you put them in order?

WE BELIEVE

What do we celebrate in Ordinary Time? We celebrate Jesus Christ! We do not remember only one event of his life. We remember and learn about his whole life, Death, and Resurrection. We celebrate Jesus Christ and everything about him!

This season is called Ordinary Time because the Church puts the Sundays in number order.

Jesus teaches the disciples to pray, "Our Father." (Matthew 6:9)

The season of Ordinary Time comes twice each year. It comes between the seasons of Christmas and Lent. Ordinary Time comes again between the Easter season and the season of Advent. The special color of Ordinary Time is green.

66

Lesson Plan

WE GATHER _____ minutes

Focus on Life Read the *We Gather* questions. Have volunteers share responses. Print five numerals on the board (22, 9, 15, 33, 4). Have the children tell you the correct numerical order for the numbers (4, 9, 15, 22, 33). Help the children to conclude that putting things in order by letter, by size, and by number is a good way to organize and keep track of things.

• **Write** one of each of the following ordinal numbers on a large index card: sixteenth, third, twenty-first, tenth. Ask four volunteers to come to the front of the room. Give one card to each volunteer. Then ask these children to arrange themselves in the correct numerical order.

WE BELIEVE _____ minutes

• **Ask** a volunteer to read the first two *We Believe* paragraphs. Have the children highlight or underline the last sentence in the first paragraph.

• **Explain:** *We use ordinal numbers for Sundays in Ordinary Time: Fifth Sunday in Ordinary Time, Seventh Sunday in Ordinary Time, and so on.*

• **Ask** the children to look at the Church year chart on page 61. Explain: *We celebrate Ordinary Time twice each year.* Have the children locate the Ordinary Time spaces on the chart. Then have a volunteer read the third *We Believe* paragraph.

During Ordinary Time we:

• learn more about Jesus

• listen to his teachings read from the Bible

• learn how to follow Jesus in our everyday lives.

Look at the pictures on these pages. What does each one show you about Jesus? What does each one show about his teachings?

ORDINARY TIME

Jesus calls us. He says, "Let the children come to me." (Matthew 19:14)

67

ACTIVITY BANK

Multiple Intelligences
Bodily-Kinesthetic
Activity Materials: costumes and props for dramatization

Have the children look at the pictures of Jesus on these pages. Read the Scripture story for each one: page 66, Matthew 6:9–15 and page 67, Matthew 19:13–15. Divide the children into two groups and assign one of the stories to each group. Provide time for the groups to practice their words and actions. Then have the groups present their dramatizations.

• **Read** together the list of things we do during Ordinary Time. Then discuss what the pictures of Jesus show about his teachings. (Possible responses: Jesus loved his Father and wanted everyone to pray to him; Jesus welcomed everyone and wants us to do the same.)

Quick Check

✔ *What do we celebrate in Ordinary Time?* (We celebrate Jesus Christ and everything about him.)

✔ *What is the special color of Ordinary Time?* (The special color of Ordinary Time is green.)

CONNECTION

To Mary

The Church celebrates some feasts of Mary during Ordinary Time, including the Feast of the Assumption of Mary on August 15, the Birth of Mary on September 8, and Our Lady of the Rosary on October 7. The Feast of Our Lady of the Rosary was established in 1571 by Pope Pius V. The purpose of the feast is to honor Mary under the title that identifies her with a devotion that began in the twelfth century. Help the children grow closer to Mary by making them aware of her feasts. Plan simple celebrations for these days.

All through the year, the most special day of the week is Sunday. Jesus rose from the dead on a Sunday.

On Sundays we gather with our parish to celebrate Mass. We listen to the Word of God and receive the Eucharist. Every Sunday, we learn more about Jesus and grow closer to him. We rest from work. We spend time with family and friends.

WE RESPOND

Draw a picture to show what your family can do on Sundays in Ordinary Time.

68

Lesson Plan

WE BELIEVE (continued)

• **Write** the word *Sunday* on the board. Stress: *Sunday is the most special day of the week because Jesus rose from the dead on a Sunday.*

• **Ask** a volunteer to read the second paragraph on the page. Then play a game of Sunday charades with the children. Invite volunteers to act out the following Sunday activities while the rest of the class tries to guess what the activities are. (During the celebration of Mass: Have children pantomime gathering, singing, listening to God's Word, receiving the Eucharist.)

(After the celebration of Mass: Have children pantomime resting, playing, reading, sharing a meal with our families, visiting our family and friends.)

• **Note** that the children will learn more about our Sunday celebration of Mass in Unit 3.

WE RESPOND ___ minutes

Read the activity directions. You may want to reread the *Chapter Story* on page 65C. Then have children work on their story boards. When the children have completed the activity, ask volunteers to share their work.

✟ We Respond in Prayer

Leader: In Ordinary Time, we also celebrate special days in honor of Mary, the mother of Jesus and our mother. One of these days is the Feast of Our Lady of the Rosary on October 7.

Side 1: Hail Mary, full of grace, the Lord is with you! Blessed are you among women, and blessed is the fruit of your womb, Jesus.

Side 2: Holy Mary, Mother of God, pray for us sinners, now and at the hour of our death.

All: Amen.

Leader: Glory to the Father, and to the Son, and to the Holy Spirit:

All: As it was in the beginning, is now, and will be for ever. Amen.

🎵 **Yes, We Will Do What Jesus Says**

Mary said, "Do what Jesus tells you."
Mary said, "Do what Jesus says."
Yes, we will do what Jesus tells us,
yes, we will do what Jesus says.

ORDINARY TIME

69

Pray Learn Celebrate Share Choose Live

Grade 2 Ordinary Time

PROJECT DISCIPLE

What is your favorite way to celebrate Ordinary Time? Underline it.

Question Corner

• learn more about Jesus
• listen to Bible stories about Jesus
• pray to Jesus everyday
• celebrate with my parish at Mass

Add another way: Possible responses: remember Jesus' life, Death, and Resurrection; celebrate everything about Jesus; honor Mary

Fast Facts

Here is a sign for Mary. The M stands for Mary and for mother. There is a cross in the M. This reminds us that we honor Mary because she is the mother of Jesus.

Color this sign for Mary.

Take Home

Test your family members' knowledge of Ordinary Time. Give them this quiz.

What is the special color of Ordinary Time? green

What do we celebrate in Ordinary Time? Jesus Christ

Why is Ordinary Time called ordinary? because the Church puts the Sundays in number order

---

We Respond in Prayer (p. 69)

Get ready by placing a green cloth on the prayer table. Also place there statues or pictures of Jesus and Mary. Play "Yes, We Will Do What Jesus Says," #6 on the Grade 2 CD. Have the children practice singing.

Invite the children to gather in the prayer space. Have them form two groups, Sides 1 and 2. Lead the children in prayer.

📖 **This Week's Liturgy**
Visit **www.webelieveweb.com** for this week's liturgical readings and other seasonal material.

Project Disciple (p. 70)

Question Corner Read the list. Ask the children to underline their favorite way. Provide a minute for them to write another way.

Fast Facts Read the explanation of the sign for Mary. Then have the children color the symbol.

Take Home

Encourage the children to share the Ordinary Time quiz with their families.

Discuss and send home copies of *Sharing Faith with My Family*, guide page 70B.

Project Disciple Additional Activities See the activities suggested on page 65C of the guide.

Find the letters hidden in the picture. Unscramble the letters to find the word that completes the prayer. Write the word on the line provided. Color the garden scene.

Jesus, in Ordinary Time we will

_____ your life and love.

SHARING FAITH
with My Family

Sharing What I Learned

Look at the pictures below. Use them to tell your family what you learned in this chapter.

A Family Prayer on Sunday Evening

On Sunday evening before going to bed, ask your family to say this prayer together:

God, we thank you for the joy and rest of this day.

A Sign for Mary

Here is a sign for Mary. The M stands for Mary and for mother. There is a cross in the M. This reminds us that we honor Mary because she is the Mother of Jesus.

Color this sign. Then be on the lookout for other places where you can find this sign.

Visit Sadlier's

www.WeBelieveweb.com

Connect to the Catechism
For adult background and reflection, see paragraph 1173.

ASSESSMENT

Unit 1 Test

Read aloud each set of test directions. Also you may choose to read aloud each test item. Wait for a minute for the children to indicate their responses in writing.

Alternative Assessment

You may want the children to complete the following alternative-assessment activity.

Imagine you are the Apostle Peter or one of the other disciples of Jesus. Write a letter home. Tell your family about things Jesus has said and done.

Additional Testing

• Unit 1 Test in Grade 2 *Assessment Book*, pages 13–14

• Unit 1 Alternative Assessment in Grade 2 *Assessment Book*, page 27

• CD-ROM *Test Generator and Resource*: Use Unit 1 Test or customize your own.

Grade 2 Unit 1

UNIT TEST

Fill in the circle beside the correct answer.

1. Jesus, Mary, and Joseph are called the _____.
   ○ Trinity   ● Holy Family   ○ Church

2. At Baptism we receive God's life, called _____.
   ○ cross   ● grace   ○ holy

3. The Church celebrates with special signs called _____.
   ○ grace   ○ Apostles   ● sacraments

4. Confirmation calls us to _____.
   ● live our faith   ○ be selfish   ○ be quiet

Circle the correct answer.

5. Did God the Father send his Son, Jesus, to be with us?   (Yes)   No

6. Are there Ten Sacraments?   Yes   (No)

7. Did Jesus promise to send the Holy Spirit to help his followers?   (Yes)   No

8. On Christmas, do we celebrate the coming of the Holy Spirit?   Yes   (No)

continued on next page   71

Grade 2 Unit 1

Write what you know about:

9. Easter Sunday

   See Chapter 2, page 29.

   _____

   _____

   _____

   _____

10. the Blessed Trinity

   See Chapter 1, page 23.

   _____

   _____

   _____

   _____

72

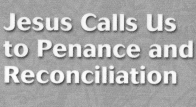

Jesus Calls Us to Penance and Reconciliation

UNIT 2

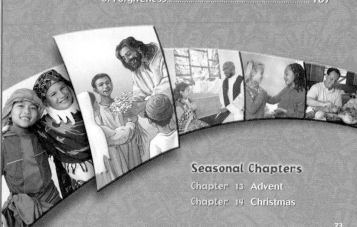

Seasonal Chapters

73

PROJECT DISCIPLE

DEAR FAMILY

In Unit 2 your child will grow as a disciple of Jesus by:

• understanding the importance of listening to the Word of God as found in the Old Testament and the New Testament

• learning how to live the Ten Commandments and the Great Commandment

• making choices that show love for God and others and avoiding sin

• recognizing that God always loves us and shows us mercy and asks us to forgive others

• preparing to celebrate God's forgiveness in the Sacrament of Penance and Reconciliation.

What's *the* Word?

In Chapter 11, the children hear the story of the shepherd and the lost sheep (Luke 15:4–6). Jesus told this story to show us that God will always love and forgive us. Read the story on page 100 with your family. This month, make it a point to ask God for his forgiveness. And pray:

Jesus, may we never wander far from you.

Pray Today
Review the list of the Ten Commandments on page 85. Then pray with your child:

God, thank you for the Ten Commandments. They help me to show love for you, for myself, and my wonderful family.

Reality Check

"The relationships within the family bring an affinity of feelings, affections and interests, arising above all from the members' respect for one another."
(Catechism of the Catholic Church, 2206)

Celebrate!

Jesus has given us a way to receive God's forgiveness. The Church celebrates this forgiveness in the Sacrament of Penance and Reconciliation. Take a moment to consider if you are receiving God's forgiveness through the sacrament on a regular basis.

Show That You Care

Point out that we can always show our love for God by forgiving one another.

Take Home

Each chapter in your child's *We Believe* Grade 2 text offers a "Take Home" activity that invites your family to support your child's journey to more fully become a disciple of Christ.

Be ready for this unit's Take Home:

Chapter 8: Discovering news about the Church

Chapter 9: Listing important family rules

Chapter 10: Discussing the qualities of a good friend

Chapter 11: Performing a scriptural puppet play

Chapter 12: Discussing the Sacrament of Penance

74

Unit 2 • Unit Opener

CLASS CONNECTION

Read aloud the unit title and the chapter titles. Ask the children: *What do you think you will be learning about in this unit?* Invite a few volunteers to respond. Then explain to the children that they will be learning about the parts of the Bible, God's forgiveness, and the Sacrament of Penance and Reconciliation.

HOME CONNECTION

Project Disciple
Dear Family

Sadlier *We Believe* calls on families to become involved in:

• learning the faith

• prayer and worship

• living their faith.

Highlighting of these unit family pages and the opportunities they offer will strengthen the partnership of the Church and the home.

For additional information and activities, encourage families to visit Sadlier's

www.WeBelieveweb.com

Chapter 8 — We Learn About God's Love

Overview

In Chapter 5 the children learned about the Sacrament of Confirmation. In this chapter the children will learn about the Bible.

Doctrinal Content	For Adult Reading and Reflection *Catechism of the Catholic Church*
The children will learn:	Paragraph
• The Bible is the book of God's Word.	104
• The Old Testament is the first part of the Bible.	121
• The New Testament is the second part of the Bible.	124
• Jesus wants us to listen to his teachings.	127

Key Words

Bible (p. 77)
Old Testament (p. 77)
New Testament (p. 79)
Gospels (p. 79)

Catechist Background

As a Catholic, where do you learn the values you live by?

If you are fortunate enough to have photos of your grandparents or even great-grandparents, you have probably looked closely at them to see whether there is a family resemblance. Our ancestors would probably want to take a good look at us, too. They would probably like to know whether the values they held dear are now embraced by our generation.

When we read the Bible we are reading the book of God's Word. We find out about our ancestors in faith and about ways that we can live out our faith. We learn that we are a chosen people, cherished by a loving and forgiving God. In the first part of the Bible, the Old Testament, we learn of God's faithfulness to his people Israel. Through reading history, poetry, prayers, and stories we hear God's promise to send a Savior.

Go to **www.webelieveweb.com**, Catechist/Teacher, We Believe Correlations for this chapter's correlation to:
• Six Tasks of Catechesis
• Catholic Social Teaching.

In the second part of the Bible, the New Testament, we learn how the life, Death, Resurrection, and Ascension of Jesus Christ fulfilled God's promise. By word and deed Jesus shows us the way to love God as our Father and the ways to love our neighbors as ourselves. Jesus asks the Father to send the Holy Spirit to help us and guide us.

In the Gospels Jesus shows us the way to live. He teaches us to be merciful, compassionate, peaceful, just, prayerful, and selfless in loving others. He invites us to listen carefully and then live our lives accordingly.

Does the way you live your life reflect Jesus' example?

Lesson Planning Guide

Lesson Steps	Presentation	Materials

WE GATHER

Lesson Steps	Presentation	Materials
page 75 **We Gather in Prayer** **Focus on Life**	• Listen to Scripture. • Respond in prayer. • Discuss favorite books.	For the prayer space: Bible, chart paper for scroll, box, gold or silver paper 🎵 "Sing for Joy," Bernadette Farrell, #4, Grade 2 CD (optional)

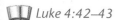 WE BELIEVE

Lesson Steps	Presentation	Materials
page 76 *The Bible is the book of God's Word.*	• Present the text about the Bible. • Design a Bible cover. • Read and discuss *As Catholics*.	• crayons or colored pencils
page 77 *The Old Testament is the first part of the Bible.*	• Read and discuss the text about the Old Testament. • Discuss ways David showed love for God.	• copies of Reproducible Master 8, guide page 75C
page 78 *The New Testament is the second part of the Bible.* 📖 *Luke 4:42–43*	• Read the Scripture story. • Present and discuss the text about the New Testament and the Gospels. • Share favorite stories about Jesus.	• chart paper for graphic organizer • pencils or colored markers
page 79 *Jesus wants us to listen to his teachings.* 📖 *Matthew 7:24–27*	• Read and discuss the Scripture story and the importance of listening.	• crayons or colored markers

WE RESPOND

Lesson Steps	Presentation	Materials
page 79	Do the *We Respond* activity.	
pages 80–81 **Project Disciple**	• Complete the Project Disciple activities. • Explain the *Take Home* activity. • Discuss/send home Sharing Faith with My Family reproducible master for this chapter.	• pencils • copies of Sharing Faith with My Family reproducible master, Chapter 8 (back of book)
page 82 **Chapter 8 Test**	• Complete Chapter 8 Test. • Work on *Alternative Assessment* activity.	• optional: copies of Scripture reproducible master, *What's the Word?*, Chapter 8 (back of book)

For additional ideas, activities, and opportunities: Visit Sadlier's **www.WeBelieve.web.com**

Here are stories about leaders we can read about in the Old Testament.

The Story of Joseph

Read Along

Joseph grew up in a large family. He had eleven brothers, but Joseph was his father's favorite. His father gave him a coat of many colors.

Joseph's brothers were jealous of Joseph. They were so jealous that they sold him to some passing merchants. These men took Joseph to Egypt, a country far from his home.

Many years later Joseph's family was starving, so his brothers went to Egypt looking for food. Joseph helped his family in Egypt. He forgave his brothers and gave his father and brothers food and a place to live.

On the back of the worksheet, write or draw what you remember about Joseph.

The Story of Queen Esther

Read Along

A beautiful young Jewish girl named Esther lived in the country of Persia a long time ago. Esther was chosen by the King of Persia to become his wife.

One day, Queen Esther's uncle came to see her. He told her that one of the king's servants had told lies about the Jews in the kingdom. The servant wanted the king to kill all the Jewish people in the country.

Esther was afraid. She went to the king and told him about the servant's lies and about the plan to kill her people. The king believed her. Esther had saved all the Jewish people living in Persia.

On the back of the worksheet, write or draw what you have learned about Esther.

PROJECT DISCIPLE

Pray
Learn
Celebrate
Share
Choose
Live

Additional Activities

Make it Happen

Teach the children the following song to sing to the tune of "Frère Jacques."

Share the Good News. Share the Good News of Jesus Christ! Of Jesus Christ!
His Good News helps us to love.
His Good News helps us to live,
Live God's Word! Live God's Word!

Ask the children to make up their own verses and to share the song with family and friends.

What's the Word?

Scripture reproducible master, Chapter 8

Materials needed: copies of *What's the Word?* (back of book), pencils

Distribute copies of the Scripture reproducible master. Read aloud the script. Then invite the children to write what the townspeople might have said.

Then choose two volunteers to be readers. For the townspeople's part, have volunteers take turns reading what they have written. You may want the children to illustrate the story in the space below the script.

Question Corner

List the following Bible story topics on the board or on chart paper. Ask volunteers to name which part of the Bible each story is in. Then have the children work in pairs to rate the stories from 1 to 6, 1 being their most favorite and 6 being their least favorite:

• God creates the world.
• the story of Noah and the ark
• the story of the birth of Jesus
• Jesus' story of the Good Samaritan
• Jesus blesses the children.

Then have the pairs share their ratings with the entire group.

More to Explore

Share and/or invite the children to share a few good-news stories about families, friends, team mates, neighbors, school faculty or students, and parish members. Keep a record of the good-news stories. Then, have the children act as reporters for a good-news TV program featuring a few of the stories.

Meeting Individual Needs
An Atmosphere of Acceptance

In the New Testament Jesus provides us with the perfect example of accepting people as they are. Make your room a place of acceptance. Consider taking a few extra minutes every day to praise the good work, behavior, or accomplishments of one or more of the children. Make sure that, over time, each child has been singled out with words of praise.

We Believe Resources

• Grade 2 *Review & Resource Book*, pages 19–21
• Grade 2 *Family Book*, pages 24–26
• Grade 2 *Assessment Book*, pages 15–16
• Grade 2 CD-ROM *Test Generator and Resource*: Use Chapter 8 Test or customize your own.

www.webelieveweb.com

Enrichment Ideas

Chapter Story

Most of Miss Miller's second grade class was outside for recess, but Marcos, Joanna, and Chris stayed inside. They helped Miss Miller decorate the bulletin board with the classes' drawings about their favorite books.

Marcos pointed to his drawing and said, "I drew a picture of Willy the dog. My favorite book is about Willy and the family who find him when they are on vacation."

Joanna asked Miss Miller, "What kind of books do you like to read?"

Miss Miller said, "Oh, I like to read many different kinds of books!"

Chris said, "Tell us about your favorite book."

Miss Miller told the children, "Well, I have a book that is very special to me. It is my favorite for two particular reasons. The first reason is that my grandmother gave me the book on my seventh birthday. It was an extra special book because she had used it in school. My grandmother said that when she was in school this book was called a reader."

"What is the book about, Miss Miller?" Marcos asked.

"Well, it's about many different things. The second reason the book is my favorite is because it has stories about famous people, animals, and children. It also has poems and songs."

Joanna asked Miss Miller, "Would you bring the reader into school for us to see?"

Miss Miller answered, "Sure, Joanna! And I will even share some of the stories and poems with you."

▶ *Why did Miss Miller think her reader was a special book?*

FAITH and MEDIA

▶ Invite the children to describe some video versions of Bible stories that they have seen. Ask them to tell why they like or dislike watching the videos. Explore with the children how watching particular videos of Bible stories can help them to grow in their faith. If possible, show the class an age appropriate video version of a Bible story and carry on a similar discussion.

CHAPTER PROJECT: A PAGEANT OF BIBLICAL PERSONS

Help the children recall their favorite stories about Jesus. Then ask them to recall their favorite stories that Jesus told when he taught his followers. You could also have the children look through *We Believe* Grade 2 for ideas or reminders. If possible, provide a few copies of *We Believe* Grade 1 for suggestions.

Then have each child choose one person from the stories. Help them to make a simple costume and select an appropriate prop to represent the biblical person. An example would be a child dressed as Zacchaeus in a colorful tunic holding a picture of a tree (because Zacchaeus was short and climbed a tree to see Jesus).

Have the children wear their costumes and carry their props in a parade. Provide time for each child to explain who he or she is dressed as and to tell a story about the person.

We Learn About God's Love

WE GATHER

✝ **Leader:** Let us gather to listen to God's Word.

Reader: God said,
"I, the LORD, your God,
teach you what is for
your good,
and lead you on the way
you should go." (Isaiah 48:17)

Leader: O God, we want to understand your Word.

All: God, help us to remember all the good things you teach us. Help us to follow your ways of love.

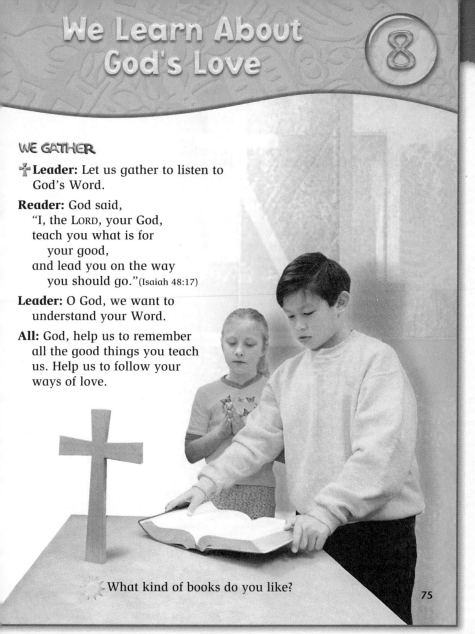

☀ What kind of books do you like?

75

PREPARING TO PRAY

For this gathering prayer, the children will listen and respond to God's Word.

• Choose a prayer leader and a reader. Provide time for them to prepare for the prayer.

• Choose a volunteer to carry the Bible and to lead the other children in a procession.

The Prayer Space

• Use chart paper to make a scroll. On the paper print *God, we want to listen to your Word.* Roll back the top and bottom of the paper to make a scroll. Display the scroll in your prayer space.

• Cover a box with gold or silver paper. Place it on a table. This can serve as a reading stand for the Bible.

• Display the Bible prominently.

📖 **This Week's Liturgy**
Visit **www.webelieveweb.com** for this week's liturgical readings and other seasonal material.

Lesson Plan

WE GATHER _____ minutes

✝ Pray

• Ask the prayer leader, the reader, and the child carrying the Bible to lead the other children in a procession to the prayer space. (Option: While the children are processing, play "Sing for Joy, " #4 on the Grade 2 CD.)

• Ask the child who is holding the Bible to place it on the special stand you have made.

• Invite all the children to gather in the prayer space and open their books to page 75. Pray the Sign of the Cross together and ask the leader to begin the prayer.

☀ Focus on Life

• Invite the children to name their favorite kinds of books. Have them describe what they like best about these books.

• Share the *Chapter Story* on guide page 75E.

Family Connection Update

Invite the children to share their family discussions about work.

Catechist Goal

• To introduce the Bible as the book of God's Word

Our Faith Response

• To identify ways we can show Jesus that we have listened to his teachings

 **Bible**

Old Testament

New Testament

Gospels

Lesson Materials

• crayons or colored pencils

• copies of Reproducible Master 8

• Scripture and Family reproducible masters (back of book)

As Catholics...

Scripture

After working on these two pages, write the words *Sacred* and *Scripture* on the board. Then read aloud the *As Catholics* text. Remind the children that you have made a special place for the Bible.

WE BELIEVE

The Bible is the book of God's Word.

God has always wanted us to know and love him. He wants us to tell others about him, too.

Long ago the Holy Spirit helped certain people to write about God's love. Different writers wrote in different ways. Some wrote stories or poems. Some wrote about people and events.

These writings were put into one large book called the Bible. God the Holy Spirit guided the people who wrote the Bible. So the **Bible** is the book in which God's Word is written.

When we read the Bible we learn:

• what God has told us about himself and his love

• what God wants us to do to live as his children.

👤 Draw a cover for the Bible. It should show that the Bible is a very special book about God's love.

As Catholics...

We also call the Bible Sacred Scripture. The word *sacred* means "holy." The word *Scripture* comes from a word that means "writings."

We keep the Bible in a special place in our homes and churches. Together make a special place in your classroom for the Bible.

76

Lesson Plan

WE BELIEVE
_____ minutes

Read the first three paragraphs on page 76. Explain that in the Bible we can read stories, poems, or accounts of people and events. All of these are God's Word.

Hold up the Bible. Stress: *The Holy Spirit guided the writers of the Bible.* Ask: *What do we learn when we read or listen to the Bible?* Have the children read the two points listed in the last paragraph on page 76.

👤 **Invite** the children to draw a cover for the Bible. When they are finished, have them show their covers to the people who are sitting near them.

Ask: *Have you ever read a book or seen a movie that has two parts?* Explain that the Bible has two parts. Print *Old Testament* on the board and tell the children that this is what the first part of the Bible is called. Hold up the Bible. Show where the Old Testament begins and ends. Then have volunteers read the paragraphs on page 77.

👤 **Invite** the children to look at the picture of David on page 77. Discuss ways David showed his love for God. Then invite the children to stand and pray David's words of praise.

The Old Testament is the first part of the Bible.

The Bible has two parts. The first part is called the **Old Testament**. In this part we learn about God's people who lived before Jesus' time on earth. We read about the many wonderful things God did for his people. We read about the ways God showed special love for them. We also learn how they showed their love for God.

In the Old Testament we learn about the lives of many people. One of the people we read about is David. David was a shepherd. God was pleased with David. God loved David very much. God chose David to become king.

David showed his great love for God by praising him. David said, "Great are you, Lord GOD!" (2 Samuel 7:22)

Key Words

Bible the book in which God's Word is written

Old Testament the first part of the Bible

 Talk about ways David showed his love for God. Pray David's prayer of praise.

77

ACTIVITY BANK

Curriculum Connection
Art
Activity Materials: drawing paper, crayons or markers

Have the children work in groups. Give each group a long sheet of paper. Encourage them to make a mural with scenes from David's, Joseph's, or Esther's life. Print captions for their pictures.

Multiple Intelligences
Bodily-Kinesthetic
Activity Materials: props and costumes for dramatizations (optional)

Have the children form three groups. Assign each group one of the Old Testament leaders that were discussed in this lesson (David, Joseph, or Esther). Ask the groups to prepare skits to tell the story of each leader.

 Distribute copies of Reproducible Master 8. (See guide page 75C.) Ask the children to read along as you read the stories of Joseph and Esther aloud. After reading, ask: *What would you tell others about these leaders?*

Quick Check

✔ *What do we learn when we read the Bible?* (We learn about God and his love. We learn how to live as God's children.)

✔ *What people do we learn about in the Old Testament?* (We learn about the people who lived before Jesus' time on earth.)

The New Testament is the second part of the Bible.

📖 Luke 4:42–43

One morning a crowd went to see Jesus. They tried to stop him from leaving their town. But Jesus said, "To the other towns also I must proclaim the good news of the kingdom of God, because for this purpose I have been sent." (Luke 4:43)

This reading is from the second part of the Bible. The second part of the Bible is the **New Testament**. The New Testament is about Jesus Christ, his disciples, and the Church.

Four of the books in the New Testament are called the **Gospels**. They are about Jesus' teachings and his life on earth.

The word *gospel* means "good news." We learn the Good News of Jesus Christ in the Gospels.

- God is our Father who loves and forgives us.
- Jesus is with us always. He teaches us how to love and do good.
- The Holy Spirit helps and guides us.

🧍 What is your favorite story about Jesus?

78

Lesson Plan

WE BELIEVE (continued)

📖 **Direct** attention to the picture of Jesus. Have a volunteer read the Scripture story on page 78. Explain: *Jesus went from town to town to announce the Good News about God's love.* Tell the group that another word for *announce* is *proclaim*.

Write the words *New Testament* and *Gospels* on the board. Explain: *The New Testament is the second part of the Bible. The Gospels are four very special books of the New Testament.* Then have volunteers read the two

paragraphs after the Bible reading. Hold up the Bible. Show the beginning and end of the New Testament. Explain: *The Gospels are the first four books of the New Testament. The word gospel means "good news." In the Gospels Jesus shows us the Good News about God and his love for us.* Then read aloud the three bulleted items listed after the fourth paragraph on page 78.

🧍 **Read** the question. Invite volunteers to share what their favorite story about Jesus is.

Key Words

New Testament the second part of the Bible

Gospels four of the books in the New Testament that are about Jesus' teachings and his life on earth

Jesus wants us to listen to his teachings.

One day Jesus had been teaching for a long time. He had taught people about believing in God and praying to him. Jesus ended by telling this story.

📖 Matthew 7:24–27

A man built his house on rock. When storms came, the wind blew. The rain beat against the house. But the house did not fall. It had been built on rock.

Jesus told the people, "Everyone who listens to these words of mine and acts on them will be like a wise man who built his house on rock." (Matthew 7:24)

When we listen to God's Word in the Bible, we hear with our ears. We remember in our minds and hearts. We show we have listened by loving God and helping others.

WE RESPOND

What can you do to show Jesus that you have listened to him?

👤 Draw a picture of or write one thing you will do.

79

ACTIVITY BANK

Multiple Intelligences
Musical

Teach the following song to sing to the tune of "Frère Jacques."

*Share the Good News, share the
    Good News,
of Jesus Christ! of Jesus Christ!
His Good News helps us to love.
His Good News helps us to live.
Live God's Word! Live God's
    Word!*

Invite the children to make up their own verses.

Curriculum Connection
Science

Activity Materials: rock, large plastic container, pitcher of water

Demonstrate the effects of water and wind on rock. Place a large rock in the center of a container. Pour water on the rock. Ask what happens. Then have children stand around the rock and blow like the wind on it. Help the children conclude that water and wind do not usually affect rocks in a short period of time.

Read aloud the statement at the top of page 79. Ask: *What are some things Jesus taught us?* Have a few volunteers share their responses. Affirm the children by saying: *You remember some things Jesus taught. That shows you have listened well.* Then invite the children to listen as volunteers read the Scripture passage.

Explain: *Rock is strong. Jesus was trying to tell us that listening to his teaching helps us to grow strong in our faith.*

Read the last paragraph on page 79. Stress: *We show we have listened to Jesus' teaching when we love and help others.*

WE RESPOND _____ minutes

Connect to Life Ask: *What can you do to show Jesus that you have listened to him?* Write the children's suggestions on chart paper or the board.

👤 **Invite** the children to look at the list and write or draw one thing that they will do this week.

Pray Invite the children to gather in the prayer space. Pray together: *Jesus, we will do what you want. We will listen to your teaching.*

Catechist Goal

• To review the chapter ideas that are key to growing as disciples of Jesus Christ

Our Faith Response

• To decide on ways to grow as disciples by living out what we have learned

Show What *you* Know

Help the children work on the web. You may want to have them expand the New Testament part of the web by drawing a rectangle below Gospels and writing Matthew, Mark, Luke, and John in the rectangle.

Pray Today Help the children write a text-message prayer. When they are finished, ask volunteers to share their prayers with the group.

Make *it* Happen

Read the recommendation form. Some children may need help identifying whether the story is in the Old Testament or New Testament. Have the children share their work with the group.

Fast Facts Ask a volunteer to read the sentence. Discuss with the group why the Bible is the best-selling book of all time.

Take Home

Explain to the children that they may find the Catholic newspaper available in the back of church. Obtain a copy and show some of the photographs and articles.

Discuss and send home copies of *Sharing Faith with My Family* reproducible master for this chapter (back of book).

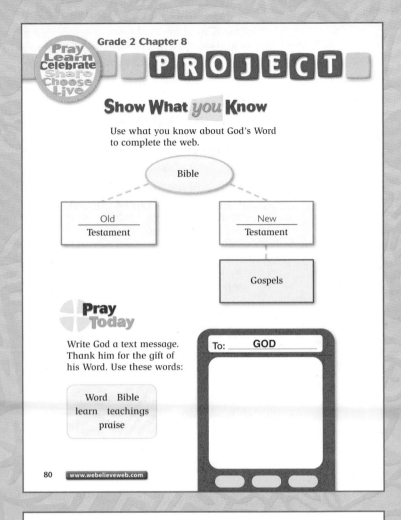

Grade 2 Chapter 8

Pray Learn Celebrate Share Choose Live

PROJECT

Show What *you* Know

Use what you know about God's Word to complete the web.

Bible

Old Testament

New Testament

Gospels

Pray Today

Write God a text message. Thank him for the gift of his Word. Use these words:

Word   Bible
learn   teachings
praise

To: **GOD**

80   www.webelieveweb.com

DISCIPLE

Pray Learn Celebrate Share Choose Live

Make *it* Happen   Recommend your favorite Bible story to a friend. Use the form below.

I recommend _____.

It can be found in the _____ Testament.

In this story, _____

_____

It is my favorite story because _____

Note: Stories about Jesus and his Apostles and stories

that Jesus told should be marked from the

New Testament.

Fast Facts

More copies of the Bible have been sold than any other book ever written.

Now, pass it on!

Take Home

Ask a family member to get a copy of your local Catholic newspaper. Find out what is happening in the Catholic community.

81

CHAPTER TEST

Fill in the circle beside the correct answer.

1. The Bible is the book of _____ Word.
   - ● God's
   - ○ David's

2. The _____ Testament is the first part of the Bible.
   - ● Old
   - ○ New

3. The _____ Testament is the second part of the Bible.
   - ○ Old
   - ● New

4. We can read about Jesus' life and teachings in the _____ Testament.
   - ○ Old
   - ● New

5. The word _____ means "good news."
   - ○ Bible
   - ● gospel

Circle the correct answer.

6. Did the Holy Spirit guide the writers of the Bible? (Yes) No

7. Are the four Gospels about God's people before Jesus' time on earth? Yes (No)

8. Did all the writers of the Bible write in the same way? Yes (No)

9–10. Write two things we can learn when we read the Bible.

Possible responses: 'what God has told us about himself; what God wants us to do to live as his children

82

CHAPTER TEST

Provide ten to fifteen minutes for the students to complete the test. After all have finished, check the answers. Clarify any misconceptions.

Alternative Assessment

You may want the students to complete the following alternative-assessment activity.

Make a poster to show the two parts of the Bible. Explain each part.

Additional Testing

• Chapter 8 Test in *Assessment Book*, pages 15–16

• CD-ROM *Test Generator and Resource*: Use Chapter 8 Test or customize your own.

Review

Review the definitions as they are presented in the chapter's *Key Word* boxes:

- Bible (page 77)
- Old Testament (page 77)
- New Testament (page 79)
- Gospels (page 79).

We Believe Statements

Review the four statements.

- The Bible is the book of God's Word.
- The Old Testament is the first part of the Bible.
- The New Testament is the second part of the Bible.
- Jesus wants us to listen to his teachings.

To use the Chapter 8 Study Guide, visit

www.webelieveweb.com

Overview

In Chapter 8 the children learned that the Bible is the book in which God's Word is written. In this chapter the children will learn that God gave us laws called commandments. By obeying these laws, we show love and respect for God, ourselves, and others.

Doctrinal Content	For Adult Reading and Reflection *Catechism of the Catholic Church*
The children will learn:	Paragraph
• Jesus taught us the Great Commandment.	2055
• The Ten Commandments help us to live as God's children.	2059
• God wants us to show him our love and respect.	2067
• God wants us to show that we love others as we love ourselves.	2069

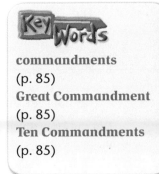

Key Words

commandments (p. 85)
Great Commandment (p. 85)
Ten Commandments (p. 85)

Go to **www.webelieveweb.com**, Catechist/ Teacher, We Believe Correlations for this chapter's correlation to:
• Six Tasks of Catechesis
• Catholic Social Teaching
• *Catechetical Formation in Chaste Living.*

Catechist Background

Who taught you the commandments?

In the Old Testament Moses is revered as the great teacher because he taught the Israelites about their covenant with God. The Israelites responded to God's love by obeying the Ten Commandments that God revealed to Moses. In the first three commandments people learn how to love and respect God while in the Fourth through the Tenth Commandments people learn how to love and respect themselves and one another.

In the Gospel of Matthew Jesus is seen as the new Moses who teaches us about our new relationship with God. From Jesus we learn that God is our loving Father. Jesus does not abolish the commandments. Rather, by his words and actions Jesus shows us how to live the commandments as loving children of God.

When Jesus is asked which is the greatest commandment, he emphasizes the importance of love. He tells us to "love the Lord, your God, with all your heart, with all your soul, and with all your mind" and "love your neighbor as yourself" (Matthew 22:37, 39). In the Great Commandment Jesus gives us the reason for obeying all of the commandments: love.

It is not always easy to imitate the love that Jesus shows us and to follow the commandments. However, we do not do this alone. Through faith we know that we have Jesus with us to guide and strengthen us.

How does the love of God and neighbor guide your actions?

Lesson Planning Guide

Lesson Steps	Presentation	Materials

1 WE GATHER

Lesson Steps	Presentation	Materials
page 83 ✚ We Gather in Prayer	• Ask God for help to follow his laws.	For the prayer space: Bible and photos of people following laws
☀ Focus on Life	• Discuss rules that we follow every day.	

2 WE BELIEVE

Lesson Steps	Presentation	Materials
page 84 *Jesus taught us the Great Commandment.* 📖 *Matthew 22:35–39*	• Read and discuss the text about the Great Commandment. 🧍 Do the picture study activity. • Reflect on the question.	
page 85 *The Ten Commandments help us to live as God's children.*	• Present the text about the Ten Commandments. • Point out the *Key Words* and the definitions. 🧍 Do the activity.	• highlighters or crayons
page 86 *God wants us to show him our love and respect.*	• Read and discuss the text about showing God love and respect. 🎵 Praise God in song. • Read and discuss *As Catholics*.	🎵 "We Celebrate with Joy," Carey Landry, #7, Grade 2 CD
page 87 *God wants us to show that we love others as we love ourselves.*	• Read and discuss the ways we show love for ourselves and others.	• pencils • copies of Reproducible Master 9, guide page 83C

3 WE RESPOND

Lesson Steps	Presentation	Materials
page 87	🧍 Complete the *We Respond* activity.	
pages 88–89 **Project Disciple**	• Complete the **Project Disciple** activities. • Explain the *Take Home* activity. • Discuss/send home **Sharing Faith with My Family** reproducible master for this chapter.	• colored pencils • copies of **Sharing Faith with My Family** reproducible master, Chapter 9 (back of book)
page 90 **Chapter 9 Test**	• Complete **Chapter 9 Test**. • Work on *Alternative Assessment* activity.	• optional: copies of Scripture reproducible master, *What's the Word?*, Chapter 9 (back of book)

For additional ideas, activities, and opportunities: Visit Sadlier's **www.WeBelieveweb.com**

Name _____

Solve the puzzle. Use the words in the box and the incomplete sentences as clues.

| Great | happy | Sunday | truth | worship |

Across

1. Jesus taught us the _____ Commandment.

4. We join our parish for Mass on _____ or Saturday evening.

5. When we _____ God, we show him our love.

Down

2. We show respect for others when we tell the _____.

3. We show our love for God and others when we are _____ and thankful for our family and friends.

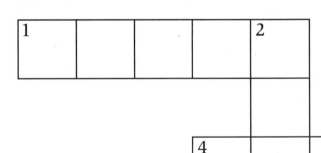

PROJECT DISCIPLE

Pray
Learn
Celebrate
Share
Choose
Live

Additional Activities

What Would *you* do?

Help the children work together to write or tell a story about following the Great Commandment.

Provide the first few sentences. Then ask the children to take turns adding sentences to the story as you record what they are saying. After the story is completed, reread or replay the story. Discuss ways the characters in the story followed the Great Commandment.

Then ask volunteers to role-play the story.

What's *the* Word?

Scripture reproducible master, Chapter 9

Materials needed: copies of *What's the Word?* (back of book), optional—props and costumes for dramatization

Distribute copies of the Scripture reproducible master. Choose three volunteers to be readers and other volunteers to mime the actions of the characters as the script is being read.

Introduce the activity by reminding the children that we read about God's People before Jesus was born in the Old Testament. Stress that Moses was a very important leader.

Make *it* Happen

Materials needed: small heart patterns, craft foam, scissors, permanent markers, hole puncher, ribbon or yarn

Have each child use a heart pattern to trace two hearts on a square of craft foam. Help each child use a permanent marker to write *God* on one heart and *others* on the other heart. Punch a hole at the top of the hearts, and then string ribbon or yarn through the holes and tie at the ends to make a band or bracelet. Explain to the children that when they look at the band they can remember to follow the Great Commandment.

Pray Today

Materials needed: drawing paper, crayons or colored pencils

Give each child a sheet of drawing paper. Read the psalm verse (Psalm 119:64) on page 83. Have the children draw a picture to illustrate these words. When the children have finished, ask them to write the verse on the back of the picture. Then encourage the children to share the psalm verse and illustrations with family and friends.

Meeting Individual Needs
English Language Learners

All children, especially those who are learning English, may have trouble understanding the vocabulary used in the Ten Commandments. Try to simplify unfamiliar terms and give a few examples so that the children know exactly what each commandment states.

We Believe Resources

- Grade 2 *Review & Resource Book*, pages 22–24
- Grade 2 *Family Book*, pages 27–29
- Grade 2 *Assessment Book*, pages 17–18
- Grade 2 CD-ROM *Test Generator and Resource*: Use Chapter 9 Test or customize your own.

• www.webelieveweb.com

Chapter Story

Liam woke up early on Monday morning and got dressed. Then he made his bed, and picked up his clothes from the floor. Liam's parents had asked him to do this every morning.

Then Liam went downstairs where his mother was getting breakfast ready. He started to climb up on a chair to reach for his favorite cereal, but his mother stopped him. "Liam, what have I said about standing on chairs?" she asked. Liam knew his mother did not think it was safe to stand on chairs. She had told him and his sister, Kelly, that she or Dad would get what he needed from the shelves.

After breakfast, Liam and Kelly climbed into the back seat of the car to go to school. They buckled their seatbelts so that they would be safe no matter what happened. Their mother started driving down the street. They didn't go far before they were stopped at the train crossing. Liam's mother was late for work, and there was no train in sight. But she stopped and waited. The very next minute a train whizzed by them.

When Liam got to school, he joined his friends. The bell rang, and everyone became quiet before walking into the building. When Liam got to his classroom, he took out his homework. While he waited for directions from his teacher, he thought about all the rules he and his family had followed that morning. He asked himself, "It's only 9:00 in the morning! How many more rules will I need to follow today?"

▶ *What are the rules or laws Liam and his family followed that morning?*

FAITH and MEDIA

▶ After the class has learned about the individual commandments and ways to follow them, consider helping the children make a Ten Commandments video. They can feature drawings of ways a second grader can follow each commandment.

CHAPTER PROJECT: GOD'S LAWS AND OUR DAILY LIFE

Write each commandment on a separate strip of paper. Put the strips on a chart or bulletin board, leaving space below each one. Encourage the children to add pictures, drawings, sentences, news-paper articles or anything else they come across that will help them to connect each of the commandments with daily life. Use the display as part of your review.

God Gives Us Laws ⑨

WE GATHER

✝**Leader:** Lord God, you give us life and love. Your laws help us to know how to love you and others. Show us how to follow you:

Reader 1: in our homes

Reader 2: in our parish

Reader 3: in our neighborhood

Reader 4: in our world.

All: "The earth, LORD, is filled with your love; teach me your laws."

(Psalm 119:64)

What are some rules that you follow every day?

PREPARING TO PRAY

In this gathering prayer the children will ask God for help in following his laws.

• Choose a prayer leader and four readers. Have these children prepare the prayer.

• Have all the children read the psalm response they will pray.

The Prayer Space

• In the prayer space display a poster on which you have placed pictures of people following laws or important safety rules.

• Place a Bible on the prayer table.

📖 **This Week's Liturgy**

Visit **www.webelieveweb.com** for this week's liturgical readings and other seasonal material.

Lesson Plan

WE GATHER _____ minutes

✝ Pray

• Invite the children to remain seated and to open their books to page 83. Have them look at the picture of the neighborhood and the people. Have them use a fingertip to trace an imaginary route beginning at the church in the upper left.

• Then have the children gather in the prayer space with their open books. Pray the Sign of the Cross together and have the leader begin.

• Have the readers pray their parts and have the entire class pray the psalm verse.

☀ Focus on Life

• Discuss the question. Help the children to realize that all people, including the principal of a school and the president of the United States, are asked to follow rules.

• Share the *Chapter Story* on guide page 83E.

Family Connection Update

Ask volunteers to share what their families have discovered in the local Catholic newspaper.

Catechist Goal

• To explain that the Great Commandment and the Ten Commandments help us to live as God's children

Our Faith Response

• To show love and respect to God and others

 commandments

Great Commandment

Ten Commandments

Lesson Materials

• copies of Reproducible Master 9

• Grade 2 CD

• Scripture and Family reproducible masters (back of book)

Teaching Tip

Teaching the Ten Commandments

   Please keep in mind that the purpose of this lesson is to give the children an overall view of the commandments. The children will study each commandment and the ways we follow it at the fourth-grade level of the *We Believe* program.

WE BELIEVE

Jesus taught us the Great Commandment.

God the Father loves us very much. He protects us by giving us laws to follow. God's laws are called **commandments**.

📖 Matthew 22:35–39

One day Jesus was teaching. Someone asked him which commandment is the greatest. Jesus answered, "You shall love the Lord, your God, with all your heart, with all your soul, and with all your mind." Then he said, "You shall love your neighbor as yourself." (Matthew 22:37, 39)

Jesus showed us how to love God, ourselves, and others. Jesus' teaching to love God and others is the **Great Commandment**. When we obey this commandment we follow all of God's commandments.

🧑 For each picture tell how Jesus is living the Great Commandment. How can you show your love like Jesus did?

84

Lesson Plan

WE BELIEVE _____ minutes

Write the word *commandments* on the board. Explain: *God's laws are called commandments.* Ask: *Why do you think God gave us laws?* Invite two or three volunteers to share their responses. Then have a volunteer read aloud the first paragraph on page 84.

Ask the children to close their eyes and imagine themselves listening to Jesus teach. Then read aloud the Scripture reading. When you have finished, ask the children to read quietly while you repeat Jesus' words. Have the children highlight or underline these words in their texts. Explain: *This teaching of Jesus is called the Great Commandment.*

Invite a volunteer to read the paragraph after the Scripture reading. Write on the board: *When we obey the Great Commandment, we love _____, _____, and _____.* Ask volunteers to tell the three words that complete the sentence (God, ourselves, others).

🧑 **Discuss** how Jesus is showing love in the pictures on page 84. Then discuss how the children can show their love like Jesus did.

The Ten Commandments help us to live as God's children.

Many years before Jesus was born, God gave his people special laws. These laws are called the **Ten Commandments**. They are written in the Old Testament in the Bible.

When Jesus was growing up, he learned these commandments. He obeyed these laws and taught his followers to obey them.

The commandments help us to live as God's children. The first three commandments help us to love God. The other seven commandments help us to love ourselves and others.

Key Words

commandments God's laws

Great Commandment Jesus' teaching to love God and others

Ten Commandments ten special laws God gave to his people

The Ten Commandments

1. I am the LORD your God: you shall not have strange gods before me.
2. You shall not take the name of the LORD your God in vain.
3. Remember to keep holy the LORD's Day.
4. Honor your father and your mother.
5. You shall not kill.
6. You shall not commit adultery.
7. You shall not steal.
8. You shall not bear false witness against your neighbor.
9. You shall not covet your neighbor's wife.
10. You shall not covet your neighbor's goods.

Use one color to underline each of the first three commandments. Use another color to underline the other seven commandments

85

ACTIVITY BANK

Multiple Intelligences
Musical

Teach the children the following verses to sing to the tune of "If You're Happy."

*Jesus taught the Great
  Commandment to help us love.
Jesus taught the Great
  Commandment to help us love,
To love God, ourselves, and others
As our sisters and our brothers.
Jesus taught the Great
  Commandment to help us love.*

*God gave us the Ten
  Commandments to help us love.
God gave us the Ten
  Commandments to help us love,
To love God, ourselves, and others
As our sisters and our brothers.
God gave us the Ten
  Commandments to help us love.*

Read the first two paragraphs on page 85. Stress: *Jesus and his followers obeyed God's commandments. The Ten Commandments are gifts from God.*

Ask a volunteer to read the third paragraph. Have the children highlight or underline the second and third sentences. Then ask the children to read quietly as you read aloud the Ten Commandments. Explain: *These laws help us to love and respect God and one another.* Stress: *We obey the Ten Commandments because we love God and want to do as he asks.* Encourage the children to see the commandments as ways to do good in our lives and to treat one another with respect.

Complete the activity.

Quick Check

✔ *What is the Great Commandment?* (The Great Commandment is Jesus' teaching to love God and others.)

✔ *What do the Ten Commandments help us to do?* (The Ten Commandments help us to live as God's children.)

✔ *Whom do we show love for when we follow the Ten Commandments?* (We show love for God, others, and ourselves.)

As Catholics...

Aspirations

After working on these two pages, read the *As Catholics* text. Encourage the children to make up their own aspirations to pray often. Ask volunteers to share their prayers with everyone.

God wants us to show him our love and respect.

Following the Ten Commandments helps us to live as children of God. We must show God our love by following the first three commandments. Here are some of the ways.

- We believe in one God and love him more than anything.
- We speak God's name only with love and respect.
- We worship God with our parish each week for Mass on Sunday or Saturday evening.

We can praise God in song.

🎵 We Celebrate with Joy

We celebrate with joy and gladness.
We celebrate God's love for us.
We celebrate with joy and gladness,
God with us today. God with us today.

God surrounding us.
God surprising us.
God in everything we do.
God surrounding us.
God surprising us.
God in all we do.

As Catholics...

God is always with us. We can talk to him anytime or anywhere. Our words to God are prayers. Sometimes we say short prayers. These prayers are called aspirations. Here are three examples.

- God, I love you.
- Jesus, be with me.
- Holy Spirit, help me.

You can make up your own aspirations. Pray them often.

86

Lesson Plan

WE BELIEVE (continued)

Remind the children: *The first three commandments help us to love God.* Then ask volunteers to read the three ways listed on page 86.

Find ways of love. Read the following list of activities aloud. Tell the children: *Stand if the activity is a way we show God love and respect. Stay in your seat if the activity is not a way we show respect.*

- Gather with our parish for Mass on Sunday. (stand)
- Do not pay attention at Mass.
- Say God's name lovingly. (stand)
- Thank God for the things he gives us. (stand)
- Race through our prayers.

Play "We Celebrate with Joy," #7 on the Grade 2 CD. Have the children practice singing. Help them to make up actions for the song. Then you may want to gather in the prayer space to sing the song.

God wants us to show that we love others as we love ourselves.

God wants us to treat one another as brothers and sisters. In the Fourth through the Tenth Commandments, we learn ways to love ourselves and others. Here are some of the ways.

- We obey our parents and all who care for us.
- We respect all human life.
- We respect our bodies and the bodies of others.
- We protect everyone, especially those who cannot protect themselves.
- We take care of what we own.
- We are fair when playing.
- We do not steal what other people own.
- We tell the truth and speak kindly of others.
- We show that we are thankful for our family and friends.
- We show that we are thankful for what we own.

WE RESPOND

Write two ways you can show love for yourself and others.

_____

_____

_____

ACTIVITY BANK

Community
Guest Speaker

Invite a law-enforcement official (police officer, park ranger, or government official) to speak to the class. Ask the speaker to stress that following laws helps many people to stay safe and healthy. After the presentation explain: *Obeying these laws is showing love for God, ourselves, and others.*

Faith and Media
Showing Love and Respect

Have the children work in small groups. Ask the members in each group to discuss characters in books, movies, or television programs and the ways those characters show or do not show love and respect for themselves and others.

Draw a large heart on the board or on chart paper. Remind the children that God wants us to love others as we love ourselves. Write *ourselves* in the center of the heart. Have volunteers tell ways that we show love and respect for ourselves (exercise, get enough sleep). Write all reasonable responses inside the heart.

Stress: *By following the Fourth through the Tenth Commandments, we are showing our love for God by loving and respecting ourselves and others.* Then have volunteers read the list of ways on page 87.

WE RESPOND _____ minutes

Connect to Life Provide time for the children to complete the *We Respond* activity.

Distribute copies of Reproducible Master 9. Have the children work in pairs to complete the puzzle. When all the pairs have finished, invite volunteers to share their answers. (Across: 1. Great; 4. Sunday; 5. worship; Down: 2. truth; 3. happy)

Pray aspirations as suggested in *As Catholics*. Then provide time for the children to pray quietly.

Catechist Goal

• To review the chapter ideas that are key to growing as disciples of Jesus Christ

Our Faith Response

• To decide on ways to grow as disciples by living out what we have learned

Show What you Know

Help the children to read the clues and find the correct *Key Words*. You may want the children to work in pairs. When all have completed the puzzle, go over the correct answers.

Reality Check

Read aloud the list of ways of living out the commandments. As the children are working, answer individual questions. Some may not consider checking *help team members*. Explain that they are all members of the Grade 2 Project Disciple team.

Picture This

Read aloud the directions. Talk about the photos. Read the three commandments. When all have completed the activity, go over the matches.

Make it Happen

Pray the psalm verse together. Encourage the children to share this prayer with their friends.

Take Home

Read the activity suggestions. Suggest some common family rules. Ask the children to complete the activity at home.

Discuss and send home copies of *Sharing Faith with My Family* reproducible master for this chapter (back of book).

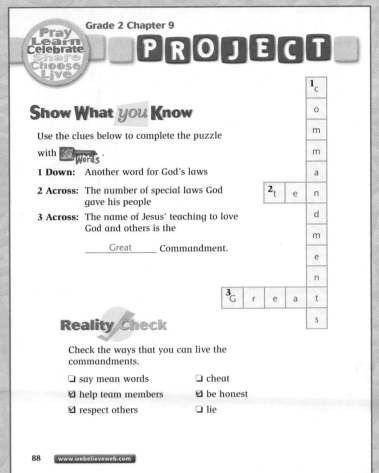

Grade 2 Chapter 9

PROJECT

Show What you Know

Use the clues below to complete the puzzle with Key Words.

1 Down: Another word for God's laws

2 Across: The number of special laws God gave his people

3 Across: The name of Jesus' teaching to love God and others is the

_____ Great _____ Commandment.

Crossword answers:
1 Down: c-o-m-m-a-n-d-m-e-n-t-s
2 Across: t-e-n
3 Across: G-r-e-a-t

Reality Check

Check the ways that you can live the commandments.

- ☐ say mean words
- ☑ help team members
- ☑ respect others
- ☐ cheat
- ☑ be honest
- ☐ lie

88   www.webelieveweb.com

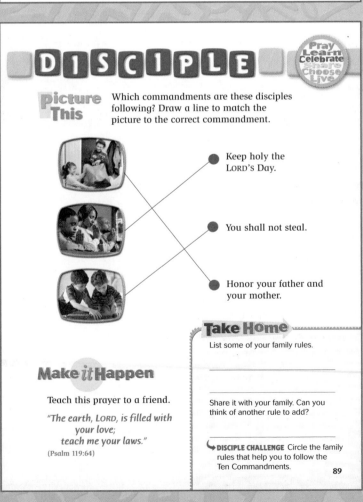

DISCIPLE

Picture This

Which commandments are these disciples following? Draw a line to match the picture to the correct commandment.

- Keep holy the LORD's Day.
- You shall not steal.
- Honor your father and your mother.

Make it Happen

Teach this prayer to a friend.

"The earth, LORD, is filled with your love;
teach me your laws."

(Psalm 119:64)

Take Home

List some of your family rules.

_____

_____

Share it with your family. Can you think of another rule to add?

_____

↳ **DISCIPLE CHALLENGE** Circle the family rules that help you to follow the Ten Commandments.

89

CHAPTER TEST

Circle the correct answer.

1. Is Jesus' teaching to love God and others the Great Commandment?　**(Yes)**　No

2. Should we always speak God's name with respect?　**(Yes)**　No

3. Are we following the commandments when we do not obey our parents?　Yes　**(No)**

4. Are we following the commandments when we steal what other people own?　Yes　**(No)**

5. Do we show our love for God when we follow the first three commandments?　**(Yes)**　No

Use the words in the box to complete the sentences.

6. In the Fourth through the Tenth Commandments, we learn to always love _____ourselves_____ and others.

all
respect
ourselves
children

7. When we obey the Great Commandment, we follow _____all_____ of God's commandments.

8. God wants us to show him our love and _____respect_____.

9. The commandments help us to live as God's _____children_____.

10. **Write one way you can follow God's commandments.**

Accept ways listed on page 86 or 87.

CHAPTER TEST

Provide ten to fifteen minutes for the students to complete the test. After all have finished, check the answers. Clarify any misconceptions.

Alternative Assessment

You may want the students to complete the following alternative-assessment activity.

Think of the Great Commandment. Write a story or draw a picture to show the ways you can love God and others.

Additional Testing

• Chapter 9 Test in *Assessment Book*, pages 17–18

• CD-ROM *Test Generator and Resource*: Use Chapter 9 Test or customize your own.

Review

Key Words

Review the definitions as they are presented in the chapter's *Key Word* boxes:

• commandments (page 85)

• Great Commandment (page 85)

• Ten Commandments (page 85).

We Believe Statements

Review the four statements.

• Jesus taught us the Great Commandment.

• The Ten Commandments help us to live as God's children.

• God wants us to show him our love and respect.

• God wants us to show that we love others as we love ourselves.

To use the Chapter 9 Study Guide, visit

www.webelieveweb.com

Overview

In Chapter 9 the children learned about the Ten Commandments. In this chapter the children will learn about following God's commandments. They will learn about God's mercy toward us when we fail to follow the commandments.

Doctrinal Content	For Adult Reading and Reflection *Catechism of the Catholic Church*
The children will learn:	Paragraph
• Jesus wants us to follow the commandments.	2074
• God gives each person free will.	1730
• Friendship with God is hurt by sin.	1850
• Jesus taught us about God's forgiveness.	981

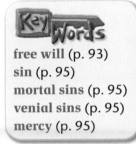

Key Words

free will (p. 93)
sin (p. 95)
mortal sins (p. 95)
venial sins (p. 95)
mercy (p. 95)

Go to **www.webelieveweb.com**, Catechist/ Teacher, We Believe Correlations for this chapter's correlation to:
• Six Tasks of Catechesis
• Catholic Social Teaching
• *Catechetical Formation in Chaste Living.*

Catechist Background

What prompts you to obey laws?

During the early years of our lives we obey rules because we are afraid of punishment. Eventually we grow old enough to see the value of rules and often obey them because they make good sense. However, rules that make common sense are still frequently ignored.

Obeying the Ten Commandments keeps us close to God and makes us happy. Our obedience to the commandments " . . . is the acknowledgement and homage given to God. . . . It is cooperation with the plan God pursues in history." (CCC 2062) Yet every day people use their free will to act in ways contrary to God's laws. They sin. If their sin is serious, people break their friendship with God, but serious or less serious, every sin damages our friendship with God and with one another.

Jesus told his followers a story to teach us how God treats those who sin. In the story of the

prodigal son (Luke 15:11–32), we encounter a selfish young man who turns his back on his father and squanders his inheritance. When he returns home in humility and sorrow, his father welcomes him as if he had never left home or done anything wrong. Instead of punishing his son, the father throws a big party to welcome him home.

Although God wants us to make loving choices and follow the commandments, each of us has free will to make our own decisions. We are responsible for the choices that we make and their consequences. If we make choices that lead to sin, God will show us love and forgive us if we are sorry.

How can you make choices that help you to live the commandments?

Lesson Planning Guide

Lesson Steps	Presentation	Materials

1 WE GATHER

page 91 **Prayer**	• Listen to God's Word. • Respond in prayer.	For the prayer space: large poster-board hearts, Bible
Focus on Life	• Talk about the choices we make every day.	

2 WE BELIEVE

page 92 *Jesus wants us to follow the commandments.*	• Read and discuss the text about following the commandments. • Complete the activity about choosing to love.	• pencils
page 93 *God gives each person free will.*	• Present the text about free will. • Reflect on the responses to the question.	• pencils or crayons • copies of Reproducible Master 10, guide page 91C
page 94 *Friendship with God is hurt by sin.*	• Read and discuss the text about the kinds of sins people commit. • Decorate the message on the poster. • Read and discuss *As Catholics*.	• colored pencils or crayons
page 95 *Jesus taught us about God's forgiveness.* *Luke 15:11–24*	• Present and discuss the text about God's forgiveness. • Read the Scripture story about God's mercy.	

3 WE RESPOND

page 95	• Reflect on the *We Respond* question. • Ask God for his mercy.	
pages 96–97 **Project Disciple**	• Complete the **Project Disciple** activities. • Explain the *Take Home* activity. • Discuss/send home **Sharing Faith with My Family** reproducible master for this chapter.	• pencils • copies of **Sharing Faith with My Family** reproducible master, Chapter 10 (back of book)
page 98 **Chapter 10 Test**	• Complete **Chapter 10 Test**. • Work on *Alternative Assessment* activity.	• optional: copies of Scripture reproducible master, *What's the Word?*, Chapter 10 (back of book)

For additional ideas, activities, and opportunities: Visit Sadlier's **www.WeBelieveweb.com**

Read the following stories.

Circle the loving choice that each child can make.

Marisela is watching her favorite TV program. Her parents are busy painting the kitchen. When her mom's phone starts to ring, Marisela can choose to

- answer the phone for her mom
- keep watching the TV and let her mom stop what she is doing to answer the phone.

Jaime is with his father in the store. He sees a racing game that he really wants. Jaime points out the game to his dad. Jaime's dad says, "We can't get the game today. I don't have enough money." Jaime can choose to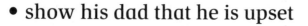

- show his dad that he is upset
- say, "I can wait, Dad. It's not that important."

Write a loving choice that John can make.

John's younger sister has just learned how to ride her new bike. When she shows him how well she can do, she falls.

John can choose to _____

_____

PROJECT DISCIPLE

Pray
Learn
Celebrate
Share
Choose
Live

Additional Activities

More *to* Explore

Read the *Take Home* paragraphs (page 97) about choosing friends. With the children brainstorm the qualities of good friends. List each response on the board. Then with the children go back over the friendship qualities listed and cross out any that most agree should not be on the list.

Picture This

Materials needed: drawing paper, crayons or colored pencils

Read the *Take Home* paragraphs about choosing friends (page 97). Have the students make a thank-you card for one of their good friends. Help the children with spelling. Encourage the children to give their cards to their friends.

Show What *you* Know

On the board draw vertical lines to make five columns. At the top of each column write one of the chapter's *Key Words*. Then ask five children to come forward and each of these children to stand at the board under one of the *Key Words*. Explain that as you read the meaning of one of the words, the child standing below that word should raise his or her hand. Continue until all the children have had the opportunity to go to the board.

What's *the* Word?

Scripture reproducible master, Chapter 10

Materials needed: copies of *What's the Word?* (back of book)

Reread the story of the forgiving father on text page 95. Then distribute copies of the Scripture reproducible master. Read the questions and provide time for the children to write their responses. Then ask volunteers to share their responses.

Meeting Individual Needs
Children Who Are Tactile Learners

Look for ways to integrate hands-on activities into your instruction. For example, when discussing moral dilemmas people face, provide children with puppets that they can use to dramatize the story.

We Believe Resources

• Grade 2 *Review & Resource Book*, pages 25–27
• Grade 2 *Family Book*, pages 30–32
• Grade 2 *Assessment Book*, pages 19–20
• Grade 2 CD-ROM *Test Generator and Resource*: Use Chapter 10 Test or customize your own.
• **www.webelieveweb.com**

Chapter Story

Hello listeners! My name is Callie. Our teacher told us that we make many kinds of choices every day. Let me tell you about last Saturday and some of the choices I made. I was watching my Saturday morning shows when Mom said she had to go to the library. I didn't want to go. I thought about making a fuss, but I didn't want to upset Mom. So I put on my jacket and met her outside.

When we were going into the library, Mom said that I could take out two books. I had a hard time choosing which ones I wanted. I finally picked one about the ocean and one about a girl my age.

On the way home we stopped at Aunt Anita's house. She was fixing lunch for my five-year-old cousin Will. Aunt Anita asked me if I was hungry. She asked me, "Do you want a grilled cheese or peanut butter sandwich?" I chose grilled cheese.

After lunch Mom and I went pumpkin picking with Aunt Anita and Will. I couldn't believe all the different sizes of pumpkins they had. I chose the biggest one I could find.

When Will saw my pumpkin, he wanted it. I thought about arguing and saying, "No, I saw it first." But I let Will have the giant pumpkin and I went to pick another one. Mom told me she was proud of me. She let me choose a special treat at the farm's bakery. I chose pumpkin cookies. We even bought a few extra that I can share with Will.

▶ *What choices did Callie make last Saturday?*

FAITH and MEDIA

▶ Invite the children to work in small groups. Explain that they will select pictures from magazines or newspapers to create a circle-shaped poster that shows people who are friends. On the back of the poster, have them write how following the commandments helps us to be friends. Connect the "Friendship Circles" by displaying them around the room.

▶ Consider videotaping the children if they act out the story of the forgiving father.

CHAPTER PROJECT: MAKING CHOICES

Begin this project after page 93. Have the children work in groups. Invite each group to think of choices children their age sometimes make. For example, some friends must choose between including a younger child in their game. Have the group decide on one choice to dramatize. Ask the groups to also dramatize the positive or negative things that may happen because of the choice made. Provide time for practice. Have the groups share their dramatizations.

We Follow God's Laws ⑩

WE GATHER

✝ **Leader:** Let us celebrate the gift of God's laws. God gives us laws because he loves us and wants us to be happy. Listen to these words Jesus said to his disciples.

Reader: "As the Father loves me, so I also love you. Remain in my love. If you keep my commandments, you will remain in my love, just as I have kept my Father's commandments and remain in his love."
(John 15:9–10)

All: Jesus, thank you for loving us. May our love for you and others grow stronger everyday.

☀ There are choices that you make each day. Talk about one choice that you made today.

91

PREPARING TO PRAY

In this gathering prayer the children will listen and respond to a Scripture reading.

• Choose a prayer leader and a reader. Allow them time to prepare for the prayer.

• Option: Have the children practice the song "Come Follow Me," #3, Grade 2 CD.

The Prayer Space

• Cut out four or five large hearts from poster board. Use the hearts to make a path on the floor in or leading up to the prayer space.

• On the prayer table place a statue or picture of Jesus. Have the Bible opened to the story of the forgiving father (Luke 15:11–24).

📖 **This Week's Liturgy**
Visit **www.webelieveweb.com** for this week's liturgical readings and other seasonal material.

Lesson Plan

WE GATHER ⎯⎯ minutes

✝ Pray

• Ask the children to open their books to page 91. Point out the heart stepping stones in the illustration. If you have made a path of hearts, invite the children to walk on the path as they gather in the prayer space. Option: Have the children sing "Come Follow Me" as they walk.

• Then pray the Sign of the Cross together. Ask the prayer leader to begin. Provide a minute of silence after the Scripture reading. Then pray the response together aloud.

☀ Focus on Life

• Help start the discussion about choices by sharing one you have made today. Then invite volunteers to tell about some of their choices.

• Share the *Chapter Story* on guide page 91E. Point out the kind of choices the main character made. Discuss why some choices are more difficult than others.

Family Connection Update

Ask volunteers to share the family rules discussed for the *Take Home* activity.

Catechist Goal

- To examine the ways that Jesus wants us to follow the commandments and what Jesus taught us about God's forgiveness

Our Faith Response

- To thank God for his great mercy

 **free will**   **sin**

mortal sins   **venial sins**

mercy

Lesson Materials

- colored pencils or crayons
- copies of Reproducible Master 10
- Scripture and Family reproducible masters (back of book)

Teaching Tip

Reproducible Master Activities

Read through the entire chapter to gauge the time you need to present the text. Then read the activity on the reproducible master. Decide whether you want the children to complete the activity during the session. Always try to check the children's work. For some of the activities you will find the answers included within the lesson plan.

WE BELIEVE

Jesus wants us to follow the commandments.

Jesus made choices all during his life on earth. He chose to love everyone. Jesus chose to help people even when he felt tired. He chose to spend time with people, both the poor and the rich. Jesus made these choices even when others did not agree with him.

Jesus wants us to follow his example of caring for everyone. He wants us to follow the commandments. Jesus knows that it is not always easy for us to choose to love God and others. That is why he sent the Holy Spirit to help us.

✗ Circle all the words that complete the sentence.

We choose to love God and others when we are _____.

(fair)   selfish   (kind)   (helpful)

92

Lesson Plan

WE BELIEVE _____ minutes

Direct the children's attention to the illustration of Jesus. Point out that Jesus is choosing to talk to a family in need. Ask: *At what other times did Jesus choose to talk to or help other people?* Have a few volunteers share their responses. Suggest: *Jesus was tired, but he chose to bless the children who came to see him. Many people did not like Zacchaeus, but Jesus chose to stop and talk to Zacchaeus.*

Choose two volunteers to read the two paragraphs on page 92. Emphasize: *Jesus sent the Holy Spirit to help us to make choices.*

✗ **Read** the directions and have the children complete the activity. Invite volunteers to share responses. Ask: *What other words would complete the sentence?* List the children's responses on chart paper.

Explain to the children that God loves us very much. Then ask children to read silently as you read aloud the first paragraph on page 93. Emphasize the definition of *free will.* Invite the children to use the term in a sentence. Ask volunteers to state whether or not the term was used correctly.

free will God's gift to us that allows us to make choices

God gives each person free will.

God never forces us to love and obey him. God lets us choose to love him and others. He lets us choose between following the commandments and not following them. God's gift to us that allows us to make choices is **free will.**

When we freely choose to do something, we are responsible for what we do. We are responsible for what happens because of our choices.

You can make good choices when you take time to think before you act. You can ask yourself these two questions:

• If I do this, will I show love for God, myself, and others?

• What would Jesus want me to do?

How can you know what Jesus would want you to do?

93

ACTIVITY BANK

Scripture
Sharing Stories

Read a Scripture story about Jesus choosing to help people. After you read the story, ask: *What choice did Jesus make?* Choose one of the following accounts.

• Cleansing of a Leper (Matthew 8:1–3)

• Healing of Two Blind Men (Matthew 20:29–34)

Curriculum Connection
Art

Activity Materials: drawing paper, crayons or markers

Demonstrate for the children how to divide their papers into four or five separate panels for a story board. Ask the children to think about a situation where two choices are given and only one can be made. Have the children prepare story boards to illustrate the situation.

Read the last two paragraphs on page 93. Tell the children that when they are faced with making a difficult decision, they can always ask themselves the two questions at the end of this section.

Distribute copies of Reproducible Master 10. If time permits at this point, have the children work on the activity. You may also want to assign the activity as work for home.

Ask the question. Invite volunteers to share their responses. Explain: *We can know what Jesus wants us to do by following his example and obeying the commandments.*

Quick Check

✔ *What are some loving choices that Jesus made?* (Jesus chose to love everyone, to help people, to forgive others.)

✔ *Whom did Jesus send to help us love God and others?* (Jesus sent the Holy Spirit.)

✔ *Which gift from God allows us to choose how we will act?* (The gift from God is free will.)

Saint Philip Neri

After working on these two pages, read the *As Catholics* paragraph. Have the children highlight or under-line the fourth and fifth sentences. Ask the children to share with their families what Saint Philip told people about God's forgiveness.

Friendship with God is hurt by sin.

Commit is another word for "do." **Sin** is any thought, word, or act that we freely choose to commit even though we know that it is wrong. We cannot commit sin by accident.

Some sins are very serious. These sins are **mortal sins**. People who commit these sins break their friendship with God. They do not share in God's grace, his life in them.

Venial sins are less serious than mortal sins. People who commit these sins hurt their friendship with God. But they still share in God's grace.

When we commit sin we hurt ourselves and others, too. But it is important to always remember the message on the poster.

Color the words on the poster.

God never stops loving us.
God will

always forgive

us when we are sorry.

As Catholics...

A person who chose to follow God's laws was Saint Philip Neri. Philip was a priest in Rome. He helped the sick and the poor. Philip told many people that Jesus loved and cared for them. He helped people understand that God would always forgive them.

94

Lesson Plan

WE BELIEVE (continued)

Write the word *sin* on the board. Explain: *Sometimes people choose not to show their love for God, themselves, or others. They choose not to follow the commandments. They choose to sin.*

Ask the children to read quietly as you read aloud the first *We Believe* paragraph on page 94. Explain: *God does not want us to judge other people's choices. Each person knows what is in her or his heart when they make choices.*

Read the second and third paragraphs on page 94. Present as simply as possible, the definitions of mortal sins and venial sins. Do not discuss these two kinds of sins in detail.

Read aloud the last paragraph on page 94 and the directions for the activity. Have the children color this important message on the poster: *God never stops loving us. God will always forgive us when we are sorry.*

Invite a volunteer to read aloud the *We Believe* state-ment on page 95. Write the word *mercy* on the board. Ask a volunteer to read aloud the first paragraph on this page. Stress: *Mercy is another word for God's love and forgiveness.*

Ask volunteers to read the Scripture story. Have the children tell how the father showed mercy to his son.

Jesus taught us about God's forgiveness.

Jesus told stories to teach about God's love and forgiveness. He taught that God always loves us and is ready to forgive us. Another word for God's love and forgiveness is **mercy**.

Here is a story about God's mercy.

 Luke 15:11–24

There was a loving father who had two sons. One day the younger son asked his father for his share of the family's money. The son took his money and left home. The young man spent his money on new friends. Soon all his money was gone. The young man began to think about the choices he had made. He remembered his father's love.

The young man was on the road home when his father saw him. The father ran to welcome him back. The young man told his father he was sorry. The father forgave his son and prepared to celebrate his son's return. "Then the celebration began." (Luke 15:24)

The father in this story showed mercy to his son. God the Father shows each of us his mercy. He will always forgive us when we are sorry.

WE RESPOND

How do you feel knowing that God is always ready to forgive you?

Pray together, "Have mercy on me, LORD." (Psalm 10:14)

Key Words

sin a thought, word, or act that we freely choose to commit even though we know that it is wrong

mortal sins sins that break our friendship with God

venial sins sins that hurt our friendship with God

mercy God's love and forgiveness

95

ACTIVITY BANK

Curriculum Connection
Language Arts
Activity Materials: poster board, yardsticks, paint (for scenery), costumes, props

Invite the children to act out the Scripture story of the forgiving father.

Make arrangements for the children to perform the play for other groups (other classes, parents' group, senior citizen's club).

Make scenery for the play. Have the children think about what props and scenery they could use for the play. Much of this can be built from poster board, yardsticks, and paint.

Discuss the choices the father and son made. Stress: *The son chose to tell his father that he was sorry. The father chose to forgive his son.* Ask: *How do you think the son felt when he was forgiven?*

WE RESPOND _____ minutes

Connect to Life Read aloud the *We Respond* question. Remind the children: *God will always forgive us when we are sorry for our sins.*

Pray Invite the children to gather in the prayer space. Together pray the psalm verse at the bottom of page 95.

Catechist Goal

- To review the chapter ideas that are key to growing as disciples of Jesus Christ

Our Faith Response

- To decide on ways to grow as disciples by living out what we have learned

Show What *you* Know

Invite the children to finish the prayer.

What Would *you* do?

Introduce the activity by discussing the possible consequences of choosing to push in line: someone might get hurt; everyone would be angry. Also discuss the consequences of waiting: less chance of someone getting hurt; people would be friendly; you might enjoy your turn more.

Make *it* Happen

When the children's charts are completed, ask volunteers to share their responses. Suggest to the children that they look at their charts at the end of each day this week. Explain that if they have made any of the choices on the charts during the day, they should circle it on the chart.

Take Home

Read aloud the *Take Home* paragraph. Discuss the suggested questions. Encourage the children to survey their family members about the qualities of good friends.

Discuss and send home copies of *Sharing Faith with My Family* reproducible master for this chapter (back of book).

Grade 2 Chapter 10

PROJECT

Show What *you* Know

Finish the prayer using Key Words from the box.

| mortal sins |
| venial sins |

God, thank you for giving me the gift of free will. With it, I will make responsible choices. I will try not to sin.

I never want to commit _____mortal sins_____ which break my friendship with you.

I never want to commit _____venial sins_____ which hurt my friendship with you.

Thank you for your mercy. Amen.

"I can push to the front of the line."

"I can wait until it's *my* turn."

What Would *you* do?

Ryan wants to go down the slide, but there is a long line of children in front of him. Circle the choice you think Ryan should make.

96   www.webelieveweb.com

DISCIPLE

Make *it* Happen

In the chart below, write choices you can make this week to show love for God, yourself, and others.

Possible responses:

At home, I can choose to	obey and help parents; do chores; help siblings; care for things
At school, I can choose to	respect classmates; listen to teachers; learn
In my neighborhood, I can choose to	play fair; help neighbors; help keep neighborhood clean
In my parish, I can choose to	go to Mass; pray; take part in parish activities

Take Home

One important decision we make in life is choosing our friends. Good friends want the best for one another. When you choose a person to be your friend, you may want to think about these questions.

- How do I act when I am with this person?
- What kind of choices do I make when I am with this person?
- Does this person want the best for me?

Survey your family members. Ask them what they look for in a friend. Together, add another question to think about when choosing friends.

_____

Now, pass it on!

97

CHAPTER TEST

Write *always* or *never* to complete the sentences.

1. God _____never_____ forces us to love and obey him.

2. God _____never_____ stops loving us.

3. God _____always_____ forgives us if we are sorry.

Draw a line to match the sentence parts.

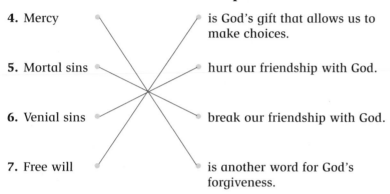

4. Mercy   is God's gift that allows us to make choices.

5. Mortal sins   hurt our friendship with God.

6. Venial sins   break our friendship with God.

7. Free will   is another word for God's forgiveness.

Circle the correct answer.

8. Can we commit sin by accident?   Yes   **(No)**

9. Does Jesus want us to follow the commandments?   **(Yes)**   No

10. **Write one thing we can learn in Jesus' story about the forgiving father.**

Possible responses: God the Father shows us his mercy. God will always forgive us when we are sorry.

Chapter 10 • Page 98

CHAPTER TEST

Provide ten to fifteen minutes for the students to complete the test. After all have finished, check the answers. Clarify any misconceptions.

Alternative Assessment

You may want the students to complete the following alternative-assessment activity.

Jesus told a story about a father who showed mercy to his son. Use your own words to tell this story. Draw a picture for each part of the story.

Additional Testing

• Chapter 10 Test in *Assessment Book*, pages 19–20

• CD-ROM *Test Generator and Resource*: Use Chapter 10 Test or customize your own.

Review

Key Words

Review the definitions as they are presented in the chapter's *Key Word* boxes:

• free will (page 93)

• sin (page 95)

• mortal sins (page 95)

• venial sins (page 95)

• mercy (page 95).

We Believe Statements

Review the four statements.

• Jesus wants us to follow the commandments.

• God gives each person free will.

• Friendship with God is hurt by sin.

• Jesus taught us about God's forgiveness.

To use the Chapter 10 Study Guide, visit

www.webelieveweb.com

We Prepare for the Sacrament of Forgiveness

Overview

In Chapter 10 the children learned about free will, sin, and God's loving forgiveness. In this chapter the children will learn about the Sacrament of Penance and Reconciliation.

Doctrinal Content	For Adult Reading and Reflection *Catechism of the Catholic Church*
The children will learn:	Paragraph
• Jesus invites us to celebrate God's forgiveness.	1441
• Jesus shares God's forgiveness and peace in the Sacrament of Penance and Reconciliation.	1446
• We examine our conscience.	1454
• We tell God we are sorry for our sins.	1451

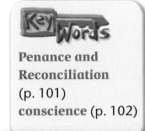

Penance and Reconciliation (p. 101)
conscience (p. 102)

Catechist Background

When can relationships cause stress in your life?

Human relationships go through periods of turmoil. Evidence of this can be found in any large card shop where you will find a variety of titles aimed at healing broken friendships. Our friendship with God and with one another experiences turmoil every time we sin. This is why we are blessed to have the Sacrament of Penance. This sacrament restores peace and harmony to our relationships.

Remote preparation for the sacrament begins with knowing God is a loving and merciful God. We reflect on Jesus, who is the healer of both body and soul and who reaches out in love to all.

In preparing for Penance we look carefully at our lives and our relationships. We seek the help of the Holy Spirit in examining our lives. The "same

Go to **www.webelieveweb.com**, Catechist/Teacher, We Believe Correlations for this chapter's correlation to:
• Six Tasks of Catechesis
• Catholic Social Teaching
• *Catechetical Formation in Chaste Living.*

Spirit who brings sin to light is also the consoler who gives the human heart grace for repentance and conversion" (CCC 1433). We confess our sins, express our sorrow, receive absolution, and do a penance.

As you prepare the children, keep in mind that the Sacrament of Penance and Reconciliation is a generous gift from a merciful and loving God who wants us to grow in love. The sacrament is a celebration of God's healing love and forgiveness.

How can the Sacrament of Penance help you grow in love?

Lesson Planning Guide

Lesson Steps	Presentation	Materials

 ① WE GATHER

Lesson Steps	Presentation	Materials
page 99 ✝ Prayer **Focus on Life**	• Pray to Jesus, the Good Shepherd. • Discuss the questions about forgiveness.	For the prayer space: containers of potting soil or sand, a picture of Jesus, the Good Shepherd • copies of Reproducible Master 11, guide page 99C • straws or craft sticks

② WE BELIEVE

Lesson Steps	Presentation	Materials
page 100 *Jesus invites us to celebrate God's forgiveness.* 📖 *Luke 15:4–6*	• Read the Scripture story and present the text about celebrating God's forgiveness. 🏃 Discuss the question about God's love.	
page 101 *Jesus shares God's forgiveness and peace in the Sacrament of Penance and Reconciliation.*	• Read and discuss the text. • Present the *Key Word* and definition. 🏃 Follow the directions and find the missing word to complete the sentence.	• crayon or highlighter
page 102 *We examine our conscience.*	• Explain the text about examining our conscience. • Reflect on questions to begin an examination of conscience. 🏃 Help children examine choices by doing an activity. • Read and discuss *As Catholics*.	• crayons or colored pencils
page 103 *We tell God we are sorry for our sins.*	• Read and discuss the text about sorrow for sin. • Present the Act of Contrition.	

③ WE RESPOND

Lesson Steps	Presentation	Materials
page 103	• Discuss the *We Respond* question. • Pray the Act of Contrition.	
pages 104–105 **Project Disciple**	• Complete the Project Disciple activities. • Explain the *Take Home* activity. • Discuss/send home Sharing Faith with My Family reproducible master for this chapter.	• crayons or colored pencils • copies of Sharing Faith with My Family reproducible master, Chapter 11 (back of book)
page 106 **Chapter 11 Test**	• Complete Chapter 11 Test. • Work on *Alternative Assessment* activity.	• optional: copies of Scripture reproducible master, *What's the Word?*, Chapter 11 (back of book)

For additional ideas, activities, and opportunities: Visit Sadlier's www.WeBelieveweb.com

Name _____

- Cut out the sheep.
- Glue cotton balls to the sheep.
- Write your name on the back of the sheep.
- Tape the sheep to a straw or stick.

PROJECT DISCIPLE

Pray
Learn
Celebrate
Share
Choose
Live

Additional Activities

What's *the* Word?

Scripture reproducible master, Chapter 11

Materials needed: copies of *What's the Word?* (back of book)

Distribute copies of the Scripture reproducible master. Read the script. Then invite the children to write the words of the shepherd on the lines provided. Ask volunteers to read the part of the script that they have written. Then read the script a few times, each time having different children take the parts of the readers and shepherd.

Make *it* Happen

In this chapter the children read the story of the shepherd and the lost sheep. Discuss together what you can do as a class for the protection and safe treatment of animals. You may want to contact a local animal shelter or organization dedicated to the protection of animals to see what their needs are. Decide together on a specific project. Ask the children to invite their families to participate in the project.

Show What *you* Know

On the board draw a word wheel or web. In the center section print *Sacrament of Penance*. Then in shapes surrounding the center section, have volunteers write words or terms associated with the sacrament. Possible responses: Reconciliation, conscience, examination of conscience, forgiveness, contrition, Act of Contrition, mercy, celebration.

Pray Today

Read the following prompts to help the children make a mini-meditation. Before you begin, ask the students to be still and quiet as they silently respond to each prompt.

- *Jesus is sitting by you. He is talking to you about God the Father. What is he telling you?*

- *What are you telling Jesus?*

- *How can you thank Jesus for his love and forgiveness?*

Meeting Individual Needs
Children with Attention-Deficit Disorder

Help the children with Attention-Deficit Disorder by breaking instruction into small segments. Ask these children to summarize paragraphs you have just read. Also have the children highlight or underline specific statements that are the important points of the chapter.

We Believe Resources

- Grade 2 *Review & Resource Book*, pages 28–30
- Grade 2 *Family Book*, pages 33–35
- Grade 2 *Assessment Book*, pages 21–22
- Grade 2 CD-ROM *Test Generator and Resource*: Use Chapter 11 Test or customize your own.
- www.webelieveweb.com

Enrichment Ideas

Chapter Story

After dinner last night Tony's mother could tell that Tony was upset about something. She asked, "What's wrong, Tony?"

"Well, Cameron doesn't like it when we tease him and call him 'Camera.' Some of the older players on the soccer team were calling him that. I joined in laughing at him and saying, 'Take my picture, Camera.' Cameron really got upset. He wouldn't walk home with me; he said he didn't want to talk to me."

Tony's mother looked at him and asked, "You do know why your friend is upset, don't you?"

Tony nodded and said, "I wanted the older boys to like me, but I hurt my friend's feelings instead. He'll never be my friend again."

"You can't know that until you talk to him," said Tony's mother.

"But I don't know what to say," Tony objected.

"Tony," said his mother. "If Cameron hurt your feelings, what would you want him to say to you? You two have been friends for a long time. I think you can find the right words. If you are truly sorry, you will know what to say."

Tony smiled. "You're right, Mom. He's my best friend. I shouldn't be afraid to tell him how sorry I am. May I call him and talk to him right now?"

Tony's mom nodded her head. Tony raced to the phone and started dialing. He told his friend, "I'm so sorry, Cameron. I promise never to tease you about your name again."

▶ *Did you ever have an experience like this? Tell about it.*

FAITH and MEDIA

▶ With the help of a librarian, select appropriate books with the theme of forgiveness. Encourage the children to read one of these stories and present an oral report.

▶ You might videotape the children as they act out the story of the lost sheep. Have one child play the shepherd, and use a plush lamb for the lost sheep. Assign a small group of children to act the parts of the shepherd's friends and have another, larger group play the ninety-nine sheep that do not stray.

CHAPTER PROJECT: LESSON BANNERS

Hang four sheets of chart paper in the room. Print one of the chapter's *We Believe* statements at the top of each sheet. Invite the children to make a collage by writing, drawing, or pasting pictures on the paper that relate to the statement. Keep each collage in place as you work through the chapter. Ask the children to add to any of the collages as they think of new ideas.

WE GATHER

✛**Leader:** Jesus is our Good Shepherd.

All: Jesus, we are the sheep of your flock.

Leader: Jesus, may we never wander far from you.

All: Jesus, Good Shepherd, hear us.

Leader: Jesus, when we have not followed your ways,

All: Forgive us and lead us back to your loving ways.

Why do you think friends and family forgive each other? How do they show their forgiveness?

99

PREPARING TO PRAY

For this gathering prayer, the children will pray to Jesus, our Good Shepherd.

• Choose a prayer leader. Give him or her time to prepare.

• Distribute Reproducible Master 11. Provide scissors for the children to cut out their sheep. Give each child a drinking straw or craft stick. Help the children tape their sheep to the straw or stick.

The Prayer Space

• In the prayer space place a few containers filled with sand or potting soil. Each child will place his or her sheep in a container.

• Set on the prayer table a picture of Jesus, the Good Shepherd.

📖 This Week's Liturgy
Visit **www.webelieveweb.com** for this week's liturgical readings and other seasonal material.

Lesson Plan

WE GATHER _____ minutes

✛ Pray

• Invite the children to open their books to page 99. Remind the children of a shepherd's role. Explain: *A shepherd cares for and guides a flock of sheep, just as Jesus guides and cares for us.* Then have the leader begin the prayer.

• Ask the children to hold the sheep they have made as they pray. At the conclusion of the prayer, invite the children to put the sheep in the containers of soil or sand.

🌟 Focus on Life

• Discuss the first *We Gather* question. Help the children conclude that forgiveness is an important part of a loving relationship.

• Discuss how people show forgiveness. (Possible responses: shake hands, hug, do something together) Share with the children the *Chapter Story* on guide page 99E.

Family Connection Update
Invite children to share their family discussions about friendships.

Catechist Goal

• To show that Jesus invites us to celebrate God's forgiveness in the Sacrament of Penance and Reconciliation

Our Faith Response

• To identify ways to show God that we are truly sorry

 Penance and Reconciliation

conscience

Lesson Materials

• drawing paper, crayons

• Scripture and Family reproducible masters (back of book)

Teaching Note

The Name of the Sacrament

The full title for the sacrament the children are learning is the Sacrament of Penance and Reconciliation. This title is presented in this chapter. However, in all future references in this program the sacrament will be called the Sacrament of Penance.

WE BELIEVE

Jesus invites us to celebrate God's forgiveness.

Jesus told people this story about God's love and forgiveness.

📖 Luke 15:4–6

There was a shepherd who took care of one hundred sheep. One day one of the sheep wandered away. The shepherd left the other sheep. He searched for the lost one until he found it. He carried it home. Then he called together his friends. He said, "Rejoice with me because I have found my lost sheep." (Luke 15:6)

Sin separates us from God and one another. When we sin, we are like the lost sheep. But Jesus has given us a way to come back together again. The word *reconciliation* comes from a word that means "coming back together again."

Jesus has given us a way to receive God's forgiveness. The Church celebrates this forgiveness in the Sacrament of Penance and Reconciliation.

🧒 What does Jesus' story of the lost sheep help you to know about God's love?

100

Lesson Plan

WE BELIEVE _____ minutes

Read together the *We Believe* statement on page 100. Then ask a volunteer to read the first paragraph. Invite the children to look at the picture of the shepherd and the sheep as you read aloud the Scripture story.

Ask the following questions:

• *Why did the shepherd leave the ninety-nine sheep to look for one?* (The shepherd wanted all the sheep to be safe.)

• *What did the shepherd do when he found the lost sheep?* (He carried it home and celebrated with his friends.)

Write the word *Reconciliation* on the board. Explain that this word means "coming back together again." Ask volunteers to read the last two paragraphs. Explain: *When we sin we are like the lost sheep, and Jesus is like the shepherd. He gives us a way to come back together again.*

🧒 **Ask** the children to think about the story of the lost sheep. Then invite the children to share their answers to the question.

Invite a child to read aloud the *We Believe* statement on page 101. Ask volunteers to read the first two paragraphs.

Jesus shares God's forgiveness and peace in the Sacrament of Penance and Reconciliation.

When we sin, we are not at peace with God, ourselves, or others. In the Gospels we read some stories about people who were not at peace with God. Jesus forgave their sins. Jesus shared God's mercy and peace with them.

Jesus gives us a way to find peace, too. He shares God's forgiveness with us. In the Sacrament of **Penance and Reconciliation** we receive and celebrate God's forgiveness of our sins. We also call this sacrament the Sacrament of Penance.

Jesus gave his Apostles the power to forgive sin in his name. Today in the Sacrament of Penance, bishops and priests forgive sins in Jesus' name. They received this power to forgive sins in the Sacrament of Holy Orders.

Key Word

Penance and Reconciliation the sacrament in which we receive and celebrate God's forgiveness of our sins

🧍 Circle every third letter to find the missing word. Write the word in the sentence.

n o (p) c d (e) y z (a) b d (c) f g (e)

The Sacrament of Penance brings us God's

_____peace_____.

101

ACTIVITY BANK

Multiple Intelligences
Bodily-Kinesthetic

Invite the children to act out the story of the lost sheep. Have all participate in the shepherd's celebration.

A Church Visit
Reconciliation Room

Show the children the Reconciliation Room in your parish church. After seeing the room, pray together the following words: *Jesus, our Good Shepherd, thank you for sharing God's forgiveness and peace with us.*

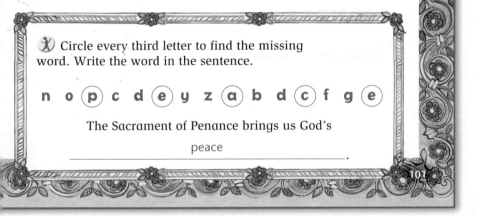

Explain: *Jesus forgave many people their sins. He shared God's forgiveness and peace with them.* Stress: *Jesus continues to share God's forgiveness and peace with us through the Sacrament of Penance and Reconciliation.* Point out that this sacrament will be referred to as the Sacrament of Penance.

Read aloud the last paragraph. Have the children highlight or underline the second sentence in this paragraph.

🧍 **Follow** the directions to find the word that completes the sentence.

Quick Check

✔ *What separates us from God and each other?* (Sin separates us.)

✔ *What is the Sacrament of Penance and Reconciliation?* (It is the sacrament in which we receive and celebrate God's forgiveness of our sins.)

✔ *How did Jesus help people who were not at peace with God and themselves?* (Jesus helped people by forgiving their sins and by sharing God's mercy and peace with them.)

As Catholics...

Daily Examination of Conscience

After working on these two pages, read the *As Catholics* text. Encourage the children to ask the Holy Spirit to help them continue to make good choices.

We examine our conscience.

God has given each person a **conscience**. This gift helps a person to know what is right and what is wrong.

We can prepare to celebrate the Sacrament of Penance by examining our conscience. This means we think about our thoughts, words, and actions.

The Holy Spirit helps us to remember the choices we have made. We think about the ways we have or have not followed the Ten Commandments. We ask ourselves questions like these.

- Did I speak God's name with respect and pray to him?
- Did I care for myself and the gifts God has given to me?
- Did I obey my parents and all those who care for me?

Think about other questions you can ask yourself to examine your conscience. Write one of them here.

_____

_____

Key Word

conscience
God's gift that helps us to know right from wrong

102

Lesson Plan

WE BELIEVE (continued)

Read aloud the *We Believe* statement on page 102. Explain that the word *examine* means "to look closely or carefully at."

Read aloud the first paragraph on page 102. Print the word *conscience* on the board. Have the children practice pronouncing the word. Explain: *When we think about the choices we make, we need to consider whether that choice follows the Ten Commandments.*

Continue reading the text on page 102. Explain: *A good way to examine our conscience is to ask ourselves questions about the ways we have shown love and respect for God, ourselves, and others.* Then read the questions listed on the page. As you read the questions, pause briefly for quiet reflection.

Invite the children to write their own questions. Ask volunteers to share their questions with the group.

Remind the children that when we sin, we turn away from God. Print the word *contrition* on the board. Explain that *contrition* means "being sorry."

102

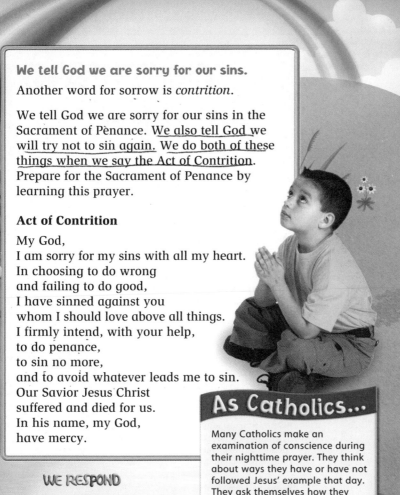

We tell God we are sorry for our sins.

Another word for sorrow is *contrition*.

We tell God we are sorry for our sins in the Sacrament of Penance. We also tell God we will try not to sin again. We do both of these things when we say the Act of Contrition. Prepare for the Sacrament of Penance by learning this prayer.

Act of Contrition

My God,
I am sorry for my sins with all my heart.
In choosing to do wrong
and failing to do good,
I have sinned against you
whom I should love above all things.
I firmly intend, with your help,
to do penance,
to sin no more,
and to avoid whatever leads me to sin.
Our Savior Jesus Christ
suffered and died for us.
In his name, my God,
have mercy.

As Catholics...

Many Catholics make an examination of conscience during their nighttime prayer. They think about ways they have or have not followed Jesus' example that day. They ask themselves how they have respected God, themselves, and others. They then ask the Holy Spirit to help them make better choices.

Ask the Holy Spirit to help you to make good choices, too.

WE RESPOND

How can you show God you are truly sorry?

Pray together the Act of Contrition on this page.

103

ACTIVITY BANK

Multiple Intelligences

Intrapersonal and Interpersonal
Activity Materials: index cards

Distribute an index card to each child. Tell the children to write *yes* on one side of the card and *no* on the other side. Explain that you will describe some choices people can make. Tell the children that if they think the choice made is one that follows the Ten Commandments, they should hold up the "yes" side of the card. If they feel the choice made is one that does not follow the commandments, they should hold up the "no" side of the card.

- *You found $5.00 on the playground and turned it in to the principal.* (yes)

- *You laughed when other teammates made fun of someone.* (no)

- *You broke a window and blamed it on your brother.* (no)

- *You helped a friend clean her room so that you could go to the park and play.* (yes)

Read aloud the *We Believe* statement and the first paragraph on page 103. Ask the children to highlight or underline the second and third sentences. Stress: *We tell God we are sorry in prayer. We show we are sorry by trying not to sin again.*

Read each line of the prayer and ask the children to repeat each line. Explain the meaning of the following phrases:

- "I firmly intend" ("I really mean to")

- "to do penance" ("to do something to make up for my sin")

WE RESPOND _____ minutes

Connect to Life Invite the children to reflect on their answers to the *We Respond* question. Stress: *We can show God we are truly sorry by trying hard not to sin. We can ask the Holy Spirit to help us make good choices and to avoid making wrong ones. We can examine our conscience and tell God we are sorry for any wrong choices we may have made.*

Pray together the Act of Contrition. Encourage the children to pray the prayer often and commit it to memory.

Catechist Goal

● To review the chapter ideas that are key to growing as disciples of Jesus Christ

Our Faith Response

● To decide on ways to grow as disciples by living out what we have learned

Show What you Know

Read aloud the directions. When all are finished coloring, point out that the priest wears a purple stole when celebrating the sacrament.

Celebrate!

Read aloud the paragraph. Have the children underline the last sentence. Ask: *What color do you think of for the terms God's forgiveness and peace?* Invite volunteers to share their responses.

Make it Happen

Have the children work in pairs. Read aloud the directions. When the children have finished their plans, allow enough time for all the pairs to act out their skits.

Take Home

Read aloud the directions. For the sheep, give the children copies of the sheep on Reproducible Master 11. The children can make their puppets in class or at home. Remind the class of your discussion of the story.

Discuss and send home copies of *Sharing Faith with My Family* reproducible master for this chapter (back of book).

104 and **105**

Pray Learn Celebrate Share Choose Live

Grade 2 Chapter 11

PROJECT

Show What you Know

Use the color code to color the Key Words.

 green — God's gift that helps us to know right from wrong

 purple — the sacrament in which we receive and celebrate God's forgiveness of our sins

conscience *green*

Penance and *purple* Reconciliation

Celebrate!

All of us are in need of God's forgiveness. The Church encourages us to celebrate God's forgiveness in the Sacrament of Penance. If we sin in a way that breaks our friendship with God, we must tell these mortal sins to the priest. We should also tell any venial sins. They hurt our friendship with God and with one another. In the Sacrament of Penance we receive forgiveness and are at peace with God and with one another.

104   www.webelieveweb.com

DISCIPLE

Pray Learn Celebrate Share Choose Live

Make it Happen

With a classmate, write a skit about forgiveness. Your skit must have a beginning, a middle, and an end. Plan it out in the space below.

Beginning	Middle	End
Problem or conflict will likely be presented by the children in the beginning.	A turning point through conversation or action will likely be presented by the children in the middle.	A resolution achieved through forgiveness will be presented by the children in the end.

Practice your skit together, and then act it out for your class.

Take Home

On a separate piece of paper, draw a picture of the shepherd and the lost sheep. Cut each one out. Use craft sticks to make your pictures into puppets. Perform a puppet play of the story of the lost sheep for your family.

DISCIPLE CHALLENGE How are we like the lost sheep? How is God like the shepherd? Tell your family.

We are all important to God. God will always love and forgive us.   105

CHAPTER TEST

Fill in the circle beside the correct answer.

1. Our _____ helps us to know right from wrong.
   - ● conscience
   - ○ contrition

2. Penance and Reconciliation is a sacrament of _____.
   - ● forgiveness
   - ○ forgetting

3. We are not at peace with God, ourselves, and others when we _____.
   - ○ love
   - ● sin

4. A word that means "coming back together again" is _____.
   - ● reconciliation
   - ○ conscience

5. When we think about our thoughts, words, and actions, we examine our _____.
   - ○ contrition
   - ● conscience

6. _____ is another word for sorrow.
   - ● Contrition
   - ○ Reconciliation

7–8. Write two ways to prepare for the Sacrament of Penance.

Possible responses: examine our conscience; learn an Act of Contrition

9–10. Write two things we tell God in the Act of Contrition.

Possible responses: We are sorry for our sins. We will try not to sin again.

106

CHAPTER TEST

Provide ten to fifteen minutes for the students to complete the test. After all have finished, check the answers. Clarify any misconceptions.

Alternative Assessment

You may want the students to complete the following alternative-assessment activity.

Jesus' story about the lost sheep on page 132 is about reconciliation with God. Draw a picture to tell the story.

Additional Testing

• Chapter 11 Test in *Assessment Book*, pages 21–22

• CD-ROM *Test Generator and Resource*: Use Chapter 11 Test or customize your own.

Review

Review the definitions as they are presented in the chapter's *Key Word* boxes:

• Penance and Reconciliation (page 101)

• conscience (page 102).

We Believe Statements

Review the four statements.

• Jesus invites us to celebrate God's forgiveness.

• Jesus shares God's forgiveness and peace in the Sacrament of Penance and Reconciliation.

• We examine our conscience.

• We tell God we are sorry for our sins.

To use the Chapter 11 Study Guide, visit

www.webelieveweb.com

Overview

In Chapter 11 the children learned about ways we prepare to celebrate the Sacrament of Penance. In this chapter the children will learn how to celebrate the sacrament.

Doctrinal Content	For Adult Reading and Reflection *Catechism of the Catholic Church*
The children will learn:	Paragraph
• We ask for God's forgiveness in the Sacrament of Penance.	1455
• We celebrate God's forgiveness in the Sacrament of Penance.	1468
• We celebrate the Sacrament of Penance with our parish community.	1469
• Jesus wants us to forgive others.	1425

Key Words

contrition (p. 109)
confession (p. 109)
a penance (p. 109)
absolution (p. 109)

Catechist Background

What steps need to be taken to heal a broken relationship?

Everyone experiences the need for forgiveness at some point. We notice a problem in a relationship and look to see if we have done something to cause it. If we are at fault, we apologize and promise not to let it happen again. The Sacrament of Penance follows a similar pattern.

When we examine our conscience, we feel sorry for our sins and ask forgiveness in Penance. After confessing our sins to the priest, we willingly accept the penance to make up for our sins. We pray an Act of Contrition and promise not to sin again. In Penance the priest acts in the person of Jesus. Although the priest says the words of absolution, it is Jesus who forgives us.

Go to **www.webelieveweb.com**, Catechist/Teacher, We Believe Correlations for this chapter's correlation to:
• Six Tasks of Catechesis
• Catholic Social Teaching.

From time to time the entire parish community gathers together to celebrate God's forgiveness in the Sacrament of Penance. After confessing our sins, we make a firm resolve not to sin again. When we receive God's forgiveness and peace, we go forth to share them with others.

Whether we receive the sacrament individually or as part of a parish celebration, it is always a sign of God's love and forgiveness. As we celebrate being forgiven, we remember that Jesus wants us to be as forgiving of others as he is of us.

How can you grow as a forgiving person?

Lesson Planning Guide

Lesson Steps	Presentation	Materials

WE GATHER

page 107 **Prayer** **Focus on Life**	 Ask God for forgiveness in song. • Talk about forgiveness.	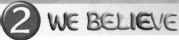 "We Come to Ask Forgiveness," Carey Landry, #8, Grade 2 CD For the prayer space: a picture of Jesus, the Good Shepherd

② WE BELIEVE

page 108 *We ask for God's forgiveness in the Sacrament of Penance.*	• Present the steps in the Sacrament of Penance. • Point out the *Key Words* and the definitions. 👤 Complete the activity about doing penance.	• pencils or pens
page 109 *We celebrate God's forgiveness in the Sacrament of Penance.*	• Present the celebration of the Sacrament of Penance. 👤 Discuss how celebrating this sacrament helps us. • Read and discuss *As Catholics.*	
page 110 *We celebrate the Sacrament of Penance with our parish community.*	• Read about celebrating Penance with the parish. 👤 Discuss the responses to the question.	
page 111 *Jesus wants us to forgive others.* 📖 *Matthew 18:21–23*	• Read and discuss the Scripture story.	• colored pencils or crayons • construction paper • copies of Reproducible Master 12, guide page 107C

③ WE RESPOND

page 111	👤 Do the *We Respond* activity about being a peacemaker.	
pages 112–113 **Project Disciple**	• Complete the **Project Disciple** activities. • Explain the *Take Home* activity. • Discuss/send home **Sharing Faith with My Family** reproducible master for this chapter.	• colored pencils • copies of **Sharing Faith with My Family** reproducible master, Chapter 12 (back of book)
page 114 **Chapter 12 Test**	• Complete **Chapter 12 Test**. • Work on *Alternative Assessment* activity.	• optional: copies of Scripture reproducible master, *What's the Word?*, Chapter 12 (back of book)

For additional ideas, activities, and opportunities: Visit Sadlier's www.WeBelieveweb.com

107B

Name _____

Make this sign to put on one of your doorknobs at home.

1. Cut along the dashed lines.

2. On construction paper, trace the sign. Cut out the shape.

3. Glue the back of your doorknob sign to the construction paper shape.

4. Color the sign. Add your own decorations to the back.

Jesus wants us to be peacemakers.

PROJECT DISCIPLE

Pray
Learn
Celebrate
Share
Choose
Live

Additional Activities

What's the Word?

Scripture reproducible master, Chapter 12

Materials needed: copies of *What's the Word?* (back of book); optional—props and costumes for dramatization

Distribute copies of the Scripture reproducible master. Choose volunteers to be the readers, Jesus, and Zacchaeus. Explain that the other children will be the people in the crowd. Have the actors mime the actions of the characters as the script is being read.

Point out that Zacchaeus showed that he was sorry for doing wrong by promising to return people's money and share with people in need.

Pray Today

Provide a few minutes of quiet time for the children to reflect on what it means to be a peacemaker. Then ask each child to pray to the Holy Spirit to ask for help in being a peacemaker at home, in school, in the neighborhood.

Picture This

Materials needed: drawing paper (8 ½ in. x 11 in.), colored pencils or crayons

Have the children work in pairs. Give each pair a sheet of drawing paper. Ask the pairs to design a three- or four- frame story board to tell the story of someone their age being a peacemaker. When the pairs are finished, ask them to share their stories with the group.

Celebrate!

On the board write the following sets of terms about the Sacrament of Penance:

- Penance, forgiveness, sacrament, water
- sins, sorry, Confirmation, a penance
- godmother, sorrow, Act of Contrition, prayer
- absolution, bread, examination of conscience, confession

Call on volunteers to cross out the term that does not belong in each group (water, Confirmation, godmother, bread). Then ask another volunteer to explain why the term does not belong.

Meeting Individual Needs
A Visual Help for Penance

Some children may find it difficult to memorize the words of the Act of Contrition. Help these children make Act of Contrition prayer cards. They can copy the words of the prayer on heavy stock paper and then cover the cards with clear plastic wrap. Tell the children that they can use these cards during the celebration of the sacrament.

We Believe Resources

- Grade 2 *Review & Resource Book*, pages 31–33
- Grade 2 *Family Book*, pages 36–38
- Grade 2 *Assessment Book*, pages 23–24
- Grade 2 CD-ROM *Test Generator and Resource*: Use Chapter 12 Test or customize your own.
- www.webelieveweb.com

Enrichment Ideas

Chapter Story

Marcy and her little sister, Jenna, shared many things. Every afternoon after school, Marcy and Jenna did their homework together at the kitchen table.

When Yolanda moved into the apartment down the hall, Marcy was very happy. More and more, Marcy spent time with Yolanda after school. Jenna tried to tell Marcy that she felt left out, but Marcy was having so much fun with her new friend that she did not listen to Jenna.

Jenna looked so sad one day that Marcy said, "I'll do something with you tomorrow. Dad said that he would take us shopping to buy a present for Mom's birthday. He said that he'd treat us to ice cream, too. We'll go tomorrow!"

The next day when Jenna arrived home from school, Marcy wasn't there. Dad said, "Marcy isn't coming with us. She is going to play soccer with Yolanda." So, Jenna and her dad went to the store by themselves.

That night, Dad told Marcy, "I know you like spending time with your new friend. But your sister misses you. Jenna was so sad, she couldn't finish her ice cream sundae."

Marcy found Jenna in their bedroom. Marcy said, "Jenna, I'm sorry I didn't go with you and Dad today."

Jenna answered, "I missed you. I guess I'll forgive you this time. Let's go find Dad so you can see the present we picked out for Mom."

▶ *What do you think Marcy can do to make her sister happy and keep her friend, too?*

FAITH and MEDIA

▶ As part of a *We Gather* discussion about stories of forgiveness, encourage the children to describe television shows or movies that have a message of forgiveness. Remind the children that such stories in the media can serve as good examples to those who watch them, and represent good use of media. As Pope John Paul II reminded us in his message for World Communications Day in 1998, "The means of social communication, properly used, can help to create and sustain a human community based on justice and charity" (as quoted in the document *Ethics in Communications*, Pontifical Council for Social Communications, June 4, 2000, #19).

CHAPTER PROJECT: A PAGEANT OF PEACEMAKERS

Give the children the names of peacemakers such as Mother Teresa, Pope John Paul II, and Saint Francis of Assisi. Ask the children to find a picture of one of the peacemakers. Then set a time for a "Pageant for Peacemakers." Suggest to the children that they ask their parents or a community librarian to help in this search. Encourage the children to find out one or two things about this peacemaker to share with the class. Display the pictures around the room.

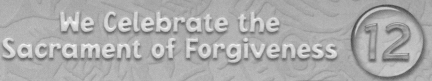

We Celebrate the Sacrament of Forgiveness (12)

WE GATHER

✝ **All:** Lord, have mercy.

🎵 **We Come to Ask Forgiveness**

We come to ask your forgiveness, O Lord,
and we seek forgiveness from each other.
Sometimes we build up walls instead
    of bridges to peace,
and we ask your forgiveness,
    O Lord.

For the times when we've been
    rude and selfish,
for the times when we have
    been unkind;
and for the times we refused
    to help our friends in need,
we ask your forgiveness,
    O Lord.

 What do you do when someone asks you to forgive them?

107

PREPARING TO PRAY

For this gathering prayer, the children will ask God for forgiveness.

• Have the children read silently as you read aloud the words of the song.

• Explain that asking God for forgiveness is building a bridge for peace.

• Play song #8 on the Grade 2 CD and have the children practice singing.

The Prayer Space

• Display a picture that shows forgiveness, such as the Good Shepherd embracing his lost sheep, or a picture of a parent hugging a child as in the story of the forgiving father.

• Also display a small bridge made from blocks, sticks, or a medium of your choice or a picture of a bridge. Explain that the bridge stands for our tries to build bridges of peace and forgiveness.

📖 **This Week's Liturgy**

Visit **www.webelieveweb.com** for this week's liturgical readings and other seasonal material.

Lesson Plan

WE GATHER _____ minutes

✝ Pray

• Invite the children to form two lines in the prayer space. Have the children in both lines face each other and make a bridge by extending their arms and hands.

• When the bridge is formed, ask the children to sing the first verse of "We Come to Ask Forgiveness." Then ask them to drop their arms and face the picture of Jesus. Sing together the second verse of the song.

• Invite the children to share a sign of peace with those who are near them.

☀ Focus on Life

• Discuss with the children what they do when people ask their forgiveness. Point out the importance of forgiving others. Share the *Chapter Story* on guide page 107E.

Family Connection Update

Ask the children to share their families' experiences of the lost sheep puppet play.

Catechist Goal

• To explain how the Sacrament of Penance is celebrated

Our Faith Response

• To learn the process of receiving the Sacrament of Penance and to identify ways to forgive others in Jesus' name

 contrition

confession

a penance

absolution

Lesson Materials

• copies of Reproducible Master 12

• Scripture and Family reproducible masters (back of book)

As Catholics...

Seal of Confession

After you have presented these two pages, read aloud the *As Catholics* text. Assure the children that the priests never tell other people what we tell them in the Sacrament of Penance.

108

WE BELIEVE

We ask for God's forgiveness in the Sacrament of Penance.

When we celebrate the Sacrament of Penance, we think about the ways we have shown or not shown love for God and for others. This is an examination of conscience. We are sorry for our sins and promise not to sin again. This is **contrition**.

We tell our sins to the priest. This is called **confession**. The priest tells us to say a prayer or to do a kind act to make up for our sins. This is called **a penance**.

We say an Act of Contrition to tell God we are sorry. We promise not to sin again. The priest acting in the name of Jesus forgives our sins. This is called **absolution**.

These steps are always part of the Sacrament of Penance. When we celebrate this sacrament, we meet with the priest. He acts in the name of Jesus. We may sit and face the priest or kneel behind a screen.

Write what we are telling God when we do the penance the priest gives us.

_____

_____

_____

Lesson Plan

WE BELIEVE ____ minutes

Ask: *What do we do when we examine our conscience?* (We think about ways we have shown or not shown love for God and for others.) *What does contrition mean?* (sorrow for sin)

Read the first two *We Believe* paragraphs on page 108. Explain: *There are times when we all need to ask for forgiveness. We do this in the Sacrament of Penance.* Remind the children that Jesus gave his Church this sacrament so that we could share in God's mercy and forgive others.

Write the words *confession, penance, absolution* on the board. Pronounce them for the children. Explain that *absolution* comes from a word that means "washing away." Then ask volunteers to read aloud the next two *We Believe* paragraphs on page 108.

Read the activity directions. Help the children to conclude that we are telling God we are sorry and are thanking him for his forgiveness.

We celebrate God's forgiveness in the Sacrament of Penance.

This is what happened when Lucy went to Father Rob to celebrate the Sacrament of Penance.

Read Along

- Father Rob welcomed Lucy, and they both made the Sign of the Cross.
- Lucy listened to a story from the Bible about God's forgiveness.
- Lucy confessed her sins to Father Rob.
- Father Rob and Lucy talked about what she could do to make right choices. Then Father gave Lucy a penance. Lucy will do her penance after the celebration of the sacrament.
- Lucy prayed an Act of Contrition.
- Lucy received absolution, or forgiveness, from her sins. Father Rob stretched out his right hand over Lucy's head. He prayed:

  "God, the Father of mercies,
  through the death and resurrection of his Son
  has reconciled the world to himself
  and sent the Holy Spirit among us
  for the forgiveness of sins;
  through the ministry of the Church may God
  give you pardon and peace, and I absolve you from your sins
  in the name of the Father, and of the Son, †
  and of the Holy Spirit."

  Lucy answered, "Amen."
- Father Rob and Lucy thanked God for his forgiveness. Father told Lucy, "Go in peace."

We can celebrate the Sacrament of Penance as Lucy did.

🕺 Talk about ways celebrating the Sacrament of Penance helps us.

Key Words

contrition being sorry for our sins and promising not to sin again

confession telling our sins to the priest in the Sacrament of Penance

a penance a prayer or a kind act we do to make up for our sins

absolution God's forgiveness of our sins by the priest in the Sacrament of Penance

As Catholics...

The parish priest is always willing to help us. He listens to us and helps us to follow Jesus. We tell the priest our sins in the Sacrament of Penance. The priest cannot tell anyone the sins we confess.

109

ACTIVITY BANK

Curriculum Connection
Language Arts
Activity Materials: writing paper or sentence strips

Direct attention to the photos on these pages. For each, ask the children to write one or two sentences to describe what is happening.

Liturgy
Priest's Vestments

Ask one of the parish priests to show the children what vestments he wears for the Sacrament of Penance. Ask the priest to explain the symbolism of the purple stole.

Read the section about Lucy's celebration of the Sacrament of Penance. Act out the celebration of the sacrament as described on this page. Take the part of Father Rob and have a volunteer take Lucy's part.

Point out that some times the priest reads the story of the father who forgave his son or the story of the shepherd finding the lost sheep.

Explain that we can celebrate the sacrament as Lucy did. Stress: *God is always willing to give us his mercy and peace when we are sorry.*

🕺 **Discuss** ways celebrating the Sacrament of Penance helps us. Explain: *Many people feel and want to be closer to Jesus after they celebrate Penance. They are happy when the priest absolves their sins, and then they try to avoid committing these sins again.*

Quick Check

✔ *What is absolution?* (It is the forgiveness of our sins by the priest in the Sacrament of Penance.)

✔ *What do we celebrate in the Sacrament of Penance?* (We celebrate God's forgiveness.)

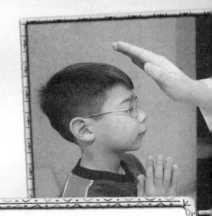

Teaching Note

Forgiving Attitude

Remind the children that Jesus wants us to forgive others, no matter how difficult that might be. As catechists we need to be sensitive to children who may feel some of their behavior is not easily forgiven. Assure the children that they are forgiven and accepted in your class. Encourage the children to ask God to help them to forgive others.

We celebrate the Sacrament of Penance with our parish community.

Our parish community sometimes gathers to celebrate the Sacrament of Penance together. This helps us see that all of us need forgiveness.

This is what happens during that celebration.

Read Along

- The parish community sings a song.
- We listen to readings from the Bible about God's love and forgiveness.
- The priest talks to us about the readings.
- We listen to questions that are part of an examination of conscience.
- We say a prayer together to tell God we are sorry for our sins. Then together we pray the Our Father.
- Each person goes alone to tell his or her sins to the priest.
- The priest gives a penance to each person.
- Each person receives absolution from the priest.
- Together we all praise and thank God for his mercy.
- The priest blesses the parish community.
- He tells us to "Go in peace."

What is special about celebrating this sacrament with your parish community?

110

Lesson Plan

WE BELIEVE (continued)

Explain to the children that their parish gathers at special times to celebrate the Sacrament of Penance. Invite the children to imagine themselves at a parish community celebration. Ask a volunteer to read the first five actions listed on page 110.

Ask: *What are some readings the priest may read and talk about?* (the story of the finding of the lost sheep; the story of the forgiving father) *What are some questions the priest may ask during the examination of conscience?* (Accept reasonable responses.)

Invite volunteers to read the next six actions. Ask the children to turn to page 109 and to read the words of absolution.

Read the discussion question. Invite volunteers to share their responses. Share your own thoughts and feelings as well. Help the children to conclude that because we are members of the Church, it is special to celebrate God's forgiveness with the Church community.

Jesus wants us to forgive others.

📖 Matthew 18:21–23

One day Peter asked Jesus, "Lord, if my brother sins against me, how often must I forgive him? As many as seven times?" Jesus answered, "I say to you, not seven times but seventy-seven times." (Matthew 18:21, 22)

In this story, Jesus is telling us that we should always forgive others. When we celebrate the Sacrament of Penance, we receive God's forgiveness and peace. Jesus wants us to forgive others and to share God's gift of peace with them.

WE RESPOND

✸ Imagine that your friend said some hurtful things to you. Then your friend said, "I am sorry. I hope you can forgive me." Write what you can say and do to be a peacemaker.

Possible response: I forgive you friend. Let's do something

together to celebrate making up.

111

ACTIVITY BANK

Multiple Intelligences
Musical, Bodily-Kinesthetic

Teach the children the following song to the tune of "Here We Go 'Round the Mulberry Bush."

This is the way we live in peace,
live in peace, live in peace.
This is the way we live in peace

* *at home with our families.*
* *when we are with friends.*
   (second verse)
* *with all our neighbors.*
   (third verse)

Have the children form a circle. Sing the song together. Invite volunteers to act out ways they can be peacemakers at home, with friends, and in their local community.

Invite the children to stand as you read aloud the Scripture story on page 111. Explain that Jesus always wants us to forgive others.

Ask a volunteer to read the paragraph after the Scripture story. Explain: *People who are peacemakers need not be famous or live in faraway places.* Ask the children to name peacemakers in their town, neighborhood, and families.

Distribute copies of Reproducible Master 12. Circulate in the room to help any child who is having difficulty. When the children are finished, encourage them to share their doorknob signs with their families.

WE RESPOND   ___ minutes

Connect to Life Read aloud the situation described in the *We Respond* section. Have the children write what they can do in this situation to be a peacemaker. Help them to conclude that when we ask for forgiveness and we forgive others, we are doing what Jesus wants. We are being peacemakers.

Pray Invite the children to gather in the prayer space. Pray together the Our Father. Invite the children to offer a sign of peace to children who are standing near them.

Catechist Goal

• To review the chapter ideas that are key to growing as disciples of Jesus Christ

Our Faith Response

• To decide on ways to grow as disciples by living out what we have learned

Show What you Know

Help the children categorize the actions of Penance. Please note that some children may write "a penance" on the priest's list. This is correct because the priest gives a penance.

Celebrate!

You may want the children to work in pairs. When they are finished, check the matches.

Saint Stories

Read the paragraph. Ask: *What did Saint Francis mean by* instrument? Help the children conclude that we can substitute the words *doers*, *makers*, or *ways* of peace. Encourage the children to pray Saint Francis's words often.

Reality Check

Have the children work independently. Remind them to respect each other's privacy as they work.

Take Home

Read the directions and encourage the children to share with their families what they have learned about the sacrament.

Discuss and send home copies of *Sharing Faith with My Family* reproducible master for this chapter (back of book).

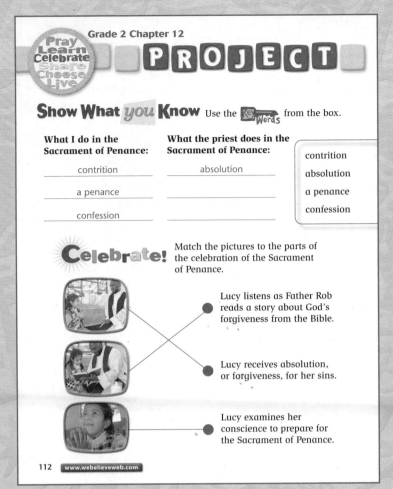

Grade 2 Chapter 12

PROJECT

Pray Learn Celebrate Share Choose Live

Show What you Know Use the Key Words from the box.

What I do in the Sacrament of Penance:	What the priest does in the Sacrament of Penance:
contrition	absolution
a penance	
confession	

contrition
absolution
a penance
confession

Celebrate!

Match the pictures to the parts of the celebration of the Sacrament of Penance.

Lucy listens as Father Rob reads a story about God's forgiveness from the Bible.

Lucy receives absolution, or forgiveness, for her sins.

Lucy examines her conscience to prepare for the Sacrament of Penance.

112 www.webelieveweb.com

DISCIPLE

Pray Learn Celebrate Share Choose Live

Saint Stories

Saint Francis of Assisi is known as a peacemaker. When one town went to war against another, Francis helped them come to a peaceful agreement. Francis wrote a prayer for peace. He wrote, "Lord, make me an instrument of your peace." For more about saints, visit "Lives of the Saints" at www.webelieveweb.com.

↳ **DISCIPLE CHALLENGE** Be a peacemaker. Pray the words of Saint Francis today.

Reality Check

Check the things someone should ask God's forgiveness for.

☑ being rude
☑ being unkind
☑ being selfish
❑ being happy

Take Home

Talk with your family about the Sacrament of Penance. Write three important things you have learned that you will share with them.

Accept information from

pages 108–111.

As a family, you might plan to visit your parish to celebrate the Sacrament of Penance.

113

Draw a line to match the sentence parts.

1. Absolution is   a prayer or kind act we do to make up for our sins.

2. A penance is   telling our sins to the priest.

3. Confession is   God's forgiveness of our sins by the priest.

4. Contrition is   being sorry for our sins and promising not to sin again.

Underline the correct answer.

5. Contrition, confession, a penance, and absolution are (**always**, sometimes) part of the Sacrament of Penance.

6. We (always, **sometimes**) gather with our parish community to celebrate the Sacrament of Penance together.

7. Jesus wants us to forgive others (**always**, sometimes).

8. In the Sacrament of Penance, the priest (**always**, sometimes) forgives us in the name of Jesus.

9–10. Write two ways you can be a peacemaker.

Possible responses: ask for forgiveness; forgive others

CHAPTER TEST

Provide ten to fifteen minutes for the students to complete the test. After all have finished, check the answers. Clarify any misconceptions.

Alternative Assessment

You may want the students to complete the following alternative-assessment activity.

Think about Lucy's celebration of the Sacrament of Penance. Put the following words in order to tell about her celebration: Act of Contrition, examination of conscience, absolution, confession, Bible reading.

Additional Testing

• Chapter 12 Test in *Assessment Book*, pages 23–24

• CD-ROM *Test Generator and Resource*: Use Chapter 12 Test or customize your own.

Review

Review the definitions as they are presented in the chapter's *Key Word* boxes:

• contrition (page 109)

• confession (page 109)

• a penance (page 109)

• absolution (page 109).

We Believe Statements

Review the four statements.

• We ask God's forgiveness in the Sacrament of Penance.

• We celebrate God's forgiveness in the Sacrament of Penance.

• We celebrate the Sacrament of Penance with our parish community.

• Jesus wants us to forgive others.

To use the Chapter 12 Study Guide, visit

www.webelieveweb.com

Advent

Advent has a twofold character: as a season to prepare for Christmas when Christ's first coming to us is remembered; as a season when that remembrance directs the mind and heart to await Christ's Second Coming at the end of time.

(Norms Governing Liturgical Calendars, 39)

Overview

In this chapter the children will learn that Advent is a season of waiting and preparing for the coming of Jesus Christ.

For Adult Reading and Reflection
You may want to refer to paragraph 524 of the *Catechism of the Catholic Church*.

Catechist Background

Go to **www.webelieveweb.com**, Catechist/Teacher, We Believe Correlations for this chapter's correlation to Six Tasks of Catechesis.

Is there anything for which you are waiting or longing?

The Church celebrates Advent as a season of joyful preparation for the coming of the Lord. We prepare for Christmas, when we celebrate that the only Son of God came to live among us on earth. We prepare for Christ's second coming at the end of time. "When the Church celebrates *the liturgy of Advent* each year, she makes present this ancient expectancy of the Messiah, for by sharing in the long preparation for the Savior's first coming, the faithful renew their ardent desire for his second coming." (CCC 524)

The Prologue of John's Gospel proclaims the Son of God as the light that overcomes our darkness. "The true light, which enlightens everyone, was coming into the world." (John 1:9) In that light, symbolized by the candles on our Advent wreaths, we see the unmistakable signs of God's love around and within us.

Jesus Christ, the greatest sign of God's love for humanity and all creation, is "the final event towards which all the events of salvation history converge" (*GDC*, 40; see Luke 24–27). During the four weeks of Advent, we respond to this gift of our loving God by joyfully expecting the Feast of his Nativity and by keeping watch for Christ's future coming. Having received the greatest gift of all in Jesus, we express our thanks by giving of ourselves to family, friends, and those in need.

How will you give of yourself during Advent?

Lesson Planning Guide

Lesson Steps	Presentation	Materials
① WE GATHER		
page 115 **Introduce the Season**	• Read the *Chapter Story*. • Introduce the Advent Season. • Proclaim words on a banner.	
page 116	♫ Sing an Advent song.	♫ "Stay Awake," Christopher Walker, #9, Grade 2 CD
② WE BELIEVE		
pages 116–117 *Advent is a season of waiting and preparing.*	• Present the text about Advent. ✗ Complete the Advent-wreath activity.	• colored pencils or crayons
③ WE RESPOND		
page 118	• Brainstorm ways to help people see God's love. ✗ Complete the Advent calendar.	
Text page 119 **Guide page 119-120** **We Respond in Prayer**	• Listen to Scripture. • Respond in prayer.	• prayer space items: photos of light shining in darkness, Advent wreath (option) • flashlight
Text page 120 **Guide pages 119–120, 120A** **Project Disciple**	• Complete the Project Disciple activities. Discuss the *Take Home* activity. • Complete the Reproducible Master 13 activity. See guide pages 120A and 115C. • Discuss/send home Sharing Faith with My Family, guide page 120B.	• colored pencils • scissors, glue, dark colored construction paper • copies of Reproducible Master 13, guide page 120A • copies of Sharing Faith with My Family reproducible master for this chapter, guide page 120B

For additional ideas, activities, and opportunities: Visit Sadlier's **www.WeBelieveweb.com**

Chapter Story

Hi! My name is Kira. My dad works on a ship. He travels on the sea, and is away from home for months at a time. When Dad is away, we talk on the phone and send messages. But I still miss seeing him every day.

My dad is on a trip right now, but he is coming home on Saturday. Yesterday Grandpop helped my brother, Eric, and me to make a Welcome Home sign. Grandpop put lights around the sign so Dad will be sure to see it.

After school tomorrow I'm going to help Mom clean. Tomorrow night we'll be finished getting everything ready for Dad.

On Saturday we are going to the docks to wait for Dad's ship. Dad's shipmates' families will be there, too. Some will carry signs; some will carry balloons and flowers. Eric and I decided that we did not want to carry anything.

We are going to wave our arms in the air until Dad walks down the ship's ramp. As Dad steps onto the dock, I'm going to run to him and give him a great big hug. I can't wait.

What is Kira's family doing to get ready for her dad's homecoming?

PROJECT DISCIPLE
Additional Activities

Make *it* Happen

Distribute Reproducible Master 13, guide page 120A.

Also give each child a large sheet of black or dark blue construction paper (11 in. by 17 in.). Explain to the children that they are going to make a Bethlehem night scene.

Ask the children to color the scene pieces on the reproducible master (moon, stable, houses, hills, and stars) and then help them cut out the pieces. Then have the children paste the pieces on construction paper.

Explain to the children that each time they do something to show God's love to others, they should add a star. They can do this by applying star stickers or drawing them by using a white crayon or chalk. Encourage the children to display their scene at home where they will see it and can add to it often.

Pray Today

Explain to the children that during Advent we can pray for others. Ask your pastor or a pastoral associate for the names of four people in the parish for whom the children could pray.

Each week of Advent have the children pray for one person and make cards to send to that person at the end of the week. Have the children draw seasonal pictures on the cards.

"In his love Christ has filled us with joy as we prepare to celebrate his birth."

Advent II Preface, Eucharistic Prayer

ADVENT

Catechist Goal
- To present Advent as a season of waiting and preparing for the Lord

Our Faith Response
- To celebrate Advent by praying and helping others

Gather In My Name Whole Community Catechesis

An Online Resource

*Celebrate **Advent** as a class, school, and/or a parish community. The Gather in My Name events come complete with detailed leader's guides, preparation charts, handouts, promotional ideas, organizational materials, and much more. Go to:*

www.webelieveweb.com

SEASONAL CHAPTER 13

This chapter prepares us to celebrate the season of Advent.

115

Lesson Plan

Introduce the Season ___ minutes

- **Pray** the Sign of the Cross and the words *Come, Lord Jesus.*

- **Read** aloud the *Chapter Story* on guide page 115C. Discuss how the family is preparing for Kira's dad's homecoming. Ask: *Is this a happy time for them?* Help the children to conclude that Kira and her family are happy getting ready for Dad. They will be happier when Dad is home with them.

- **Have** the children open their texts to page 115. Read aloud the chapter title. Explain: *Advent is the first season of the Church year. It is a happy time for us as we prepare to celebrate the coming of Jesus.*

- **Invite** the children to look at the photo on the pupil page. Ask: *What are the children doing to get ready to celebrate Christmas?* Invite volunteers to share what they know about the Advent wreath.

- **Proclaim** together the words on the banner.

Lesson Materials
- Grade 2 CD
- colored pencils, crayons, or markers
- flashlight
- copies of Reproducible Master 13
- dark colored construction paper
- drawing paper for cards

Teaching Tip

Guest Speaker

You may want to invite a member of your parish's liturgical committee to speak to the children about Advent. Ask the speaker to talk about parish Advent celebrations and ways parish members are preparing to celebrate the Feast of Christmas.

Advent is a season of waiting and preparing.

WE GATHER

🎵 **Stay Awake**

Stay awake, be ready.
You do not know the hour when the
 Lord is coming.
Stay awake, be ready.
The Lord is coming soon!
Alleluia, alleluia!
The Lord is coming soon!

WE BELIEVE

The season of Advent is a time to prepare to celebrate the coming of Jesus. During Advent we watch and wait.

We watch for signs of God's love in the world. We can see signs of God's love in:

- the gifts of his creation
- the loving ways people treat one another
- the work of the Church.

Think about some other signs of God's love. Talk about them.

Jesus is the greatest sign of God's love. Jesus is the Son of God who came into the world. Jesus brings life and light to all people.

Lesson Plan

WE GATHER ___ minutes

Focus on Life Have the children think about getting ready to celebrate a special day at school (Thanksgiving, Presidents' Day, and Valentine's Day). Ask volunteers to share ways in which they get ready. Point out: *Sometimes you help decorate. Sometimes you learn special songs to sing.*

Explain: *Today you will learn a special Advent song.* Have the children open their books to page 116. Play "Stay Awake," #9 on the Grade 2 CD. Have the children practice singing. Then invite the children to stand and sing the song together.

WE BELIEVE ___ minutes

• **Read** together the *We Believe* statement. Have volunteers read the first three *We Believe* paragraphs. Invite the children to share the signs of God's love we can see in the world.

• **Remind** the children that during Advent, we prepare to celebrate Jesus' coming to live among us. Read aloud the fourth *We Believe* paragraph.

• **Show** the children a branch of an evergreen tree. Explain that the branches of these trees are green throughout the year. When we look at them, we can think about God's love that never ends.

The four weeks of Advent are filled with joy and hope. We celebrate this season at home and in our parish. One way of celebrating is by gathering around an Advent wreath. This wreath is made of evergreen branches and has four candles. There is one candle for each week of Advent. We pray as we light the candle each week.

 On the first Sunday of Advent we light the first purple candle.

Week One

On the second Sunday of Advent we light the first and second purple candles.

Week Two

 On the third Sunday of Advent we light the first and second purple candles and the rose candle.

 **On the fourth Sunday of Advent** we light all four candles.

Week Three

Show how the wreath changes as the weeks of Advent go by.

We light the Advent wreath to remind us to watch and wait for the coming of Jesus. The light from the candles reminds us that Jesus is the Light of the World.

Week Four

117

ADVENT

ACTIVITY BANK

Parish
Make an Advent Wreath
Activity Materials: four battery-operated candles, purple and rose ribbon, styrofoam wreath form, evergreen branches

Visit your parish church to see the Advent wreath. When you return to your classroom, invite the children to help you make an Advent wreath to put in your prayer space. Tie purple ribbon around three candles, and rose-colored ribbon around one candle. Then place the wreath form on the prayer table. Put the candles inside or outside the wreath form. Then give the children evergreen branches to place on the form. Invite one of the priests from the parish to bless the Advent wreath. Light the appropriate candles whenever your class meets during the Advent season.

• **Invite** the children to look at the Advent wreath on page 115. Then read aloud the text about the Advent wreath on this page.

Help the children complete the wreath activity. On the second wreath, two purple candles should have flames. On the third wreath, two purple candles and one rose candle should have flames. On the fourth wreath, the four candles should have flames.

• **Read** the last *We Believe* paragraph. Have the children highlight or underline *Jesus is the Light of the World.*

Quick Check

✔ *What is Advent?* (Advent is the first season of the Church year. During Advent we prepare to celebrate the coming of Jesus.)

✔ *Why do we light the Advent wreath?* (We light the Advent wreath to remind us to watch and wait for the coming of Jesus.)

CONNECTION

Multicultural Connection
Aguinaldos

Have the children sing again "Stay Awake" on page 116. Then tell them about the Latin American custom of celebrating *de aguinaldos*. Each morning between December 16 and December 24 many families rise early to go to church. Along the way they wake up others to join them. In church they say special prayers or participate in the celebration of Mass. They offer their prayers and participation as gifts, *aguinaldos*, to Jesus. After some families return home from church, they share a special breakfast treat.

WE RESPOND
Jesus asks us to share his light with others. During the season of Advent, we can help people to see God's love.

Fill out the Advent calendar. For each week of Advent, write or draw one thing you will do to help others see God's love.

The things you choose to do may be with your family, class, or parish.

First Week

Second Week

Third Week

Fourth Week

118

Lesson Plan

WE RESPOND   ___ minutes

Connect to Life Remind the children that there are four weeks of Advent. Read the first paragraph. Brainstorm with the children what they can do to help people see God's love. Write all the responses on the board or on chart paper. (Some possible responses: Be kind; keep my room clean; help with the dishes; do my homework; pray often; help my teacher and classmates; learn more about Jesus.)

Read the activity directions. Explain to the children that they can choose things that are written on the board or make up their own. When the children have finished writing, encourage them to do the things they have written on their Advent calendar. Explain: *Remember that when you do these things, you are sharing the light of Jesus.*

• **Share** the following prayer. Encourage the children to pray it often during Advent. *Jesus, we want to share your light, every day and every night.*

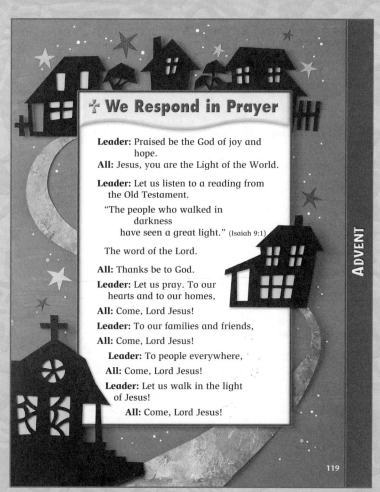

We Respond in Prayer

Leader: Praised be the God of joy and hope.
All: Jesus, you are the Light of the World.

Leader: Let us listen to a reading from the Old Testament.

"The people who walked in darkness
have seen a great light." (Isaiah 9:1)

The word of the Lord.

All: Thanks be to God.

Leader: Let us pray. To our hearts and to our homes,

All: Come, Lord Jesus!

Leader: To our families and friends,

All: Come, Lord Jesus!

Leader: To people everywhere,

All: Come, Lord Jesus!

Leader: Let us walk in the light of Jesus!

All: Come, Lord Jesus!

ADVENT

119

We Respond in Prayer (p. 119)

Get ready by placing a purple cloth on the prayer table. If you have an Advent wreath on the table, light the appropriate candles for this week. You may want the students to sing "Stay Awake" as they gather in the prayer space. Pray the Sign of the Cross and the prayer.

This Week's Liturgy

Visit **www.webelieveweb.com** for this week's liturgical readings and other seasonal material.

Project Disciple (p. 120)

Picture This Before the children begin the activity, have them look at the Advent wreaths on page 117. When you have checked the children's answers, help them identify what the current week of Advent is.

Make *it* Happen

Help the children work on their postcards. You may want to give the children construction paper to make the postcards to send to their family members or friends.

Take Home

Encourage the children to work with their families on writing a family Advent prayer. If you meet again in Advent, ask volunteers to share their prayers.

Discuss and send home copies of *Sharing Faith with My Family*, guide page 120B.

Project Disciple Additional Activities
See the activities suggested on page 115C of the guide.

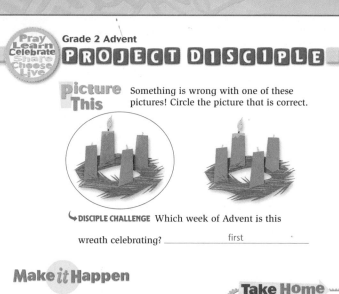

Pray Learn Celebrate Share Choose Live

Grade 2 Advent

PROJECT DISCIPLE

Picture This Something is wrong with one of these pictures! Circle the picture that is correct.

↳**DISCIPLE CHALLENGE** Which week of Advent is this wreath celebrating? _____ first

Make *it* Happen

Write a postcard to another disciple to tell him or her what you learned about Advent. Include how you will celebrate Advent.

Possible responses: Advent is a season of waiting and preparing to celebrate the coming of Jesus. Advent lasts four weeks. To celebrate Advent children may pray, watch for signs of God's love, and light an Advent wreath.

Take Home

With your family use these words to write your own prayer for Advent. Pray it together.

light   Advent

prepare

wreath   candle

Name

Make an Advent picture. Cut out each piece of scenery.

SHARING FAITH
with My Family

Sharing What I Learned

Look at the pictures below. Use each picture to tell your family what you learned in this chapter.

Around the Table

With your family, make special place mats for Sunday meals during Advent. Decorate large pieces of paper or fabric with gifts of creation, which are signs of God's love. Write Advent messages and prayers on the place mat, too. Use these messages and add your own!

Come, Lord Jesus!
Jesus is the Light of the World.
We wait for Jesus with hope
   and joy.

An Advent Prayer

At your family meals, place a candle in the center of the table. Ask an adult to light it. Then pray together.

Jesus, you are the Light
   of the World.
As we prepare to receive you
   into our hearts this
   Christmas,
help us to share your light
   with one another,
with everyone we meet,
and with the whole world.
Amen.

Visit Sadlier's
www.WEBELIEVE.web.com

 Connect to the Catechism
For adult background and reflection,
see paragraph 524.

120B

Christmas

Next to the yearly celebration of the Paschal Mystery, the Church holds most sacred the memorial of Christ's birth and early manifestations. This is the purpose of the Christmas season.

(Norms Governing Liturgical Calendars, 32)

Overview

In this chapter the children will learn that Christmas is a season to give glory to God.

For Adult Reading and Reflection
You may want to refer to paragraph 526 of the *Catechism of the Catholic Church*.

Go to **www.webelieveweb.com**, Catechist/ Teacher, We Believe Correlations for this chapter's correlation to Six Tasks of Catechesis.

Catechist Background

What was your most memorable celebration of Christmas? Why?

In some of our cultural settings, we are apt to think of Christmas as one single day rather than an entire season. For the Church, however, Christmas Day is a beginning: the beginning of the Christmas season.

For about two weeks we celebrate the mystery of the Incarnation, the coming of the Word made flesh to us. As we profess in the Nicene Creed,

". . . for our salvation,
   he came down from heaven;
by the power of the Holy Spirit,
   he was born of the Virgin Mary,
   and became man."

Each day of the Christmas season renews the celebration of the birth of Jesus Christ. In the northern hemisphere, the Christmas season is a celebration of light at the darkest time of the year. The traditional Christmas lights of this season remind us that Jesus, "the light [which] shines in the darkness," (John 1:5) is the true light who enlightens our lives every day of this season and throughout the year. Jesus truly is light for all people.

The feasts of this season reflect the light of Christ, each in its own way. As we celebrate the Feasts of the Holy Innocents, the Holy Family, the Solemnity of Mary, Mother of God, the Epiphany, and the Baptism of the Lord, we rejoice in the everlasting truth that Jesus Christ is our light and our life. Each day of the Christmas season we have reason to sing: "Today is born our Savior, Christ the Lord" (Christmas antiphon).

Throughout the Christmas season how will you celebrate that Jesus Christ is our light and our life?

Lesson Planning Guide

Lesson Steps	Presentation	Materials

1 WE GATHER

page 121 **Introduce the Season**	• Read the *Chapter Story*. • Introduce the Christmas Season. • Praise God.	
page 122	• Share responses to the questions.	

2 WE BELIEVE

pages 122–124 *Christmas is a season to give glory to God.*	• Present the text about the Christmas season. Act out the Scripture story about Jesus' birth and the visit of the shepherds.	• costumes and props, including a doll for the infant Jesus.

3 WE RESPOND

page 124	• Reflect on the questions. Decorate the message on a banner.	• crayons or colored pencils
Text page 125 **Guide page 125–126** **We Respond in Prayer**	• Praise God. 🎵 Respond in song.	🎵 "O Come, All Ye Faithful," #10, Grade 2 CD • prayer space items: white table-cloth, Christmas crèche
Text page 126 **Guide pages 125–126, 126A** **Project Disciple**	• Complete the Project Disciple activities. Discuss the *Take Home* activity. • Complete the Reproducible Master 14 activity. See guide pages 126A and 121C. • Discuss/send home Sharing Faith with My Family, guide page 126B.	• colored pencils or crayons • scissors • envelopes • copies of Reproducible Master 14, guide page 126A • copies of Sharing Faith with My Family reproducible master for this chapter, guide page 126B

For additional ideas, activities, and opportunities: Visit Sadlier's **www.WeBelieveweb.com**

Chapter Story

It was the Sunday after Christmas day, the Feast of the Holy Family. After Mass, Dominic, his parents, and his friend were going to Aunt Cecilia's for a celebration. Dominic said, "I wonder what gift I will get from Jesus this year."

Dominic's friend asked, "What do you mean?"

Dominic explained, "Every year my aunt makes cards. On the cards she writes God's gifts of creation. She puts the cards near the Christmas crèche. Then each person picks one card as a gift from Jesus. Last year my gift card said, 'I give you the gift of animals. When you see them or hear them, remember I want you to learn about them and take care of them.'"

That afternoon, Aunt Cecilia invited everyone to gather near the crèche. Dominic waited until his friend picked a card. His friend read the card. "Wow. My gift is the moon and stars. When I see them shining, I should remember that Jesus is the Light of the world."

When everyone had picked a gift card, they sang Christmas carols together and then had dinner.

What do you think was special about Dominic's family celebration?

PROJECT DISCIPLE
Additional Activities

Celebrate!

Reread the *Chapter Story*. Then distribute copies of Reproducible Master 14, guide page 126A. Explain to the children that they are going to make "Gifts from Jesus" cards. Read aloud the cards. Then give the children time to color and cut out the cards. Also give each child an envelope in which to place the completed cards.

Explain to the children that during the Christmas season, they can invite each family member to choose a "Gift from Jesus" card during a special family celebration.

Pray Today

Distribute copies of the *Sharing Faith with My Family* reproducible master, guide page 126B. Read "For All to See and Pray." Demonstrate the following as you bless the classroom.

• Dip a pine branch in holy water. Walk around the classroom.

• Swing the pine branch as you sprinkle the water praying the words of blessing.

• Suggest to the children that they do the same actions and pray the words of blessing when they gather with their families during the Christmas season.

"Glory to God in the highest."
Luke 2:14

SEASONAL CHAPTER 14

This chapter addresses the entire Christmas season.

121

Chapter 14 • Christmas

Catechist Goal

• To present Christmas as the season of celebrating God's greatest gift, his Son, Jesus

Our Faith Response

• To celebrate that Jesus, the Light of the World, is with us now and forever

Gather In My Name

Whole Community Catechesis

An Online Resource

Celebrate **Christmas** *as a class, school, and/or a parish community. The* Gather in My Name *events come complete with detailed leader's guides, preparation charts, handouts, promotional ideas, organizational materials, and much more. Go to:*

www.webelieveweb.com

Lesson Plan

Introduce the Season ___ minutes

• **Pray** the Sign of the Cross and the words *God, thank you for sending Jesus to us.*

• **Read** aloud the *Chapter Story* on guide page 121C. Ask the children: *Why was Dominic happy about going to his Aunt Cecilia's house?* Help the children to conclude that he was happy he was going to be with his family. He was excited about receiving a gift from Jesus.

• **Have** the children open their texts to page 121. Read aloud the chapter title. Explain: *Christmas is the second*

season of the Church year. It is the season when we give glory to God for sending Jesus to us.

• **Invite** the children to look at the photo. Remind the children that Christmas is a happy time that we celebrate in prayer and song. Point out: *The children are singing Christmas carols that tell the story of the birth of Jesus.*

• **Proclaim** together the words on the banner.

Lesson Materials

- Grade 2 CD
- costumes and props including a doll for the infant Jesus
- copies of Reproducible Master 14
- crayons, markers, scissors
- envelopes (one for each child)

Teaching Tip

When to Present the Lesson

Because you will not meet with the children during the Christmas season, present this lesson during the week before Christmas. Emphasize that Christmas is not just one day we celebrate, but it is a season which lasts about two weeks.

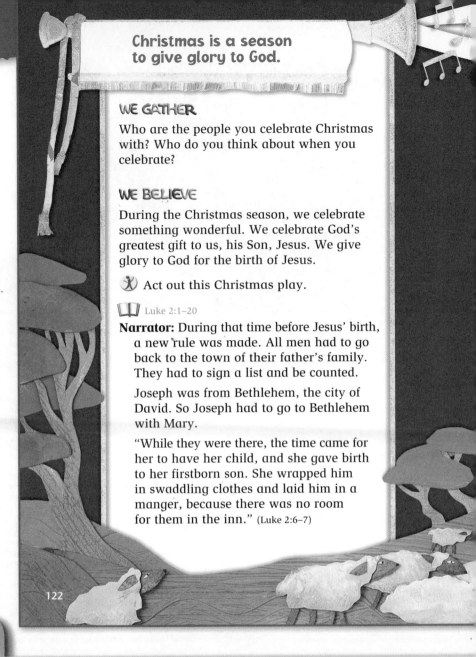

Christmas is a season to give glory to God.

WE GATHER

Who are the people you celebrate Christmas with? Who do you think about when you celebrate?

WE BELIEVE

During the Christmas season, we celebrate something wonderful. We celebrate God's greatest gift to us, his Son, Jesus. We give glory to God for the birth of Jesus.

Act out this Christmas play.

Luke 2:1–20

Narrator: During that time before Jesus' birth, a new rule was made. All men had to go back to the town of their father's family. They had to sign a list and be counted.

Joseph was from Bethlehem, the city of David. So Joseph had to go to Bethlehem with Mary.

"While they were there, the time came for her to have her child, and she gave birth to her firstborn son. She wrapped him in swaddling clothes and laid him in a manger, because there was no room for them in the inn." (Luke 2:6–7)

122

Lesson Plan

WE GATHER ___ minutes

Focus on Life Read aloud the *We Gather* questions. Provide quiet time for the children to reflect on their answers. Then ask volunteers to share their responses.

• **Invite** volunteers to share their family's favorite Christmas stories presented in books, movies, or television programs. Take an informal survey of favorites and list the titles on the board. Tell the children that in this lesson they will act out the greatest Christmas story ever told.

WE BELIEVE ___ minutes

• **Invite** a volunteer to read aloud the *We Believe* statement and the first *We Believe* paragraph. Ask: *How do we give glory to God?* Have volunteers share their responses. Point out: *We gather to celebrate Mass; we sing Christmas carols; we listen to the story of Jesus' birth.*

• **Show** the children Nazareth and Bethlehem on a world map or map of Israel. Explain: *Mary and Joseph had to travel almost 150 miles by donkey and on foot. It took them several days to travel.* Ask: *How do you think they felt when they reached Bethlehem?* (Possible responses: tired, hungry, upset when they could not find a room)

On the hills nearby, some shepherds were watching their sheep.

Shepherds: Look! Look! The sky is filled with light!

Narrator: All of a sudden, an angel appeared. The shepherds were afraid.

Angel: "Do not be afraid; for behold, I proclaim to you good news of great joy that will be for all the people. For today in the city of David a savior has been born for you who is Messiah and Lord. You will find an infant wrapped in swaddling clothes and lying in a manger." (Luke 2:10–12)

Narrator: Suddenly, many angels were there. They were all praising God and saying:

All Angels: "Glory to God in the highest." (Luke 2:14)

Narrator: The shepherds hurried to Bethlehem. They found Mary and Joseph, and the baby lying in the manger. The shepherds told them what the angels had said about this child. All were amazed. The shepherds went back to their fields, saying:

Shepherds: Praise God! Glory and praise to God forever! Amen!

CHRISTMAS

123

ACTIVITY BANK

Meeting Individual Needs

English Language Learners

Activity Materials: recordings and/or lyrics to Christmas carols in any language spoken as a first language by a second grader

Children who are in the process of learning to speak English need opportunities to share their primary language. Singing Christmas carols in their first language (Spanish, French, Polish, or other languages) provides these children an opportunity to share with their classmates. Invite the children to teach a carol or song with or without a recording. You can search the Internet for lyrics. For Spanish speakers, recommend the album "Diciembre en México," by Donna Peña (GIA). This album includes "Noche de Paz" ("Silent Night") and other familiar Christmas songs.

• **Prepare** for the children to act out the Christmas play. If possible, have two children serve as narrators. Ask for volunteers to portray Mary, Joseph, the shepherds, the angel, and the choir of angels. Read the play once. Then distribute the costumes and props for the children to use when acting out the play.

• **Invite** the children to look at the art on pages 122 and 123. Ask: *How do you think the shepherds felt after they visited Jesus?* (Possible responses: happy, special that they were told by angels about Jesus' birth, so excited they wanted to tell their friends and families)

Quick Check

✔ *What do we celebrate during the Christmas season?* (We celebrate God's greatest gift to us, his Son, Jesus.)

✔ *What is one way we celebrate the birth of Jesus?* (We give glory to God by praying, singing, and listening to the story of the birth of Jesus.)

CONNECTION

To Liturgy

The Christmas season begins on Christmas Day and ends on the Feast of the Baptism of the Lord. During this season we gather with our parish for the celebration of Mass. We join our parish for Mass on the Sunday after Christmas Day. On that day we celebrate together the Feast of the Holy Family.

We also gather with our parish for Mass on January 1, the Solemnity of Mary, the Mother of God. We gather on the Sunday after January 1 to celebrate the Feast of the Epiphany. On this day we remember the visit of the three kings to the Child Jesus in Bethlehem.

Show the children a calendar page for December and January. Have volunteers point out the days we gather with our parish to celebrate the Mass.

The Christmas season lasts about two weeks. It begins on Christmas Day, December 25. The special color of the Christmas season is white. White is a color of light and joy. You will see this color during the celebration of the Mass.

During the Christmas season, we celebrate that Jesus is the Light of the World. He is with us now and forever.

We remember this all during the season, especially when we take part in Mass.

WE RESPOND

Decorate this banner.
Who will you share this Good News with? How will you share it?

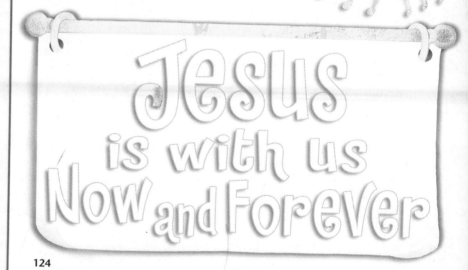

Jesus is with us Now and Forever

124

Lesson Plan

WE BELIEVE (continued)

• **Ask** a volunteer to read aloud the first paragraph on the page. Explain: *When we gather for Mass during the Christmas season, the priest wears white.*

• **Read** aloud the second paragraph. Have the children highlight or underline the first two sentences.

WE RESPOND
___ minutes

Connect to Life Remind the children: *The angel announced Jesus' birth to the shepherds. After visiting Jesus, the shepherds told their friends and family.* Stress: *God wants us to share with others that Jesus is with us now and forever.*

• **Provide** time for the children to decorate the banner. While the children are working, play a recording of inspirational Christmas music.

• **Read** the *We Respond* questions. Give the children a few minutes of quiet time to reflect on their responses. Then invite volunteers to share their responses.

✝ We Respond in Prayer

Leader: Blessed be the name of the Lord.

All: Now and for ever.

Leader: Lord our God,
we praise you for the light of creation:
the sun, the moon, and the stars of
the night.

We praise you for Jesus Christ, your Son:
he is Emmanuel, God-with-us,
the Prince of Peace,
who fills us with the wonder of
your love.

All: We praise you, Lord God.

 O Come, All Ye Faithful

O come, all ye faithful,
joyful and triumphant,
O come ye, O come ye to Bethlehem;
Come and behold him,
born the King of angels;

O come, let us adore him,
O come, let us adore him,
O come, let us adore him,
Christ, the Lord!

CHRISTMAS

125

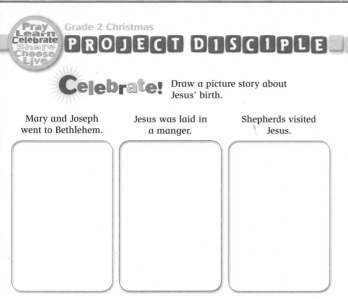

Pray Learn Celebrate Share Choose Live

Grade 2 Christmas

PROJECT DISCIPLE

Celebrate! Draw a picture story about Jesus' birth.

Mary and Joseph went to Bethlehem.	Jesus was laid in a manger.	Shepherds visited Jesus.

Pray Today

The Christmas season is a good time to bless your home.

*Lord, Creator of heaven and earth,
bless our home.
Make it a place of peace and love.
Amen.*

Take Home

Talk about ways you can fill your home with peace and love during the Christmas season.

126   www.webelieveweb.com

Chapter 14 • Christmas

We Respond in Prayer (p. 125)

Get ready by placing a Christmas crèche in the prayer space. Give a few children bells to ring three times after the all responses are prayed. Have the children gather in the prayer space. Lead them in prayer. Play "O Come, All Ye Faithful," #10 on the Grade 2 CD as background while the children are singing. Conclude the prayer by inviting the children to ring the bells three times.

📖 This Week's Liturgy

Visit **www.webelieveweb.com** for this week's liturgical readings and other seasonal material.

Project Disciple (p. 126)

Celebrate!

Reread the play on text pages 122–123. While the children are working, you may want to play inspirational Christmas music.

Pray Today

Refer to *Pray Today* on guide page 121C. Also pray to ask God to make the classroom a place of peace and love.

Take Home

Have the children suggest ways of making their homes places of peace and love during the Christmas season. Possible responses include: helping our families at mealtimes; obeying our parents; taking care of and being thankful for our gifts.

Discuss and send home copies of *Sharing Faith with My Family*, guide page 126B.

Project Disciple Additional Activities
See the activities suggested on page 121C of the guide.

125 and **126**

Name _____

Color and cut out the "Gifts from Jesus" cards. Share
them with your family during the Christmas season.

I give you trees and plants.
When you see them,
remember I want you to
grow in God's love.

I give you the animals.
When you see them or
hear them, remember I
want you to care for them.

I give you the wind.
When you hear it or feel
it, remember that the
Holy Spirit is with you.

I give you the moon and
stars. When you see them
shining, remember that I
am the Light of the World.

I give you the oceans,
rivers, and lakes. When
you see them, remember
that God shares his life
with you.

I give you stones and
rocks. When you see them
or hold them, remember
the Holy Spirit will help
you to be strong.

SHARING FAITH
with My Family

Sharing What I Learned

Look at the pictures below. Use each picture to tell your family what you learned in this chapter.

For All to See and Pray

The Christmas season is a good time to bless your home. Together with your family, pray this blessing.

Lord, Creator of heaven and earth,
   bless our home.
Make it a place of peace and love.
May all who live here bring
   the light and love of Christ
   to one another.
May we welcome visitors with joy.
May we always care for the weak
   and the poor.
We ask this through Christ
   our Lord.

Amen.

Visit Sadlier's

www.WEBELIEVEweb.com

Connect to the Catechism
For adult background and reflection,
see paragraph 526.

126B

ASSESSMENT

Unit 2 Test

Read aloud each set of test directions. Also you may choose to read aloud each test item. Wait for a minute for the children to indicate their responses in writing.

Alternative Assessment

You may want the children to complete the following alternative-assessment activity.

Make a booklet to show what you have learned about the Bible and the stories of God's forgiveness.

Additional Testing

• Unit 2 Test in Grade 2 *Assessment Book*, pages 25–26

• Unit 2 Alternative Assessment in Grade 2 *Assessment Book*, page 28

• Semester Test (Units 1–2) in Grade 2 *Assessment Book*, pages 29–30

• CD-ROM *Test Generator and Resource*: Use Unit 2 Test or customize your own.

Grade 2 Unit 2

UNIT TEST

Fill in the circle beside the correct answer.

1. God will _____ forgive us if we are sorry.
   ○ sometimes   ○ never   ● always

2. _____ is God's forgiveness of our sins by the priest in the Sacrament of Penance.
   ● Absolution   ○ Celebration   ○ Contrition

3. God's gift that allows us to make choices is _____.
   ○ penance   ● free will   ○ mercy

4. The _____ Testament is the part of the Bible about Jesus and the beginning of the Church.
   ● New   ○ Old   ○ Free

Draw a line to match the sentence parts.

5. The Act of Contrition •   • helps us to know right from wrong.

6. The Great Commandment •   • is a prayer of sorrow.

7. God's gift of conscience •   • is Jesus' teaching to love God and one another.

continued on next page   127

Grade 2 Unit 2

8. **Write a sentence to tell what you have learned about the Ten Commandments.**

   See Chapter 9, pages 85–87. _____

   _____

   _____.

9. **Look at the photograph. Write two different things that the child can choose to do.**

   The child could choose to

   wear the helmet or _____

   not wear the helmet

   _____

   _____.

10. **Circle the choice Jesus would want the child to make.**

128

---

127 and **128**

Jesus Gives Himself in the Eucharist

UNIT 3

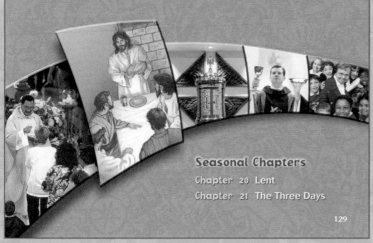

Seasonal Chapters

129

Pray Learn Celebrate Share Live

PROJECT DISCIPLE
DEAR FAMILY

In Unit 3 your child will grow as a disciple of Jesus by:

- appreciating that Jesus gave us the gift of himself at the Last Supper
- gathering at Mass to celebrate what Jesus did at the Last Supper
- listening to God's Word during the Liturgy of the Word
- recognizing that Jesus is truly present in the Eucharist
- sharing God's love and peace with others.

What's the Word?

In Chapter 15, the children hear the Scripture story of Jesus feeding the crowd of people. Read the story together from the Bible (John 6:1–14), or retell it in your own words. Point out that it was a child who offered the five barley loaves and two fish. With the loaves and fish, Jesus performed a miracle and fed thousands of people. What are some ways that children help others today? Affirm your child's talents and abilities, and suggest ways to use those talents to help others. Remind your child that we hear stories from the Bible every Sunday at Mass during the Liturgy of the Word.

Picture This

Look at the photos of the celebration of the Mass on pages 142–143. Talk about your own parish celebration of Mass. How do the people in your parish participate in the Mass? Decide on one way your family will participate more fully this Sunday.

Reality Check

"Parents have the mission of teaching their children to pray and to discover their vocation as children of God."
(Catechism of the Catholic Church, 2226)

Celebrate!

Make your next family meal a special one—maybe by serving a favorite food or dessert, or eating "picnic" style in the family room. Talk about how sharing a meal brings us closer together and how Jesus must have felt when he shared the Last Supper with his friends. Use this as an opportunity to build your child's anticipation of receiving first Holy Communion.

Make it Happen

After Mass on Sunday point out the tabernacle to your child. Pray together to Jesus in the Blessed Sacrament. As you leave the church, talk about one thing you will do together to share God's love. Do it!

Take Home

Each chapter in your child's *We Believe* Grade 2 text offers a "Take Home" activity that invites your family to support your child's journey to more fully become a disciple of Christ.

Be ready for this unit's Take Home:

Chapter 15: Preparing and sharing a family meal

Chapter 16: Participating at Mass

Chapter 17: Praying for the needs of others

Chapter 18: Presenting the gifts at Mass

Chapter 19: Promoting peace in the family

130

CLASS CONNECTION

Read aloud the unit title and the chapter titles. Ask the children: *What do you think you will be learning about in this unit?* Invite a few volunteers to respond. Then explain to the children that they will be learning about the Mass, the celebration of the Eucharist. Also have a class discussion about the photographs and illustrations on this page.

HOME CONNECTION

Project Disciple
Dear Family

Sadlier *We Believe* calls on families to become involved in:

- learning the faith
- prayer and worship
- living their faith.

Highlighting of these unit family pages and the opportunities they offer will strengthen the partnership of the Church and the home.

For additional information and activities, encourage families to visit Sadlier's

www.WeBelieveweb.com

Overview

In Chapter 12 the children learned about the celebration of the Sacrament of Penance. In this chapter the children will learn that in the Eucharist we remember and celebrate what Jesus did for us.

Doctrinal Content	For Adult Reading and Reflection *Catechism of the Catholic Church*
The children will learn:	Paragraph
• Jesus brings us life.	1401
• Jesus celebrated a special meal with his disciples.	1339
• In the Eucharist we remember and celebrate what Jesus did at the Last Supper.	1341
• The Mass is a meal and a sacrifice.	1382

Key Words

Last Supper (p. 133)
Eucharist (p. 135)
Mass (p. 135)
Holy Communion (p. 135)

Catechist Background

Go to **www.webelieveweb.com**, Catechist/Teacher, We Believe Correlations for this chapter's correlation to:
• Six Tasks of Catechesis
• Catholic Social Teaching.

How do you nourish your spiritual life?

Nourishment is a universal need of living things—as many vacationers discover when they return home to find their neglected plants wilted or even dead. In our personal lives, both our physical and spiritual needs must be nourished so that we can thrive and grow.

The Passover meal that Jesus celebrated with his disciples on Holy Thursday satisfied their physical need for food, but the meal fulfilled a spiritual dimension as well. As observant Jews, the disciples gathered to remember God's goodness and give him thanks and praise.

At the Last Supper Jesus blessed and shared bread and wine that became his Body and Blood. Each time that we gather for the eucharistic celebration, we are honoring these words of Jesus, "do this in memory of me" (Luke 22:19).

At every Mass we recall the sacrifice of Jesus when he died on the cross to save us from our sins. Through Jesus' life, Death, and Resurrection we have new life. When we receive Holy Communion, we grow in holiness. "Through the Eucharist those who live from the life of Christ are fed and strengthened." (CCC 1436) We are fed that we might, with God's grace, nourish others with the Gospel.

What difference does the Eucharist make in your life?

Lesson Planning Guide

Lesson Steps	Presentation	Materials

 WE GATHER

Lesson Steps	Presentation	Materials
page 131 ✝ **Prayer** **Focus on Life**	🎵 Pray in song to Jesus. • Discuss questions.	For prayer space: crucifix, Bible, container for wheat stalks or basket with bread and grapes 🎵 "We Remember You," Bernadette Farrell, #12, Grade 2 CD

② WE BELIEVE

page 132 *Jesus brings us life.* 📖 *John 6:2–14*	🏃 Read and dramatize the Bible story. • Read the text about Jesus, the Living Bread. 🎵 Sing the song "We Remember You."	• costumes and props for Scripture dramatization (optional) 🎵 "We Remember You," Bernadette Farrell, #12, Grade 2 CD
page 133 *Jesus celebrated a special meal with his disciples.* 📖 *Mark 14:22–24*	• Share the Bible story about the Last Supper. • Point out the *Key Word* and definition. 🏃 Write the response to the question.	• colored pencils or markers
page 134 *In the Eucharist we remember and celebrate what Jesus did at the Last Supper.*	• Present the text about the celebration of the Eucharist. 🏃 Write ways to show thanks to God.	• highlighter or crayon • writing and drawing materials
page 135 *The Mass is a meal and a sacrifice.*	• Read about and discuss the Mass as a meal and a sacrifice. • Point out the *Key Words* and definitions.	• copies of Reproducible Master 15, guide page 131C

③ WE RESPOND

page 135	• Share responses to the picture study question. • Present the *As Catholics* text.	
pages 136–137 **Project Disciple**	• Complete the **Project Disciple** activities. • Explain the *Take Home* activity. • Discuss/send home **Sharing Faith with My Family** reproducible master for this chapter.	• crayons or colored pencils • copies of **Sharing Faith with My Family** reproducible master, Chapter 15 (back of book)
page 138 **Chapter 15 Test**	• Complete **Chapter 15 Test**. • Work on *Alternative Assessment* activity.	• optional: copies of Scripture reproducible master, *What's the Word?*, Chapter 15 (back of book)

For additional ideas, activities, and opportunities: Visit Sadlier's **www.WeBelieveweb.com**

Name _____

Find the words of Jesus. Circle every third letter below. Print the letters in the empty spaces on the sign. Then color the sign.

C D (A) E F M G H T I J H

K L E M N L O P I Q R V

S T I U V N W X G Y Z B

Z Y R X W E V U A T S D

Jesus said,

"I _____ _____   _____ _____ _____

_____ _____ _____ _____ _____

_____ _____ _____ _____ _____ ."

John 6:51

PROJECT DISCIPLE

Pray
Learn
Celebrate
Share
Choose
Live

Additional Activities

What's the Word?

Scripture reproducible master, Chapter 15

Materials needed: copies of *What's the Word?* (back of book); pencils

Choose volunteers to be readers and the other characters in the story on text page 132. Have these volunteers reread the script. Then distribute copies of the reproducible master. Invite the children to write their answers on the sheet. When the children are finished writing, ask them to share their responses with the group.

Reality Check

Materials needed: drawing paper and crayons or colored pencils

Have the children brainstorm gifts that God has given us. Write each response on the board. Distribute drawing paper. Along the bottom edge of the paper, have the children print "Thank you, God." Then have the children choose from the board list five gifts for which they are most thankful. Then above the prayer words, have the children draw the five gifts. Collect the papers and put them in a folder. Place the folder in the prayer space.

Picture This

Materials needed: drawing paper, colored pencils or crayons

After you present *As Catholics*, have the children look at the altar shown in the photo on page 134 and the diagram of the sanctuary on text pages 238–239.

Visit the parish church. Have the children look at the altar. Then, when you return, ask the children to draw a picture of the altar in your parish church. Ask the children to explain what is the same about the three altars and what is different.

Pray Today

Pray with the children a short prayer for the following groups of people:

• farmers who plant and grow food we need

• people who prepare and ship food

• people who cook/bake food

• people who are hungry

• groups who help feed hungry people.

Meeting Individual Needs
English Language Learners

Children who are learning to speak English may have difficulty participating in class discussions. When possible pair each of these children with a helper who can clarify and summarize discussion points. Keep in mind that the attitude of the helper is as important as his or her skill in the English language. Assign helpers who are sensitive to the dignity of the children.

We Believe Resources

• Grade 2 *Review & Resource Book*, pages 34–36
• Grade 2 *Family Book*, pages 43–45
• Grade 2 *Assessment Book*, pages 31–32
• Grade 2 CD-ROM *Test Generator and Resource*: Use Chapter 15 Test or customize your own.

• **www.webelieveweb.com**

Enrichment Ideas

Chapter Story

Hello, my name is Anthony. A few days ago we received a package from Cousin Paula. She sent us a statue of Saint Joseph. The card said: "This is for your Saint Joseph's table this year. May God bless you all."

Let me explain what our cousin meant. Last year Cousin Paula came from Italy to visit us in the United States. She and Nana Gallo came to our house for dinner a few days before the feast of Saint Joseph, March 19. She told us how the families in her town celebrated the feast.

Cousin Paula said, "We gather to honor Saint Joseph on his feast. We ask Saint Joseph to help our families. We share a special meal. Some families invite people who are poor or lonely to celebrate with them.

"Families set up a Saint Joseph's table. On the table they put special feast-day food. Families spend a few days preparing for the meal. They make bread in the shapes of stars, angels, and other objects that remind people of the Holy Family. Families also prepare different kinds of fish and vegetables. They bake many different kinds of desserts."

When Cousin Paula was finished talking, Mom asked her to help our family prepare a special Saint Joseph's feast-day meal. My aunt, uncle, cousins, and two of Nana's neighbors shared our first Saint Joseph's Day dinner. During dessert we all agreed to have a family celebration every year. My aunt said, "Cousin Paula, please give us your recipes. I think we'll need them."

▶ *What was special about the meal Anthony's family shared?*

FAITH and MEDIA

▶ Consider videotaping the children as they act out the Scripture story.

▶ Consider using the family illustrations the children bring in, perhaps along with stories and drawings from the children's family celebration books (*Activity Bank*, page 133), to set up a family celebration bulletin board.

CHAPTER PROJECT: CELEBRATING WITH SNACKS

With the children and a few parent volunteers, plan a special snack celebration. Explain that you are going to celebrate being Jesus' disciples. Some can work on decorations. Others can work with you to plan the snack food. (Some type of bread and juice would be appropriate.) A group can write a grace to pray before the celebration. Check each group's progress leading up to the celebration.

God Gives Us the Eucharist

WE GATHER

✝ Let us thank Jesus by singing.

🎵 **We Remember You**

Jesus, we remember you.
Jesus, we remember you.
We remember you gave your
    life for us.
We remember. We believe.

We praise you, we remember you.
We bless you, we remember you,
and we thank you that we belong to you.
We remember. We believe.

☀ What special meals have you
shared with others? Why do you
like to remember them?

131

PREPARING TO PRAY

During this gathering prayer, the children will thank Jesus for giving his life for us.

• Have the children read aloud the lyrics for "We Remember You." Explain that when we gather together to pray, we remember all Jesus taught us and did for us.

• Play "We Remember You," #12 on the Grade 2 CD. Have the children practice singing.

The Prayer Space

• On the table place a crucifix, a container for wheat stalks, or a basket filled with bread and grapes. Also have a Bible opened to John 6:2–16 on the table.

 This Week's Liturgy
Visit **www.webelieveweb.com** for this week's liturgical readings and other seasonal material.

Lesson Plan

WE GATHER   ___ minutes

✝ Pray

• Ask the children to open their books to the gathering prayer. Invite the children to gather in the prayer space.

• Begin by praying the Sign of the Cross. Then sing together "We Remember You."

• If time permits, invite each child to share one thing he or she remembers about Jesus' life or teaching.

☀ Focus on Life

Encourage the children to share memories of special meals that they have shared with others. Discuss why the children like to remember these meals. Share the *Chapter Story* on guide page 131E.

Family Connection Update

Invite the children to tell their experiences about sharing what they know about the Sacrament of Penance.

Catechist Goal

• To present that in the Eucharist we remember and celebrate what Jesus said and did at the Last Supper

Our Faith Response

• To remember and appreciate Jesus' gift of himself in the Eucharist

 **Last Supper   Eucharist**

Mass

Holy Communion

Lesson Materials

• optional: costumes and props

• Grade 2 CD

• copies of Reproducible Master 15

• Scripture and Family reproducible masters (back of book)

Teaching Tip

A Drama Center

   Set aside a staging area for Scripture dramatizations or role-plays. In this area hang an old sheet or large piece of fabric to serve as a backdrop or curtain. For Scripture dramatizations, have volunteers bring in props appropriate for the story.

WE BELIEVE
Jesus brings us life.

Act out the following story.

 John 6:2–14

Reader 1: One day thousands of people were listening to Jesus. He knew that the people were hungry. Jesus asked his disciples to get food for all the people.

Philip: Jesus, we could never find enough food to feed this many people!

Andrew: There is a boy here who has five loaves of bread and two fish.

Reader 2: Jesus took the loaves and gave thanks. He asked his disciples to give out the bread and fish. There was food for everyone and some leftover.

All: What a wonderful thing Jesus has done for us!

Jesus told us, "I am the living bread that came down from heaven; whoever eats this bread will live forever." (John 6:51)

All of us need bread to live and grow.

All of us need Jesus to grow closer to God and share in God's life. Jesus is the living bread. He is the Son of God who was sent to bring us life.

Sing "We Remember You."

132

Lesson Plan

WE BELIEVE   ____ minutes

Remind the children about the crowds of people that went to see and hear Jesus teach. Explain: *Traveling was not easy and there were no roadside places to eat.*

Read the activity directions. Assign the different roles for the play about Jesus feeding many people. Give the children a few minutes to prepare their parts. Then have the actors read their parts. After the children have finished reading the play, ask: *What would you have said to or about Jesus that day?*

Read aloud John 6:51 and the last two paragraphs on page 132. Stress: *We need Jesus to grow closer to God and share in God's life.*

Invite the children to join in singing "We Remember You." The words may be found on page 131.

Direct attention to the picture on page 133. Ask the following questions:

• *Who is with Jesus?* (his disciples)

• *What are they doing together?* (sharing a meal)

Jesus celebrated a special meal with his disciples.

Every year the Jewish people celebrate the feast of Passover. During this holy time, they gather to share a special meal. At this meal they say prayers of blessing. They thank God for all he has done.

On the night before he died, Jesus was with his disciples to celebrate the Passover meal with them.

 Mark 14:22–24

During the meal Jesus took bread and said a blessing. He broke the bread and gave it to his disciples. He said, "Take it; this is my body." (Mark 14:22)

Then Jesus took a cup of wine and gave thanks. All the disciples drank from this cup. Jesus said, "This is my blood." (Mark 14:24)

The meal Jesus shared with his disciples on the night before he died is called the **Last Supper**. At this meal the bread and wine became the Body and Blood of Jesus Christ.

 Why was the Last Supper a special meal?

The bread and wine became the Body

and Blood of Jesus Christ.

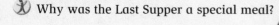

Key Word

Last Supper the meal Jesus shared with his disciples on the night before he died

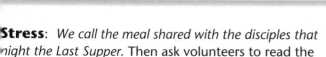

133

ACTIVITY BANK

Multiple Intelligences
Bodily-Kinesthetic
Activity Materials: costumes and props for dramatization

Help the children prepare a dramatization of Jesus feeding the people. Allow them time to practice. Invite another class or adult guests for a presentation at a later time.

Family
Family Celebration Books
Activity Materials: writing paper and drawing paper; crayons or colored pencils

Ask the children to recall a time when they shared a special family meal. Ask them to write a story about this meal, explaining why it was so special. Tell the children to include details about who was there, where they celebrated the meal, and the ways they showed their thanks to God. Then ask them to illustrate the story. Combine all the stories into one large book. Bind it together and ask volunteers to make a colorful cover for the book. Keep the book in the prayer space.

Stress: *We call the meal shared with the disciples that night the Last Supper.* Then ask volunteers to read the first two paragraphs on page 133. Ask the children to stand as you read aloud the Scripture passage.

Ask a volunteer to read the question. Have the children write their responses. Discuss the children's responses.

Quick Check

✔ *What did Jesus tell us about himself?* (He said, "I am the living bread.")

✔ *What is the last meal that Jesus shared with his disciples called?* (The Last Supper is the last meal Jesus shared with his disciples.)

✔ *What did the bread and wine blessed by Jesus become at the meal?* (The bread and wine became the Body and Blood of Jesus Christ.)

As Catholics...

The Altar

After working on these two pages, read the *As Catholics* text. Have volunteers describe the altar in your parish church. If possible, arrange a visit to the church to see the altar up close.

In the Eucharist we remember and celebrate what Jesus did at the Last Supper.

At the Last Supper Jesus told the disciples to remember what he had just done. Jesus wanted them to remember and celebrate this special meal again and again. Jesus said, "Do this in memory of me." (Luke 22:19)

The Church continues to do as Jesus asked when we celebrate the Eucharist. The **Eucharist** is the sacrament of the Body and Blood of Jesus Christ. In this sacrament, the bread and wine become the Body and Blood of Christ. This is done by the power of the Holy Spirit and through the words and actions of the priest.

The word *eucharist* means "to give thanks." When we celebrate this sacrament, we thank God the Father for his many gifts. We praise Jesus for all he has done. We ask the Holy Spirit to help us grow closer to God and others.

What can you do this week to show that you are thankful for God's gifts? Write your answer.

_____

_____

_____

_____

As Catholics...

Every Catholic church has an altar. At the altar the sacrifice of Jesus is made present. The altar is a table and it reminds us of the table of the Last Supper. From this table we receive Jesus in Holy Communion.

Think about the church where your parish community gathers for Mass. Where is the altar? What does the altar look like?

134

Lesson Plan

WE BELIEVE (continued)

Explain: *Jesus wanted his disciples to remember and celebrate the Last Supper again.* Stress: *We do this when we celebrate the Eucharist.*

Ask a volunteer to read aloud the first two paragraphs on page 134. Have the children highlight or underline the last three sentences of the second paragraph.

Write the word *eucharist* on the board. Explain that the word means "to give thanks." Have a volunteer read the third paragraph on page 134.

Invite the children to do the activity on page 134. If some children are having difficulty, suggest the following: *pray; take care of God's gifts; share God's gifts with others.* Encourage volunteers to share what they have written. Then talk together about the gifts God has given us and the ways to thank God for these gifts.

Explain: *Another name for the celebration of the Sacrament of the Eucharist is the Mass.* Write on the board: *The Mass is a meal.* Read aloud the first paragraph on page 135.

The Mass is a meal and a sacrifice.

Another name for the celebration of the Eucharist is the **Mass**. The Mass is a meal. During the Mass we remember what Jesus did at the Last Supper. The bread and wine become the Body and Blood of Christ. **Holy Communion** is receiving the Body and Blood of Christ. Holy Communion makes the life of God within us stronger.

The Mass is a sacrifice. A *sacrifice* is an offering of a gift to God. The word *offer* means "to give" or "to present." Jesus offered the greatest sacrifice of all time. He died to bring us new life. At every Mass we remember Jesus' sacrifice.

Key Words

Eucharist the sacrament of the Body and Blood of Jesus Christ

Mass the celebration of the Eucharist

Holy Communion receiving the Body and Blood of Christ

When we take part in the Mass, we remember and celebrate that:

- Jesus offered his life for us on the cross. He died to save us from sin.
- Jesus rose to new life so that we could live happily with God forever.
- Jesus gives us his own Body and Blood in Holy Communion.

WE RESPOND

Look at the pictures. What can each picture help you to remember about the Mass?

135

ACTIVITY BANK

Curriculum Connection
Art

Activity Materials: drawing paper, crayons, colored pencils, or markers, Grade 2 CD

Have the children draw pictures to illustrate the lyrics for "We Remember You." (See page 131.) While the children are working, play the recording, #12 on the Grade 2 CD.

Catholic Social Teaching
Option for the Poor and Vulnerable

Explain that one way children can prepare to receive Holy Communion for the first time is to help those in need. Each week during the time of preparation ask the children to think of ways they can help others. Choose one act that the children can do together and write it on the board. Some possible acts: showing respect for people who are different from you; preparing a basket of foodstuffs; collecting money to give to poor families.

Write on the board: *The Mass is a sacrifice.* Then read aloud the second paragraph on page 135. Then together read aloud the list of what we remember and celebrate at Mass.

Ask a volunteer to read the words and their definitions in the *Key Words* box. Ask: *How are the words related to one another?* (We receive Holy Communion during the Mass, and Mass is another name for the Eucharist.)

WE RESPOND _____ minutes

Connect to Life Have the children look at the pictures as you read the *We Respond* question. Ask volunteers to share their responses.

Invite the children to gather in the prayer space. Sing together "We Remember You." Give each child a copy of Reproducible Master 15. Have the children work on the activity now or work on it at home. (Jesus' words: "I am the living bread.")

Catechist Goal

- To review the chapter ideas that are key to growing as disciples of Jesus Christ

Our Faith Response

- To decide on ways to grow as disciples by living out what we have learned

Show What *you* Know

Help the children read the clues and complete the *Key Word* cards. When all have completed the activity, check the answers.

Pray Today

Read the prayer together. Suggest that the children decorate the frame by drawing their favorite foods.

Reality Check

Children can check any or all items. Discuss other ways that they and their families can help others who are in need of food: find out more about helping organizations who have food or fund drives; Be respectful when helping others.

Make *it* Happen

If time permits, review the *We Believe* paragraphs on page 135.

Take Home

Encourage the children to work with their families on planning a special meal.

Discuss and send home copies of *Sharing Faith with My Family* reproducible master for this chapter (back of book).

 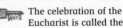 Grade 2 Chapter 15

PROJECT

Show What *you* Know Fill in each Key Word card.

The meal that Jesus shared with his disciples on the night before he died is the **Last Supper**	The sacrament of the Body and Blood of Jesus Christ is the **Eucharist**
Receiving the Body and Blood of Christ is **Holy Communion**	The celebration of the Eucharist is called the **Mass**

Pray Today

This prayer is called *Grace Before Meals.* You can pray it before you enjoy a meal.

Decorate the frame.

Pray this prayer with your family and friends.

> *Bless us, O Lord, and these your gifts which we are about to receive from your goodness, through Christ, our Lord. Amen.*

136 www.webelieveweb.com

DISCIPLE

Reality Check

In the Bible, we read that Jesus fed many hungry people. We can follow Jesus' example. Check the ways that you and your family can help other families who are hungry.

- ☑ Give to food collections
- ☑ Try not to waste food
- ☑ Help out at your parish soup kitchen
- ☑ Pray for those people who are hungry

PARISH KITCHEN

- ❑ Another way: _____

Make *it* Happen

Before Mass, talk with your family. Explain that the Mass is a meal and a sacrifice.

Take Home

This week, make one of your family meals a special celebration. Together, plan the menu and decorations.

Menu

_____

_____

Decorations

_____

_____

Ask each family member to help prepare for the meal in some way. Then, before your meal, pray the *Grace Before Meals.*

137

CHAPTER TEST

Use the words in the box to complete the sentences.

1. The word *eucharist* means to
   _____give thanks_____.

2. The _____Mass_____ is the celebration of the Eucharist.

3. Jesus wants us to ____remember____ and celebrate what he did at the Last Supper.

4. The Mass is a _____meal_____ and a sacrifice.

5. A ____sacrifice____ is an offering of a gift to God.

6. ___Holy Communion___ is receiving the Body and Blood of Christ.

> remember
>
> meal
>
> sacrifice
>
> Mass
>
> give thanks
>
> Holy Communion

7–8. What did Jesus do at the Last Supper?

He gave us the gift of his Body and Blood.

9–10. What do we remember and celebrate at every Mass?

We remember and celebrate what Jesus did at the Last Supper.

138

CHAPTER TEST

Provide ten to fifteen minutes for the students to complete the test. After all have finished, check the answers. Clarify any misconceptions.

Alternative Assessment

You may want the students to complete the following alternative-assessment activity.

> *Find a creative way to share with others that the Mass is:*
> - *a sacrifice*
> - *a meal*
> - *a memory of Jesus.*

Additional Testing

• Chapter 15 Test in *Assessment Book*, pages 31–32

• CD-ROM *Test Generator and Resource*: Use Chapter 15 Test or customize your own.

Review

Review the definitions as they are presented in the chapter's *Key Word* boxes:

- Last Supper (page 133)
- Eucharist (page 135)
- Mass (page 135)
- Holy Communion (page 135).

We Believe Statements

Review the four statements.

- Jesus brings us life.
- Jesus celebrated a special meal with his disciples.
- In the Eucharist we remember and celebrate what Jesus did at the Last Supper.
- The Mass is a meal and a sacrifice.

To use the Chapter 15 Study Guide, visit

www.webelieveweb.com

138

Chapter 16 — We Gather for the Celebration of the Eucharist

Overview

In Chapter 15 the children learned that the Mass is both a sacrifice and a meal. In this chapter the children will learn that at Mass we are united to Jesus Christ and one another.

Doctrinal Content	For Adult Reading and Reflection *Catechism of the Catholic Church*
The children will learn:	Paragraph
• We are united to Jesus Christ and to one another.	1348
• The Church celebrates the Mass.	1368
• The parish gathers for the celebration of Mass.	1389
• When Mass begins, we praise God and ask for his forgiveness.	2643

Key Word

assembly (p. 142)

Go to **www.webelieveweb.com**, Catechist/ Teacher, We Believe Correlations for this chapter's correlation to:
• Six Tasks of Catechesis
• Catholic Social Teaching.

Catechist Background

How does the Eucharist strengthen you?

As a young child you probably began to go to Mass on Sunday. It was an automatic thing; you hardly even thought about it. Besides, how could you think about Mass when its meaning was such a mystery?

As adults, we gain insight into the meaning of Mass by reading Chapter 15 of Saint John's Gospel. There we learn that Jesus is the vine; we, the Church, are the branches. In sacred art wheat and a vine are used to symbolize the Eucharist. The vine signifies the union we have through Jesus. During the eucharistic celebration, we announce our union with Christ and with one another each time we hear, "The Lord is with you," and we say, "And also with you."

When we gather for Mass, we also acknowledge our sinfulness and seek God's forgiveness and mercy. Knowing that we are weak, we seek the strength of Jesus in the Eucharist so that we can become more like him.

Saint Paul emphasized our union with Jesus. When he wrote to the Christians at Corinth, he challenged them, "Examine yourselves to see whether you are living in faith. Test yourselves. Do you not realize that Jesus Christ is in you?" (2 Corinthians 13:5).

Perhaps the challenge of Mass is not so much the mystery of its meaning but the mystery of being transformed into Jesus. If we were to test ourselves as Saint Paul suggests, would we find ourselves living in faith?

In your words and deeds are you becoming more like Jesus?

Lesson Planning Guide

Lesson Steps	Presentation	Materials

① WE GATHER

page 139 ✝ **Prayer** 📖 *Matthew 18:20* ☀ **Focus on Life**	• Listen to Scripture. • Respond in prayer. • Discuss groups to which the children belong.	• prayer space items: vine plant, tablecloth, Bible, statue or picture of Jesus

② WE BELIEVE

page 140 *We are united to Jesus Christ and to one another.*	• Discuss being united to Jesus as a vine to a branch. 🧍 Do the activity and share responses to the question.	• crayons or colored pencils
page 141 *The Church celebrates the Mass.*	• Read about gathering to celebrate the Mass. 🧍 Share ways to live Sunday as the Lord's Day. • Read and discuss the *As Catholics* text.	• pencils
page 142 *The parish gathers for the celebration of Mass.*	• Present who takes part in the celebration of Mass. 🧍 Reflect and respond to the questions about Mass participation.	• copies of Reproducible Master 16, guide page 139C
page 143 *When Mass begins, we praise God and ask for his forgiveness.* *The Roman Missal*	• Present what happens when Mass begins.	🎵 "God Is Here!" Carey Landry, #13, Grade 2 CD • highlighter or crayon

③ WE RESPOND

page 143	🧍 Do the *We Respond* activity. 🎵 Pray by singing.	
pages 144–145 **Project Disciple**	• Complete the **Project Disciple** activities. • Explain the *Take Home* activity. • Discuss/send home **Sharing Faith with My Family** reproducible master for this chapter.	• crayons or colored pencils • copies of **Sharing Faith with My Family** reproducible master, Chapter 16 (back of book)
page 146 **Chapter 16 Test**	• Complete **Chapter 16 Test**. • Work on *Alternative Assessment* activity.	• optional: copies of Scripture reproducible master, *What's the Word?*, Chapter 16 (back of book)

For additional ideas, activities, and opportunities: Visit Sadlier's **www.WeBelieveweb.com**

139B

Name _____

When celebrating Mass, priests and deacons wear special clothes called vestments.

A priest wears a long, white robe that is called an alb.

Over the alb the priest wears a stole.

Over the stole the priest wears a chasuble.

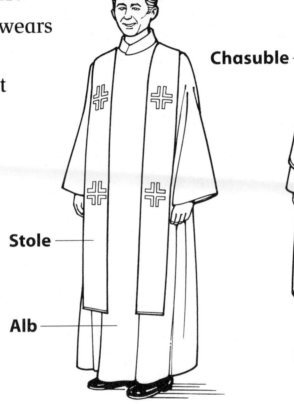

Chasuble

Stole

Alb

Stole

Alb

When a deacon is present at Mass, he wears an alb and a stole that stretches from his left shoulder to his right side.

What season of the Church year are you celebrating now? Color the priest's stole and chasuble the color of the season. If it is the Christmas season or Easter season, color the neckline and center of the chasuble gold.

PROJECT DISCIPLE

Pray
Learn
Celebrate
Share
Choose
Live

Additional Activities

What's the Word?

Scripture reproducible master, Chapter 16

Materials needed: copies of *What's the Word?* (back of book); crayons or colored pencils

Distribute copies of the Scripture reproducible master. Explain that the Jewish People prayed this psalm often when they gathered together to worship God and that we still pray these words sometimes when we gather for Mass.

Have the children form two groups: Groups A and B. Read the psalm once. Then have the children gather in the prayer space, having Group A stand to one side and Group B to another side. Pray the psalm. Then if time permits, have the children draw illustrations for the verses to the right of the words.

Show What you Know

Have the children look at text page 143. Then do a role-play of the assembly participating in the beginning part of the Mass (the Introductory Rites). It may be helpful at first for you to take the part of the priest.

Question Corner

Ask the children to write their response to the following question: *What is special about gathering with your parish on Sunday?* After the children have finished writing, invite volunteers to share their responses.

What Would you do?

Assign the children to small groups. Give the groups about seven minutes to discuss the following situation. Then ask the groups to share with others what the members decided Luke should do.

Luke likes to sing the hymns at Mass. His cousin Paula went to church with Luke's family last Sunday. After Mass, Paula made fun of Luke's singing. What do you think Luke should do?

Meeting Individual Needs
Children with Auditory Needs

Seat children with auditory needs where they can see as much of the group as possible. While speaking, avoid facing away from the children. If the children sign, ask them to share with the group how they sign the Mass responses.

We Believe Resources

- Grade 2 *Review & Resource Book*, pages 37–39
- Grade 2 *Family Book*, pages 46–48
- Grade 2 *Assessment Book*, pages 33–34
- Grade 2 CD-ROM *Test Generator and Resource*: Use Chapter 16 Test or customize your own.
- **www.webelieveweb.com**

Enrichment Ideas

Chapter Story

Roberto's sister, Maris, is in fifth grade. Almost every day after school Maris talks and laughs with her friend Patrice. Last Tuesday afternoon Roberto was surprised when he got home from school. Maris was very serious as she walked back and forth in the kitchen. She was carrying a broom, and Patrice was walking behind her.

Roberto asked, "What are you two doing? Last week you told me you were too old to play games. Now you look like you're playing one."

Maris answered, "Well, for your information, little brother, we are not playing a game. I'm going to be one of the altar servers for the Saturday evening Mass. I'm going to carry the cross when Mass begins. Patrice is helping me to practice."

Dad was standing by the sink. He said, "Roberto, don't make fun of your sister. Saturday will be the first time she is serving. She's going to practice during the week, and we're going to help her."

On Wednesday night Roberto helped Maris. He timed her to see how long she could stand without fidgeting. On Thursday night Roberto listened as their dad read the Mass prayers and Maris said the responses. Roberto knew some of the responses and said them aloud with Maris.

After Mass on Saturday night, Maris met Roberto and their dad outside. She said, "Thanks for all your help. And guess what, Roberto? Father Perez said I did so well tonight that I can be one of the altar servers for Mass on your first Holy Communion Day!"

▶ *Would you like to be an altar server? Why?*

FAITH and MEDIA

▶ After discussing the questions on page 142, you might mention that some television stations provide broadcasts of the Mass for those who cannot attend.

▶ Use "God Is Here," #13 on the Grade 2 CD to begin a discussion about singing as a form of prayer. Consider extending the discussion to music as a medium. What sort of music do we listen to or sing in our daily lives? What sort of messages do we get and send as we play and sing our favorite songs? How do different kinds of music make us feel?

CHAPTER PROJECT: VISIT TO CHURCH

Arrange to take the children to church. Ask a parish priest to show the children the altar, the ambo (also called the lectern), and the books used at Mass: the Sacramentary, the Lectionary, and the Book of the Gospels. Ask the priest to show the children the vestments he wears and the sacred vessels he uses at Mass.

When the children have returned to the classroom, have them draw pictures and write about their visit. Ask the children to share their work.

We Gather for the Celebration of the Eucharist 16

WE GATHER

✝ **Leader:** Join hands to form a circle. Let us listen to God's Word.

Reader: Jesus said, "For where two or three are gathered in my name, there am I in the midst of them." (Matthew 18:20)

Leader: Jesus, we gather in your name. Together we thank God our Father for his many gifts.

All: God our Father, we thank you.

Leader: Jesus, we gather in your name. Together we praise you for all you have done for us.

All: God the Son, we praise you.

Leader: Jesus, we gather in your name. Together we ask the Holy Spirit to help us to grow closer to God and to others.

All: God the Holy Spirit, help us.

Think of groups to which you belong. When do you gather? What do you do together?

139

PREPARING TO PRAY

Children gather to pray in Jesus' name.

• Choose a prayer leader and a reader. Give them time to prepare for the prayer.

The Prayer Space
• In the space place a plant that has a vine, branches, and leaves.

• Cover the prayer table with a tablecloth. On the table place the Bible and a picture or statue of Jesus.

This Week's Liturgy
Visit www.webelieveweb.com for this week's liturgical readings and other seasonal material.

Lesson Plan

WE GATHER ___ minutes

✝ Pray

• Invite the children to gather in the prayer space.

• Ask the leader to begin praying. Pause briefly to give children time to form a circle.

• Have the reader stand in the center of the circle to read Jesus' words. Then continue praying.

Focus on Life

• Read aloud the directive and question. Allow time for reflection. Then ask volunteers to share the group activities in which they participate.

Family Connection Update
Invite volunteers to share their experiences of their families' meal celebrations.

Catechist Goal

• To explain that Jesus unites us, especially in our parish celebration of Mass

Our Faith Response

• To know ways in which we can participate at Mass as fully as possible

 assembly

Lesson Materials

• crayons or colored pencils
• copies of Reproducible Master 16
• Grade 2 CD
• Scripture and Family reproducible masters (back of book)

As Catholics...

Mass Obligation

After you have presented the material on these two pages, read aloud the *As Catholics* text. You may want to tell the children that Christmas is a holy day of obligation. Also explain that there are five other holy days that we celebrate in the United States. The children will learn about these holy days at a later time.

WE BELIEVE

We are united to Jesus Christ and to one another.

At the Last Supper, Jesus told his disciples that he would always be with them. He also told them to stay close to him and to one another. He said, "I am the vine, you are the branches." (John 15:5) He told them that they were joined to him and one another as branches are joined to a vine.

Jesus wanted his disciples to work and pray together. He wanted them to share God's love with the whole world.

We are Jesus' disciples, too. Jesus is with us always. When we celebrate the Sacrament of the Eucharist, Jesus is with us in a special way. He gives himself to us. We receive the bread and wine that have become the Body and Blood of Christ. Holy Communion unites us to Jesus and to one another. Jesus is the vine and we are the branches.

Write Jesus' name on the vine. Write your name on a branch. How can you stay close to Jesus?

140

Lesson Plan

WE BELIEVE

___ minutes

Read aloud the *We Believe* statement. Remind the children that Jesus used everyday things to teach important concepts. Explain: *He told people about a plant's vine to teach that we are joined to him and to each other.* Then have volunteers read the three paragraphs on page 140.

Follow the directions for the activity. Then ask volunteers to share responses to the question. Remind the children that we are able to stay close to Jesus by praying to him and by sharing his love with others.

Remind children of the third commandment: *Remember to keep holy the Lord's Day.* Explain: *For us every Sunday is the Lord's Day.* Ask a volunteer to read aloud the first two paragraphs on page 141.

Read together the list of what we do when we gather for Mass.

Have the children complete the activity. Invite the children to share ideas in response to the question.

The Church celebrates the Mass.

Sunday is a special day. It is also called the *Lord's Day* because Jesus Christ rose to new life on this day. Every Sunday Catholics gather in their parishes for the celebration of the Mass.

The Mass is the greatest way to worship God. This is why the Church tells us to take part in the Mass every Sunday of the year. We can also celebrate the Sunday Mass on Saturday evening.

During Mass we gather to:
• praise and thank God
• listen to God's Word
• remember Jesus' life, Death, and Resurrection
• celebrate Jesus' gift of himself in the Eucharist.

At the end of Mass we are sent out to live as Jesus taught us.

As Catholics...

One of the laws of the Church is that we participate in the Mass every Sunday and on other special days. These other special days are called *holy days of obligation*. An obligation is a requirement. In many places, Mass is celebrated each day of the week. We are invited to take part in Mass every day. How does taking part in the Mass help us to live as Jesus taught us?

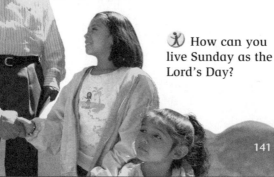

How can you live Sunday as the Lord's Day?

141

ACTIVITY BANK

Multicultural Connection
Churches Around the World
Activity Materials: resource books, magazines for churches around the world

Help the children find pictures of different parish churches around the world. As the children look at these different places of worship, point out the differences due to the location of the church and the cultural influences. Then be sure to emphasize: *These are all places to worship God; no one church is superior to another. Jesus loves us and will be with us where two or more are gathered in his name.*

Quick Check

✔ *How are we all united to one another?* (We are united with one another through Jesus Christ.)

✔ *Why is Sunday a special day?* (It is the Lord's Day. Jesus Christ rose to new life on this day.)

✔ *What is the greatest way to worship God?* (The Mass is the greatest way to worship God.)

Teaching Tip

Games As Learning Tools

Help the children remember the important points they are learning by playing games based on familiar game shows. For example, for one game set up categories (parts of the Mass, people we are learning about, prayers). Have the children provide questions for given answers in each category.

The parish gathers for the celebration of Mass.

The community of people who join together for the celebration of the Mass is called the **assembly**. We are part of the assembly. The assembly gives thanks and praise to God throughout the Mass. A priest leads the assembly in this celebration.

Sometimes a deacon takes part in the celebration of the Mass. The deacon reads the Gospel and prays some special prayers. He also helps the priest at the altar.

The priest offers our prayers to God. He does what Jesus did at the Last Supper.

Altar servers do many things to help the priest and deacon. Readers read the first two Bible readings. Extraordinary ministers of Holy Communion help give out Holy Communion. After Mass, they may bring Holy Communion to those who are not able to be at Mass.

 What can you do to participate at Mass now? What can you do to participate at Mass as you get older?

Key Word

assembly the community of people who join together for the celebration of the Mass

142

Lesson Plan

WE BELIEVE (continued)

Ask a volunteer to read aloud the *We Believe* statement on page 142. Write the word *assembly* on the board. Explain: *The assembly is the community who have joined together for the celebration of Mass.* Read aloud the first paragraph. If time permits, have the children draw their families as part of the assembly at Mass.

Invite volunteers to read the remaining paragraphs on page 142.

Distribute Reproducible Master 16. Explain: *At Mass priests and deacons wear special clothes called vestments.* On the board write the names of the vestments. Explain: *The color of the priest's stole and chasuble is the color of the Church season.* Have the children identify the current Church season. Then have them color the priest's stole and chasuble.

Discuss together the questions on page 142. Explain: *Each person participates at Mass in different ways.* Name some forms of participation children may have now or in the future. (Note that now they may sing in a children's choir or help their parents to welcome people to the celebration.)

Read together the *We Believe* statement at the top of page 143. Stress: *It is important that we take part in the celebration of Mass.* Then have a volunteer read the first paragraph. Read together the list of ways we take part in the beginning of Mass.

When Mass begins, we praise God and ask for his forgiveness.

When we join together at Mass, we show God our love and thanks. The beginning of the Mass unites us as members of the Church. It prepares us to hear God's Word and to celebrate the Eucharist. Here are the ways we take part as Mass begins.

Read Along

- We greet one another.

- We stand and sing to praise God as a community. The priest, deacon, and others helping at Mass walk to the altar.

- We pray the Sign of the Cross.

- The priest prays,

    "The Lord be with you."
    We respond,
    "And ~~also with you~~." *with your spirits*

- We ask God and one another for forgiveness.

- We ask for God's mercy. We pray with the priest:

    "Lord, have mercy. *may*
    Christ, have mercy.
    Lord, have mercy."

- We praise God by praying:

    "Glory to God in the highest, and peace to ~~his~~ people ~~on earth~~." *of good will*

- The priest says an opening prayer. We respond, "Amen."

WE RESPOND

What are some ways you take part in the beginning of the Mass? Highlight or underline the words we pray.

🎵 God Is Here!

God is here! Come, let us celebrate!
God is here! Let us rejoice!
God is here! Come, let us celebrate!
God is here! Let us rejoice!

143

ACTIVITY BANK

Parish
Thanking Altar Servers
Activity Materials: drawing paper; crayons, markers, or colored pencils

Find out who is in charge of your parish's altar servers. Ask this coordinator how many altar servers are in your parish.

Have the children fold 8½-in. by 11-in. sheets of drawing paper to make cards. On the board write the following message: *Thank you for helping us celebrate the Eucharist.* Ask the children to copy the message on the inside part of the card. Then ask them to draw a picture on the card cover. Some children may make two cards to have a sufficient number for all the altar servers.

When the cards are finished, collect them and give them to the altar-server coordinator to give to each server.

WE RESPOND   ___ minutes

Connect to Life   Discuss the *We Respond* question.

Point out the prayers "Lord, have mercy" and "Glory to God." Have the children highlight or underline these prayers and the other responses.

You may want to help the children make their Mass booklets, pages 241–244. Review the prayers they have learned in this chapter. You may want to refer the children to the booklet throughout this unit.

Pray   Play "God Is Here!," #13 on the Grade 2 CD. Have the children sing this song of praise. Explain that this song may be sung at the beginning of Mass.

Catechist Goal

• To review the chapter ideas that are key to growing as disciples of Jesus Christ

Our Faith Response

• To decide on ways to grow as disciples by living out what we have learned

Show What *you* Know

Help the children unscramble the *Key Word*. Suggest that the children include themselves in their drawings of the assembly.

Picture This

When the children have completed the web, ask volunteers to share their responses. Then remind the group how important it is to participate at Mass. Have the children highlight or underline the verbs, action words in the web: listen, celebrate, praise, remember.

Make *it* Happen

Read the paragraph. Then discuss with the children different ways to greet people at Mass.

Fast Facts

If possible, use the computer in the classroom to show the children how to find Latin Hall at **www.weliveourfaith.com**.

Take Home

Encourage the children to work with their families to complete the activity.

Discuss and send home copies of *Sharing Faith with My Family* reproducible master for this chapter (back of book).

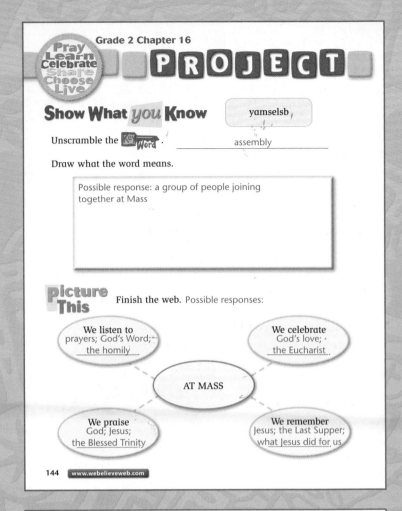

Grade 2 Chapter 16

PROJECT

Pray Learn Celebrate Share Choose Live

Show What *you* Know

yamselsb

Unscramble the Key Word. _____ assembly

Draw what the word means.

Possible response: a group of people joining together at Mass

Picture This

Finish the web. Possible responses:

We listen to prayers; God's Word; the homily

We celebrate God's love; the Eucharist

AT MASS

We praise God; Jesus; the Blessed Trinity

We remember Jesus; the Last Supper; what Jesus did for us

144   www.webelieveweb.com

DISCIPLE

Pray Learn Celebrate Share Choose Live

Make *it* Happen

In many parishes, there are people who welcome us to the celebration of Mass. These people greet us as we enter the church. Their words help us to feel welcome and to know that we belong to the Church. We should greet one another, too. Greeting one another is a good way to prepare for the celebration of the Eucharist. What is one way you will greet someone at the celebration of Mass this Sunday? Possible responses: smile; shake hands; say hello; be friendly

Fast Facts

For many years, the Church celebrated Mass only in the Latin language. Today, some parishes offer Latin Masses.

↳ **DISCIPLE CHALLENGE** Go to Latin Hall at **www.weliveourfaith.com**. Listen to the Sign of the Cross in Latin.

Take Home

This Sunday, pay close attention to what happens at Mass. Talk about what your family does to take part in Mass. Write one thing on each line below.

Possible responses: listen to

God's Word; pray; receive

Holy Communion

145

CHAPTER TEST

Check the things we do at the beginning of Mass.

1. ____ We receive Holy Communion.

2. _✔_ We ask God for forgiveness.

3. _✔_ We stand and sing.

4. _✔_ We prepare to hear God's Word.

Fill in the circle beside the correct answer.

5. It is important for _____ in the assembly to take part in the celebration of Mass.
   ○ only children   ● each person

6. Glory to God is a prayer of _____.
   ● praise   ○ sorrow

7. The _____ leads the assembly at Mass.
   ● priest   ○ deacon

8. The beginning of Mass _____ us as members of the Church.
   ○ divides   ● unites

9–10. Write two reasons Catholics gather for Mass every Sunday.

Possible responses: to praise and thank God; to listen to God's Word; to remember and celebrate Jesus' life, Death, and Resurrection; to celebrate Jesus' gift of himself in the Eucharist

---

CHAPTER TEST

Provide ten to fifteen minutes for the students to complete the test. After all have finished, check the answers. Clarify any misconceptions.

Alternative Assessment

You may want the students to complete the following alternative-assessment activity.

Begin to make a Mass booklet. Draw pictures and write sentences to tell what we do as Mass begins. You will add to your booklet in the next three chapters.

Additional Testing

• Chapter 16 Test in *Assessment Book*, pages 33–34

• CD-ROM *Test Generator and Resource*: Use Chapter 16 Test or customize your own.

Review

Review the definition as it is presented in the chapter's *Key Word* box:

• assembly (page 142).

We Believe Statements

Review the four statements.

• We are united to Jesus Christ and to one another.

• The Church celebrates the Mass.

• The parish gathers for the celebration of Mass.

• When Mass begins, we praise God and ask for forgiveness.

To use the Chapter 16 Study Guide, visit

www.webelieveweb.com

Overview

In Chapter 16, the children learned that we are united to Christ and one another at Mass. In this chapter the children will learn that the Liturgy of the Word is an integral part of the Mass.

Doctrinal Content	For Adult Reading and Reflection *Catechism of the Catholic Church*
The children will learn:	Paragraph
• We listen to God's Word during the Liturgy of the Word...... 1349	
• We listen and respond to readings from the Old Testament and the New Testament.......... 1349	
• We listen as the Gospel is proclaimed................... 1349	
• Together we pray the Creed and the Prayer of the Faithful.............................. 197	

Key Words

Liturgy of the Word (p. 149)
psalm (p. 149)
homily (p. 150)

Catechist Background

How does listening to the Word of God influence your life?

Have you ever listened to a public speech and discussed it with a friend afterward? Each person usually hears it a little differently because each person's history influences the hearing.

When we gather at Mass to hear a public proclamation of the Word of God, we bring our own histories with us. As we mature, our understanding of Scripture deepens, and we can gain new insights into the readings. We need to open our minds and hearts to truly hear what God is saying to us at this moment of our lives.

In the Old Testament readings, we hear God's Words to his people Israel. We listen to discover how these words remind us of our own lives and the way God calls us to live. In the readings from the New Testament, we learn the Good News of Jesus Christ. We hear about the events of his life. We read about the first followers of Jesus and their understanding of Jesus and his teachings.

Go to **www.webelieveweb.com**, Catechist/Teacher, We Believe Correlations for this chapter's correlation to:
• Six Tasks of Catechesis
• Catholic Social Teaching.

The reading of the Gospel prepares us to accept Jesus more deeply into our lives. As Saint John explains, "these are written that you may [come to] believe that Jesus is the Messiah, the Son of God, and that through this belief you may have life in his name" (John 20:31). By listening to the Gospel we see Jesus more clearly and allow him to influence our thoughts and actions. The same Holy Spirit, who guided the authors of Scripture, helps us to listen carefully and to live as followers of Jesus.

How will you respond to God's Word?

Lesson Planning Guide

Lesson Steps	Presentation	Materials

1 WE GATHER

page 147 ✝ **Prayer** ☀ **Focus on Life**	🎵 Pray to Jesus in song. • Listen to Scripture. • Discuss the question about listening.	• prayer space items: illustrations of Bible stories, Bible 🎵 "Alleluia, We Will Listen," Paul Inwood, #14, Grade 2 CD

2 WE BELIEVE

page 148 *We listen to God's Word during the Liturgy of the Word.*	• Read and discuss the text about the Liturgy of the Word. 🏃 Unscramble the letters to complete the sentence.	• colored pencils, crayons or markers
page 149 *We listen and respond to readings from the Old Testament and the New Testament.* *The Roman Missal*	• Present the text. • Point out the *Key Words* and definitions. 🏃 Discuss ways we can prepare for the readings at Mass. • Read and discuss the *As Catholics* text.	• large sheet of white paper
page 150 *We listen as the Gospel is proclaimed.* *The Roman Missal*	• Read the text and discuss what we do when the Gospel is proclaimed. 🏃 Share ways we show we are ready to listen to Jesus Christ's Good News.	
page 151 *Together we pray the Creed and the Prayer of the Faithful.* *The Roman Missal*	• Present the text about the Creed and the Prayer of the Faithful. • Work on Reproducible Master 17.	• copies of Reproducible Master 17, guide page 147C

3 WE RESPOND

page 151	🏃 Do the *We Respond* activity. • Reflect on the *We Respond* question.	
pages 152–153 **Project Disciple**	• Complete the **Project Disciple** activities. • Explain the *Take Home* activity. • Discuss/send home **Sharing Faith with My Family** reproducible master for this chapter.	• crayons or colored pencils • copies of **Sharing Faith with My Family** reproducible master, Chapter 17 (back of book)
page 154 **Chapter 17 Test**	• Complete **Chapter 17 Test**. • Work on *Alternative Assessment* activity.	• optional: copies of Scripture reproducible master, *What's the Word?*, Chapter 17 (back of book)

For additional ideas, activities, and opportunities: Visit Sadlier's **www.WeBelieveweb.com**

Name _____

Find the following words hidden in the puzzle.
Use two words in a sentence about the Liturgy of
the Word. Write the sentence below the puzzle.

listen
sing

homily
Gospel

psalm
Creed

g p s a l m b z
o a e i o u w c
s i n g j x b r
p c e h k m n e
e h o m i l y e
l i s t e n o d

_____

_____

PROJECT DISCIPLE

Pray
Learn
Celebrate
Share
Choose
Live

Additional Activities

More *to* Explore

Have the children turn to the diagram of the church on page 238–239 of their texts. Draw attention to #6. Explain that this stand is called the ambo or pulpit. It is the place where the Word of God is proclaimed.

If possible, visit the parish church. Point out the ambo. Also invite a reader from your parish to speak to the children about their experiences of sharing God's Word with all gathered for Mass.

Make *it* Happen

Materials needed: drawing paper, colored pencils or crayons

Have the children work in pairs to design screen savers that proclaim a Gospel message. Brainstorm some messages that they would like to share with others. After some ideas have been recorded, invite the pairs to work on pictorial images that will invite others to read the messages. When the children are finished, display the screen savers in the prayer space.

What's *the* Word?

Scripture reproducible master, Chapter 17

Materials needed: copies of *What's the Word?* (back of book); optional—props and costumes for dramatization

Distribute copies of the Scripture reproducible master. Choose volunteers to be the narrator, readers, and Martha. Have other volunteers mime the actions of the people in the story as the script is being read.

What Would *you* do?

Reread the story of Jesus' visit to Martha and Mary on the Scripture reproducible master. Have the children put themselves in Martha's place after Jesus spoke to her. Discuss: *What should you do now?* Then have the children role-play the story, including what your group decides Martha should do. Encourage the students to conclude that it might be helpful for Martha to sit and listen to Jesus.

Meeting Individual Needs
Children with Special Needs

Try to see children with special needs as providing you with opportunities for you to help them to do their best. Focus on the opportunities rather than the challenges these children present.

We Believe Resources

• Grade 2 *Review & Resource Book*, pages 40–42

• Grade 2 *Family Book*, pages 49–51

• Grade 2 *Assessment Book*, pages 35–36

• Grade 2 CD-ROM *Test Generator and Resource*: Use Chapter 17 Test or customize your own.

• **www.webelieveweb.com**

Enrichment Ideas

Chapter Story

When Alyssa was finished talking to her Grandma, she was excited. Her grandmother had called to invite her family for the holiday. Alyssa likes to visit Grandma and Grandpa Robicheaux. Grandpa always had many stories to tell Alyssa and all her cousins.

After every holiday meal, Grandpa Ro sat in his favorite chair. Alyssa and her cousins all sat on the floor around him. They listened to Grandpa tell stories about people who lived long ago. He told funny stories about Alyssa's mom and aunts and uncles. He even told stories about when he was growing up. These stories about Grandpa were Alyssa's favorites. Grandpa Ro told them what it was like before there were microwave ovens, video games, cell phones, and computers. He told them about doing dances like the twist and the mashed potatoes. After one holiday dinner, Grandpa and Grandma taught the children how to do these dances.

Alyssa has learned a lot about her family because she has listened to Grandpa Ro's stories. She has listened to some so many times that she knows them by heart. Alyssa hopes she can remember her favorite stories when she is older. She wants to tell them to her children and their cousins when they come to her house for a holiday dinner.

▶ *What is one of your favorite family stories?*

FAITH and MEDIA

▶ On page 149, the *We Respond* question asks what we can do during the week to prepare for the readings at Sunday Mass. Remind the children that reflections on the readings for every Sunday can be found online at webelieveweb.com and on other Catholic Web sites.

▶ In connection with the *As Catholics* text about Saint Paul's letters, consider discussing how easy it is to spread Jesus' message today and how hard it was in Saint Paul's time. Today Jesus' message is spread instantly via television, radio, and the Internet. In contrast, Saint Paul had to travel on foot, on horseback, or by ship. He wrote his letters by hand and gave them to messengers to carry to Jesus' followers. Those who received the letters had to read them aloud to gatherings of Christians and then copy the words by hand to send the letters on to others.

CHAPTER PROJECT: LISTEN TO AND RESPOND TO SCRIPTURE

Whenever possible, read a story from the Gospels. You can read one of the stories in the *We Believe* text. Before reading, ask the children to listen carefully. After reading the story, have the children write about or make a storyboard, telling the story in their own words or drawings. Display the children's work in the prayer space.

WE GATHER

✝ **Leader:** Let us pray.

🎵 **Alleluia, We Will Listen**

Alleluia, alleluia,
We will listen to your word.
Alleluia!

Reader: A reading from the holy Gospel according to Luke.

 Luke 8:1

Jesus "journeyed from one town and village to another, preaching and proclaiming the good news of the kingdom of God."

The Gospel of the Lord.

All: Praise to you, Lord Jesus Christ.

JESUS SHARES GOOD NEWS WITH US

Think about a time when you really listened. How did it help you?

147

PREPARING TO PRAY

In this prayer, children will celebrate the Word of God.

• Play "Alleluia, We Will Listen," #14 on the Grade 2 CD. Have the children practice singing.

• Choose a reader and provide time for this person to prepare the reading.

The Prayer Space
• Display illustrations of stories in the Gospels.

• Place the Bible on the prayer table.

This Week's Liturgy
Visit **www.webelieveweb.com** for this week's liturgical readings and other seasonal material.

Lesson Plan

WE GATHER ___ minutes

✝ Pray

• Have the children open their books to the opening prayer on page 147. Begin by praying the Sign of the Cross. Then sing together "Alleluia, We Will Listen."

• Ask the reader to begin reading the Scripture passage from Luke.

• Pray the response together.

☀ Focus on Life

• Read the question. Discuss how listening carefully to others can help us.

• Share the *Chapter Story* on guide page 147E.

Family Connection Update

Invite volunteers to share their families' discussions about participating at Mass.

Catechist Goal

• To emphasize that we listen and respond to God's Word during the Liturgy of the Word

Our Faith Response

• To listen to God's Word and to put it into practice

 **Liturgy of the Word**

　　　　　psalm　　　　　homily

Lesson Materials

• copies of Reproducible Master 17
• Grade 2 CD
• Scripture and Family reproducible masters (back of book)

As Catholics...

The Letters of Saint Paul

　　After working on these two pages, read aloud the *As Catholics* text. Explain: *Each Christian group would gather in one place to hear Paul's letter read.* Read the names of some groups to whom he wrote: Romans, Corinthians, and Galatians.

WE BELIEVE

We listen to God's Word during the Liturgy of the Word.

The Mass has two main parts. The first main part of the Mass is the **Liturgy of the Word**. During the Liturgy of the Word, we worship God by listening to his Word. We listen to readings from the Bible.

At Sunday Mass we usually hear three readings from the Bible. When we listen to these readings, we hear about God's love for us. We learn ways to show our love for God and others.

God's Word has always been an important part of the Church's worship. We hear God's Word during the celebration of all the sacraments.

　Unscramble these letters to complete this sentence.

　　　　　　　　e g i l n s t i n

By ＿l＿＿i＿＿s＿＿t＿＿e＿＿n＿＿i＿＿n＿＿g＿ to God's

Word, we learn to be better followers of Jesus.

148

Lesson Plan

WE BELIEVE ＿＿ minutes

Review with the children what they learned about the beginning of Mass. (See Chapter 16.) Also review what the children have learned about the Bible. (See Chapter 8.)

Write on the board *Liturgy of the Word.* Pronounce the words and have the children repeat them. Read together the *We Believe* statement on page 148. Then have volunteers read the text. Stress: *When we listen to God's Word at Mass we are worshiping him. Listening to God's Word at Mass helps us to grow in faith and love for God and others.*

　Help the children unscramble the letters of the missing word.

Invite a child to read aloud the *We Believe* statement at the top of page 149. Then have a volunteer read the first paragraph. Ask: *What is the first reading usually about?* (all the things God did for his people before Jesus was born)

Write the word *psalm* on the board. Help the children to pronounce the word. Have volunteers read the remaining paragraphs on page 149. Ask: *What is the second reading usually about?* (the teaching of the Apostles and the beginning of the Church)

Explain: *We respond "Thanks be to God" after the first and second readings. This helps us to show our thanks to God for his Word.*

We listen and respond to readings from the Old Testament and the New Testament.

The Liturgy of the Word begins with the first reading. The first reading is usually from the Old Testament. We hear about all the things God did for his people before Jesus was born. We remember that God has always been with his people. We believe that God is with us now.

After the first reading we let God's Word enter our hearts. Then we sing a psalm. A **psalm** is a song of praise from the Bible.

Next we listen to the second reading from the New Testament. It is about the teachings of the Apostles and the beginning of the Church. We learn how to be followers of Jesus. We remember and give thanks that we are the Church.

At the end of the first and second readings, the reader says, "The word of the Lord."

We respond, "Thanks be to God."

 What can you do during the week to prepare for the readings at Mass?

Key Words

Liturgy of the Word the first main part of the Mass when we listen to God's Word

psalm a song of praise from the Bible

As Catholics...

After Pentecost, Jesus' disciples spread his message to the people of many lands. Saint Paul was one of these disciples. After he visited a group of Christians, he sent letters back to them. In the letters Paul reminded the people that they were Jesus' followers and members of the Church.

Many of the letters in the New Testament are from Paul. We often listen to parts of these letters in the second reading at Mass.

See if you and your family can find the letters of Saint Paul in the Bible. They are named for the people Paul wrote to.

ACTIVITY BANK

Practice Listening Skills

Play the game "Telephone." Have the children form two groups. Choose a "starter" for each group. To the starter whisper a short message about Jesus' teaching. Then ask the starter to pass the message to the person closest to him or her. Tell the groups that they should pass the message along until the last person has heard it. The last person in each group should then say the message aloud. Explain: *You have been good listeners if the message said aloud is the same one that I shared with the starter.* You may want to use the following messages.

- Jesus is with us always.
- God always forgives us when we are sorry.
- The Holy Spirit helps and guides us.

149

Invite the children to look at the photos on these pages. Ask: *Would you like to be a reader when you are older? Why or why not?*

 Discuss different ways that people prepare to hear God's Word at Mass.

Quick Check

✔ *What is the Liturgy of the Word?* (It is the first main part of the Mass when we listen to God's Word.)

✔ *How does listening to the first reading help us?* (We remember that God has always been with his people. We believe that God is with us now.)

✔ *What do we learn by listening to the second reading?* (We learn how to be followers of Jesus.)

Teaching Tip

Listening

Children sometimes struggle with listening to the homily at Mass. Encourage them to listen for key words that they have learned in religion class. Share with the children the message that you heard in the past Sunday's homily.

We listen as the Gospel is proclaimed.

There are four books in the New Testament called Gospels: Matthew, Mark, Luke, and John. In these Gospels we learn the Good News about Jesus' life and teaching. The third reading of the Liturgy of the Word is from one of the Gospels.

The deacon or priest proclaims the Gospel. To proclaim the Gospel means to announce the Good News of Jesus Christ with praise and glory.

This is what we do:

- We stand. We sing the alleluia or other words of praise. This shows we are ready to listen to the Good News of Jesus Christ.

- We listen as the deacon or priest proclaims the Gospel.

- Then the deacon or priest says, "The Gospel of the Lord."

  We respond, "Praise to you, Lord Jesus Christ."

After the Gospel, the priest or deacon talks about the readings at Mass. In this talk he helps us to understand the readings. This talk is called the **homily**. Through the homily we learn what it means to believe and what we can do to be followers of Jesus.

 How do we show we are ready to listen to the Good News of Jesus Christ?

Key Word

homily the talk given by the priest or deacon at Mass that helps us understand the readings and how we are to live

150

Lesson Plan

WE BELIEVE (continued)

Write the word *Gospels* on the board. Explain: *There are four Gospels in the New Testament.* Then have a volunteer read the first paragraph on page 150. Stress: *The third reading of the Liturgy of the Word is from one of the Gospels.*

Write the word *proclaim* on the board. Read aloud the second paragraph. Then ask the children to stand as you read aloud together what we do when the Gospel is proclaimed.

Write the word *homily* on the board. Pronounce it for the children and have them repeat it. Ask a volunteer to read the last paragraph on page 150. Discuss how the homily gives us a better understanding of how to be followers of Jesus.

Discuss how we show we are ready to listen to the Good News of Jesus Christ.

Together we pray the Creed and the Prayer of the Faithful.

After the homily we stand to pray the Creed. In this prayer we show our faith. We say what we believe as Christians.

The word *creed* comes from a word that means "believe." We say that we believe in God the Father, Jesus Christ, and the Holy Spirit. We also say that we believe in the Church and in God's forgiveness of our sins.

After the Creed, we pray for the needs of all God's people. This prayer is called the Prayer of the Faithful.

WE RESPOND

Read what good listeners do. Put a check beside each thing you can do next Sunday during the Liturgy of the Word.

_____ Look at the person who is reading or speaking.

_____ Pay close attention to what the reader or speaker is saying.

_____ Picture in your mind what the reader or speaker is talking about.

What else will you do to take part in the Liturgy of the Word?

151

ACTIVITY BANK

Faith and the Media
Good News Screen Savers
Activity Materials: drawing paper, crayons or markers

Have the children work in small groups to design screen savers that proclaim a Gospel message. Brainstorm some messages that they would like to share with others. After some ideas have been recorded, invite the groups to work on pictorial images that will attract others to read their message.

Cooperative Learning
Playing a Review Game

Form two groups. Ask each group to write four questions about the Liturgy of the Word. Point out that the children should look at the chapter in their books. When each group has finished, check the questions. Then have the groups ask their questions in turn. Have the group members consult with each other before giving an answer. Keep score on the board. When a group answers correctly, write an Alleluia in the group's column.

Invite a volunteer to read the first two paragraphs on page 151. Explain: *The Prayer of the Faithful are prayers for many different people and their needs.*

Distribute copies of Reproducible Master 17. Have the children work in pairs to complete the activities. (across: first row, psalm; third row, sing; fifth row, homily; sixth row, listen. down: first row, Gospel; last row, Creed.)

WE RESPOND   _____ minutes

Connect to Life Ask the children to do the checklist. Then read the *We Respond* question and invite the children to share their responses. Review the prayers the group learned in this chapter.

Pray Invite the children to gather in the prayer space. Ask volunteers to pray for specific people. (for world leaders, for families, for people in need) After each petition pray: *Lord, hear our prayer.*

Catechist Goal

- To review the chapter ideas that are key to growing as disciples of Jesus Christ

Our Faith Response

- To decide on ways to grow as disciples by living out what we have learned

Show **W**hat *you* **K**now

Read the definitions. When the children have finished coloring the words, check their answers. Clarify any misconceptions.

More *to* **E**xplore

Ask a volunteer to read the paragraph. Remind the children that the homily takes place after the Gospel is read. Then have volunteers share what the priest or deacon said last Sunday to help people live as disciples.

Make *it* **H**appen

Have the students work in pairs to write their columns. Then have the pairs share with the group what they have written.

Pray Today

Provide a few minutes of silence for the children to pray by themselves for world leaders.

Take Home

Encourage the children to pray with their families for the people listed.

Discuss and send home copies of *Sharing Faith with My Family* reproducible master for this chapter (back of book).

 152 and 153

  Grade 2 Chapter 17

PROJECT

Show **W**hat *you* **K**now

Use this color code to color the .

red	the first main part of the Mass when we listen to God's Word
blue	a song of praise from the Bible
yellow	the talk given by the priest or deacon that helps us understand the readings and how we are to live

psalm *blue*
Liturgy of the Word *red*
homily *yellow*

More *to* **E**xplore

At Mass this Sunday, listen closely to the priest's or deacon's homily. Then ask yourself these questions. When did the homily take place? What did the priest or deacon say that helps me to live as a disciple?

DISCIPLE

Make *it* **H**appen

Help proclaim the Good News! Write an advice column to other disciples about ways they can be like Jesus in their communities.

Dear Disciples,

Pray Today

Leaders of the world have great responsibilities. That is why it is important to pray for them. We pray together for them during the Prayer of the Faithful on Sunday. We can also pray for them at other times. Say a prayer now for world leaders.

Take Home

Lead your family members in this prayer. Have them say, "Lord, hear our prayer" after each part of the prayer.

For the whole Church,
For all those in our parish,
For those who are sick or in need,
➥ **DISCIPLE CHALLENGE** Add your own.

_____

CHAPTER TEST

Fill in the circle beside the correct answer.

1. The first reading at Mass is usually from the _____.
   - ● Old Testament
   - ○ New Testament

2. The second reading at Mass is usually from the _____.
   - ○ Old Testament
   - ● New Testament

3. In the _____ we say what we believe as Christians.
   - ● Creed
   - ○ homily

4. The _____ is the talk given by the priest or deacon that helps us understand the readings and the Gospel and how we are to live.
   - ○ Creed
   - ● homily

5. A _____ is a song of praise from the Bible.
   - ○ Gospel
   - ● psalm

6. We learn the Good News about Jesus' life and teachings by listening to the _____.
   - ○ first reading
   - ● Gospel

7–8. Who do we pray for in the Prayer of the Faithful?

Possible response: We pray for the needs of all God's people.

9–10. What do we learn by listening to God's Word at Mass?

Possible responses: to be better followers of Jesus; ways to show our love for God and others

CHAPTER TEST

Provide ten to fifteen minutes for the students to complete the test. After all have finished, check the answers. Clarify any misconceptions.

Alternative Assessment

You may want the students to complete the following alternative-assessment activity.

Add to your Mass booklet. Draw a picture and write a sentence to tell about each reading and prayer of the Liturgy of the Word.

Additional Testing

• Chapter 17 Test in *Assessment Book*, pages 35–36

• CD-ROM *Test Generator and Resource*: Use Chapter 17 Test or customize your own.

Review

Review the definitions as they are presented in the chapter's *Key Word* boxes:

• Liturgy of the Word (page 149)

• psalm (page 149)

• homily (page 150).

We Believe Statements

Review the four statements.

• We listen to God's Word during the Liturgy of the Word.

• We listen and respond to readings from the Old Testament and the New Testament.

• We listen as the Gospel is proclaimed.

• Together we pray the Creed and the Prayer of the Faithful.

To use the Chapter 17 Study Guide, visit

www.webelieveweb.com

Overview

In Chapter 17 the children learned the importance of the Liturgy of the Word in the celebration of the Mass. In this chapter the children will learn about the Liturgy of the Eucharist.

Doctrinal Content	For Adult Reading and Reflection *Catechism of the Catholic Church*
The children will learn:	Paragraph
• We bring forward the gifts of bread and wine..	1350
• The Eucharistic Prayer is the great prayer of thanks and praise.	1353
• We pray the Our Father and ask God for forgiveness and peace.	1355
• We receive Jesus Christ in Holy Communion.	1386

Liturgy of the Eucharist (p. 157)
Eucharistic Prayer (p. 157)

Catechist Background

What do you bring to—and from—the eucharistic celebration?

Our own experiences of family gatherings help us appreciate the parish family gathering for the eucharistic meal. Just as families and their guests share, we bring gifts of bread and wine forward to the priest at the beginning of the Liturgy of the Eucharist.

By offering gifts we acknowledge our gratefulness and dependence on God, the source of all that is good. The bread and wine that we offer will become the Body and Blood of Jesus through the power of the Holy Spirit. The money we add to the collection shows our desire to help the Church and those in need.

We prepare to receive Jesus by praying together the Our Father and by offering a sign of peace. After Communion we praise and thank God for the gift of the Eucharist. When we leave Mass, we bring the peace and love that we have received to others.

Go to **www.webelieveweb.com**, Catechist/Teacher, We Believe Correlations for this chapter's correlation to:
• Six Tasks of Catechesis
• Catholic Social Teaching.

In the early years of the Church, the community in Jerusalem had special needs so Saint Paul took up a collection for them. He urged his fellow Christians to imitate the generosity and concern of Jesus. "I say this is not by way of command, but to test the genuineness of your love by your concern for others" (2 Corinthians 8:8). By receiving the Eucharist, we become more like Jesus. As we leave Sunday Mass, we can imitate Jesus by bringing his concern, love, and generosity to others.

In what specific ways do you express your Christian love in concern for others?

Lesson Planning Guide

Lesson Steps	Presentation	Materials

 ① WE GATHER

page 155 **Prayer** **Focus on Life**	• Pray the "Echo Prayer." • Discuss ways to show thanks.	For the prayer space: three gift boxes, photographs of people sharing God's love, bread, grapes

② WE BELIEVE

page 156 *We bring forward the gifts of bread and wine.*	• Present the text about the beginning of the Liturgy of the Eucharist. 🎵 Sing about the presentation of the gifts. • Read and discuss the *As Catholics* text.	🎵 "A Gift from Your Children," Nancy Bourassa and Carey Landry, #16, Grade 2 CD
page 157 *The Eucharistic Prayer is the great prayer of thanks and praise.* *The Roman Missal*	• Read about the Eucharistic Prayer and consecration. • Point out the *Key Words* and definitions. 🏃 Follow the direction to review the Eucharistic Prayer.	• highlighters or crayons
page 158 *We pray the Our Father and ask God for forgiveness and peace.* *The Roman Missal*	• Read and discuss the Our Father, the sign of peace, and the Lamb of God. 🏃 Discuss responses to the question.	• pencils or pens
page 159 *We receive Jesus Christ in Holy Communion.* *The Roman Missal*	• Continue the presentation on the Liturgy of the Eucharist. • Practice praying the Mass responses.	• copies of Reproducible Master 18, guide page 155C

③ WE RESPOND

page 159	🏃 Respond to the question.	🎵 "Jesus, You Are Bread for Us," Christopher Walker, #17, Grade 2 CD
pages 160–161 **Project Disciple**	• Complete the **Project Disciple** activities. • Explain the *Take Home* activity. • Discuss/send home **Sharing Faith with My Family** reproducible master for this chapter.	• crayons or colored pencils • copies of **Sharing Faith with My Family** reproducible master, Chapter 18 (back of book)
page 162 **Chapter 18 Test**	• Complete **Chapter 18 Test**. • Work on *Alternative Assessment* activity.	• optional: copies of Scripture reproducible master, *What's the Word?*, Chapter 18 (back of book)

For additional ideas, activities, and opportunities: Visit Sadlier's  **www.WeBelieveweb.com**

Name _____

Color the picture on the song card.

♪ Jesus, You Are Bread for Us ♫

Jesus, you are bread for us.

Jesus, you are life for us.

In your gift of Eucharist

We find love.

When we feel we need a friend,

You are there with us, Jesus.

Thank you for the friend you are.

Thank you for the love we share.

PROJECT DISCIPLE

Pray
Learn
Celebrate
Share
Choose
Live

Additional Activities

What's the Word?

Scripture reproducible master, Chapter 18

Materials needed: copies of the *What's the Word?* (back of book)

Distribute copies of the Scripture reproducible master. Choose volunteers to be readers and three children to mime the actions of Jesus and the two disciples. Then ask the children to highlight or underline the exact words from Scripture: see Readers 3, 5, and 6.

Picture This

Materials needed: modeling clay or homemade modeling dough (recipes may be found on the Internet) and newspaper

Give each child newspaper to cover the working area. Also give each enough clay or dough to make a cup and plate. Have the children look at the Scripture art on text page 133. When the children are finished, put their work somewhere to dry. When the cups and plates are dry, have the children take them home. Suggest that they ask their parents if they may place the cups and plates as centerpieces on their tables and talk about Jesus' gift of himself in the Eucharist.

Celebrate!

Have the children form four small groups. Assign each group one of the four *We Believe* statements of the chapter. Have the children in each group reread in the text the paragraphs pertaining to the group's assigned statement. Then have the group members prepare and practice a role-play to demonstrate what happens during the particular part of the Liturgy of the Eucharist to which the statement refers. Then have the children present their role-plays to the other groups in the correct order of the parts of the Liturgy of the Eucharist.

Saint Stories

On the Internet go to *Lives of the Saints* at **www.webelieveweb.com**. In the Archive section you will find the story of Pope Saint Pius X, who in 1910 made it possible for children to receive the Eucharist at a younger age than previously practiced. Read the story to the children. Then have the children work in pairs to list three reasons why the Church honors this saint.

Meeting Individual Needs
Children with Attention-Deficit Disorder

The children may need practice walking reverently in church to receive Holy Communion. If you are having the children practice in the classroom, have them focus on the prayer table as they are walking. If they are practicing in church, ask them to focus on the altar as they are walking.

We Believe Resources

- Grade 2 *Review & Resource Book*, pages 43–45
- Grade 2 *Family Book*, pages 52–54
- Grade 2 *Assessment Book*, pages 37–38
- Grade 2 CD-ROM *Test Generator and Resource*: Use Chapter 18 Test or customize your own.
- **www.webelieveweb.com**

Enrichment Ideas

Chapter Story

On Saturday Danny's family was going to have a birthday party for his Aunt Vivian. Danny wanted to give his aunt a special gift because she was his godmother. On the Tuesday before the party, Danny still did not know what he should give Aunt Viv. Danny's father suggested that Danny make a gift. His dad said, "If you make something, I know it will mean a lot to your aunt."

Danny asked, "What should I make, Dad?" His father answered, "Take some time to think about it. I'm sure you'll think of something special."

That night Danny and his dad looked through the family's photo album. There were pictures of Danny's Baptism. Danny's father pulled out a piece of paper that was underneath one of the large photos. It was a letter that Aunt Viv had written to Danny about the day he was baptized. In the letter Aunt Viv told Danny that it was an honor to be his godmother.

After reading the letter, Danny thought of the gift he would make for Aunt Viv. He talked to his dad about his idea. Danny's dad said, "I'll help you." Danny and his dad worked on the gift all week. At the party, Aunt Viv was surprised when she unwrapped Danny's gift. Aunt Viv said, "This gift is very special, Danny. I will treasure it always."

The gift was a collage of pictures of Danny and his aunt together. Danny had used photos and drew pictures for the collage. At the bottom of the collage, Danny had written, "My gift to you comes from my heart. Thank you for always being there for me."

▶ *Would you like to give or receive a gift like the one Danny made? Tell why or why not.*

FAITH and MEDIA

▶ Make a "Prayer of Peace" bulletin board for the parish. Help a few children to write a short prayer and print it on poster paper. Help the children take photographs of other students working as peacemakers. If they do not have cameras, have them draw or paint pictures of their observations. Arrange the pictures on the bulletin board.

CHAPTER PROJECT: THE GIFTS OF GOD

Invite the children to make a collage about the gifts of God in their lives. Have the class work in four groups: family, friends, the world, the Church. Have the children work together to find photographs in magazines or draw pictures that depict the gifts God has given them in each of these categories. Set a day for a "Thank You, Jesus!" celebration. Have the members of each group display and explain their collage. Allow time for questions and comments by the other groups. Display each work on a bulletin board entitled "The Gifts of God" and celebrate together the love of Jesus.

We Celebrate the Liturgy of the Eucharist

WE GATHER

✝ **Leader:** Write your initials in each gift box to show that you offer God all that you think, say, and do.

Now stand and lift up your books. Echo each line of the prayer.

We lift our minds and hearts in prayer. (Echo)
God, we offer to you today (Echo)
All we think, and do, and say, (Echo)
Uniting it with what was done (Echo)
On earth by Jesus Christ, your Son. (Echo)

 What are some different ways to show your thanks to others?

155

PREPARING TO PRAY

Children will gather to offer their thoughts, words, and actions in prayer.

• Explain to the children that you will lead them in prayer.

The Prayer Space
• Option: Make three gift boxes like the ones shown on this page. Display them in the prayer space.

• Display photographs of people sharing God's love with others.

• On the prayer table place bread and grapes.

📖 **This Week's Liturgy**
Visit **www.webelieveweb.com** for this week's liturgical readings and other seasonal material.

Lesson Plan

WE GATHER _____ minutes

✝ Pray

• Pray the Sign of the Cross together. Then have the children open their books to page 155. Invite the children to follow the directions for the activity on this page, and write their initials on each gift box.

• Ask the children to stand and lift their opened books.

• Read each line of the prayer and have the children echo the words.

☀ Focus on Life
• Ask the children to share ways that they can show thanks to others in their lives.

• Read aloud the *Chapter Story* on guide page 155E.

Family Connection Update
Ask volunteers to share their families' petitions for the Prayer of the Faithful.

Catechist Goal

• To present what we say and do during the Liturgy of the Eucharist

Our Faith Response

• To be thankful for the gift of the Eucharist

 Liturgy of the Eucharist
Eucharistic Prayer

Lesson Materials

• Grade 2 CD
• copies of Reproducible Master 18
• highlighters or crayons
• Scripture and Family reproducible masters (back of book)

As Catholics...

Communion Vessels

After working on these two pages, read aloud the *As Catholics* text. If possible, ask one of the priests in the parish to show the children a paten, a chalice, and an unconsecrated host.

WE BELIEVE

We bring forward the gifts of bread and wine.

The **Liturgy of the Eucharist** is the second main part of the Mass. During the Liturgy of the Eucharist we present the gifts of bread and wine. A very special prayer is prayed. The bread and wine become the Body and Blood of Christ. We receive the Body and Blood of Christ.

The Liturgy of the Eucharist begins as the priest prepares the altar. This is also the time when we give money or other gifts for the Church and the poor.

Then members of the assembly bring forward the gifts of bread and wine. We remember that everything we have is a gift from God. We will offer these gifts and ourselves back to God. The priest prepares these gifts of bread and wine with special prayers.

We can respond:

"Blessed be God for ever."

Then we pray that the Lord will accept these gifts.

🎵 A Gift From Your Children

Here is our gift, the bread and the wine:
A symbol of sharing, a beautiful sign:
A gift, a gift from your children;
A gift, a gift of our love.

156

As Catholics...

The Church uses a special plate and cup at Mass. The plate is called a *paten*. The paten holds the bread that will become the Body of Christ. The cup is called a *chalice*. The chalice holds the wine that will become the Blood of Christ. The next time you are at Mass, notice the paten and chalice.

Lesson Plan

WE BELIEVE _____ minutes

Write *Liturgy of the Eucharist* on the board. Read aloud the first paragraph on page 156. Have the children read aloud the definition of *Liturgy of the Eucharist* in the *Key Words* box on page 157.

Invite volunteers to read the remaining paragraphs on page 156. Ask: *Has anyone here brought forward the gifts of bread and wine?* Encourage the children to share their experiences.

Invite the children to highlight or underline the words we pray as the priest prepares the gifts. ("Blessed be God for ever.")

🎵 **Play** "A Gift from Your Children," #16 on the Grade 2 CD. Invite the children to join in singing.

👤 **Ask** the children to circle our gifts to God named in the song. (bread, wine, love)

Write *Eucharistic Prayer* on the board. Explain: *The Eucharistic Prayer is the most important prayer in the Mass.* You may want to tell the children that in many parishes the assembly kneels during the Eucharistic Prayer.

The Eucharistic Prayer is the great prayer of thanks and praise.

After the preparation of the gifts, the priest prays in our name. He prays the most important prayer in the Mass. This prayer is called the **Eucharistic Prayer**. It is the great prayer of praise and thanksgiving.

During this prayer we pray for many things. We praise God by singing "Holy, holy, holy. . . ." We remember what Jesus said and did at the Last Supper. The priest takes the bread. He says:

> "Take this, all of you, and eat it: *of*
> this is my Body which will be given up for you."

Then the priest takes the cup of wine. He says:

> "Take this, all of you, and drink from it: this is the ~~cup~~ of my Blood. . . ."

chalice

Read Along

This part of the Eucharistic Prayer is called the Consecration. By the power of the Holy Spirit and through the words and actions of the priest, the bread and wine become the Body and Blood of Christ. What looks like bread and wine is not bread and wine anymore. The bread and wine are now the Body and Blood of Christ. As Catholics we believe that Jesus Christ is really present in the Eucharist.

The priest invites us to proclaim our faith. We pray:

"Christ has died,
Christ is risen,
Christ will come again."

We pray that the Holy Spirit will unite all those who believe in Jesus. We end the Eucharistic Prayer by responding "Amen." We are saying "yes" to the prayer the priest has prayed in our name.

Circle the words the priest says when he takes the bread and wine.

Key Words

Liturgy of the Eucharist the second main part of the Mass in which the gifts of bread and wine become the Body and Blood of Christ

Eucharistic Prayer the most important prayer of the Mass

157

Gift of Ourselves

Activity Materials: construction paper, drawing paper, ribbons, crayons, markers, glue, scissors

Help the children cut and fold a piece of construction paper to form a box. The children may want to decorate the box with ribbons and drawings. Then have the children use a piece of drawing paper and illustrate their response to the following: *What gift of yourself would you choose to offer to God during the presentation of the gifts?* Have them place their completed picture inside of their gift box. Invite the children to prayerfully process to the prayer space with their gift box as they sing, "A Gift from Your Children."

Ask volunteers to read the first three paragraphs on page 157. Point out: *The priest says the same words that Jesus said to his disciples during the Last Supper.* You may want to read the Gospel story of the Last Supper in Mark 14:22–24.

Write the word *Consecration* on the board. Then read the *Read Along* paragraphs.

Have the children circle the words of the priest.

Quick Check

✔ *Why is the Liturgy of the Eucharist such an important part of the Mass?* (During the Liturgy of the Eucharist the gifts of bread and wine become the Body and Blood of Christ.)

✔ *What are we saying when we pray "Amen" at the end of the Eucharistic Prayer?* (We are saying "yes" to the prayer the priest has prayed in our name.)

Teaching Note
The Our Father

The meaning of the words of the Our Father is presented in the Grade 1 *We Believe* pupil's text. (See Chapter 8.) The meaning of the prayer words are also explained in the Grade 2 text. (See Chapter 24.)

We pray the Our Father and ask God for forgiveness and peace.

After the Eucharistic Prayer, we prepare to receive the Body and Blood of Christ. We join ourselves with the whole Church. We pray the Our Father.

After the Our Father, the priest prays, "Peace I leave ~~with~~ you; my peace I give ~~to~~ you." (John 14:27)

We pray that Christ's peace may be with us always. We offer a sign of peace to one another. This action shows that we are united to Christ and to one another.

Then we ask Jesus for forgiveness and peace:

"Lamb of God, you take away
the sins of the world:
have mercy on us.

Lamb of God, you take away
the sins of the world:
have mercy on us.

Lamb of God, you take away
the sins of the world:
grant us peace."

As we pray the "Lamb of God," the priest breaks the Bread or Host that has become the Body of Christ.

Why do we share a sign of peace at Mass?

158

Lesson Plan

WE BELIEVE (continued)

Invite a volunteer to read the *We Believe* statement and the first paragraph on page 158. Remind the children that the Our Father is a prayer that Jesus taught us. Explain: *When we pray these words at Mass, we join ourselves with the whole Church.*

Read the other paragraphs on page 158. Point out: *We should be prayerful and respectful when sharing the sign of peace with others.* Ask: *What is another word for mercy?* (forgiveness) Then read together the words of the "Lamb of God."

Direct the children to discuss in pairs why we share the sign of peace at Mass. Help all to conclude: *We show that we are united to Christ and to one another.* Have the children share a sign of peace with the people near them.

Read aloud the text on page 159. Have the children highlight or underline the responses we pray.

Direct attention to the photographs on these pages. Talk about what is happening in each one. Stress: *When we go forward to receive Holy Communion, we should be respectful.* Explain: *We may receive the Host in the hand or on the tongue.*

We receive Jesus Christ in Holy Communion.

After the "Lamb of God," the priest holds up the Host that has become the Body of Christ. He says,

"~~This is~~ Behold the Lamb of God who takes away the sins of the world. ~~Happy~~ Blessed are those who are called to ~~his~~ the supper." of the Lamb.

We respond,
"Lord, I am not worthy ~~to receive you~~ that you should enter under my roof, but only say the word and ~~I~~ my soul shall be healed."

Then people go forward to receive Communion. The priest, deacon, or extraordinary minister of Holy Communion shows the Host to each person and says, "The body of Christ." Each person responds, "Amen" and receives Holy Communion.

Then the priest, deacon, or extraordinary minister of Holy Communion may hand the cup to each person saying, "The blood of Christ." Each person responds, "Amen" and drinks from the cup.

We all sing a song of thanksgiving. Then there is quiet time. We thank Jesus for the gift of himself in Holy Communion.

WE RESPOND

Write what you can do to thank Jesus for the gift of himself in the Eucharist.

_____

159

ACTIVITY BANK

Multiple Intelligences
Intrapersonal

Activity Materials: writing paper, pencils, construction paper, markers and crayons

Give each child a sheet of writing paper. Ask the children to write thank-you notes to Jesus expressing why they are thankful for His gifts, especially the gift of the Eucharist. After the children have written the notes, help them mount the notes on construction paper, and decorate the notes to Jesus. Encourage the children to share their notes with their families.

Parish

Extraordinary Ministers of Holy Communion

Invite extraordinary ministers of Holy Communion to speak to the group. Encourage the ministers to talk about their roles in the parish, especially during the celebration of the Mass.

Help the children to understand that it is important to talk to Jesus during the quiet time of prayer. During this time we thank Jesus for giving himself to us in Holy Communion.

WE RESPOND   ___ minutes

Connect to Life Have a volunteer read the *We Respond* question. Ask the children to share their answers.

🎵 **Distribute** copies of Reproducible Master 18. Then play "Jesus, You Are Bread for Us," #17 on the Grade 2 CD. Have the children practice singing. Then invite the children to bring their song sheets (Reproducible Master 18) as they gather in the prayer space. Invite them to sing the song.

Review the Mass prayers the children have learned so far. You may want to have the children use their Mass booklets (pages 241–244). Continue to encourage the children to use these booklets at Mass.

Catechist Goal

• To review the chapter ideas that are key to growing as disciples of Jesus Christ

Our Faith Response

• To decide on ways to grow as disciples by living out what we have learned

Show What *you* Know

Read each set of directions. When the children have completed the activity, choose volunteers to use each of the terms in one sentence.

Celebrate!

Have the children work in pairs. You may want to allow the children to refer to the pages in the chapter while working.

Picture This

Direct attention to the photograph. Ask: *Where is the priest standing?* Help with the spelling of Eucharistic Prayer.

Make *it* Happen

Read the directions. Most of the children in your group may be preparing to receive first Holy Communion. If this is so, assign pairs of children to be prayer partners. Ask the children to pray for their prayer partner every day.

Take Home

Discuss with the children why it is an honor to bring forward the gifts at Mass. Encourage the children to discuss their thoughts at home.

Discuss and send home copies of *Sharing Faith with My Family* reproducible master for this chapter (back of book).

Grade 2 Chapter 18

PROJECT

Show What *you* Know

Circle the  that names the second main part of the Mass in which the gifts of bread and wine become the Body and Blood of Christ.

Underline the that names the most important prayer of the Mass.

| Liturgy of the Eucharist | Eucharistic Prayer |

Celebrate!

Put the parts of the Liturgy of the Eucharist in order. The first one has been done for you.

4	Sign of peace
1	Presentation of gifts
3	Our Father
5	Lamb of God
6	Holy Communion
2	Eucharistic Prayer

160 www.webelieveweb.com

DISCIPLE

Picture This

Look at the photo. What important prayer is the priest praying in our name?

E u c h a r i s t i c

P r a y e r

Make *it* Happen

In some parishes, people volunteer to be prayer partners with those preparing for their first Holy Communion. In the space below, write a prayer for prayer partners to pray together.

↳ **DISCIPLE CHALLENGE** Pray your prayer for those receiving first Holy Communion in your parish.

Take Home

Discuss with your family why it is an honor to bring forward the gifts at Mass. Write your thoughts here.

Possible responses: We are offering

the gifts and ourselves back to God.

We show we are thankful for God's

gifts.

161

CHAPTER TEST

Fill in the circle beside the correct answer.

1. The second main part of the Mass is the _____.
   ○ Our Father   ● Liturgy of the Eucharist

2. Bread and wine become the Body and Blood of Christ during the _____.
   ○ Our Father   ● Eucharistic Prayer

3. When we pray "Amen," we are saying _____.
   ○ have mercy   ● Yes, I believe

4. Right after we pray the _____, we are invited to share in the Eucharist.
   ● Lamb of God   ○ Creed

Order these actions of the Liturgy of the Eucharist, 1 to 4.

5. We offer each other a sign of peace.   3

6. We receive Holy Communion.   4

7. We bring forward gifts of bread and wine.   1

8. The Eucharistic Prayer begins.   2

9–10. Why is the Eucharistic Prayer the most important prayer of the Mass?

Possible responses: It is the great prayer of praise and thanksgiving. The bread and wine become the Body and Blood of Christ.

162

CHAPTER TEST

Provide ten to fifteen minutes for the students to complete the test. After all have finished, check the answers. Clarify any misconceptions.

Alternative Assessment

You may want the students to complete the following alternative-assessment activity.

Add to your Mass booklet. Draw a picture and write a sentence to tell what happens during the Liturgy of the Eucharist.

Additional Testing

• Chapter 18 Test in *Assessment Book*, pages 37–38

• CD-ROM *Test Generator and Resource*: Use Chapter 18 Test or customize your own.

Review

Review the definitions as they are presented in the chapter's *Key Word* boxes:

• Liturgy of the Eucharist (page 157)

• Eucharistic Prayer (page 157).

We Believe Statements

Review the four statements.

• We bring forward the gifts of bread and wine.

• The Eucharistic Prayer is the great prayer of thanks and praise.

• We pray the Our Father and ask God for forgiveness and peace.

• We receive Jesus Christ in Holy Communion.

To use the Chapter 18 Study Guide, visit

www.webelieveweb.com

Overview

In Chapter 18 the children learned about the Liturgy of the Eucharist. In this chapter the children will learn about ways we continue the celebration of the Eucharist in our lives.

Doctrinal Content	For Adult Reading and Reflection *Catechism of the Catholic Church*	
The children will learn:		Paragraph
• We are sent to share God's love with others.		1332
• Jesus is present in the Blessed Sacrament.		1418
• Jesus is with the Church as we share God's love.		1397
• Jesus is with us as we share his peace with others.		1416

Key Words

Blessed Sacrament (p. 165)
tabernacle (p. 165)

Catechist Background

When you hear the words "Christian community," what comes to mind?

Go to **www.webelieveweb.com**, Catechist/ Teacher, We Believe Correlations for this chapter's correlation to:
• Six Tasks of Catechesis
• Catholic Social Teaching.

Hundreds of years ago Saint Francis of Assisi started a Christian community that was inspired by the New Testament. His community, like the early Church community described in Acts 4:12—5:16, shared Eucharist, prayer, work, and everything they had. These communities were based on the reality of Jesus among them, working through them.

As we leave our celebration of the Eucharist, we can still hear the closing words ringing in our ears: "Go in peace to love and serve the Lord." These words challenge the parish community to carry on the work of Jesus in the world. This is the mission of the Church.

We carry Jesus' spirit of forgiveness and peace from Mass to others. We do what we can to lessen violence in our own area of life and pray for those parts of the world that are burdened with hatred and violence.

The love and generosity of Jesus become second nature to us when he lives in us through the Eucharist. We make this love real by caring for others, especially the poor, the needy, and those whose rights have been denied. We can visit Jesus in the Blessed Sacrament, knowing that he is there to motivate us and strengthen us. By our Christlike words and actions we should be bringing others to believe in Jesus.

How do your words and actions bring others to believe in Jesus?

Lesson Planning Guide

Lesson Steps	Presentation	Materials

1 WE GATHER

Lesson Steps	Presentation	Materials
page 163 ✚ Prayer ☀ **Focus on Life**	• Listen to Scripture. • Respond in prayer. • Discuss responses to the questions.	• prayer space items: packet of seeds, small pot of soil, plant • Bible

2 WE BELIEVE

Lesson Steps	Presentation	Materials
page 164 *We are sent to share God's love with others.* *The Roman Missal*	• Present what happens at the end of Mass. • Practice praying the Mass responses. 🏃 Find the hidden word.	• colored pencils or crayons
page 165 *Jesus is present in the Blessed Sacrament.*	• Read the text about the presence of Jesus in the Blessed Sacrament. 🏃 Discuss ways to share God's love with people who are sick. • Read and discuss the *As Catholics* text.	• construction paper, colored markers or crayons (optional)
page 166 *Jesus is with the Church as we share God's love.*	• Present the text about the early Christians. 🏃 Complete the writing activity.	• pens or pencils • highlighter or crayon
page 167 *Jesus is with us as we share his peace with others.*	• Read about and discuss how we share Jesus' peace.	• copies of Reproducible Master 19 guide page 163C • world map or globe (option) 🎵 "Take the Word of God with You," James Harrison and Christopher Walker, #18, Grade 2 CD

3 WE RESPOND

Lesson Steps	Presentation	Materials
page 167	• Discuss the *We Respond* questions. 🎵 Sing "Take the Word of God with You."	
pages 168–169 **Project Disciple**	• Complete the Project Disciple activities. • Explain the *Take Home* activity. • Discuss/send home **Sharing Faith with My Family** reproducible master for this chapter.	• pencils • copies of Sharing Faith with My Family reproducible master, Chapter 19 (back of book)
page 170 **Chapter 19 Test**	• Complete Chapter 19 Test. • Work on *Alternative Assessment* activity.	• optional: copies of Scripture reproducible master, *What's the Word?*, Chapter 19 (back of book)

For additional ideas, activities, and opportunities: Visit Sadlier's **www.WeBelieveweb.com**

Name _____

Think of ways you can spread Jesus' peace with others.
Use each letter in the word peace. Write ways you can
be a peacemaker. One is done for you.

P

BE kind

A

C

E

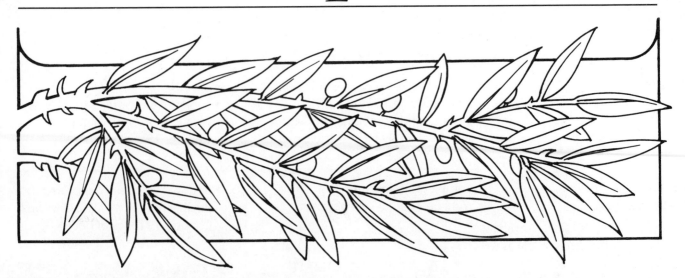

PROJECT DISCIPLE

Pray
Learn
Celebrate
Share
Choose
Live

Additional Activities

Picture This

Materials needed: copies of Reproducible Master 19; sheets of colored construction paper; scissors and glue sticks; crayons or colored pencils

Make peace signs. Distribute copies of Reproducible Master 19. Explain that the branches shown are olive branches, which are symbols of peace. Have the children color one of the branches. Then help them cut out and glue the branch to a separate sheet of construction paper. On the sheet have the children print **Peace to all in our home.** Encourage the children to display this sign in a place in their home where family members will see it often.

What's the Word?

Scripture reproducible master, Chapter 19

Materials needed: copies of *What's the Word?* (back of book); pencils

Distribute copies of the Scripture reproducible master. Choose volunteers to be readers.

Then have children work in pairs. Invite the children in each pair to imagine being an Apostle on the mountain that day. Ask the partners to role-play talking together on their way back to Jerusalem. Then have the pairs present their role-plays to the entire group.

Question Corner

Materials needed: small index cards; pencils

Give an index card to each child. Invite the children to think of Jesus' promise to be with us always. Then ask: *Who are three people with whom you will share this message?* Have the children write the names on the index cards. Then see the following *Make It Happen* activity.

Make it Happen

Lead a discussion with the children about ways that they can share the message that Jesus is with us always. List the suggestions on the board. Then have each child choose a way of action. Ask the children to write their chosen ways of action on the index cards where they have written the names for the *Question Corner* activity.

Have the children fold the index cards and then collect them. Place the cards in the prayer space. Encourage the children to carry out their plans to share the message with others.

Meeting Individual Needs
Illness in Families

Children are affected when family members are sick for an extended period of time. Be sensitive to these children and give them extra help when needed. Have the entire group pray often for family members who are sick or hospitalized. Make get-well cards to send.

We Believe Resources

- Grade 2 *Review & Resource Book*, pages 46–48
- Grade 2 *Family Book*, pages 55–57
- Grade 2 *Assessment Book*, pages 39–40
- Grade 2 CD-ROM *Test Generator and Resource*: Use Chapter 19 Test or customize your own.
- **www.webelieveweb.com**

Enrichment Ideas

Chapter Story

Last Saturday Lanna's dad asked her brother Alex to go with his sister to the park and watch out for her. When Alex and Lanna got there, Lanna saw her friend Keisha in line at the water fountain. "I'll stay here, Alex, while you play basketball." Lanna was thirsty so she cut in the line in front of Keisha. Keisha pushed Lanna and started yelling. Both girls said they were not going to move.

When Alex walked by, he saw and heard the two friends fighting. Alex asked, "Why are you two fighting? I thought you were best friends." Keisha told Alex what happened. He asked Lanna, "Why did you cut in the line?" Lanna explained that she wanted to be first. Alex asked her, "How would you feel if Keisha had cut in the line in front of you?"

Lanna answered, "I wouldn't like it. I would have pushed her, too." Alex just shook his head and said, "Don't you want to be friends any more?" When Lanna and Keisha looked at each other, they realized they wanted to be friends.

Keisha said, "I'm sorry for pushing you. I hope you are not hurt. I want to be your friend."

Alex said, "That's good, Keisha. Now Lanna, it's your turn. What do you want to say to Keisha?"

Lanna said, "I'm sorry for cutting in the line. I don't want to fight." Keisha and Lanna hugged each other and walked away together. As they walked home Keisha said, "I'm glad Alex talked to us. I guess you and I were both having a bad day."

Lanna said, "Why don't we do something for Alex? He helped get us to be friends again!"

▶ *How did Alex help Lanna and Keisha?*

FAITH and MEDIA

▶ Before the hidden-word activity on page 164, help the children find examples in print media (magazines and newspapers) of people in the local community who have shared God's love with others as volunteers, in acts of generosity and/or bravery. Discuss the ways these people are following Jesus' example.

▶ Consider discussing the ways people can use various media (television, radio, the Internet, Catholic books, magazines, and newspapers) to share God's love with others.

▶ After the *We Respond* song on page 167, remind the children that the media can be used to spread peace and love. Ask the children to name television programs, movies, music videos, songs, or video games that encourage peace and love.

CHAPTER PROJECT: MISSION POSSIBLE

Make a voice recording or videotape to play at the end of each lesson. Read a special mission for the children to do; for example: *Your mission today is to help out at home.*

Make a sign entitled "Mission Accomplished."

Have index cards or pieces of drawing paper available. Each time, before giving the children their next mission, have them write about or draw on the cards what they did to accomplish the previous mission. Display the sign and cards in the prayer space

We Go in Peace to Share God's Love

19

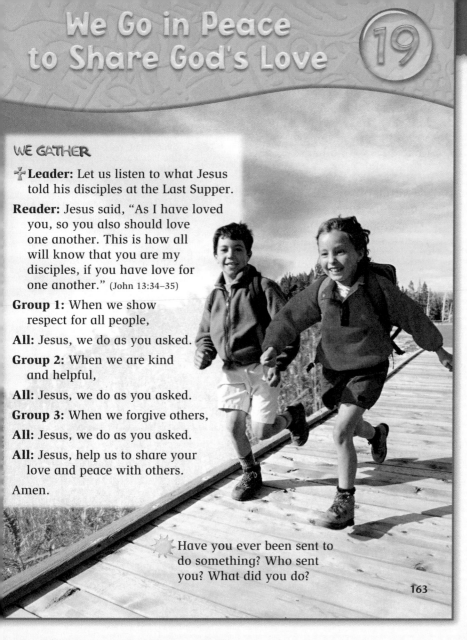

WE GATHER

✝ **Leader:** Let us listen to what Jesus told his disciples at the Last Supper.

Reader: Jesus said, "As I have loved you, so you also should love one another. This is how all will know that you are my disciples, if you have love for one another." (John 13:34–35)

Group 1: When we show respect for all people,

All: Jesus, we do as you asked.

Group 2: When we are kind and helpful,

All: Jesus, we do as you asked.

Group 3: When we forgive others,

All: Jesus, we do as you asked.

All: Jesus, help us to share your love and peace with others.

Amen.

Have you ever been sent to do something? Who sent you? What did you do?

163

PREPARING TO PRAY

Children will listen to and respond to Jesus' words in Scripture.

• Choose a leader and a reader.

• Have the other children form three groups. Provide time for all to read the words they will pray.

The Prayer Space
• On the prayer table place a packet of seeds, a small pot of soil, and a plant.

This Week's Liturgy
Visit **www.webelieveweb.com** for this week's liturgical readings and other seasonal material.

Lesson Plan

WE GATHER
___ minutes

✝ Pray

• Invite the children to gather in the prayer space. Ask them to bring their books and open to this page.

• Pray the Sign of the Cross. Then ask the leader to begin the prayer.

• When the reader has finished, pause briefly. Then ask Group 1 to begin praying. Continue the prayer.

• Point to the packet of seeds and plant on the prayer table. Explain that when we share Jesus' love and peace, we help God's love to grow.

☀ Focus on Life

• Read and discuss the questions. Have the children share how they felt being trusted to do something for someone.

• Share the *Chapter Story*, guide page 163E.

Family Connection Update
Invite volunteers to share their families' discussions about presenting the gifts at Mass.

Catechist Goal

• To highlight that we are sent to share God's love and peace with others

Our Faith Response

• To identify ways to share God's love and peace with others

 **Blessed Sacrament**

tabernacle

Lesson Materials

• Grade 2 CD

• copies of Reproducible Master 19

• highlighters or crayons

• Scripture and Family reproducible masters (back of book)

As Catholics...

Visits to the Blessed Sacrament

After you have presented the *As Catholics* text, take the children to church. Point out the tabernacle and sanctuary light. Provide about five minutes of quiet time for the children to pray by themselves. Then pray together: *Jesus, help us to remember that you are with us always.*

WE BELIEVE

We are sent to share God's love with others.

The first disciples were sent out to continue Jesus' work. We are also disciples. Jesus asks us to continue his work, too. At the end of every Mass, the priest sends us out to share God's love with others.

Before we are sent out, the priest blesses us. We make the Sign of the Cross as he says,

"May almighty God bless you, the Father, and the Son, † and the Holy Spirit."

We respond, "Amen."

Then the deacon or priest says, ~~may~~

"Go in peace ~~to love~~ ~~and serve the Lord.~~"

We respond, "Thanks be to God."

 Color all the ♡ spaces green. Color all the ☆ spaces blue. Read the word you see. It comes from a word that means "sending out."

164

As Catholics...

The Blessed Sacrament is kept in the tabernacle in church. Jesus is really present in the Blessed Sacrament. We can visit Jesus in the Blessed Sacrament. During our visits, we can talk to Jesus and tell him that we love him. We can be with Jesus our friend and thank him for all of his love and care. We can ask him to help us love and care for others.

Find out where the tabernacle is in your parish church.

Lesson Plan

WE BELIEVE _____ minutes

Read aloud the first paragraph. Remind the children: *Disciples are those who follow Jesus and as his disciples we are to carry on his work.*

Continue to read the text. Ask the children to read our prayer responses. Tell the children that sometimes the priest uses other words to send us out to do Jesus' work. Explain: *Even though the priest uses other words, we are sent to love and serve others.*

Read the directions for the hidden-word activity. Allow time for the children to complete and share what they discovered.

Read aloud the three paragraphs on page 165. Explain: *Catholics have an action to show that they believe Jesus is present in the Blessed Sacrament. They genuflect before going into the pews in church.*

Demonstrate how we genuflect by bending your right knee to the floor.

Read aloud the text. Then have the children share their ideas. If time permits, give the children drawing paper to use to make get-well cards. Give the cards to a pastoral associate and ask him or her to give the cards to parishioners who are sick.

Jesus is present in the Blessed Sacrament.

After Holy Communion there may be Hosts that have not been received. These Hosts are called the Blessed Sacrament. **The Blessed Sacrament** is another name for the Eucharist.

The Blessed Sacrament is kept in the special place in the church called the **tabernacle**. A special light or candle near the tabernacle reminds us that Jesus is really present in the Blessed Sacrament.

After Mass and at other times, priests, deacons, and extraordinary ministers of Holy Communion take the Blessed Sacrament from the tabernacle. They bring the Blessed Sacrament as Holy Communion to those who are not able to join the parish community for Mass. The Blessed Sacrament strengthens all those who receive it.

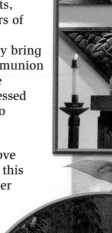

Jesus wants us to share God's love with those who are sick. We can do this by praying for them. Talk about other ways we can share God's love with those who are sick.

Key Words

Blessed Sacrament another name for the Eucharist

tabernacle the special place in the church in which the Blessed Sacrament is kept

ACTIVITY BANK

Multiple Intelligences
Bodily-Kinesthetic
Activity Materials: index cards, bag

On index cards write situations in which children can make a choice to love and serve or not to love and serve. Here are two examples:

• You want to watch a TV show. Your father asks you to help put the groceries away.

• You see a younger child fall down in the playground. You want to play a game with your friends.

Put the cards in a bag. Have the children form groups. Invite one child from each group to draw a card from the bag. Have the group members discuss what a disciple of Jesus would choose to do and act out the situation and the loving choice.

165

Quick Check

✔ *What do we do when the priest blesses us at the end of Mass?* (We make the Sign of the Cross.)

✔ *What does the priest ask us to do at the end of the Mass?* (The priest asks us to go in peace to love and serve God and others.)

✔ *Why is there always a special light near the tabernacle?* (The light helps us remember that Jesus is really present in the Blessed Sacrament.)

Chapter 19 ● Pages 166–167

Teaching Tip

Global Awareness

Point out on a globe or a world map where the children live. Help them to see the vastness of the world. Stress: *Jesus has given us the mission to spread his peace throughout the world. We can start by spreading his peace in our home, school, neighborhood, town, and country.*

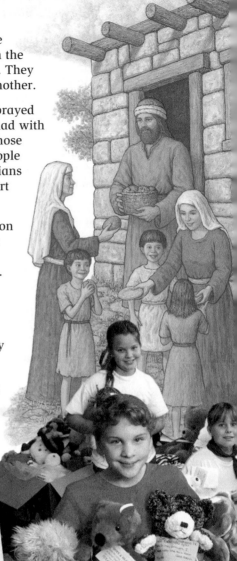

Jesus is with the Church as we share God's love.

The early Christians celebrated the Eucharist often. Receiving Jesus in the Eucharist helped their community. They were united with Jesus and one another.

The early Christians learned and prayed together. They shared what they had with those in need. They tried to help those who were sad or lonely. When people looked at the way the early Christians lived, they wanted to become a part of Jesus' community, the Church.

Receiving Jesus in Holy Communion helps us to love God and others. It helps us to be followers of Jesus. It helps us to be part of our parish. Together we show others what God's love is like.

Look at the picture of the early Christians. Write one way we can follow their example.
Possible responses: try to be kind at home and at school; pray with others; take part in the Mass and other Sacraments; give to those in need

Please give

166

Lesson Plan

WE BELIEVE (continued)

Invite the children to read aloud the *We Believe* statement on page 166. Have the children look at the picture of the early Christians as volunteers read the first two paragraphs. Stress:

• *Celebrating the Eucharist helped the early Christians to be united to Jesus and to one another.*

• *The example of the early Christians made others want to join the Church and follow Jesus Christ.*

Read aloud the third paragraph on page 166. Have the children highlight or underline the ways receiving Holy Communion helps us.

Ask a volunteer to read the activity directions. Discuss with the group what is happening in the picture. Encourage the children to share their written responses.

Invite the children to read aloud the *We Believe* statement at the top of page 167. Then ask volunteers to read the two paragraphs.

Share the following example to explain how we can help spread Jesus' peace.

Rita shared her crayons with her younger sister, Dana. Because Rita had shared with her, Dana shared candy with Rita and their friends.

Jesus is with us as we share his peace with others.

During Mass we ask Jesus to give us peace. At the end of Mass, the deacon or priest tells us, "Go in peace." Jesus wants us to share his peace with others.

Every time we make a choice to be peaceful, we spread Jesus' love and peace throughout the world.

WE RESPOND

How can you be a disciple of Jesus and share his love with your family? with people in your school? with people in your neighborhood?

> ♫ **Take the Word of God with You**
>
> Take the peace of God with you as you go.
> Take the seeds of God's peace and make them grow.
>
> Go in peace to serve the world, in peace to serve the world.
> Take the love of God, the love of God with you as you go.

167

ACTIVITY BANK

The Church
Role-Play

Have the children work in pairs. Explain that one partner should play the role of an early Christian child and the other partner a child today. Ask the children to imagine that they are visiting each other. Explain that they should have a conversation about the way receiving Holy Communion helps them and their communities.

Faith and Media
Television Themes

Many of the plots of television shows aimed at younger viewers center around conflict resolution. Ask the children to recall examples from their favorite television programs where a problem or conflict is resolved in a peaceful way. Encourage them to describe their emotions towards the show's characters as they interact.

WE RESPOND ___ minutes

Connect to Life Discuss the *We Respond* questions. Have the children form groups. Ask each group to think of ways they can spread Jesus' peace. Then invite the members of each group to act out their example.

♫ **Play** "Take the Word of God with You," #18 on the Grade 2 CD. Have the children practice singing. Explain: *When we are kind, fair, and caring, we help God's peace and love to grow.*

Distribute copies of Reproducible Master 19. Have the children complete the acrostic activity in their free time.

Pray Sing "Take the Word of God with You."

Catechist Goal

● To review the chapter ideas that are key to growing as disciples of Jesus Christ

Our Faith Response

● To decide on ways to grow as disciples by living out what we have learned

Show What *you* Know

Read the directions. When the children are finished writing, ask volunteers to read their sentences.

What Would *you* do?

Introduce the activity by reading a simple recipe for a treat (cookies, cake). Then after reading the directions, explain that the children should include things that we can not see: peace, love, kindness.

Make *it* Happen

Have the children work in pairs. Read the directions. When the children are finished writing, you may want the partners to share their stories by doing a role-play for the group.

Take Home

Brainstorm together things that might make the class environment more peaceful. Then read the directions for the family activity. Encourage all to do the activity with their families.

Discuss and send home copies of *Sharing Faith with My Family* reproducible master for this chapter (back of book).

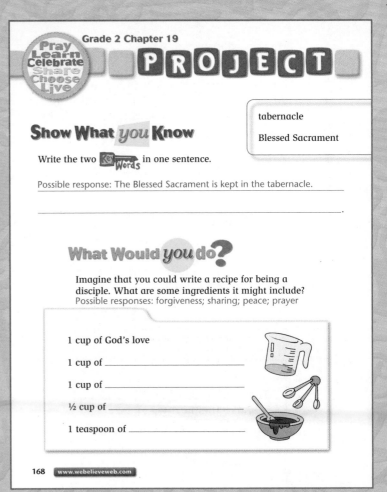

Pray Learn Celebrate Share Choose Live

Grade 2 Chapter 19

PROJECT

tabernacle

Blessed Sacrament

Show What *you* Know

Write the two Key Words in one sentence.

Possible response: The Blessed Sacrament is kept in the tabernacle.

_____ .

What Would *you* do?

Imagine that you could write a recipe for being a disciple. What are some ingredients it might include?
Possible responses: forgiveness; sharing; peace; prayer

1 cup of God's love

1 cup of _____

1 cup of _____

½ cup of _____

1 teaspoon of _____

168   www.webelieveweb.com

DISCIPLE

Pray Learn Celebrate Share Choose Live

Make *it* Happen

Write a story about an early Christian who was a friend and follower of Jesus. Then, share the story with your classmates and family. Talk about ways this early Christian is like a disciple today.

See page 166.

Take Home

Make a list of things that make family life more peaceful.

_____

_____

As a family, talk about your list.

↳ **DISCIPLE CHALLENGE** Decide on one thing you all can do this week to make your home more peaceful.

169

CHAPTER TEST

Circle the correct answer.

1. Does the word *Mass* come from a word that means "giving thanks"? Yes **(No)**

2. Is Jesus present in the Blessed Sacrament? **(Yes)** No

3. Is the tabernacle the special place in the church in which the Blessed Sacrament is kept? **(Yes)** No

4. Did the early Christians celebrate the Eucharist only a few times a year? Yes **(No)**

5–6. Write two things that happen at the end of Mass.

Possible responses: The priest blesses us and we pray the Sign of the Cross. The priest sends us to share God's love with others.

7–8. Write two ways the early Christians shared God's love.

Possible responses: They shared what they had with those in need. They tried to help those who were sad or lonely.

9–10. Write two ways receiving Holy Communion helps us.

Possible responses: It helps us to love God and others. It helps us to be followers of Jesus.

170

Chapter 19 ● Page 170

CHAPTER TEST

Provide ten to fifteen minutes for the students to complete the test. After all have finished, check the answers. Clarify any misconceptions.

Alternative Assessment

You may want the students to complete the following alternative-assessment activity.

Complete your Mass booklet. Draw a picture and write a sentence that tells how you will go in peace to love and serve God and one another.

Additional Testing

• Chapter 19 Test in *Assessment Book*, pages 39–40

• CD-ROM *Test Generator and Resource*: Use Chapter 19 Test or customize your own.

Review

Review the definitions as they are presented in the chapter's *Key Word* boxes:

• Blessed Sacrament (page 165)

• tabernacle (page 165).

We Believe Statements

Review the four statements.

• We are sent to share God's love with others.

• Jesus is present in the Blessed Sacrament.

• Jesus is with the Church as we share God's love.

• Jesus is with us as we share his peace with others.

To use the Chapter 19 Study Guide, visit

www.webelieveweb.com

Lent

Lent is a preparation for the celebration of Easter. For the Lenten liturgy disposes both catechumens and the faithful to celebrate the Paschal Mystery: catechumens, through the several stages of Christian initiation; the faithful, through reminders of their own baptism and through penitential practices.

(Norms Governing Liturgical Calendars, 27)

Overview

In this chapter the children will learn that Lent is a season of preparing.

For Adult Reading and Reflection
You may want to refer to paragraph 540 of the *Catechism of the Catholic Church*.

Catechist Background

Go to **www.webelieveweb.com**, Catechist/Teacher, We Believe Correlations for this chapter's correlation to the Six Tasks of Catechesis.

How have you observed Lent in the past?

Lent is the season of preparation for the celebration of Easter, the greatest feast of the Church year. For catechumens (those preparing for Baptism) and for all the faithful, it is a time to focus on Sacraments of Christian Initiation, the first of which is Baptism, the sacrament through which we die to sin and rise to new life in Christ. We remember that:

"The God of power and Father of our Lord Jesus Christ
has freed [us] from sin
and brought [us] to new life
through water and the Holy Spirit."
(Rite of Baptism, 62)

Lent is a penitential season, a time for ongoing conversion, not only for catechumens but also for all the baptized. We gradually turn our hearts more towards God and towards the needs of others. For forty days, from Ash Wednesday until the Evening Mass of the Lord's Supper on Holy Thursday, we pray, fast, and give alms to those in need. The forty days of this season remind us of the forty days Jesus spent in the desert, alone in prayer, totally dependent upon his God and Father.

We enter Lent knowing our need for a deeper turning, a deeper conversion, as disciples of the risen Lord. We enter Lent needing God's guidance amid myriad choices of modern life. We enter Lent with the mark of ashes on our foreheads. This ancient ritual of repentance helps us to "Remember how brief is my life," (Psalm 89:48) and challenges us to proclaim the Gospel, in the time we have been given, with our lives.

How will you observe Lent this year? How will you help the children to celebrate the season?

Lesson Planning Guide

Lesson Steps	Presentation	Materials
① WE GATHER		
page 171 **Introduce the Season**	• Read the *Chapter Story*. • Introduce the season of Lent. • Proclaim words on a banner.	
page 172	• Share responses to the directive and question.	
② WE BELIEVE		
pages 172–173 *Lent is a season of preparing.*	• Present the text about what we remember during Lent. • Discuss how people in photos are following Jesus.	
③ WE RESPOND		
page 174	🏃 Work on the chart for Lent.	• purple crayons or colored pencils
Text page 175 **Guide page 175–176** **We Respond in Prayer**	📖 Listen to a Scripture story. 🎵 Respond in song.	🎵 "We Are Yours, O Lord," Janet Vogt, #19, Grade 2 CD • prayer space items: cross, Bible, purple tablecloth
Text page 176 **Guide pages 175–176, 176A** **Project Disciple**	• Complete the **Project Disciple** activities. Discuss the *Take Home* activity. • Complete the Reproducible Master 20 activity. See guide pages 176A and 171C. • Discuss/send home **Sharing Faith with My Family**, guide page 176B.	• cross patterns • crayons or colored pencils • brad fasteners, scissors, and glue • purple and other colors of construction paper • copies of Reproducible Master 20, guide page 176A • copies of **Sharing Faith with My Family**, guide page 176B

For additional ideas, activities, and opportunities: Visit Sadlier's **www.WeBelieveweb.com**

Chapter Story

Yesterday Mark went to his friend Robert's house. Robert's mom and brothers and sisters were at the kitchen table. Mark asked, "What are you doing?"

Robert answered, "We're decorating paper crosses to send to my Uncle Stan."

Robert's uncle was a priest who was a missionary. Mark met him last year when he visited Robert's family. Father Stan worked in a country in Africa, teaching and helping the poor and sick. Robert explained, "When Uncle Stan travels from village to village, he gives crosses to the people he teaches. When the people look at the crosses, they may remember what Uncle Stan has taught them."

Mark told his friend, "I can help you make crosses now. And maybe you could ask Miss Torres if we could make them in class. Then we would have a lot of crosses to send to your uncle. We would be helping many people remember all Jesus has done for us."

Robert's mom said, "That's a great idea, Mark. I'll call Miss Torres now and ask her. Father Stan would certainly appreciate everyone's help."

How are Robert's family and Mark showing their love for God and others?

PROJECT DISCIPLE
Additional Activities

Celebrate!

Distribute copies of Reproducible Master 20, guide page 176A. Also give each child a sheet of purple construction paper. Have the children color the parts of the Lent wheel. Then ask them to cut out the wheel and the pointer. Tell the children to glue the back of the wheel to the construction paper. Help them use a brad fastener to attach the pointer. Encourage the children to display the wheel in a place where their families will see it often. Explain that they can move the pointer each day or week during Lent to show how they will share their love with God and others.

Make *it* Happen

Have available patterns of crosses, colored construction paper, scissors, and glue sticks. Begin by rereading the *Chapter Story*. Then ask the children to look at the crosses on the pages of this chapter. Help the children make crosses to send to the missions. Ask your pastor or call your diocesan office for names and addresses of where you can send the crosses.

Chapter 20

Chapter

Catechist Goa

- To explain that Le preparing

Our Faith Respo

- To show our love for God and others during Lent

"Turn away from sin and be faithful to the gospel."

The Marking of Ashes

SEASONAL

CHAPTER 20

This chapter offers preparation for the season of Lent.

LENT

171

Gather In My Name

Whole Community Catechesis

An Online Resource

Celebrate Lent as a class, school, and/or a parish community. Gather In My Name events come complete with detailed leader's guide, preparation charts, handouts, promotional ideas, organizational materials, and much more. Go to:

www.webelieveweb.com

Lesson Plan

Introduce the Season —— minutes

- **Pray** the Sign of the Cross.

- **Read** aloud the *Chapter Story* on guide page 171C. Ask the children: *Why does Father Stan give crosses to the people he teaches?* Help the children to understand that the cross is a sign of the followers of Jesus.

- **Have** the children open their texts to page 171. Read aloud the chapter title. Explain: *Lent is the season in which we get ready to celebrate Easter.*

- **Invite** the children to look at the photo on the pupil page. Point out that the children are celebrating what we can learn about Jesus by listening to Gospel stories about him and his followers.

- **Proclaim** together the words on the banner below the photo.

...on Materials
- copies of Reproducible Master 20
- purple crayons or colored pencils
- scissors and glue
- brad fasteners
- colored construction paper
- Grade 2 CD

Teaching Note

Blessing of Ashes

The ashes used to sign our fore-heads on Ash Wednesday are made by burning the palm branches blessed for the previous year's procession on Passion Sunday. During Mass on Ash Wednesday, the priest blesses the ashes after the homily. He then prays:

"Lord,
bless the sinner who asks for your
    forgiveness
and bless † all those who receive
    these ashes.
May they keep this lenten season
    in preparation for the joy of
    Easter.
We ask this through Christ our
    Lord."

Lent is a season of preparing.

WE GATHER

Sometimes a special logo or mark stands for something or someone. Think about some logos or marks that you know. What do they stand for?

WE BELIEVE

Lent is a time of remembering all that Jesus did to save us. It is a time to get ready. We get ready for the celebration of Easter and the new life that Jesus brings us.

The season of Lent lasts forty days. During that time we pray to God and ask for his forgiveness. We thank him for his mercy.

Lent begins on a day called Ash Wednesday. On Ash Wednesday, Catholics are marked with blessed ashes. The ashes are used to make a cross on our foreheads.

The cross reminds us that Jesus suffered and died for each of us. He did this so that we could live with God forever.

The cross of ashes on our foreheads is a sign that we are sorry for our sins and want to follow Jesus.

172

Lesson Plan

WE GATHER ___ minutes

Focus on Life Read the *We Gather* text. Discuss with the children the logos with which they are familiar. Have volunteers draw a few on the board and identify what these marks represent.

• **Invite** each child to think of a logo to represent himself or herself. Ask volunteers to share their own logos with the group.

WE BELIEVE ___ minutes

• **Ask** the children to identify the symbol on these pages (cross). Point out the photo on this page. Explain: *At the beginning of Lent we are marked with a cross. This is a sign that we are sorry for our sins and want to follow Jesus.*

• **Have** volunteers read the first five *We Believe* paragraphs. Stress: *The cross reminds us that Jesus suffered and died so that we could live with God forever.*

• **Draw** a large cross on the board or on chart paper. Have the children read the last *We Believe* paragraph. Then have volunteers write on the cross the things we do during Lent to follow Jesus.

Lent is a time when we try to grow closer to Jesus. We follow Jesus by praying, doing good things for others, and helping the poor. We treat people with love and respect, the way Jesus did.

Look at the photos on this page.

Talk about the ways people are following Jesus.

LENT

173

ACTIVITY BANK

Catholic Social Teaching

Call to Family, Community, and Participation

Activity Materials: traditionally formed soft or hard pretzels

Explain to the children: *Long ago when people prayed, they put their right hands on their left shoulders and their left hands on their right shoulders to form crosses.* Demonstrate this for the children. Then tell them: *In Lent some Christians twisted their bread dough into "little arms" crossed in prayer. This bread became known as* bracellae *in Latin. The English word is pretzels. Pretzels were baked on Ash Wednesday, and people ate them during Lent.*

Once each week during Lent, invite the children to gather in the prayer space. Pray the Our Father together; then share a snack of pretzels and juice.

Direct attention to the photos on page 173. For each photo ask: *How are the people following Jesus?*

Possible responses include:

Upper right: (Children are following Jesus by doing their work at school.);

Lower left: (Children are following Jesus by helping their families.);

Large photo: (Children are following Jesus by playing peacefully with others.).

Quick Check

✔ *What do we get ready for in Lent?* (We get ready for the celebration of Easter and the new life that Jesus brings us.)

✔ *What happens on Ash Wednesday?* (Catholics are marked with a cross of blessed ashes.)

CONNECTION

To Scripture

In Chapter 15 of the Gospel of Luke, there are three "lost and found" parables: the lost sheep, the lost son, and the lost coin. The lesson of each story is that God is always ready to welcome home the repentant sinner. The finding of the lost is the cause of great rejoicing. During the season of Lent, share these stories with the children. Refer the children to the story of the lost son, on page 95 of Chapter 10 and the story of the lost sheep on pages 100 and 101 of Chapter 11.

WE RESPOND

The color of the season of Lent is violet or purple. On the chart, color the word *Lent*. During Lent, each time you show your love for God and others, draw a cross in one of these boxes.

LENT

174

Lesson Plan

WE RESPOND   ___ minutes

Connect to Life Stress that the color of the season of Lent is purple or violet. Then read the directions for the Lenten chart activity.

• Brainstorm with the children what they can do during Lent to show their love for God and others. Write the children's responses on chart paper. Display the paper near the prayer space. Have the children look at the paper often during Lent. Remind the children that doing one or two things each day during Lent will help them prepare to celebrate Easter in a special way.

Some suggested acts: pray; do without a special treat; share with others; compliment someone; save money to donate to a food pantry or shelter; read a Bible story; ask God and others for forgiveness; forgive someone who has hurt you; give a little extra time to studying; talk to a classmate or teammate whom you usually do not talk to; be fair and peaceful when playing games; obey parents, guardians, and teachers.

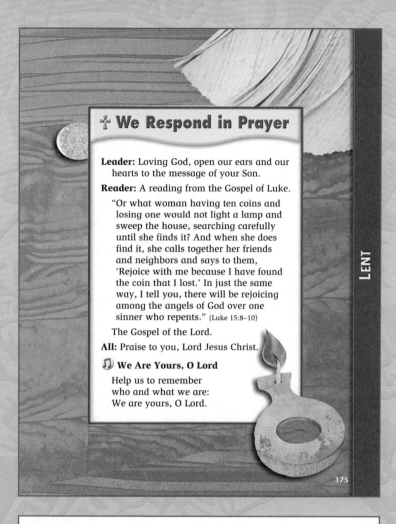

✝ We Respond in Prayer

Leader: Loving God, open our ears and our hearts to the message of your Son.

Reader: A reading from the Gospel of Luke.

"Or what woman having ten coins and losing one would not light a lamp and sweep the house, searching carefully until she finds it? And when she does find it, she calls together her friends and neighbors and says to them, 'Rejoice with me because I have found the coin that I lost.' In just the same way, I tell you, there will be rejoicing among the angels of God over one sinner who repents." (Luke 15:8–10)

The Gospel of the Lord.

All: Praise to you, Lord Jesus Christ.

🎵 **We Are Yours, O Lord**

Help us to remember
who and what we are:
We are yours, O Lord.

LENT

175

We Respond in Prayer (p. 175)

Get ready by placing a purple cloth and a cross on the prayer table. Then lead the children in prayer. Ask them to listen carefully to the Scripture story. Then respond together by singing "We Are Yours, O Lord," #19 on the Grade 2 CD.

📖 **This Week's Liturgy**

Visit **www.webelieveweb.com** for this week's liturgical readings and other seasonal material.

Project Disciple (p. 176)

Picture This Help the children complete the chart.

Celebrate!

Have the children start at #1 to connect the dots in numerical order. Also explain that they should draw a line to connect the #14 dot to the #1 dot.

Take Home

Read and discuss the *Take Home* activity. Decide on someone the class can pray for during Lent. Then pray. Encourage the children to share the prayer activity with their families.

Discuss and send home copies of *Sharing Faith with My Family*, guide page 176B.

Project Disciple Additional Activities
See the activities suggested on page 171C of the guide.

 Pray Learn Celebrate Share Choose Live

Grade 2 Lent

PROJECT DISCIPLE

Picture This Complete the chart about Lent. Use words or pictures.

The color of Lent is	Lent begins on	A sign of Lent is	The number of days in Lent
purple or violet	Ash Wednesday	a cross	forty days

Celebrate!

Connect the dots to find a sign of Lent. Then, color it in.

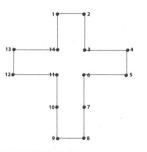

Take Home

Think of a person who needs your prayer during Lent. Write his or her name in this prayer.

Let the light of God shine on

_____

Say your prayer together.

↳ **DISCIPLE CHALLENGE**
Talk about what you can do during the season to help this person.

Name _____

1. Cut out the wheel. Attach the pointer.

2. Decide what you will do each week of Lent to show God and others your love.

3. Move the pointer to the part of the wheel that tells what you will do.

Lent is

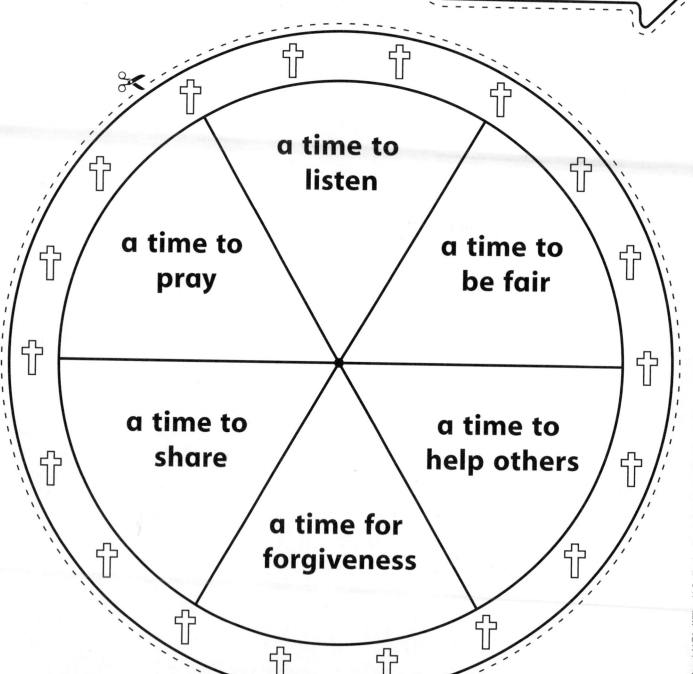

a time to
listen

a time to
pray

a time to
be fair

a time to
share

a time to
help others

a time for
forgiveness

SHARING FAITH
with My Family

Sharing What I Learned

Look at the pictures below. Use each picture to tell your family what you learned in this chapter.

The Giving Box

Find a special box or jar. During Lent, ask your family to think about people who are poor. Instead of spending money on treats or toys, put the money in the box or jar for people who are poor. With your family, choose a way to use this money to help people.

Our Lenten Prayer

Pray this prayer together often during Lent.

Jesus,
may we know you more clearly,
love you more dearly,
and follow you more nearly.

Amen.

(Saint Richard of Chichester)

Visit Sadlier's

www.WeBelieveweb.com

Connect to the Catechism
For adult background and reflection, see paragraph 540.

176B

The Three Days

Christ redeemed us all and gave perfect glory to God principally through his paschal mystery: dying he destroyed our death and rising he restored our life. Therefore the Easter Triduum of the passion and resurrection of Christ is the culmination of the entire liturgical year.

(Norms Governing Liturgical Calendars, 18)

Overview

In this chapter the children will learn that we celebrate the Death and Resurrection of Jesus during the Easter Triduum.

For Adult Reading and Reflection
You may want to refer to paragraph 628 of the *Catechism of the Catholic Church*.

Go to **www.webelieveweb.com**, Catechist/Teacher, We Believe Correlations for this chapter's correlation to the Six Tasks of Catechesis.

Catechist Background

What do you consider to be the most important three days of the liturgical year?

The Church's celebration of the Triduum, the Three Days, begins on Holy Thursday and ends on Easter Sunday evening. Each liturgical celebration from the Mass of the Lord's Supper on Holy Thursday to Evening Prayer on Easter Sunday is part of the celebration of the Paschal Mystery, Christ's Passion, Death and Resurrection. If we sincerely participate in these celebrations, we may sense that our ordinary lives are truly lived in Christ, with him and through him in sorrow and joy.

Within the Triduum, the Easter Vigil is the high point, because this is the celebration of the night when Christ passed from death to life, the night when hope and joy are once again restored to us. Celebrating our belief in Christ crucified, buried, and risen—and thus handing on our faith in him—is a baptismal ministry shared by all believers.

During the Triduum, as we enter deeply into the "hour" of Christ's Passover, we are asked to join him. We are asked to leave sin and death behind, and walk with Jesus into new life, love, peace, and forgiveness. Jesus Christ whom we follow has conquered death and sin. "You too must think of yourselves as [being] dead to sin and living for God in Christ Jesus" (Romans 6:11).

How will you participate in the Church's celebration of the Triduum, the Three Days?

Lesson Planning Guide

Lesson Steps	Presentation	Materials
① WE GATHER		
page 177 **Introduce the Season**	• Read the *Chapter Story*. • Introduce the Three Days. • Proclaim words on a banner.	
page 178	• Share responses to the questions.	
② WE BELIEVE		
pages 178–180 *The Three Days celebrate the Death and Resurrection of Jesus.*	• Present the text about celebrating the Death and Resurrection of Jesus. 🏃 Do the activity to show the beginning and end of the Three Days.	• crayons or colored pencils
③ WE RESPOND		
page 180	🏃 Share responses to the question. Decorate a prayer frame.	• crayons or colored pencils
Text page 181 **Guide page 181–182** **We Respond in Prayer**	• Listen to a Scripture reading. Respond in song.	🎵 "Alleluia, We Will Listen," Paul Inwood, #20, Grade 2 CD • prayer space items: tree branch, squares of red tissue paper, white tablecloth, Bible
Text page 182 **Guide pages 181–182, 182A** **Project Disciple**	• Complete the Project Disciple activities. Discuss the *Take Home* activity. • Complete the Reproducible Master 21 activity. See guide pages 182A and 177C. • Discuss/send home Sharing Faith with My Family, guide page 182B.	• crayons or colored pencils • copies of Reproducible Master 21 guide page 182A • copies of Sharing Faith with My Family, guide page 182B

For additional ideas, activities, and opportunities: Visit Sadlier's **www.WeBelieveweb.com**

Chapter Story

Allie's birthday was on April 10. She was looking forward to having her party this year. One day last week she asked her dad about what they could do for her party.

Allie's dad looked at the calendar. He said, "Allie, I think we'll have to have your party the week after your birthday. This year your birthday is on Good Friday, the day we remember that Jesus suffered and died for us."

Allie asked if they could have her party on the night before her birthday. But her mom told her, "Allie, that's Holy Thursday. I'll be reading at the Mass of the Lord's Supper. We'll have to have an early dinner and then get ready for church."

Allie thought for a few minutes. Instead of being upset, she told her parents, "Jesus did a lot for me. I can wait until after Easter for my party."

Do you think Allie reacted in a loving way? Why or why not?

PROJECT DISCIPLE
Additional Activities

picture This

Distribute copies of Reproducible Master 21, guide page 182A. Read the directions. Explain that a triptych is an art piece that has three panels. Discuss the symbol on each panel and identify which Three-Day celebration it represents.

Have the children color the panels; then help them cut out the triptych. Glue the triptych and fold the panels along the fold lines shown.

Encourage the children to share the triptych with their families and friends. Also encourage them to share what they learned about the Church's celebration of the Three Days.

Make it Happen

Distribute copies of Reproducible Master 21, guide page 182A. Have the children make triptychs for the people who will be baptized during the Easter Vigil Mass. Have the children color and cut out the triptychs and then glue them onto a piece of white construction paper. Then ask the children to print *Welcome to the Church* on the other side of the paper. Collect the triptychs and ask the pastor or RCIA director to give the welcoming cards to the new Church members.

"We should glory in the cross of our Lord Jesus Christ."
Evening Mass of the Lord's Supper

SEASONAL

CHAPTER 21

This chapter includes the three days from Holy Thursday evening until Easter Sunday.

177

Chapter 21 • Three Days

Catechist Goal

• To introduce the Church's celebration of the Three Days

Our Faith Response

• To recall the importance of the Three Days

Gather In My Name
Whole Community Catechesis

An Online Resource

For the **Triduum** *season use the Easter* GIMN *event or the Eucharist* GIMN *event to highlight the season. Gather In My Name events come complete with a detailed leader's guide, preparation charts, handouts, promotional ideas, organizational materials, and much more. Go to:*

www.webelieveweb.com

Lesson Plan

Introduce the Season ____ minutes

• **Pray** Pray the Sign of the Cross and pause for the children to reflect quietly about all Jesus has done for us.

• **Read** aloud the *Chapter Story*, guide page 177C. Discuss Allie's response to her parents.

• **Have** the children open their texts to page 177. Read together the title of the chapter. Have the children turn to page 61. Then have the children point to the Three Days' space on the Church year chart. Ask: *What seasons does the Three Days come between?*

• **Ask** the children to look at the photo. Explain: *When we gather with our parish on Good Friday, we venerate the cross. This means we show our love and thanks to Jesus for dying on the cross for us.*

• **Read** together the words on the banner.

Lesson Materials

- copies of Reproducible Master 21
- crayons or colored pencils
- Grade 2 CD
- white and red construction paper
- scissors and glue, paste, or tape

Teaching Tip

Being Flexible

Veteran teachers often point out that a lesson plan is a plan, not a contract that must be carried out to the letter of the law. Remember a lesson plan is a guide that can be changed. Be open to possibilities raised by your needs or the needs of the children: more review, more explanations, more creative activities, change in length of class. Keep in mind the children's creativity as well as their needs.

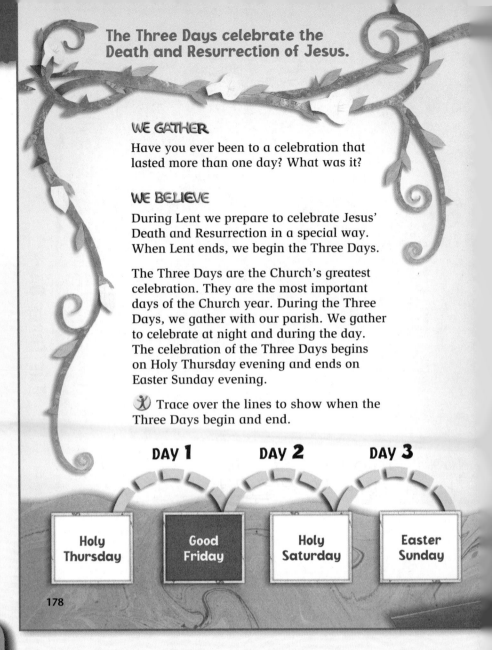

The Three Days celebrate the Death and Resurrection of Jesus.

WE GATHER

Have you ever been to a celebration that lasted more than one day? What was it?

WE BELIEVE

During Lent we prepare to celebrate Jesus' Death and Resurrection in a special way. When Lent ends, we begin the Three Days.

The Three Days are the Church's greatest celebration. They are the most important days of the Church year. During the Three Days, we gather with our parish. We gather to celebrate at night and during the day. The celebration of the Three Days begins on Holy Thursday evening and ends on Easter Sunday evening.

Trace over the lines to show when the Three Days begin and end.

DAY 1   **DAY 2**   **DAY 3**

| Holy Thursday | Good Friday | Holy Saturday | Easter Sunday |

178

Lesson Plan

WE GATHER   ___ minutes

Focus on Life Read the *We Gather* questions. Ask volunteers to share their responses. Point out that sometimes family celebrations (reunions, weddings, birthdays, anniversaries) last two or more days. Tell the children that in this lesson they will learn about the Church's most special celebration, the celebration of the Three Days.

WE BELIEVE   ___ minutes

- **Have** a volunteer read aloud the two *We Believe* paragraphs on page 178. Ask the children to highlight or underline the first and last sentences of the second paragraph.

Read the *We Believe* activity directions. Have the children complete the activity.

- **Ask** the children to look at page 133 in Chapter 15. Have volunteers explain what happened at the Last Supper. Explain: *Every year on Holy Thursday evening we gather to celebrate Jesus' gift of the Eucharist in a special way.*

- **Ask** a volunteer to read the first *We Believe* paragraph on page 179. You may want to point out that on the night of the Last Supper Jesus washed his disciples' feet. Have the children look at the top right photo on page 179. Explain: *During the Mass of the Lord's Supper on Holy*

The celebration begins on Holy Thursday night. We remember what happened at the Last Supper. We celebrate that Jesus gave himself to us in the Eucharist. We remember the ways Jesus served others. We have a special collection for those who are in need.

On Good Friday, we listen to the story of Jesus' Death and pray before the cross. The cross reminds us of Jesus' dying and rising to new life. We pray for the whole world. We wait and pray.

THE THREE DAYS

179

ACTIVITY BANK

Catholic Social Teaching
Call to Family, Community, and Participation
Activity Materials: duplicated copies of recipe for hot-cross buns, construction paper, markers, tape or glue, commercially prepared hot-cross buns (optional)

To focus on the Good Friday symbol of the cross, consider providing commercially prepared hot-cross buns for the children to share. Explain that these yeast rolls may have originated in an English monastery hundreds of years ago. The monks made the buns and used frosting to draw a cross on them. They distributed the buns to the poor on Good Friday. Give each child a copy of any basic hot-cross-bun recipe. Recipes are available on numerous Web sites. Then distribute the art materials and have the children mount the recipe on construction paper to take home to their families.

Thursday evening, the priest washes the feet of twelve people in the assembly. This helps us to remember that Jesus served others and wants us to do the same.

• **Ask** a volunteer to read the second paragraph on page 179. Have the children look at the bottom photo and look again at the photo of the veneration of the cross on page 177.

Quick Check

✔ *What do the Three Days celebrate?* (The Three Days celebrate the Death and Resurrection of Jesus.)

✔ *When does the celebration of the Three Days begin and end?* (The celebration of the Three Days begins on Holy Thursday evening and ends on Easter Sunday evening.)

CONNECTION

To Liturgy

A Three-Day Procession

Processions are part of the liturgical celebrations of Holy Week, beginning with the palm procession on Passion Sunday. On Holy Thursday the Blessed Sacrament is carried in silent procession to the altar of repose. On Good Friday the congregation processes to the sanctuary to venerate the cross. At the Easter Vigil the paschal candle is carried in procession from the bonfire outside into the church. Plan a class procession into the church any time while presenting this chapter. Have the children take turns carrying a cross with a flower wreath. Sing together a familiar version of "Christ has died." Process to the altar, bow, and then process around the church.

On Holy Saturday night, we light the Easter candle. Jesus has risen! He brings light to the darkness. We listen to Bible readings about all the great things God has done for us. We sing with joy to celebrate that Jesus rose from the dead. We remember our Baptism in a special way. We also welcome new members of the Church as they are baptized.

Holy Saturday turns into Easter Sunday. We sing songs of joy and praise as we begin the Easter season. Alleluia!

WE RESPOND

Think about the things we do to celebrate the Three Days. How does your parish celebrate the Three Days?

Pray this prayer. Then color the frame.

When we eat this Bread and drink this Cup, we proclaim your Death O Lord, ~~Christ has died.~~ ~~Christ is risen.~~ ~~Christ will~~ until you come again.

180

Lesson Plan

WE BELIEVE (continued)

• **Read** aloud the *We Believe* paragraphs on page 180. You may want to take the children to church to show them the Paschal or Easter candle. Also have the children look at the candle on the page. Explain: *Outside the church on Holy Saturday night the priest starts a new fire and lights the Easter candle with this fire. The candle is carried in procession into the church and the members of the assembly light their candles by the flame of the Easter candle.*

WE RESPOND ___ minutes

Connect to Life Read the *We Respond* question. Invite one of the members of the parish liturgy committee to talk with the children about the celebration of the Three Days.

Ask the children to pray the *We Respond* prayer. Then have them color the frame.

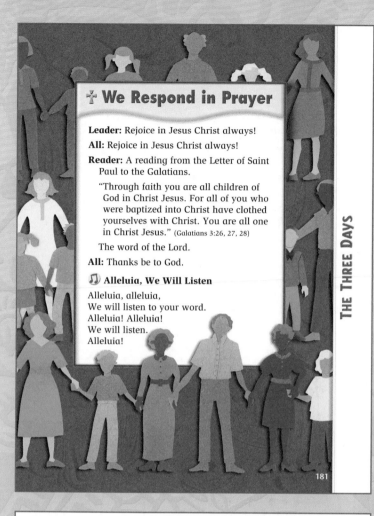

✝ We Respond in Prayer

Leader: Rejoice in Jesus Christ always!

All: Rejoice in Jesus Christ always!

Reader: A reading from the Letter of Saint Paul to the Galatians.

"Through faith you are all children of God in Christ Jesus. For all of you who were baptized into Christ have clothed yourselves with Christ. You are all one in Christ Jesus." (Galatians 3:26, 27, 28)

The word of the Lord.

All: Thanks be to God.

♫ **Alleluia, We Will Listen**

Alleluia, alleluia,
We will listen to your word.
Alleluia! Alleluia!
We will listen.
Alleluia!

THE THREE DAYS

181

 Grade 2 The Three Days

PROJECT DISCIPLE

Show What *you* Know

Put these events in the order that they are celebrated during the Three Days.

third

first

second

Celebrate!

Draw a picture of one way that you will celebrate during the Three Days.

Possible responses: gather to celebrate with parish community; give to a collection for those in need; listen to stories about Jesus; pray; sing; welcome new members to the Church

Take Home

Now that the above pictures are in order, use them to talk about the Three Days. Touch each picture as you tell your family why it is important.

We Respond in Prayer (p. 181)

Get ready by placing a white cloth on the prayer table. Then invite the children to gather in the prayer space. Ask them to join hands as they pray and listen to the reading from Scripture. Lead the children in prayer and singing "Alleluia, We Will Listen," #20 on the Grade 2 CD.

 This Week's Liturgy

Visit www.webelieveweb.com for this week's liturgical readings and other seasonal material.

Project Disciple (p. 182)

Show What *you* Know

Discuss the pictures; then help the children put them in order.

Celebrate!

Share with the children a few ways you are planning to celebrate during the Three Days.

Take Home

Read the directions. Invite volunteers to share with the group what they tell their families about the illustrations. Encourage the children to share with their families what they have learned about the Three Days.

Discuss and send home copies of *Sharing Faith with My Family*, guide page 182B.

Project Disciple Additional Activities
See the activities suggested on page 177C of the guide.

Name

Show what we celebrate during the Three Days.
Color each picture of the triptych.

Fold   Fold

SHARING FAITH
with My Family

Sharing What I Learned

Look at the pictures below. Use each picture to tell your family what you learned in this chapter.

Around the Table

The Church's celebration of the great Three Days begins on Holy Thursday evening and ends on Easter Sunday evening. See the calendar boxes below.

Mark these days on your family calendar. Talk together about ways your parish celebrates on these days.

DAY 1   **DAY 2**   **DAY 3**

Holy Thursday	Good Friday	Holy Saturday	Easter Sunday

The Three Days

For All to Pray

"We should glory in the cross of our Lord Jesus Christ."

Visit Sadlier's

www.WeBelieve.web.com

Connect to the Catechism
For adult background and reflection, see paragraph 628.

182B

ASSESSMENT

Unit 3 Test

Read aloud each set of test directions. Also you may choose to read aloud each test item, pausing for a few minutes for children to write their responses.

Alternative Assessment

You may want the children to complete the following alternative-assessment activity.

Write two things that happen during each of the following parts of the Mass:

- *Beginning*
- *Liturgy of the Word*
- *Liturgy of the Eucharist*
- *End of Mass.*

Additional Testing

• Unit 3 Test in Grade 2 *Assessment Book*, pages 41–42

• Unit 3 Alternative Assessment in Grade 2 *Assessment Book*, page 55

• CD-ROM *Test Generator and Resource*: Use Unit 3 Test or customize your own.

Grade 2 Unit 3

UNIT TEST

Use the words in the box to complete the sentences.

| giving thanks |
| celebrate |
| Creed |
| assembly |
| Holy Communion |
| Eucharistic Prayer |

1. In the Eucharist we remember and ___celebrate___ what Jesus did at the Last Supper.

2. The word *eucharist* means ___giving thanks___.

3. We receive the Body and Blood of Christ in ___Holy Communion___.

4. The ___Eucharistic Prayer___ is the most important prayer of the Mass.

5. The ___Creed___ is a prayer in which we say what we believe as Christians.

6. The community of people who join together for the celebration of the Mass is the ___assembly___.

continued on next page   183

Grade 2 Unit 3

7–8. **Draw or write about two things that happen during the Liturgy of the Word.**
See Chapter 17.

9–10. **Draw or write about two things that happen during the Liturgy of the Eucharist.**
See Chapter 18.

184

We Live Our Catholic Faith

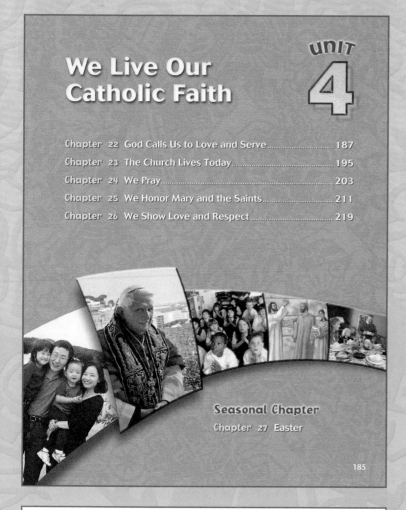

185

PROJECT DISCIPLE

DEAR FAMILY

In Unit 4 your child will grow as a disciple of Jesus by:

- learning about the ways people can serve God as married or single people, ordained men, and religious
- praying, celebrating at Mass and the sacraments, and with our parish community caring for those in need
- learning about the ways the pope and the bishops lead and serve the Church
- talking and listening to God in prayer
- honoring Mary and the saints by following their example of discipleship.

Saint Stories

Some popes and bishops who served the Church have been named saints. Saint Pius X was the pope from 1903–1914. As Pope, he wanted to ensure that children received their first Holy Communion at an early age. He is the patron saint of first communicants.

Saint Charles Borromeo was the Archbishop of Milan, Italy. Saint Charles began Sunday school for children, showed great care for the sick, and served his diocese with great love. He is the patron saint of bishops.

Share these saint stories with your child. Ask these two saints to help our pope and bishops.

Pray Today

Chapter 22 presents the different vocations to which God calls people. Pray together:

God, you call each of us to serve you.
Bless your people:
single and married,
priests and deacons,
brothers and sisters.
Help each of us to answer your call
and to serve you with love.
Amen.

Reality Check

"The Christian family is the first place of education in prayer."
(Catechism of the Catholic Church, 2685)

Fast Facts

The Mass is celebrated in many languages throughout the United States, according to the native language of the people who are gathered. Mass is also celebrated in the Latin language, which was until the mid-1960s the only language used for Mass in most countries.

Show That You Care

In Chapter 26, your child will learn about God's many gifts to us—including the gift of creation. Talk about the ways your family cares for creation. Decide on one extra thing you all can do to care for the environment this week.

Take Home

Each chapter in your child's *We Believe* Grade 2 text offers a "Take Home" activity that invites your family to support your child's journey to more fully become a disciple of Christ.

Be ready for this unit's Take Home:

Chapter 22: Discussing your child's vocation

Chapter 23: Sharing family faith traditions

Chapter 24: Praying an evening prayer

Chapter 25: Finding works of art depicting Mary

Chapter 26: Being a disciple of Jesus Christ

186

CLASS CONNECTION

Read aloud the unit title and the chapter titles. Ask the children: *What do you think you will be learning about in this unit?* Invite a few volunteers to respond. Then explain that in this unit they will be learning about the ways we live our faith. Also have a class discussion about the photographs and illustrations on this page.

HOME CONNECTION

Project Disciple Dear Family

Sadlier *We Believe* calls on families to become involved in:

- learning the faith
- prayer and worship
- living their faith.

Highlighting of these unit family pages and the opportunities they offer will strengthen the partnership of the Church and the home.

For additional information and activities, encourage families to visit Sadlier's

www.WeBelieveweb.com

Overview

In Chapter 19 the children learned about sharing God's love with others. In this chapter the children will learn that everyone is called by God to love and serve him.

Doctrinal Content	For Adult Reading and Reflection *Catechism of the Catholic Church*
The children will learn:	Paragraph
• We are called by God.	1604
• Married people and single people are called by God.	1658
• Priests are called by God.	1578
• Religious sisters and brothers are called by God.	1618

called by God
(p. 188)

Catechist Background

Go to **www.webelieveweb.com**, Catechist/ Teacher, We Believe Correlations for this chapter's correlation to:
- Six Tasks of Catechesis
- Catholic Social Teaching
- *Catechetical Formation in Chaste Living.*

How have you been called by God?

God has called each of us by name to love and serve him. In Baptism we receive the grace to answer God's call. We live out our calling in many ways. For example, when you teach, you are serving God through your profession as a teacher.

We also serve God through our particular state in life. Some people remain single throughout their lives and serve God in their relationships with their family, coworkers, and others. Other people celebrate the Sacrament of Matrimony and serve God first by loving their spouse and children. They also serve God in relationships with others.

Some men are called to the Sacrament of Holy Orders. There are actually three orders, or degrees, to this sacrament: deacons, priests, and bishops. Some deacons are ordained for the purpose of helping and serving and assisting priests in their role. This is called the permanent diaconate. Other men are ordained deacons as a step in the process

of becoming a priest. Some priests are called to serve the Church in the role of bishop, and thus receive "the fullness of the sacrament of Holy Orders" (CCC 1557).

Finally, some people are called by God to serve as religious brothers and sisters. These people belong to religious communities and serve God through working and praying in their communities and loving and serving others.

Although we may have different states in life: single, married, ordained, or vowed religious, all of us are called by God to love and serve him. The way we live our lives is our answer to God's call.

How do you see people around you responding to God's call?

Lesson Planning Guide

Lesson Steps	Presentation	Materials

1 WE GATHER

page 187 ✝ **Prayer**	• Praise and thank God.	For the prayer space: magazine and newspaper photos of people helping; bowl of holy water
☀ **Focus on Life**	• Reflect and discuss the directive and question.	

2 WE BELIEVE

page 188 *We are called by God.*	• Read the text about ways we can serve God. • Point out the *Key Word* and definition. ⟳ Do the activity.	• highlighters or crayons • pencils
page 189 *Married people and single people are called by God.*	• Present the text about single and married people. ♫ Pray by singing.	♫ "God Has Made Us a Family," Carey Landry, #21, Grade 2 CD
page 190 *Priests are called by God.*	• Read the text about ways priests serve God and others. ⟳ Do the activity about the ways priests serve. • Read and discuss the *As Catholics* text.	• pencils
page 191 *Religious sisters and brothers are called by God.*	• Read the text about religious sisters and brothers. ⟳ Share the questions the children would like to ask.	• crayons • copies of Reproducible Master 22, guide page 187C • scissors, glue, construction paper

3 WE RESPOND

page 191	⟳ Respond to the question in writing.	
pages 192–193 **Project Disciple**	• Complete the **Project Disciple** activities. • Explain the *Take Home* activity. • Discuss/send home **Sharing Faith with My Family** reproducible master for this chapter.	• crayons or colored pencils or markers • copies of Sharing Faith with My Family reproducible master, Chapter 22 (back of book)
page 194 **Chapter 22 Test**	• Complete **Chapter 22 Test**. • Work on *Alternative Assessment* activity.	• optional: copies of Scripture reproducible master, *What's the Word?*, Chapter 22 (back of book)

For additional ideas, activities, and opportunities: Visit Sadlier's **www.WeBelieveweb.com**

Follow these puzzle directions:

- Cut out the "**Serve God**" sign.
- Glue it to the bottom of a piece of construction paper.
- Color the puzzle pieces red. Cut them out.
- Put the puzzle pieces together to form a shape.
- Glue the pieces above the "**Serve God**" sign.

PROJECT DISCIPLE

Pray
Learn
Celebrate
Share
Choose
Live

Additional Activities

What's the Word?

Scripture reproducible master, Chapter 22

Materials needed: copies of *What's the Word?* (back of book)

Distribute copies of the Scripture reproducible master. Have the students close their eyes and imagine that they are on a mountainside listening to Jesus teach. Explain that they are with thousands of people.

Then ask volunteers to take the parts of Narrator, Joseph, and Marah. Have these volunteers read the script. Discuss what being light for others means; then ask the children to answer Marah's question by listing a few ways children their age can be light for others.

Show What you Know

Choose volunteers to role-play the following parts: a married woman, a married man, a single woman, a man who is a deacon, a religious sister, a religious brother, and a priest. Have the children who are role-playing introduce themselves and share a few ways that they serve the Church. An example would be: *I am Sister Lucy. I work in a hospital. I visit patients and comfort their families.* Ask the children to prepare by referring to their texts.

More to Explore

Materials needed: traditionally shaped pretzels and fruit juice

If you have not presented the activity in the Lent chapter activity bank on guide page 173, you may want to do this activity with the children. Explain the following:

Long ago monks, religious brothers or priests, taught the children, who came to the monastery school, their prayers. At this time people prayed by putting the right hand on the left shoulder and the left hand on the right shoulder. (Demonstrate for the children and ask them to do the same.)

One day a monk was baking. He twisted bread dough into "little arms" crossed in prayer. (Show the children a pretzel.) *The monks in the monastery decided they would give the twisted bread to the children as "little rewards" for learning their prayers. The Latin word for "little rewards" is* pretiola.

You may want to find a recipe for pretzels online or have traditionally shaped pretzels available. Share a pretzel and fruit juice snack with the children. (Before doing this check with parents about food allergies their children may have.)

Meeting Individual Needs
Families in Crisis

Be sensitive to all the children's family situations. Keep discussions objective. In the presentation of this chapter, have the children think about families in general, not about their own families.

We Believe Resources

- Grade 2 *Review & Resource Book*, pages 49–51
- Grade 2 *Family Book*, pages 62–64
- Grade 2 *Assessment Book*, pages 43–44
- Grade 2 CD-ROM *Test Generator and Resource*: Use Chapter 22 Test or customize your own.
- **www.webelieveweb.com**

Enrichment Ideas

Chapter Story

Lorenzo came running into the house all excited. "Guess what, Mom and Dad! The children's choir is going to sing for Sister Angela's anniversary celebration on Sunday. Father Albert heard us today and invited us to sing on Sunday. Can you believe that Sister has been at Saint Jerome's for twenty years?"

Lorenzo's father said, "Sister Angela has helped me many times. Once I dropped books I was carrying. Sister stopped and helped me to pick up all the books."

Lorenzo's mother said, "Sister Angela will be so surprised by everything the parish is doing for her. Sister has worked hard to help the parish. She is always finding ways to help families, especially those who are in need. She has started many of the successful programs that the parish offers for single people, families, children, and teenagers."

On Sunday afternoon the members of Saint Jerome's parish gathered in the parish hall. Many families and parish members had decorated and made food for the celebration. As Sister walked into the hall, everyone said, "Surprise" and then clapped. Then Father Albert spoke. He said, "Thank you, Sister, for sharing God's love with the parish through all the years you've been here." Father then invited the children's choir to sing the special song Brother Fredrick had taught them.

Then Sister Angela went to the microphone. She said, "How special you make me feel. I came to Saint Jerome's to do God's work, and I've enjoyed doing this work with many of you. Thank you for your kindness. Now, let's continue the celebration."

▶ *Why were the people of Saint Jerome's parish having a celebration for Sister Angela?*

FAITH and MEDIA

▶ After reading page 188 with the children, remind them that many people, among them writers, editors, actors, directors, and newscasters, serve God through work in media. Point out that those who serve God through media include many priests, religious sisters and brothers, and others working in Church ministries around the world.

▶ Before the children complete the reproducible master puzzle, show them both the print publications and the Web sites of one or more communities of religious sisters and brothers.

CHAPTER PROJECT: RECORDED GREETINGS

Help the children make a recording to share with the residents of a local retirement home, continuing care facility, or participants in your parish's senior citizens' group. Have each child write a greeting he or she would like to record. Also ask the group to decide what song they would like to sing. Set aside time to record the children's greetings and their song. Then ask a pastoral minister to deliver the recording to the group you have chosen.

God Calls Us to Love and Serve

WE GATHER

✝ **Leader:** God, our Father, in Baptism you called us by name making us members of your people, the Church.

All: We praise you for your goodness. We thank you for your gifts.

Leader: We ask you to strengthen us to live in love and service to others as your Son, Jesus, did.

We ask this through Christ, our Lord.

All: Amen.

☀ Think about a time when someone you love called your name. What did you do?

187

PREPARING TO PRAY

In this gathering prayer the children praise and thank God the Father and ask for his help.

• Ask a volunteer to be the prayer leader. Have this person read the leader's words.

The Prayer Space
• Display photographs from magazines and newspapers showing people helping one another. (Try to include pictures of priests or religious sisters and brothers.) If possible include photos of people in your parish. These pictures will help illustrate our baptismal call to love and serve others.

• On the prayer table place a bowl of holy water to remind the children of their Baptism.

📖 **This Week's Liturgy**
Visit **www.webelieveweb.com** for this week's liturgical readings and other seasonal material.

Lesson Plan

WE GATHER ___ minutes

✝ Pray
• Say each child's name and ask him or her to gather in the prayer space.

• Have the children dip their fingers in the holy water and pray the Sign of the Cross quietly.

• Ask the prayer leader to begin the prayer.

☀ Focus on Life
• Ask the children to read the directive and question. Invite them to share experiences they have had when parents called them by name. Tell the children that in this chapter they will learn that we are all called by God to love and serve him. Share the *Chapter Story* on guide page 187E.

Family Connection Update
Ask the children to share their family discussion about ways of making their home more peaceful.

Catechist Goal

- To explain that all people are called to serve God as married, single, priests, or religious brothers and sisters

Our Faith Response

- To answer God's call to love and serve him and to show our gratitude for priests and religious brothers and sisters

 called by God

Lesson Materials

- highlighters or crayons
- Grade 2 CD
- copies of Reproducible Master 22
- Scripture and Family reproducible masters (back of book)

Teaching Tip

Using Music in the Classroom

Singing in unison promotes positive feelings among group members. Play a song on the Grade 2 CD a few times. When the children become comfortable with the melody, invite them to sing along.

WE BELIEVE

We are called by God.

We read in the Bible that God says, "I have called you by name: you are mine." (Isaiah 43:1)
When we are **called by God**, we are invited by God to love and serve him.

We love and serve God now in many ways. As members of the Church we pray and respect God's name. We take part in the Mass and the other sacraments. We learn about God from the teachings of Jesus and the Church. We tell others the wonderful things God has done for us.

As we grow older we are called to serve God in different ways. We may serve God as single or married people, religious brothers or sisters or priests or deacons. These ways of serving God are all important to the Church. Together we work to bring God's love to others.

Write the name of a person you know who loves and serves God.

How does that person show love for God?

Key Word
called by God
invited by God to love and serve him

Lesson Plan

WE BELIEVE ____ minutes

Invite a volunteer to read aloud the *We Believe* statement and the first paragraph on page 188. Ask the children to highlight or underline the last sentence.

Ask the children to think of ways they can love and serve God now. Write these ways on chart paper. Then ask a volunteer to read the second paragraph on page 188. Have the children look at the list on the chart paper and compare their list with the ways mentioned in the text.

Ask: *When you are older, do you think there will be other ways you will love and serve God?* Have a volunteer read the third paragraph. Emphasize: *We are called to love and serve God throughout our lives.*

Give the children a few moments of silence to think of people they know who love and serve God. Then have each child write one person's name. Invite volunteers to share the names of the persons and how they love and serve God.

Have a volunteer read aloud the first two sentences on page 189. Then ask volunteers to read the listed sentences aloud. Stress: *Married people and single people love and serve God by helping others.*

Married people and single people are called by God.

In our families there are single people and married people. They serve God in many of the same ways.

- They love and care for their families.
- They take part in parish activities.
- They tell others about Jesus and the Church.
- They work to make their communities better places.
- They help people in need.
- They pray for others.

Single people share God's love in their families, communities, and the Church. Married people celebrate the Sacrament of Matrimony. A husband and wife share God's love with each other and with their children. They teach their children about Jesus and the Church. They show them how to live as Catholics.

🎵 **God Has Made Us a Family**

God has made us a family
and together we will grow in love.
God has made us a family
and together we will grow in love.

189

ACTIVITY BANK

Scripture
Called by Name
Activity Materials: poster board or heavy construction paper cut into 12-in. by 2-in. strips, one for each child, colored markers, (glitter and glue—option)

Invite the children to make personalized name plaques. Give each child a pre-cut paper strip. Have the children carefully print their name and then decorate the plaque by using their favorite colors and designs. On the back of the plaque have them write *God calls me by name.* Suggest to the children that they may want to display their name plaque on their bedroom door. You may want to collect all the plaques to display on a bulletin board with the title: "God Calls Each of Us by Name."

Point out that married and single people help us to celebrate the Eucharist. Explain: *Some volunteer to be readers at Mass or extraordinary ministers of Holy Communion. Some volunteer to play musical instruments or sing.* Then ask about other ways that married and single people help the parish community.

Read aloud the last paragraph. Point out: *Married people celebrate the Sacrament of Matrimony. They have certain responsibilities to each other and their children.*

🎵 **Play** "God Has Made Us a Family," #21 on the Grade 2 CD. Then replay the song as the children sing along.

Pray Invite the group to gather in the prayer space and sing "God Has Made Us a Family."

Quick Check

✔ *What does being called by God mean?* (God invites us to love and serve him.)

✔ *What are some of the same ways that married and single people can serve God?* (any of the ways described on page 189)

As Catholics...

Deacons

Have volunteers read the paragraphs. If a deacon is serving in your parish, ask him to come and speak to the children. When inviting the deacon, ask him to allow time for a question and answer period.

Priests are called by God.

Some men are called, or invited, to serve God and the Church as priests. A man becomes a priest when he receives the Sacrament of Holy Orders.

Priests spend their lives sharing God's love with people. They share the message of Jesus and help us to live as Jesus did.

Priests lead the celebration of the Mass and other sacraments. They teach us about our Catholic faith. They work in parishes, schools, hospitals, and communities all over the world.

Write one way priests serve God and others. Remember to thank them.

Accept what is given in the third

paragraph.

190

As Catholics...

Deacons are baptized men who have received the Sacrament of Holy Orders. Some men are deacons for life, or permanent deacons. These men may be married or single. Other men become deacons as a step before they become priests.

Deacons serve the Church by assisting the bishops and priests. Deacons serve in their parishes by baptizing new members into the Church and by witnessing at marriages. They can proclaim the Gospel and give the homily at Mass. Deacons also have a special responsibility to serve people in need.

Is there a deacon serving in your parish?

Lesson Plan

WE BELIEVE (continued)

Ask a volunteer to read the *We Believe* statement on page 190. Then read the three paragraphs that follow. Have the children tell about the priests whom they know. Encourage them to mention times that they have seen a priest serving God by caring for the people of the parish.

Discuss the photographs on page 190. Help the children name the activities pictured.

Read the directions. Have the children write their responses. Remind the children to remember to thank the priests of the parish for all they do.

Ask volunteers to read the first two paragraphs on page 191. Stress: *Religious brothers or sisters live, pray, and work together in communities.*

Ask volunteers to read the remaining text. Encourage the children to share stories of religious brothers and sisters about whom they know or whom they have heard.

Talk with the children about questions they would like to ask religious sisters or brothers. Give the children time to share how they think the sisters and brothers would answer each question. If possible, invite a religious sister or brother to answer the questions either in person, by letter, or by e-mail.

Religious sisters and brothers are called by God.

Some women and men are called by God to love and serve him as religious sisters and brothers. They belong to religious communities.

These women and men pray and work together. They live a life of loving service to God, the Church, and their religious communities.

Religious sisters and brothers serve in many ways.

- They tell others about Jesus either in our country or in faraway places.
- They teach in schools and parishes.
- They work in hospitals and spend time with those who are sick or elderly.
- They care for people who are in need.

What questions would you like to ask religious sisters and brothers about the work they do?

WE RESPOND

What is the one thing you will do to serve God this week?

_____

_____

_____

191

ACTIVITY BANK

Church
Guest Speaker

Activity Materials: crayons or markers, drawing paper

Ask a priest or a religious brother or sister to speak in person to the children about their lives and work. If this is not possible, ask the speakers to record an audio or videotape to play for the children.

Curriculum Connection
Language Arts

Activity Materials: chart paper, colored pencils

Have the children work in groups. Give each group a sheet of chart paper. Each group is to design a word-search puzzle. Ask the children to use words or terms in this chapter. (Possible words: serve, sister, brother, priest, married, single, name, community) Go to each group and check the progress of the puzzles. Then invite the groups to exchange puzzles and solve them. You might want to list on the board the terms from each group's puzzle and use this list as a way to evaluate the children's understanding of the chapter.

Distribute copies of Reproducible Master 22. Read the directions. Have the children put the puzzle pieces together. (The pieces form a heart.) Encourage the children to share the puzzle message with their families and friends.

WE RESPOND
_____ minutes

Connect to Life Ask a volunteer to read aloud the *We Respond* question. Discuss the children's responses. Provide a minute of quiet time in which they can think about their response.

Pray Ask the children to pray quietly about loving and serving God.

Catechist Goal

• To review the chapter ideas that are key to growing as disciples of Jesus Christ

Our Faith Response

• To decide on ways to grow as disciples by living out what we have learned

Show What *you* Know

Help the children to complete the web.

Make *it* Happen

Show a sports trading card to the children. Read the statistics on the card. Then read aloud the activity directions.

Have each child draw the person's picture in the space on the left. Then help with the spelling of the person's name. Ask volunteers to show their trading cards to the group.

Saint Stories

Read the paragraph about Saint Elizabeth Ann Seton. You may want to read more about Elizabeth. Go to *Lives of the Saints* Archive at **www.webelieveweb.com.** Download the primary activity.

Take Home

Read the activity suggestion. Encourage the children to discuss with their families ways that they will show God's love when they are adults.

Discuss and send home copies of *Sharing Faith with My Family* reproducible master for this chapter (back of book).

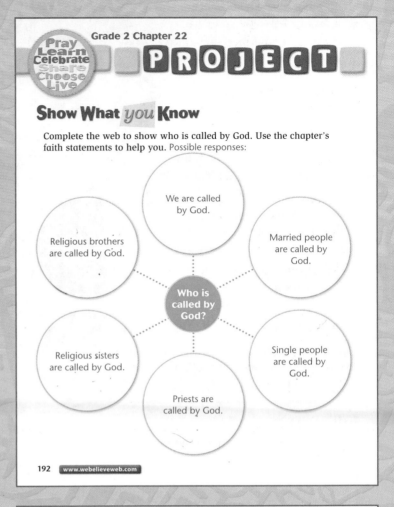

Pray Learn Celebrate Share Choose Live

Grade 2 Chapter 22

PROJECT

Show What *you* Know

Complete the web to show who is called by God. Use the chapter's faith statements to help you. Possible responses:

- We are called by God.
- Religious brothers are called by God.
- Married people are called by God.
- Who is called by God?
- Religious sisters are called by God.
- Single people are called by God.
- Priests are called by God.

192   www.webelieveweb.com

DISCIPLE

Pray Learn Celebrate Share Choose Live

Make *it* Happen

Complete this trading card about a person you know who serves God.

Name: _____

Shows love for God and others by:
_____
_____

Saint Stories

Elizabeth Ann Seton is the first person from the United States to be named a saint. She taught and helped the poor. She started the first Catholic school in the United States. She started a religious community called the Sisters of Charity. They teach in schools, work in hospitals, and help in parishes today.

Take Home

Talk with your family about the person you want to be when you grow up. Make a list of ways that you will show your love for God when you are a grown-up.

_____
_____
_____
_____

193

CHAPTER TEST

Circle the correct answer.

1. Does God call all the members of the Church to love and serve him? **(Yes)** No

2. Does a man become a priest when he celebrates the Sacrament of Matrimony? Yes **(No)**

3. Do married people and single people serve God in many of the same ways? **(Yes)** No

4. Are only women called to serve God in religious communities? Yes **(No)**

Check the ways you are called to love and serve God.

5. ✔ Respect God's name.

6. ✔ Learn about God from the teachings of Jesus and the Church.

7. ___ Not share all the wonderful things God has done for us.

Write one way each of the following groups is called to love and serve God.

8. Married people See page 189.

9. Religious brothers and sisters See page 191.

10. Priests See page 190.

194

CHAPTER TEST

Provide ten to fifteen minutes for the students to complete the test. After all have finished, check the answers. Clarify any misconceptions.

Alternative Assessment

You may want the students to complete the following alternative-assessment activity.

As we grow older we are called to serve God in different ways. Make up a booklet to show the different ways. Draw pictures and write sentences.

Additional Testing

• Chapter 22 Test in *Assessment Book*, pages 43–44

• CD-ROM *Test Generator and Resource*: Use Chapter 22 Test or customize your own.

Review

Review the definition as it is presented in the chapter's *Key Word* box:

• called by God (page 188).

We Believe Statements

Review the four statements.

• We are called by God.

• Married people and single people are called by God.

• Priests are called by God.

• Religious sisters and brothers are called by God.

To use the Chapter 22 Study Guide, visit

www.webelieveweb.com

Chapter 23 The Church Lives Today

Overview

In Chapter 22 the children learned that everyone is called by God to love and serve him. In this chapter the children will focus on today's Church.

Doctrinal Content	For Adult Reading and Reflection *Catechism of the Catholic Church*
The children will learn:	Paragraph
• Catholics belong to parish communities.	2179
• Bishops lead and serve the Church.	886
• The pope is the leader of the Church.	882
• The Church is in every part of the world.	831

Key Words

pastor (p. 197)
bishops (p. 197)
diocese (p. 197)
pope (p. 199)

Catechist Background

Go to **www.webelieveweb.com**, Catechist/ Teacher, We Believe Correlations for this chapter's correlation to:
• Six Tasks of Catechesis
• Catholic Social Teaching.

What would your school be like without order and people in charge?

Just as Jesus is the Sacrament of God, a visible sign of an invisible God, so the Church is the Sacrament of the risen Christ. Thus the Church is visible and tangible, readily available for the world to see.

Part of this visibility is the witness we provide by living our lives according to God's will. Another part of this visibility is the order or structure of the Church.

Catholics are united at the local level in parishes where we worship together, work together to help others, and celebrate the sacraments. Each parish has a pastor, the priest appointed to lead and serve the parish. Parishes are grouped in geographical regions called dioceses. The diocese is led by a bishop. The Church worldwide is led by the pope, who is called the Bishop of Rome.

In his lifetime, Jesus appointed certain people, called Apostles, to carry out his ministry after his Death. He appointed Peter as the very foundation of this mission: "And so I say to you, you are Peter and upon this rock I will build my church" (Matthew 16:18). The pope is the successor of Peter, and the bishops today continue to carry out the work of the Apostles. We call this apostolic succession, because it goes back to the time of the Apostles.

The Catholic faith is practiced throughout the world. We are one, united by common belief and the leadership of the pope. But there is much diversity in our expression of belief and worship. Our diversity reminds us of the vastness and greatness of God. In our unity and diversity the Church is a Sacrament of God to the world.

What might you do to support and encourage Church leaders?

Lesson Planning Guide

Lesson Steps	Presentation	Materials

① WE GATHER

Lesson Steps	Presentation	Materials
page 195 ✠ **Prayer** ☀ **Focus on Life**	• Listen to Scripture. 🎵 Respond by singing. • Discuss the questions.	• For prayer space: globe or world map, Bible 🎵 "Rejoice in the Lord Always," G. B. Brown and D. M. Hebert, #22, Grade 2 CD

② WE BELIEVE

Lesson Steps	Presentation	Materials
page 196 *Catholics belong to parish communities.*	• Present our role and the pastor's role in the parish. 🚶 Do the activity about participating in the parish.	• colored pencils
page 197 *Bishops lead and serve the Church.*	• Present the text about the roles of bishops in the Church. • Point out the *Key Words* and definitions. 🚶 Share responses to the questions.	• the name of your diocese and of the bishop of your diocese
page 198 *The pope is the leader of the Church.*	• Read and discuss the text about the role of the pope. 🚶 Write and share responses to the question. • Read and discuss the *As Catholics* text.	• crayon or highlighter
page 199 *The Church is in every part of the world.*	• Read and discuss the text and photographs.	• highlighter or crayon • copies of Reproducible Master 23, guide page 195C • crayons or colored pencils

③ WE RESPOND

Lesson Steps	Presentation	Materials
page 199	• Discuss responses to the question.	
pages 200–201 **Project Disciple**	• Complete the Project Disciple activities. • Explain the *Take Home* activity. • Discuss/send home Sharing Faith with My Family reproducible master for this chapter.	• crayons or colored pencils or markers • copies of Sharing Faith with My Family reproducible master, Chapter 23 (back of book)
page 202 **Chapter 23 Test**	• Complete Chapter 23 Test. • Work on *Alternative Assessment* activity.	• optional: copies of Scripture reproducible master, *What's the Word?*, Chapter 23 (back of book)

For additional ideas, activities, and opportunities: Visit Sadlier's **www.WeBelieveweb.com**

Name _____

Find the word that completes the sentence.
Use the following clues.

1. This letter is in wake but not in bake. _____

2. This letter is in rock but not in rack. _____

3. This letter is in cart but not in cast. _____

4. This letter is in love but not in dove. _____

5. This letter is in card but not in cart. _____

Catholics live in every part of the

___ ___ ___ ___ ___.
 1   2   3   4   5

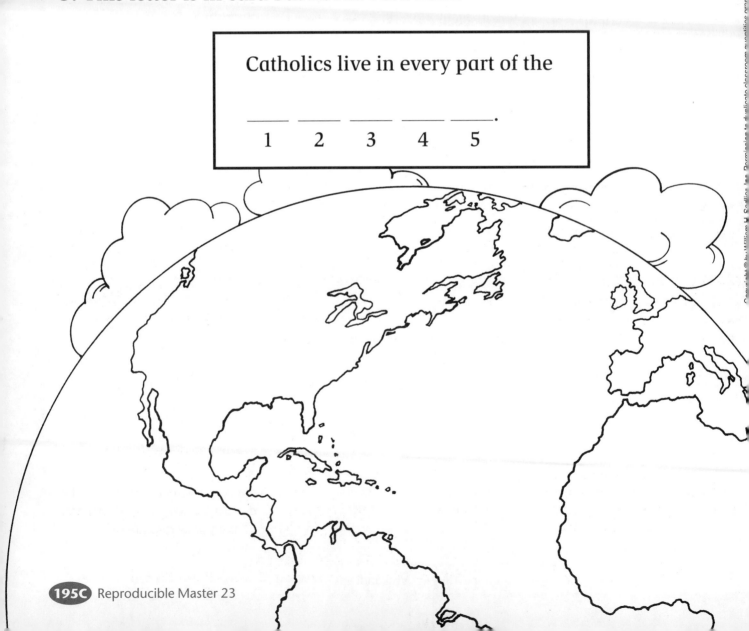

PROJECT DISCIPLE

Pray
Learn
Celebrate
Share
Choose
Live

Additional Activities

What's the Word?

Scripture reproducible master, Chapter 23

Materials needed: copies of *What's the Word?* (back of book)

Distribute copies of the Scripture reproducible master. Remind the children that after the Holy Spirit came to the Apostles on Pentecost, they traveled to different lands to spread the Good News. Choose volunteers to take the parts of the readers, the angel, Philip, and the man in the chariot. After the script is read, ask the students to underline the words taken directly from Scripture: the words spoken by the angel, Philip, and the man in the chariot.

Picture This

Materials needed: drawing paper; crayons or colored pencils

Distribute the drawing paper. Have the students design a story board for the story of the Apostle and the man in the chariot. Explain that the students may use speech and thought balloons above the characters' heads. When the students have completed their story boards, display them in your prayer space.

More to Explore

Materials needed: map of the world; books and/or downloads from the Web of photos of Vatican City

On a world map, point to the city of Rome, Italy. Also point to the Mediterranean Sea and the countries on the sea's coast. Explain to the children that when Jesus was teaching, the Romans ruled many of these countries. Also explain that after the Holy Spirit came on Pentecost, Saint Peter and Saint Paul traveled through many of these lands to Rome.

Show the children the photographs of the Vatican. Point out that if the pope is in Rome, he speaks to the crowds who gather in Saint Peter's Square on Sundays. Ask the children to discuss: *Would you like to visit the Vatican? What would you like to see?*

Show What you Know

Have the children work in small groups. Ask each group to identify two times when Catholics gather together. Then have the groups share these times with the other groups. Follow this procedure, having the groups identify two beliefs of Catholics throughout the world and then two ways that Catholics respond to God's love.

Meeting Individual Needs
Children with Special Needs

Keep in mind that group activities are physically demanding for children with special needs. Look for signs of frustration or fatigue in these children. Limit the time spent in group activities.

We Believe Resources

- Grade 2 *Review & Resource Book*, pages 52–54
- Grade 2 *Family Book*, pages 65–67
- Grade 2 *Assessment Book*, pages 45–46
- Grade 2 CD-ROM *Test Generator and Resource*: Use Chapter 23 Test or customize your own.
- **www.webelieveweb.com**

Enrichment Ideas

Chapter Story

Hello! My name is Alicia. My family and I belong to Saint John the Baptist parish. Saint John's feast day is June 24. Every year during this week, our parish has a fair. Many people of the parish work at the fair. They try to raise money to help people of the parish. They also share money with people in need.

Before the fair opens, the workers gather in the church to pray. Then our pastor, Father Ramone, says a special blessing. We pray together and ask God for good weather.

Last year at the fair, I helped my parents work at the lemonade booth. I handed the lemons to my dad. He cut the lemons and squeezed them for the juice. I also helped to sell the cups of lemonade.

We were not working all the time at the fair. My family went on the rides and played some of the games. We talked with other people from our parish. We also met some people who live in other nearby parishes.

It is two weeks until this year's fair. I think my parents and I are going to help out at the pizza booth. Mom told me I could help her sprinkle the toppings on top of the dough.

I know that I will have a lot of fun at the fair, working at the booth, going on the rides, and playing some games. I hope the next two weeks go quickly.

▶ *Would you like to help out at a parish fair? What would you like to do?*

FAITH and MEDIA

▶ Before the *We Respond* question on page 199, consider searching online for more pictures and descriptions of Catholic customs in other countries. These might include the countries of some of the children's ancestors or countries the children would like to visit.

▶ After discussing the work of missionaries in the Project Disciple *Make It Happen* activity, remind the children that missionary organizations such as Maryknoll and Catholic Relief Services (CRS) use media—including magazines, television, radio, and the Internet—to tell the world about their work.

CHAPTER PROJECT: SENDING LETTERS

Contact a second-grade teacher from another parish in your diocese. Explain that you would be interested in having the children in your class exchange letters with the children in his or her class. Suggest that the children write and tell one another what they are learning about their faith. Then help the children write the letters to send to the other parish's second-grade class.

The Church Lives Today

WE GATHER

✝ **Leader:** Let us listen to a reading from the letter of Paul to the Philippians.

Reader: "Rejoice in the Lord always. I shall say it again: rejoice! Your kindness should be known to all."
(Philippians 4: 4–5)

The word of the Lord.

All: Thanks be to God.

🎵 **Rejoice in the Lord Always**

Rejoice in the Lord always,
　Again I say, rejoice!
Rejoice in the Lord always,
　Again I say, rejoice!
Rejoice! Rejoice!
　Again I say, rejoice!
Rejoice! Rejoice!
　Again I say, rejoice! (Repeat)

☀ You belong to your family and to your class in school. How are these groups the same? How are they different?

195

PREPARING TO PRAY

For this gathering prayer the children will celebrate the Word of God by listening and responding in song.

• Choose a prayer leader and reader.

• Play "Rejoice in the Lord Always," #22 on the Grade 2 CD. Have the children practice singing. Ask a few volunteers to make up dance steps for the song and to teach them to the entire group.

The Prayer Space

• Display a globe or world map.

• On the prayer table place a Bible opened to Philippians 4:4–5.

📖 **This Week's Liturgy**
Visit **www.webelieveweb.com** for this week's liturgical readings and other seasonal material.

Lesson Plan

WE GATHER　　　___ minutes

✝ Pray

• Invite the children to gather in the prayer space. Ask the leader to begin.

• Ask the reader to pause briefly after the reading. Then invite the children to respond by singing and dancing.

☀ Focus on Life

• On chart paper or on the board, draw a two-column chart. Ask volunteers to name things the children do with their families. List these things in the first column

of the chart. Then ask volunteers to identify things they do with their classmates. List these activities in the second column. Help the children to identify what activities are the same and what ones are different. You may also prompt the discussion by having children talk about the numbers of members of the groups. Then share the *Chapter Story* on guide page 195E.

Family Connection Update

Ask volunteers to share their family discussions about serving God as grown-ups.

Catechist Goal

• To describe the duties of parish members, bishops, the pope, and explain the practices of Catholics around the world

Our Faith Response

• To express appreciation for our parish and Church leaders

 **pastor   bishops**

diocese   pope

Lesson Materials

• Grade 2 CD

• copies of Reproducible Master 23

• Scripture and Family reproducible masters (back of book)

Teaching Tip

A Visual Aid

Use a graphic organizer to help the children understand the scope of their bishop's responsibilities. Write the name of the diocese and bishop in the center of a circle. Insert the names of some of the nearby parishes within the circle. Tell the children that the bishop of the diocese leads and cares for all the people in these parishes.

WE BELIEVE

Catholics belong to parish communities.

As Catholics we belong to a parish family. A parish is a community of Catholics who worship and work together. As a parish, we come together to pray. We celebrate the sacraments. We care for those in need. We learn to live as followers of Jesus.

A parish has a pastor who is chosen by the bishop. The **pastor** is the priest who leads and serves the parish. He leads the parish in celebrating the sacraments, in prayer, and in teaching.

Together with the pastor, the members of the parish continue the work of Jesus. Some of these people help in parish ministries. Together the whole parish serves the needs of others.

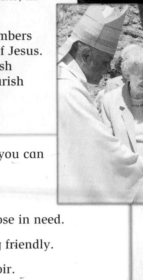

Put a check by each thing you can do to take part in your parish.

_____ Join the parish for Mass.

_____ Help with projects for those in need.

_____ Welcome others by being friendly.

_____ Sing in the children's choir.

_____ Be part of activities for children and families.

196

Lesson Plan

WE BELIEVE   _____ minutes

Read the *We Believe* statement on page 196. Explain: *Our parish is a community of people who support and help one another.* Have a volunteer read the first two paragraphs. Emphasize: *As a parish community we worship and work together.*

Write the word *pastor* on the board. Explain: *The pastor leads and serves all the people of the parish. He works with them to help others.* Ask a volunteer to read the last paragraph.

Read the directions for the activity. Invite the children to work in pairs. Allow enough time for the partners to report their responses to the group, citing reasons for their choices.

Read aloud the *We Believe* statement on page 197. Ask a volunteer to read aloud the first two paragraphs. Ask: *Who were the first leaders of the Church?* (Peter and the other Apostles)

Write the word *diocese* on the board. Pronounce it for the children and then have them pronounce it. Read aloud the third and fourth paragraphs.

Bishops lead and serve the Church.

Jesus chose the twelve Apostles to lead and care for his followers. He chose the Apostle Peter to be the leader of the Apostles. Peter and the other Apostles were the first leaders of the Church.

Peter and the Apostles chose other men to lead and serve the Church. These leaders became known as bishops. Bishops still lead and serve the Church today. **Bishops** are leaders of the Church who carry on the work of the Apostles.

A bishop is chosen by the pope to lead and care for a diocese. A **diocese** is an area of the Church led by a bishop. A diocese is made up of all the Catholics who live in a certain area.

The bishop guides and serves the members of his diocese. He passes on the teachings of Jesus. He helps the people to grow closer to God.

What diocese is your parish part of? Who is the bishop of your diocese?

Key Words

pastor the priest who leads and serves the parish

bishops leaders of the Church who carry on the work of the Apostles

diocese an area of the Church led by a bishop

197

ACTIVITY BANK

Multiple Intelligences
Musical

Teach the following song to the tune of "Go 'Round and 'Round the Village."

We worship God together.
We worship God together.
We worship God together,
as a parish community.

We try to help all people.
We try to help all people.
We try to help all people
in our parish community.

Greeting to the Bishop
Activity Materials: voice recorder or video camera

With the children prepare a hello and thank-you greeting for the bishop of your diocese. Record the children reading the message. Have some of the children explain to the bishop what they have learned this year about Jesus, the Church, and the sacraments. Then have everyone sing an appropriate song. Ask for the address of the bishop's office and send the recording with an explanatory note.

Ask for three volunteers to pretend that each is a bishop. Give each one a slip of paper on which you have written a way a bishop serves his diocese: *I guide and serve the people in my diocese; I pass on the teaching of Jesus; I help my people grow closer to God.* Ask the volunteers to introduce themselves as bishops and read the way they help the people of their diocese.

Read aloud the questions. Write the names of your diocese and the bishop of your diocese on the board or on chart paper. Remind the children: *The bishop leads and serves the people of all the parishes in your diocese.*

Quick Check

✔ *What is a parish?* (It is a community of Catholics who worship and work together.)

✔ *What is a diocese?* (It is an area of the Church led by a bishop.)

The pope is the leader of the Church.

The pope is the Bishop of Rome in Italy. The **pope** is the leader of the Church who continues the work of Saint Peter. With the other bishops, the pope helps Catholics to be disciples of Jesus.

The pope serves and cares for the Church. He preaches the Good News of Jesus Christ to everyone. The pope travels to other countries. Wherever he is, the pope celebrates Mass and talks to the people. He teaches them about God's love. He asks people to love and care for one another.

As Catholics...

Vatican Radio

After working on these two pages, read the *As Catholics* text. Encourage the children to listen to broadcasts of Vatican Radio and to check the Vatican's Web site and report what they learn to the group.

If the pope were coming to your parish, what would you tell or ask him?

_____

_____

_____

_____

_____

As Catholics...

The pope lives in a special part of Rome called Vatican City. Every day the pope's messages and other programs can be heard on Vatican Radio in forty different languages. They are also broadcast on the radio and over the Internet on the Vatican's own Web site at www.vatican.va.

Listen to the pope's message on Vatican Radio or log on to the Vatican's Web site.

198

Lesson Plan

WE BELIEVE (continued)

Have the children form two groups. Assign one of the paragraphs on page 198 to each group. Explain: *Each group will read the paragraph and then discuss the important points in the paragraph.* Then ask a representative from each group to share the important points with the other groups. Possible group responses are the following.

• First paragraph: The pope is the Bishop of Rome; he continues the work of Saint Peter; he helps Catholics to be disciples of Jesus.

• Second paragraph: The pope serves and cares for the entire Church; he preaches the Good News of Jesus

Christ; he celebrates Mass. The pope travels and listens to people; he asks people to take care of one another; he teaches about God's love.

Encourage the children to imagine what it would be like if the pope visited their parish. Ask: *What would you ask or tell the pope?* Have the children write their answers. Invite volunteers to share their responses. Act out an imaginary parish visit from the pope.

Ask a volunteer to read the first paragraph on page 199. Have the children highlight or underline what beliefs all Catholics share and celebrate.

The Church is in every part of the world.

Catholics in every part of the world have the same beliefs. They share and celebrate the same beliefs about the Blessed Trinity, Jesus, the Son of God, the Church, Mary, and the saints. They all celebrate the Eucharist and the other sacraments. They look to the pope as the leader of the Church.

However, Catholics around the world also show their faith in different ways. Look at the pictures and some of the ways Catholics pray and show their faith.

> **Key Word**
>
> **pope** the leader of the Church who continues the work of Saint Peter

These Catholics are Polish. It is Christmas Eve. The father of this family is breaking a wafer called *oplatki*. He will give a piece of the wafer to each member of his family. This is a sign of love and peace.

These Catholics are celebrating the Feast of Corpus Christi, or the Feast of the Body and Blood of Christ. The priest is carrying the Eucharist for all to worship. The priest and people sing songs to Jesus as they walk through their town.

WE RESPOND

What could you tell children from another country about the way your parish prays and celebrates?

199

ACTIVITY BANK

Multiple Intelligences
Verbal-Linguistic
Activity Materials: writing paper

Have the children recall the many things the pope does to lead the Church. Ask them to write one question an interviewer might ask the pope such as, *"Why do you travel to other countries?"* Children should base questions on the information in their text. Encourage volunteers to share their questions and elicit answers from the group.

Church
Celebrations
Activity Materials: writing paper

Direct attention to the photos on this page. Have the children choose one celebration in which they would like to participate. Ask each child to write why he or she would like to celebrate our Catholic faith in this way.

Read aloud the text about each photograph. Ask: *Are any of these people celebrating their faith in the same ways you do?* Point out that some of the Catholic celebrations that occur in other countries are also celebrated by families in the United States.

Distribute copies of Reproducible Master 23. Read the directions. After the children have answered the clues, invite a volunteer to complete the sentence. (w, o, r, l, d; world)

WE RESPOND _____ minutes

Connect to Life Have a volunteer read aloud the *We Respond* question. Ask volunteers to share their responses.

Pray Conclude the lesson by having the children pray silently to God for all of their Catholic brothers and sisters around the world.

Catechist Goal

• To review the chapter ideas that are key to growing as disciples of Jesus Christ

Our Faith Response

• To decide on ways to grow as disciples by living out what we have learned

Show What you Know

Read aloud the directions. You may want the children to work in pairs to complete the activity.

Fast Facts Read the paragraphs. If possible, invite one of the priests of the parish to show the children the vestments he wears at Mass.

Make it Happen

Discuss with the children words that they may print on the banner. Possible wording: Jesus is the light of the world; Jesus is the living bread. Jesus is the Son of God.

Picture This Read aloud the activity directions. Share with the children ways your family members celebrate their faith. Help the children recall special Christmas or Easter customs. Or suggest to the children that they draw themselves celebrating their faith with your class.

Take Home

Read the activity suggestion. Encourage the children to interview family members.

Discuss and send home copies of *Sharing Faith with My Family* reproducible master for this chapter (back of book).

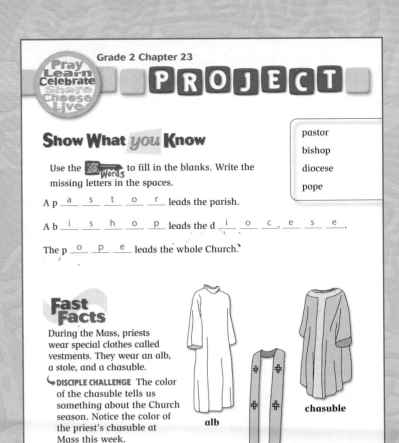

Pray Learn Celebrate Share Choose Live

Grade 2 Chapter 23

PROJECT

Show What you Know

pastor
bishop
diocese
pope

Use the **Key Words** to fill in the blanks. Write the missing letters in the spaces.

A p a s t o r leads the parish.

A b i s h o p leads the d i o c e s e.

The p o p e leads the whole Church.

Fast Facts

During the Mass, priests wear special clothes called vestments. They wear an alb, a stole, and a chasuble.

↳ **DISCIPLE CHALLENGE** The color of the chasuble tells us something about the Church season. Notice the color of the priest's chasuble at Mass this week.

alb

stole

chasuble

DISCIPLE

Pray Learn Celebrate Share Choose Live

Make it Happen

Missionaries teach others about Jesus. They follow Jesus' example. We can be missionaries in our homes, schools, neighborhoods, and world. We can share our belief in Jesus and live as he did. Make a banner that shares your belief in Jesus.

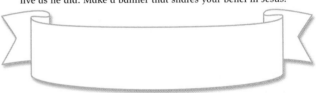

Picture This Look at the picture of the children celebrating their faith. Then draw a picture of yourself celebrating your faith.

Take Home

Interview friends and relatives about the different ways their families might have celebrated their faith. Write questions to ask.

_____

_____

_____

CHAPTER TEST

Use the words in the box to complete the sentences.

1. A _____parish_____ is a community of Catholics who worship and work together.

2. The _____pope_____ is the leader of the Church who continues the work of Saint Peter.

3. A _____bishop_____ is a leader of the Church who carries on the work of the Apostles.

4. A _____diocese_____ is an area of the Church led by a bishop.

pope

bishop

diocese

parish

Circle the correct answer.

5. Is a pastor the Bishop of Rome? Yes (No)

6. Do Catholics around the world have different beliefs about the Blessed Trinity? Yes (No)

7. Did Jesus choose Peter to be the leader of the Apostles? (Yes) No

8. Do Catholics around the world show their faith in different ways? (Yes) No

9–10. Write two things all Catholics share and celebrate.

Possible responses: beliefs about the Blessed Trinity, Jesus, the Son of

God, the Church, Mary and the saints; the sacraments

Chapter 23 ● Page 202

CHAPTER TEST

Provide ten to fifteen minutes for the students to complete the test. After all have finished, check the answers. Clarify any misconceptions.

Alternative Assessment

You may want the students to complete the following alternative-assessment activity.

Make up a question for each of these answers: parish, people, pastor, diocese, bishop, and pope. Share your questions with a partner. Answer your partner's questions, too.

Additional Testing

• Chapter 23 Test in *Assessment Book*, pages 45–46

• CD-ROM *Test Generator and Resource*: Use Chapter 23 Test or customize your own.

Review

Review the definitions as they are presented in the chapter's *Key Word* boxes:

• pastor (page 197)

• bishops (page 197)

• diocese (page 197)

• pope (page 199).

We Believe Statements

Review the four statements.

• Catholics belong to parish communities.

• Bishops lead and serve the Church.

• The pope is the leader of the Church.

• The Church is in every part of the world.

To use the Chapter 23 Study Guide, visit

www.webelieveweb.com

Overview

In Chapter 23 the children learned about belonging to a parish community and about Church leadership. In this chapter they will learn about the way Jesus prayed and the way prayer brings us closer to God.

Doctrinal Content	For Adult Reading and Reflection *Catechism of the Catholic Church*
The children will learn:	Paragraph
• Prayer keeps us close to God.	2560
• Jesus prayed to God his Father.	2599
• Jesus teaches us to pray.	2759
• We pray as Jesus did.	2767

prayer (p. 205)
Temple (p. 205)

Catechist Background

Why do you pray?

Go to **www.webelieveweb.com**, Catechist/ Teacher, We Believe Correlations for this chapter's correlation to:
 • Six Tasks of Catechesis
 • Catholic Social Teaching.

No relationship can exist without some form of communication. That communication may involve talking, listening, writing, being together in silence, or simply being held in one another's thoughts. So, too, our relationship with God cannot exist without communication. We call that communication prayer. Prayer, which can take many forms and be in many places, is the basis for our relationship with God.

Our greatest example of how to pray is Jesus, who prayed often to God his Father. Jesus learned to pray from his family and the Jewish community of faith. Like other Jews of his time, Jesus would travel to the Temple in Jerusalem to pray. Our gathering together for Mass has its beginnings in these ancient community forms of prayer. Jesus also went off alone to pray.

In addition to being an example of how to pray, Jesus also taught us how to pray. When his disciples asked him how to pray, Jesus taught them the Our Father. We find this prayer in Scripture in Matthew 6:9–13 and Luke 11:1–4. The early Church gave this prayer to catechumens preparing for Baptism as a great gift, one of the treasures of the Church. Today, we continue to teach this prayer to our children, not simply words to memorize, but as the treasure that it is: the very way to pray and remain in communion with God.

We pray, then, as Jesus prayed. We pray in community, especially as we gather weekly to celebrate the Mass together. And we pray alone, spending time quietly with our God. Without prayer our relationship with God could not exist.

How can the example of Jesus improve the quality of prayer in your life?

Lesson Planning Guide

Lesson Steps	Presentation	Materials

① WE GATHER

Lesson Steps	Presentation	Materials
page 203 ✚ **Prayer** ☀ **Focus on Life**	• Pray the beginning of the Eucharistic Prayer from the Mass. ♫ Respond by singing "Sing Hosanna." • Discuss the questions.	For the prayer space: picture or statue of Jesus, colorful streamers ♫ "Sing Hosanna," Jack Miffleton, #23, Grade 2 CD

② WE BELIEVE

Lesson Steps	Presentation	Materials
page 204 *Prayer keeps us close to God.*	• Read and discuss the text about prayer. ⊙ Complete the activity.	• highlighter or crayon
page 205 *Jesus prayed to God his Father.*	• Present the text about Jesus and prayer. ⊙ Share times of prayer.	
page 206 *Jesus teaches us to pray.*	• Read the text about the Lord's Prayer. • Discuss the meaning of the words we pray in the Lord's Prayer. ⊙ Make up actions to use while praying the Our Father.	
page 207 *We pray as Jesus did.*	• Present the text about the importance of prayer. ⊙ Discuss times when our parish prays together. • Read and discuss the *As Catholics* text.	• crayons or colored pencils • copies of Reproducible Master 24, guide page 203C • instrumental music (option)

③ WE RESPOND

Lesson Steps	Presentation	Materials
page 207	• Offer a quiet prayer to God.	
pages 208–209 **Project Disciple**	• Complete the Project Disciple activities. • Explain the *Take Home* activity. • Discuss/send home Sharing Faith with My Family reproducible master for this chapter.	• crayons or colored pencils or markers • copies of Sharing Faith with My Family reproducible master, Chapter 24 (back of book)
page 210 **Chapter 24 Test**	• Complete Chapter 24 Test. • Work on *Alternative Assessment* activity.	• optional: copies of Scripture reproducible master, *What's the Word?*, Chapter 24 (back of book)

For additional ideas, activities, and opportunities: Visit Sadlier's **www.WeBelieveweb.com**

Name _____

We pray to God for many reasons. When we talk to
God we can use our own words. In each box below
write a prayer to God.

Ask for help

_____

_____

_____

_____

Give praise

_____

_____

_____

Ask for forgiveness

_____

_____

_____

Give thanks

_____

_____

_____

PROJECT DISCIPLE

Pray
Learn
Celebrate
Share
Choose
Live

Additional Activities

Make *it* Happen

Materials needed: poster board; crayons or markers; construction paper; scissors and glue sticks

Have the children work in small groups. Give each group a poster board. Ask the members of each group to make a poster to remind people to make time every day to pray. Then ask permission of the appropriate parish leader to display the posters in the parish.

Celebrate!

Point out that when we sing during the celebration of the sacraments or during other prayer celebrations, we are praying. Ask: *What is your favorite prayer song you learned this year?* Give the children about ten minutes to look through their *We Believe* texts and choose their favorite song.

Then have the children take turns naming their favorite songs. Write the titles on the board as the children are sharing. Then keep a tally and ask the students to help you make a Top Ten Prayer Song List.

What's *the* Word?

Scripture reproducible master, Chapter 24

Materials needed: copies of *What's the Word?* (back of book); crayons or colored pencils

Distribute copies of the Scripture reproducible master. Invite the children to gather in the prayer space. Have the children form two groups, designating one group as A and the second group as B. Then lead the children in praying the psalm verses. When the children return to their seats, ask them to illustrate the psalm to the right of the verses.

Saint Stories

Go to **www.webelieveweb.com**, *Lives of the Saints* Archive to find the story of Saint Thérèse of Lisieux. Emphasize the prayer life of the saint. You may want to download the primary activity sheet for the children.

Meeting Individual Needs
Children with Attention-Deficit Disorder

When doing an art project, assign the children who have difficulty staying on task to be special art helpers. Ask them to distribute and collect art supplies as needed. Look for ways to thank the children for their help.

We Believe Resources

- Grade 2 *Review & Resource Book*, pages 55–57
- Grade 2 *Family Book*, pages 68–70
- Grade 2 *Assessment Book*, pages 47–48
- Grade 2 CD-ROM *Test Generator and Resource*: Use Chapter 24 Test or customize your own.

www.webelieveweb.com

Enrichment Ideas

Chapter Story

Nick and Natalie Grapkis were twins. They enjoyed doing things together. Their father was a forest ranger who often took the twins on trips to learn about trees, birds, and animals. But today was the first time their dad was taking them for a hike up Mount Agamenticus. The twins were so excited. Their wish was finally coming true. Their backpacks were already filled with snacks, bottled water, binoculars, and a first-aid kit.

As the twins and their dad hiked along the trail, they sang songs. Soon the trail grew steeper. Their dad asked, "Do you want to stop and rest now?" But the twins called out, "No way, Dad! Keep going."

Mr. Grapkis noticed that a tree had fallen across the trail up ahead. He told the twins to stay where they were while he went ahead to clear the trail. But Nick and Natalie were anxious to explore. So they wandered off the trail. Suddenly Nick's foot slipped on a mossy rock and he sprained his ankle. Natalie called out, "Dad, help!" But Dad could not hear her.

Nick and Natalie were both afraid. What if their father could not find them? How could Natalie help Nick by herself? Natalie said to Nick, "Dad always says not to panic and to pray for God's help." The twins started to pray. They asked God to let their dad find them soon.

About two hours had passed. Then the twins heard sounds on the trail above them. They shouted, "Dad, Dad, we're over here!" In a few moments they saw their father come over the ridge. Mr. Grapkis hugged both of his children and said, "Thank you, God." As Dad and Natalie helped Nick back down the hiking trail, they thanked God that they were all together again.

▶ *How did prayer help the Grapkis family?*

FAITH and MEDIA

▶ Consider visiting the Web sites of one or more contemplative communities to show the children pictures of these men and women as they go about their lives of work and prayer. Remind the children that the Internet is now one of the main places where people can go to find out more about vocations, both to the priesthood and to the religious life. This is just one more example of how media can help the Church do the work of Jesus in the world.

CHAPTER PROJECT: A PRAYER BANNER

Invite the children to make a prayer banner that will remind them that prayer keeps us close to God. Obtain a large piece of felt cloth. Use stencils to make letters that spell "We Pray," and attach them to the top of the banner. Have smaller, circular-shaped pieces of felt and felt scraps of different colors for the children to make "faces" for the banner. Encourage the children to use the felt scraps to make eyes, a nose, a mouth, and hair for their faces. Tell them they can use a variety of colors so that there will be a "rainbow of faces" on the banner. When the children have finished gluing the felt pieces on the circles, attach all the faces to the banner. Invite the children to write their prayer requests on index cards. Pin their prayer request cards to the banner. Hang the banner in a prominent place.

We Pray

24

WE GATHER

✝ **Leader:** The Lord be with you.

All: And ~~also~~ with your *spirit*

Leader: Lift up your hearts.

All: We lift them up to the Lord.

Leader: Let us give thanks to the Lord our God.

All: It is right ~~to give him thanks and praise~~ *and just*.

🎵 Sing Hosanna

Sing hosanna! Sing hosanna!
Sing it for Jesus. Sing it for Jesus.
Sing it for friendship.
Sing it for friendship.

Sing it forever. Sing it forever.
Sing hosanna! Sing hosanna!
Sing hosanna! Sing!

Play the conga! Play the conga!
Play it for Jesus. Play it for Jesus.
Play it for friendship.
Play it for friendship.

Play it forever. Play it forever.
Play the conga! Play the conga!
Play the conga drum!

When do you talk to other people? When do you listen to other people?

203

PREPARING TO PRAY

Children will offer God their praise and thanks in word and song.

• Play "Sing Hosanna," #23 on the Grade 2 CD. Have the children practice singing.

• Give a few children percussion instruments to play while singing the song.

• Have the other children cut scraps of construction paper into pieces to serve as confetti as they sing during prayer.

The Prayer Space

• Display a picture or statue of Jesus.

• Decorate the space with colorful streamers.

📖 This Week's Liturgy

Visit **www.webelieveweb.com** for this week's liturgical readings and other seasonal material.

Lesson Plan

WE GATHER ___ minutes

✝ Pray

• Invite the musicians to bring their instruments to the prayer space.

• Have the other children bring a handful of confetti. Ask these children to toss the confetti in the air each time you sing the name Jesus.

• Lead the children in their prayer of praise.

☀ Focus on Life

• Invite the children to share responses to the questions. Ask: *Whom do you talk to every day? How do you feel when someone you like talks to you? Why is it also important to listen to the other person?* Give examples of when listening is truly important—even lifesaving.

• Share the *Chapter Story* on guide page 203E.

Family Connection Update

Invite the children to share the different ways their families celebrate their faith.

Catechist Goal

• To explore how prayer keeps us close to God, how Jesus prayed, and the meaning of the Lord's Prayer

Our Faith Response

• To celebrate the gift of prayer and name ways we can pray

 **prayer   Temple**

Lesson Materials

• highlighter or crayon
• Grade 2 CD
• copies of Reproducible Master 24
• Scripture and Family reproducible masters (back of book)

Teaching Tip

Importance of Listening

Point out to the children that listening helps us to know people better. Have the children sit in a circle. Have each child take a turn telling the group about something that he or she likes to do. Encourage the children to listen carefully. Then invite volunteers to repeat what they heard. Ask: *Have you been a good listener?*

WE BELIEVE

Prayer keeps us close to God.

We can grow closer to God through prayer. **Prayer** is talking and listening to God. No matter how we pray, God is with us.

We talk to God about different things. We share the things we are thinking about. Sometimes we ask for help or forgiveness. Other times we thank God for his love, or ask his blessing.

God is always there to hear our prayer. He knows what we need and takes care of us.

Prayer is listening to God, too. God speaks to us at Mass, through the sacraments, and through the words of the Bible. He speaks to us through Church leaders and through all who show us his love.

Who has taught you to pray?

_____

_____

_____

204

Lesson Plan

WE BELIEVE ____ minutes

Invite a volunteer to read aloud the *We Believe* statement and the first paragraph. Emphasize the following points:

• *God wants us to know him better.*
• *God is always with us, both when we talk to him and when we are quiet and listen.*

Ask: *What can we talk to God about?* (Accept all reasonable responses and list them on the board.) Then have a volunteer read the second and third paragraphs.

Ask: *How can we listen to God?* Then read together the last paragraph. Have the children highlight or underline the ways God speaks to us.

Read the question and ask the children to write their responses.

Read together the *We Believe* statement on page 205. Invite volunteers to read aloud the paragraphs. Then ask:

• *Where did Jesus and his family pray?* (at home, in the Temple)

• *How did Jesus pray?* (Sometimes he prayed alone. Other times he prayed with family, friends and disciples.)

The Solitude of Christ by Maurice Denis, 1918/© 2009
Artists Rights Society (ARS), New York/ADAGP, Paris

Jesus prayed to God his Father.

When Jesus was growing up, he learned to pray. He prayed with Mary and Joseph. They also gathered with other Jewish families to pray.

They all traveled to Jerusalem to celebrate religious holidays. The **Temple** is the holy place in Jerusalem where the Jewish People worshiped God.

As Jesus grew older he continued to pray. He wanted to be close to God his Father. He asked his Father to be with him. He thanked his Father for his many blessings.

Jesus often went off by himself to pray. Jesus also prayed when he was with his family, friends, and disciples.

Ⓧ Name some times when you pray by yourself. Name some times when you pray with others.

Key Words

prayer talking and listening to God

Temple the holy place in Jerusalem where the Jewish People worshiped God

205

ACTIVITY BANK

Curriculum Connection
Music, Language Arts
Activity Materials: rhythm-band instruments

Have the children use simple, familiar melodies such as "Row, Row, Row Your Boat," "The Farmer in the Dell," or "Here We Go 'Round the Mulberry Bush." Help them to make up their own prayer lyrics to fit these melodies. Have a variety of instruments for the children to use for musical accompaniment. Allow the children time to practice and then play for a group of younger children or parents.

Draw the children's attention to the picture of Jesus. Ask: *What do you think Jesus is saying to God?*

Ⓧ **Read** the directives. Make a two-column chart on the board. At the top of the first column, write *by yourself.* At the top of the second column, write *with others.* In each column write the times the children mention.

Quick Check

✔ *What is prayer?* (Prayer is talking and listening to God.)

✔ *What is the Temple?* (It is the holy place in Jerusalem where the Jewish people worshiped God.)

Jesus teaches us to pray.

Jesus' disciples wanted to learn how to pray as Jesus did. One day they asked Jesus, "Lord, teach us to pray." (Luke 11:1)

Jesus taught them the Lord's Prayer. It is also called the Our Father.

As Catholics...

Morning and Evening Prayer

After working on these two pages, read the *As Catholics* text. The explanation is referring to the Liturgy of the Hours.

The Lord's Prayer

Our Father, who art in heaven, hallowed be thy name;	We talk to God. We praise him as our loving Father.
thy kingdom come; thy will be done on earth as it is in heaven.	We ask that all people will know and share God's love. This is what God wants for all of us.
Give us this day our daily bread;	We ask God to give us what we need. We remember all people who are hungry or poor.
and forgive us our trespasses as we forgive those who trespass against us;	We ask God to forgive us. We need to forgive others.
and lead us not into temptation, but deliver us from evil. Amen.	We ask God to keep us safe from anything that goes against his love.

As a class make up prayerful actions for each part of the Our Father. Then pray the prayer using the actions.

206

Lesson Plan

WE BELIEVE (continued)

Read aloud together the *We Believe* statement on page 206. Then ask volunteers to read the first paragraph.

Explain: *Jesus taught his disciples the Lord's Prayer. We also call this prayer the Our Father.* Ask: *Why do you think we call this prayer the Our Father?* (We are praying to God our Father. Our and Father are the first two words of the prayer.)

Point out the chart. Ask the children sitting on the left side of the room to read the prayer verse in the left column. Ask the children on the right side of the room to read the explanation of the verse in the right-hand column.

Direct attention to the prayer chart. Help the children make up an action for each section of the prayer.

Invite a volunteer to read aloud the *We Believe* statement at the top of page 207. Read together the list of reasons we pray. Remind the children: *We can use our own words to pray.*

Distribute copies of Reproducible Master 24. Read the directions and provide time for the children to write their own prayers. While the children are writing, you may want to play instrumental music.

We pray as Jesus did.

There are many reasons to pray.
We pray:

- to ask God for help
- to tell God how beautiful
  the world is
- to ask God to forgive us
- to pray for someone in need
- to thank God for his love
- to ask for God's blessing for us
  and others.

When we pray we can use our own
words. We can also use prayers that
we have learned. We use many of these
prayers when we pray together.

Praying together is an important part
of being a member of the Church. As a
parish we join together to celebrate the
Eucharist and the other sacraments.

There are other times when our
parish prays together. Talk about
some of these times.

WE RESPOND

Think about one way you and your
family will pray this week. Now sit
quietly. Talk and listen to God.

As Catholics...

At special times of the day, many
members of the Church come
together to pray. Morning and
evening are two of these special
times. At morning prayer and
evening prayer, people gather to
pray and sing psalms. They listen
to readings from the Bible. They
pray for the whole world. They
thank God for his creation. Many
religious communities gather in
their chapels for morning and
evening prayer. Your parish may
gather, too.

Find out if your parish gathers to
celebrate morning and evening
prayer.

ACTIVITY BANK

Multiple Intelligences
Linguistic, Spatial
Activity Materials: sentence strips
   Prepare a set of sentence strips.
Write a verse of the Lord's Prayer on
each strip. Distribute the strips to a
group of children. Have the group
arrange themselves in the correct
prayer-verse order. Then invite everyone to say the prayer together.

Catholic Social Teaching
*Call to Family, Community, and
Participation*
   Gather in the prayer space.
Remind the children that they are
part of the parish's learning community. Invite the children to join hands
to form a circle. Have the children
take turns praying for the person
standing on their right: *God bless
(child's name)*. After the last person
has prayed, pray aloud: *God, bless
each person in our learning community. Amen.*

207

Read the second and third paragraphs on page 207.

Discuss with the children times when our parish
prays together. Point out: *We pray together for special
feast days. We gather to pray to ask for God's help.*

WE RESPOND
_____ minutes

Connect to Life Have a volunteer read aloud the
We Respond text. Provide the children time to reflect on
one way their families will pray with your parish.

Pray Have the children pray quietly. You may want to
dim the lights and play instrumental music while the
children are praying.

Catechist Goal

- To review the chapter ideas that are key to growing as disciples of Jesus Christ

Our Faith Response

- To decide on ways to grow as disciples by living out what we have learned

Show What you Know

Read aloud the directions. Give the children about five minutes to complete the activity.

More to Explore

Direct the children's attention to the photographs on the page. Then read the paragraph. Point out to the children that the sisters and brothers pray for them and their families every day.

Pray Today

Read the directions. Help the children work through the maze.

Make it Happen

Have the children look at *My Prayer Book* in the back of their texts before sharing their favorite prayers. Then share what your favorite prayer is.

Take Home

Encourage the children to pray the Evening Prayer with their families.

Discuss and send home copies of *Sharing Faith with My Family* reproducible master for this chapter (back of book).

Pray Learn Celebrate Share Choose Live

Grade 2 Chapter 24

PROJECT

Show What you Know

Write the Key Words into the word shapes.

prayer
Temple

Talking and listening to God

p r a y e r

The holy place in Jerusalem where the Jewish People worshiped God

T e m p l e

More to Explore

People in religious communities live a life of prayer. They pray together at different hours each day. They also spend time alone to think about and pray to God. Their prayers are very important to the Church and the world.

DISCIPLE

Pray Learn Celebrate Share Choose Live

Pray Today

Choose the correct way through the maze by praying the Our Father.

Our Father, who art in heaven, hallowed be thy name;

Give us this day our daily bread;

thy kingdom come; thy will be done on earth as it is in heaven.

and forgive us our trespasses as we forgive those who trespass against us;

and lead us not into temptation; but deliver us from evil.

Amen.

Take Home

Learn this prayer as a family. Pray it together in the evenings.

Evening Prayer
Dear God, before we go to sleep, we want to thank you for this day so full of your kindness and your joy. We close our eyes to rest safe in your loving care.

Make it Happen

What is your favorite prayer? Share it.

CHAPTER TEST

Circle the correct answer.

1. Did Jesus always pray by himself? Yes (No)

2. Is prayer talking and listening to God? (Yes) No

3. Is the Hail Mary the prayer Jesus taught to his disciples? Yes (No)

4. Can we use our own words to pray? (Yes) No

Fill in the circle beside the correct answer.

5. God _____ listens to our prayer.
   ● always   ○ sometimes

6. Praying together is _____ part of being a member of the Church.
   ○ not an important   ● an important

7. Another name for the Lord's Prayer is the _____.
   ○ Hail Mary   ● Our Father

8. Prayer was _____ to Jesus.
   ○ not important   ● important

9–10. **Write two things we ask God when we pray the Lord's Prayer.**

Possible responses: that all people will know and share God's love; to

give us what we need; to forgive us; to keep us safe

210

CHAPTER TEST

Provide ten to fifteen minutes for the students to complete the test. After all have finished, check the answers. Clarify any misconceptions.

Alternative Assessment

You may want the students to complete the following alternative-assessment activity.

Make a prayer calendar for this week. Write ways you will pray each day. At the end of the week, see how many different ways you talked to and listened to God.

Additional Testing

• Chapter 24 Test in *Assessment Book*, pages 47–48

• CD-ROM *Test Generator and Resource*: Use Chapter 24 Test or customize your own.

Review

Review the definitions as they are presented in the chapter's *Key Word* boxes:

• prayer (page 205)

• Temple (page 205).

We Believe Statements

Review the four statements.

• Prayer keeps us close to God.

• Jesus prayed to God his Father.

• Jesus teaches us to pray.

• We pray as Jesus did.

To use the Chapter 24 Study Guide, visit

www.webelieveweb.com

Overview

In Chapter 24 the children learned that Jesus taught us the Lord's Prayer. In this chapter they will learn that we can honor Mary and the saints and learn from their example.

Doctrinal Content	For Adult Reading and Reflection *Catechism of the Catholic Church*
The children will learn:	Paragraph
• The Church honors the saints.	957
• The Church honors Mary.	963
• We honor Mary with special prayers.	2676
• We honor Mary on special days.	971

Key Words

saints (p. 212)
procession
(p. 215)

Catechist Background

How have you learned to teach by observing others?

We are called to be saints, good and holy people who live in right relationship with God and one another. All of us are called to this high and holy calling. And just as we learn a trade or a skill, such as teaching, by being apprentices under a mentor, so we learn how to be a good Christian by following the example of others.

In the Church we honor saints as people who lived faithfully and show us by their example how to live as Christians. We acknowledge all the members of the Church who have died and now live with God in everlasting life as saints. In addition we formally acknowledge particular people as saints through a process called canonization. Canonization is the solemn proclamation that a person has "practiced heroic virtue and lived in fidelity to God's grace" (*CCC* 828). These saints become models and intercessors for us, aiding us in our journey of faith.

Go to **www.webelieveweb.com**, Catechist/ Teacher, We Believe Correlations for this chapter's correlation to:
• Six Tasks of Catechesis
• Catholic Social Teaching.

The supreme model for us of Christian discipleship is Mary, the Blessed Mother. By her obedience and faithfulness to God, our salvation was made possible. We honor Mary in special ways, through devotions, prayers, feast days, and processions as our mentor and intercessor in Christian holiness.

Remembering the faithful who have gone before us, honoring those saints who have been canonized, and being devoted to Mary are all ways we learn to live a faithful life as Christians.

What holy person, canonized or not, has helped you live as a Christian?

Lesson Planning Guide

Lesson Steps	Presentation	Materials

1 WE GATHER

page 211 ✝ **Prayer** ☀ **Focus on Life**	♪ Pray by singing. • Discuss the questions about honoring people.	For prayer space: pictures of Mary and other saints, Bible ♪ "Litany of the Saints," John Schiavone, #24, Grade 2 CD

2 WE BELIEVE

page 212 *The Church honors the saints.*	• Read the text and discuss some of the saints. • Point out the *Key Word* and definition. ⚲ Do the activity.	• highlighter or crayon
page 213 *The Church honors Mary.* 📖 *Luke 1:28–30*	• Read the Scripture story about Mary. ⚲ Share ways of honoring Mary as the greatest saint.	• pictures of Mary with Jesus, statue of Mary • crayons or colored pencils
page 214 *We honor Mary with special prayers.* 📖 *Luke 1:39–42*	• Read the Scripture story. • Learn the Hail Mary. ⚲ Complete the activity. • Read and discuss the *As Catholics* text.	
page 215 *We honor Mary on special days.*	• Present the text about ways the Church honors Mary.	• rosary beads (option) • copies of Reproducible Master 25, guide page 211C

3 WE RESPOND

page 215	⚲ Discuss the *We Respond* question. ♪ Honor Mary in song.	♪ "Immaculate Mary," #25, Grade 2 CD
pages 216–217 **Project Disciple**	• Complete the **Project Disciple** activities. • Explain the *Take Home* activity. • Discuss/send home **Sharing Faith with My Family** reproducible master for this chapter.	• crayons or colored pencils or markers • copies of **Sharing Faith with My Family** reproducible master, Chapter 25 (back of book)
page 218 **Chapter 25 Test**	• Complete **Chapter 25 Test**. • Work on *Alternative Assessment* activity.	• optional: copies of Scripture reproducible master, *What's the Word?*, Chapter 25 (back of book)

For additional ideas, activities, and opportunities: Visit Sadlier's **www.WeBelieveweb.com**

Name _____

The rosary is a special prayer in honor of Mary.
Color in the beads.

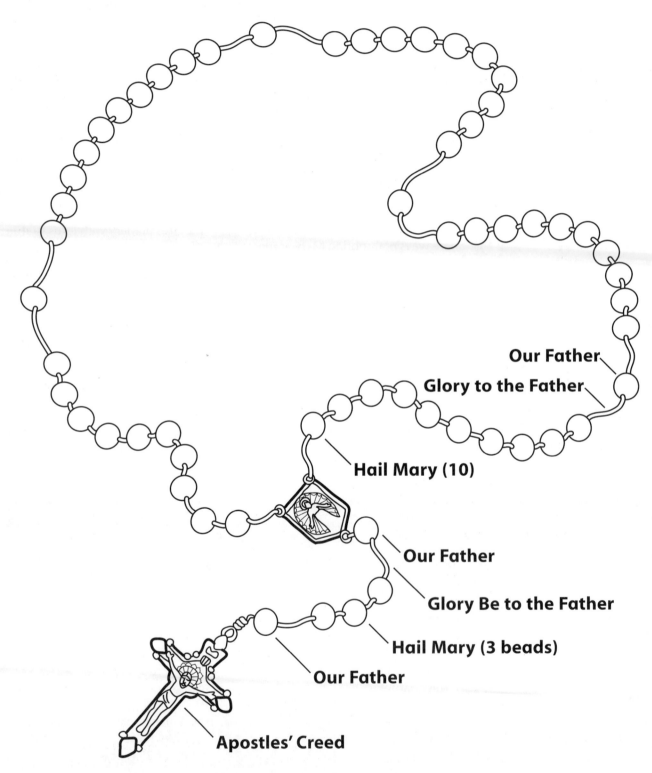

Our Father

Glory to the Father

Hail Mary (10)

Our Father

Glory Be to the Father

Hail Mary (3 beads)

Our Father

Apostles' Creed

PROJECT DISCIPLE

Pray
Learn
Celebrate
Share
Choose
Live

Additional Activities

What's the Word?

Scripture reproducible master, Chapter 25

Materials needed: copies of *What's the Word?* (back of book)

Distribute copies of the Scripture reproducible master. You may want the children to work in pairs. Read the directions, and then provide about ten minutes for the children to solve the riddles. Check the children's responses: Saints John the Baptist, Peter, Joseph, and Elizabeth.

Picture This

Materials needed: large index cards; crayons or colored pencils

As an alternative to the *Chapter Project* activity, have the children make "saint trading cards." Ask them to use the model they did for the Project Disciple activity on page 193. Give each child about three cards for three saints. The picture of each saint should go on one side of the card and the facts about the saint on the other side of the card. Explain to the students that they can look through their texts to find the names of the saints.

Celebrate!

Materials needed: props and costumes for favorite saints; Grade 2 *We Believe* CD

Have the students look at the photo on page 211. Before sponsoring a saints' celebration, involve the children in the planning. Explain that the children may dress as their favorite saints and bring in props that are appropriate for the saints to carry. You may want to invite the children's families.

For the celebration, have the children process to the prayer space as they sing "Litany of the Saints," #24 on the Grade 2 CD. Remind the children that Mary is the greatest saint. Pray the Hail Mary together. As the children process to their seats, ask them to sing "Immaculate Mary," #25 on the Grade 2 CD.

To conclude the celebration, you may want to have a healthy snack available for the participants.

Meeting Individual Needs
Children with Attention-Deficit Disorder

Help everyone in your group be understanding of children with attention-deficit disorder. Share with them stories about these children. Consult a children's librarian to ask about books and other resources to use with the class.

We Believe Resources

- Grade 2 *Review & Resource Book*, pages 58–60
- Grade 2 *Family Book*, pages 71–73
- Grade 2 *Assessment Book*, pages 49–50
- Grade 2 CD-ROM *Test Generator and Resource*: Use Chapter 25 Test or customize your own.
- **www.webelieveweb.com**

Enrichment Ideas

Chapter Story

Keri liked to listen to her grandfather tell stories about the saints. This is Keri's favorite because it is about Mary and Saint Bernadette.

There once was a young girl named Bernadette. She lived in Lourdes, a small town in France. Her family was happy, and they loved each other very much.

One day Bernadette was with two other girls near the bank of a river. She heard a noise and then looked toward a cave. There Bernadette saw a beautiful lady whom she later learned was Mary, our Blessed Mother.

Mary visited Bernadette eighteen times that year. Mary told Bernadette to tell the priests to bring people there to build a church. Mary also told Bernadette to drink water from the spring, but Bernadette did not see a spring. Mary told her to dig with her hands in a sandy spot. Bernadette did what Mary told her and a spring of water began to flow there. Soon many people came to know that this water was a sign of God's love and power. People came to the spring to pray and to wash with the water. A blind man and a sick baby were healed because they believed in God's love and power.

Today a beautiful church stands in Lourdes near the place where Mary visited Bernadette. Every year thousands of people from all over the world visit there. They pray and sing in honor of Mary. Many people who have gone to Lourdes have received special blessings from God.

▶ *Would you like to visit Lourdes? Tell why.*

FAITH and MEDIA

▶ You might want to tell the children about some saints who are the patrons of various media and the people who work in them: Saint Clare of Assisi (radio and television), Saint Francis de Sales (journalists), Saint Bernadine of Siena (public relations and advertising), Saint Genesius (actors), Saint Cecilia (composers and musicians), Saint Luke (artists), and Saint Isidore of Seville (proposed patron of the Internet).

▶ On page 215, as part of the *We Respond* activity, discuss the ways families can thank mothers and grandmothers for all that they do. Then consider asking the children to name movies and television programs they have seen that show families honoring mothers and grandmothers.

CHAPTER PROJECT: SAINT MOBILES

Explain to the children that they will be learning about ways to honor Mary and the saints. Provide the children with access to age-appropriate reading materials about various saints. Invite the children to make special mobiles in honor of a saint. Provide markers, paper plates, string, and hangers. Encourage the children to draw the face of their chosen saint on a white paper plate and print the saint's name around the outside rim of the plate. They might also add other pictures or symbols that represent the saint. When they have finished, help the children attach their plates to hangers. Display the mobiles around the room and invite each child to tell something about his or her chosen saint.

We Honor Mary and the Saints

WE GATHER

✝ Let us pray by singing.

🎵 **Litany of Saints**

Holy Mary, Mother of God,
Holy Mary, born without sin,
Holy Mary, taken into heaven:

Chorus
Pray for us.
Pray with us.
Help us to share God's love.

Saint Peter and Saint Paul,
Saint Mary Magdalene,
Saint Catherine of Siena:
(Chorus)

 What does it mean to honor someone? What are some ways we honor people?

211

PREPARING TO PRAY

For this gathering prayer the children pray by singing a litany of Mary and the saints.

• Play a recording of "Litany of the Saints," #24 on the Grade 2 CD. Ask the children to practice singing.

The Prayer Space

• Decorate the prayer space with pictures of Mary and other saints.

• On the prayer table, place a Bible opened to the beginning of the Gospel of Luke.

📖 **This Week's Liturgy**
Visit **www.webelieveweb.com** for this week's liturgical readings and other seasonal material.

Lesson Plan

WE GATHER

___ minutes

✝ Pray

• Remind the children: *Saint Peter and Saint Paul helped the Church to grow.* Explain: *Saint Mary Magdalene was a friend and follower of Jesus.* Also tell the children that Saint Catherine of Siena lived many years after Saints Peter, Paul, and Mary Magdalene. Explain: *Saint Catherine was a peacemaker. She helped other people to be peacemakers, too.*

• Invite the children to begin singing.

 Focus on Life

• Read the questions and ask volunteers to respond. Help the children to understand that we honor and celebrate people we respect and admire. Share the *Chapter Story* on guide page 211E.

Family Connection Update

Ask volunteers to share their family's experience when praying "Evening Prayer."

Catechist Goal

• To examine the ways the Church honors Mary and the saints

Our Faith Response

• To follow the example of Mary and the saints

 **saints   procession**

Lesson Materials

• highlighter or crayon
• Grade 2 CD
• copies of Reproducible Master 25
• picture or statue of Mary
• rosary beads (option)
• Scripture and Family reproducible masters (back of book)

Teaching Note

About the Saints

Before presenting this chapter, you may want to refer to the Kindergarten and Grade 1 texts of the *We Believe* program. The stories of specific saints are presented in these books.

WE BELIEVE

The Church honors the saints.

God is good and holy and wants us to be holy, too. So he shares his life with us. The sacraments help us to be holy. Loving God and others helps us to be holy, too.

The Church community honors holy people. The saints are holy people. The **saints** are all the members of the Church who have died and are happy with God forever in Heaven.

The saints followed Jesus' example. We remember and try to do what the saints did. Here are some of the saints we remember.

• Saint Peter and Saint Paul helped the Church to spread and grow.

• Saint Brigid of Ireland and Saint Catherine of Siena were peacemakers.

• Saint Rose of Lima and Saint Martin de Porres helped the poor and the sick.

• Saint John Bosco and Saint Frances Cabrini began schools to teach children about God's love.

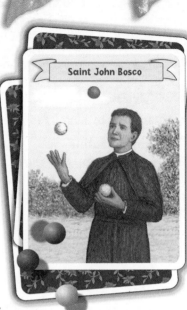

Saint John Bosco

 What saint do you know about? Write a sentence to tell some ways you can follow this saint's example.

_____

_____

saints all the members of the Church who have died and are happy with God forever in Heaven

212

Lesson Plan

WE BELIEVE _____ minutes

Invite a volunteer to read aloud the *We Believe* statement on page 212. Ask the children to share what they have previously learned about the saints.

Ask the children to read silently the first two paragraphs as you read them aloud. Have them highlight or underline the definition of saints in the second paragraph. Stress: *The saints were kind and caring during their lifetime. They shared God's love with many people.*

Read aloud the third paragraph and the introduction to the list of saints. Have volunteers read aloud about each pair of saints listed.

Brainstorm with the children ways we can follow the saints' example. Write all responses on the board or chart paper. (Possible responses: Be peacemakers; help people who are poor or sick; share what we know about God's love.) Then have the children write how they can follow one saint's example.

Present the reasons why the Church honors Mary as explained in the first paragraph on page 213.

Ask the children to stand as a volunteer reads the Scripture story of the angel's visit to Mary. Have two volunteers act out the story.

The Church honors Mary.

God chose Mary to be the Mother of his own Son, Jesus. So God blessed her in a special way. Mary was free from sin from the very first moment of her life. She was always filled with grace. All through her life she did what God wanted. A few months before Jesus was born, God sent an angel to Mary.

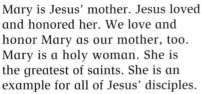 Luke 1:28–30, 38

The angel said to Mary, "Hail, favored one! The Lord is with you." (Luke 1:28) Then the angel told Mary not to be afraid. The angel said that God wanted her to be the Mother of his own Son. Mary told the angel she would do what God wanted.

Mary is Jesus' mother. Jesus loved and honored her. We love and honor Mary as our mother, too. Mary is a holy woman. She is the greatest of saints. She is an example for all of Jesus' disciples.

How can we honor Mary as the greatest saint?

Virgin and Child Enthroned, Sister Corita Kent c. 1960

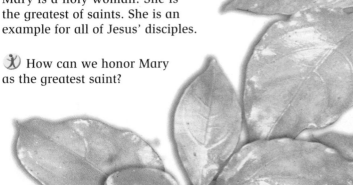

213

ACTIVITY BANK

Family
Saint Interview
Activity Materials: chart paper, writing paper

Ask the children to interview family members about their favorite saints. Have the children write these questions for their interview: *Who is your favorite saint? What do you like or admire about this saint?* Suggest to the children: *Ask your family to share their answers with you as you write their responses for each question.* Invite the children to share the results of their interviews with the group. You may wish to chart the interview data on a large sheet of chart paper.

nvite a volunteer to read the last paragraph on page 13. Write on chart paper: *Mary is ———.* Have volunteers tell you five different ways of finishing the sentence. (Jesus' mother, our mother, a holy woman, the greatest of saints, an example for all)

Help the children to understand that we can honor Mary by following her example in our everyday lives. Explain: *God wants us to learn from Mary and the saints. He wants us to love and care for others.*

Call attention to the fine art on page 213. Explain that Mary is pictured with Jesus as a child. They are surrounded by figures of some of the saints.

Quick Check

✔ *Who are saints?* (They are all the members of the Church who have died and are happy with God forever in heaven.)

✔ *How did Mary know that God had chosen her to be the Mother of his Son, Jesus?* (An angel visited her and told her what God wanted.)

The Rosary

After working on these two pages, read *As Catholics*. Show the children a rosary. Distribute copies of Reproducible Master 25. Point out the prayers we say on the different beads. Have the children color the beads in their free time. Encourage them to share the rosary diagram with their families.

We honor Mary with special prayers.

Mary had a cousin named Elizabeth. Elizabeth was going to have a baby, too. Mary went to visit and help her cousin.

📖 Luke 1:39, 40–42

When Elizabeth saw Mary, she was very happy and excited. The Holy Spirit helped Elizabeth to know that God had chosen Mary to be the Mother of his own Son. Elizabeth said to Mary, "Most blessed are you among women, and blessed is the fruit of your womb." (Luke 1:42)

These words to Mary are part of one of the Church's prayers, the Hail Mary.

Hail Mary

Hail Mary, full of grace,
the Lord is with you!
<u>Blessed are you among women,
and blessed is the fruit of your
    womb</u>, Jesus.
Holy Mary, Mother of God,
pray for us sinners,
now and at the hour of our death.
Amen.

Add your own decorations to the prayer frame. Underline Elizabeth's words to Mary. Pray the Hail Mary now.

214

Lesson Plan

WE BELIEVE (continued)

Direct attention to the illustration. Explain: *The picture shows Mary and Elizabeth. Elizabeth was Mary's cousin. Mary was going to have a baby. She visited Elizabeth, who was also going to have a baby.* Point out that Elizabeth's baby was Jesus' cousin, John. John later became known as John the Baptist.

Share the Scripture story on page 214. Explain: *Elizabeth greeted Mary with words of praise. We pray these words when we pray the Hail Mary.*

Direct attention to the prayer. Explain that the word *hail* means "hello." It can also mean "rejoice." Help the children to understand that we address Mary in this way to express our joy. Then invite the children to read the words of the Hail Mary aloud with you.

Have the children underline Elizabeth's words. Then ask the children to add decorations to the prayer frame. When they have finished, ask them to share their drawings. Then pray the Hail Mary together.

We honor Mary on special days.

Catholics honor Mary during the year. On special days, called feast days, the whole parish gathers for Mass. Here are some of Mary's feast days.

Date	We gather to celebrate
January 1	Mary is the Mother of God.
August 15	Mary is in Heaven with God forever.
December 8	Mary was free from sin from the very first moment of her life.

Sometimes parish communities gather to honor Mary by having a procession. A **procession** is a prayer walk. While walking, people pray and sing. On December 12, many parishes have a procession to honor Mary as Our Lady of Guadalupe.

Inside and outside homes and churches, people often put statues and pictures of Mary. Looking at the statues and pictures helps people to remember Mary.

WE RESPOND

What can your class do to honor Mary?

🎵 Immaculate Mary

Immaculate Mary,
your praises we sing.
You reign now in heaven
with Jesus our King.
Ave, Ave, Ave, Maria!
Ave, Ave, Maria!

Key Word

procession a prayer walk

As Catholics...

The Rosary is a prayer in honor of Mary. When we pray the Rosary, we use beads as we pray. We begin with the Sign of the Cross, the Apostles' Creed, Our Father, three Hail Marys and a Glory Be to the Father. Then there are five sets of ten beads to pray Hail Marys. Each set begins with the Our Father and ends with the Glory Be to the Father.

As we pray each set of ten beads, we think about the lives of Jesus and Mary. Plan a time this week to pray the Rosary with your family.

215

ACTIVITY BANK

Multicultural Connection

Honoring Mary

Activity Materials: world map, construction paper, scissors, glue or tape, colored markers

Locate Guatemala on a world map. Explain that to honor Mary, artists in Guatemala made a beautiful crown to place on their favorite statue of her. The crown is made of diamonds, emeralds, and pearls. During the month of October (the month dedicated to the Rosary), the people of Guatemala honor Our Lady of the Rosary with celebrations, songs, feasts, and prayers.

Invite the children to imagine they are taking part in the celebrations in Guatemala. Distribute construction paper, scissors, glue or tape, and markers. Have the children design crowns for Mary, the Mother of God.

Read aloud the first paragraph on page 215. Help the children understand the chart. Stress: *On these days we gather with our parish to celebrate the Mass.* Point out that we honor Mary in different ways on other days throughout the year.

Ask volunteers to read the second and third paragraphs. Then stress: *We can honor Mary every day of the year.* Ask the children to describe their favorite pictures of Mary.

Distribute Reproducible Master 25, guide page 211C. Have the children do the activity now or work on it at home.

WE RESPOND ___ minutes

Connect to Life Read the *We Respond* question. Invite volunteers to share their responses. Then plan together a celebration to honor Mary.

🎵 **Read** the words of "Immaculate Mary." Explain that *Ave* means "hail" or "hello," and that Maria is the Latin, Spanish, and Italian name for Mary. Play "Immaculate Mary," #25 on the Grade 2 CD, and have the children practice singing.

Pray Have the children walk in a procession. Ask them to sing "Immaculate Mary."

Catechist Goal

- To review the chapter ideas that are key to growing as disciples of Jesus Christ

Our Faith Response

- To decide on ways to grow as disciples by living out what we have learned

Show What you Know

Help children locate the two *Key Words*. Ask them if there is another word in the puzzle. Provide this clue: the word represents an action that all disciples should do each day. Have a volunteer share the word *pray* (in the upper left corner). Ask children to circle the word.

Saint Stories

Read aloud the story about Saint Frances of Rome. Point out that Saint Frances was married and had children. Ask the children to think of ways that they can follow the saint's example.

Make it Happen

Read aloud the activity directions. When the children are finished with their cards, collect them and make a poster for the parish.

Pray Today

Provide about five minutes for the children to pray the Hail Mary and to talk about the meaning of "full of grace."

Take Home

You may want to have available art books that have art work featuring Mary. Show the children. Encourage them to do the activity with their families.

Discuss and send home copies of *Sharing Faith with My Family* reproducible master for this chapter (back of book).

216 and **217**

Grade 2 Chapter 25

PROJECT

Show What you Know

Find the hidden in the word search.

P	R	A	Y	I	S	X	I	O	N
A	O	T	X	J	A	S	H	O	S
N	C	D	P	M	I	R	U	J	T
T	E	H	S	Y	N	L	P	A	Z
B	Y	C	A	N	T	Q	T	S	A
P	R	O	C	E	S	S	I	O	N

saints

procession

Saint Stories

Saint Frances of Rome, Italy, took food to those who were poor. She comforted people who were sad and lonely. She cared for children who had no families. Her feast day is March 9.

216　www.webelieveweb.com

DISCIPLE

Make it Happen

Mary is the greatest of saints. Make a card to honor Mary. Share it with your parish.

Pray Today

Pray the Hail Mary quietly with a friend.

↳ **DISCIPLE CHALLENGE** Talk together about what "full of grace" means.

filled with God's life

Take Home

As a family, find paintings and stained-glass windows and other works of art that tell us about Mary. Visit your parish church or look online. Choose your family favorite. Write about it here.

_____

_____

_____

217

CHAPTER TEST

Fill in the circle beside the correct answer.

1. Mary _____ did what God wanted.
   - ● always
   - ○ never

2. Mary was free from _____ from the first moment of her life.
   - ○ work
   - ● sin

3. _____ told Mary that God wanted her to be the Mother of his own Son.
   - ○ Elizabeth
   - ● An angel

4. Mary is the _____ saint.
   - ● greatest
   - ○ newest

Complete the following sentences.

5. _____The Hail Mary_____ is one of the Church's prayers to Mary.

6. A procession is a _____prayer walk_____.

7. _____Saints_____ are all the members of the Church who have died and are happy with God forever in Heaven.

8. Feast days are ways to _____honor_____ Mary.

9–10. Write two ways you can follow the example of Mary and the saints.

Possible responses: follow Jesus' example; be kind and caring; share God's love with others

218

CHAPTER TEST

Provide ten to fifteen minutes for the students to complete the test. After all have finished, check the answers. Clarify any misconceptions.

Alternative Assessment

You may want the students to complete the following alternative-assessment activity.

Make a chart. List the ways parishes honor Mary and the saints. Draw pictures and write sentences.

Additional Testing

• Chapter 25 Test in *Assessment Book*, pages 49–50

• CD-ROM *Test Generator and Resource*: Use Chapter 25 Test or customize your own.

Review

Review the definitions as they are presented in the chapter's *Key Word* boxes:

• saints (page 212)

• procession (page 215).

We Believe Statements

Review the four statements.

• The Church honors the saints.

• The Church honors Mary.

• We honor Mary with special prayers.

• We honor Mary on special days.

To use the Chapter 25 Study Guide, visit

www.webelieveweb.com

Overview

In Chapter 25 the children learned that the Church honors Mary and the saints. In this chapter they will learn about loving and respecting all of God's creation.

Doctrinal Content	For Adult Reading and Reflection *Catechism of the Catholic Church*
The children will learn:	Paragraph
• We live in God's love.	1694
• Jesus taught us to love others.	1823
• We love and respect others.	1825
• We respect God's creation.	307

Key Word

new commandment (p. 221)

Catechist Background

What is the greatest gift you have ever received?

Go to **www.webelieveweb.com**, Catechist/Teacher, We Believe Correlations for this chapter's correlation to:
- Six Tasks of Catechesis
- Catholic Social Teaching
- *Catechetical Formation in Chaste Living.*

God created us out of love to live in love with him. As Saint John tells us, "God is love, and whoever remains in love remains in God and God in him" (1 John 4:16). God lavishes us with many gifts, and we call God's gifts to us "grace." Grace abounds all around us. We receive grace in a special way in the sacraments, which help to open our eyes and hearts to see the grace present all around us.

The greatest gift God has given to us is his Son, Jesus Christ. Through Jesus' Death and Resurrection we have new and everlasting life. Through Jesus' life and teaching we learn the way to that new life. Jesus taught us how to live a life faithful to God's love. Before his death, Jesus told his disciples, "I give you a new commandment: love one another. As I have loved you, so you also should love one another. This is how all will know that you are my disciples, if you have love for one another" (John 13:34–35).

Following Jesus' new commandment and being faithful to who God created us to be, we love and respect one another. All of the Church's teachings on social justice and personal morality stem from this core belief: that we are created in God's image and must treat one another with love and respect. This belief extends to the environment as well. We become good stewards of God's creation by caring for what God has made.

By caring for the world and loving one another we accept God's gift of love for us, and we become gift-givers like our God.

How do you show love and respect for God's creation?

Lesson Planning Guide

Lesson Steps	Presentation	Materials

 1 WE GATHER

Lesson Steps	Presentation	Materials
page 219 ✚ **Prayer** **Focus on Life**	• Listen to Scripture. 🎵 Respond by singing. • Discuss the questions.	🎵 "A Circle of Love," Felicia Sandler, #26, Grade 2 CD • pictures of families enjoying and caring for creation (option)

2 WE BELIEVE

Lesson Steps	Presentation	Materials
page 220 *We live in God's love.*	• Present the text about the gifts of faith, hope, and love. 🚶 Do the missing word activity.	• colored pencils or crayons
page 221 *Jesus taught us to love others.*	• Present the text about the ways to love God and others. • Read the Scripture story about Jesus' new commandment. 🚶 Do the picture study activity.	• large sheets of drawing paper (one sheet per set of partners) • colored pencils or crayons
page 222 *We love and respect others.*	• Read the text about showing love and respect. 🚶 Complete the activity.	
page 223 *We respect God's creation.*	• Present the text about respecting God's creation. • Read and discuss the *As Catholics* text.	• colored pencils • copies of Reproducible Master 26, guide page 219C • scissors, glue, drawing paper 🎵 "God Made the World," by Jack Miffleton, #27, Grade 2 CD

3 WE RESPOND

Lesson Steps	Presentation	Materials
page 223	🚶 Complete the checklist.	
pages 224–225 **Project Disciple**	• Complete the Project Disciple activities. • Explain the *Take Home* activity. • Discuss/send home **Sharing Faith with My Family** reproducible master for this chapter.	• crayons or colored pencils or markers • copies of Sharing Faith with My Family reproducible master, Chapter 26 (back of book)
page 226 **Chapter 26 Test**	• Complete Chapter 26 Test. • Work on *Alternative Assessment* activity.	• optional: copies of Scripture reproducible master, *What's the Word?*, Chapter 26 (back of book)

For additional ideas, activities, and opportunities: Visit Sadlier's **www.WeBelieveweb.com**

Name _____

Celebrate God's world in song. Make a song booklet. Cut along the dotted lines. Paste each verse to a page in your booklet. Draw a picture of the gifts of creation for each verse.

God Made the World

God made the world so broad and grand,
filled it with blessings from his hand.
God made the sky so high and blue,
and all the little children too.

God made the sun, the moon and stars,
lighting the world from near and far.
God made the world with tender care
and all the little children there.

God made the sparrow and the rose,
gifts for the ear, the eye and nose.
God made the beauty voices bring,
when all the little children sing.

PROJECT DISCIPLE

Pray
Learn
Celebrate
Share
Choose
Live

Additional Activities

What's *the* Word?

Scripture reproducible master, Chapter 26

Materials needed: copies of *What's the Word?* (back of book); crayons or colored pencils; drawing paper and/or construction paper; scissors and glue sticks

Distribute copies of the Scripture reproducible master. Read the words of Jesus. Ask the children to choose one of the quotes. Help each child cut out the quote and then glue it to the center of a sheet of drawing paper or construction paper. Then have the children decorate the border around the quote. Encourage the children to share the words of Jesus with their families and display the sign where family members may see it often.

Show What *you* Know

Materials needed: index cards, each card having one of the Grade 2 *Key Words* printed on it

Play "What's the Question?" Stack the index cards. Assign sets of partners. Have each set take turns drawing a card from the stack.

The partners should consult briefly and then say aloud a question for the *Key Word* on the card. If the partners are incorrect, have them give the card to the next set of partners to come up with a question.

Make *it* Happen

Materials needed: slips of paper; container for the slips of paper; note paper

Explain to the children that one of the ways we show our love for others is by praying for them. Give each child a slip of paper. Have the children write their names on the papers. Ask the children to fold the slips of paper in half and collect them in the container.

Place the container in the prayer space. Then have the children take turns coming to the prayer space and drawing one of the papers from the container. If any child draws her or his own name, have the child draw another. Then explain that during the summer they will be praying for the people whose names they have drawn.

Give a sheet of note paper to each child, having him or her write a note to the person the child will be praying for this summer. Ask all the children to gather in the prayer space and give their notes to the appropriate children. Pray the Our Father together. Encourage the children to remember to pray for each other often during the summer.

Meeting Individual Needs
Children with Allergies

Keep a list of children who have allergies. Notify these children's parents before field trips or engaging in outdoor activities. Ask the parents to talk to the children about what they should avoid. Encourage the children to tell you immediately about any problems they might have.

We Believe Resources

- Grade 2 *Review & Resource Book*, pages 61–63
- Grade 2 *Family Book*, pages 74–76
- Grade 2 *Assessment Book*, pages 51–52
- Grade 2 CD-ROM *Test Generator and Resource*: Use Chapter 26 Test or customize your own.
- **www.webelieveweb.com**

Enrichment Ideas

Chapter Story

Cindy and her friends were walking together. Cindy told everybody to stop when she heard a noise in the nearby bushes. The friends wondered what was making the noise. They looked hard but could not see anything in the bushes. Then they heard the noise again. They saw a small bird on the grass near the edge of the bushes.

At first Cindy wanted to scoop up the bird and take it home. Something inside her told her not to do that. She asked her friends, "What do you think we should do?"

Now invite the children to write an ending to the story of Cindy's friends and the bird. They can work independently, in pairs, or in groups. Have the children share the endings they have written. The children can also prepare story boards to share with each other and their families.

FAITH and MEDIA

▶ After discussing the responses to the questions at the bottom of page 219, you might ask the children to name some stories they have seen, heard, or read in the media (on television, in the movies, on the Internet, or in newspapers or magazines) about people who are setting a good example for others.

▶ After completing the *We Respond* activity on page 223, you might point out to the children that the media help increase our awareness and appreciation of the gifts of God's creation. We can also learn through the media ways to care for God's gifts and to share what we have with people who are in need. Consider having the children visit the Web site of an organization such as the Catholic Conservation Center that uses the Internet to promote prayerful stewardship of God's creation.

CHAPTER PROJECT: FIELD TRIPS

Together visit a nearby park. Invite the park's caretakers or rangers to speak to the children about what they do to protect the environment. Or, visit an animal shelter or bird sanctuary. Also show the children videotapes about the care of animals and plants of different ecological systems. Have the children sign a group pledge to do what they can to be God's stewards.

We Show Love and Respect

WE GATHER

✝ **Leader:** Let us listen to a reading from Paul to the Corinthians.

Reader: "Love is patient, love is kind. Love never fails. Faith, hope, love remain, these three; but the greatest of these is love." (1 Corinthians 13:4, 8, 13) The word of the Lord.

All: Thanks be to God.

🎵 **A Circle of Love**

Chorus
A circle of love, yes a circle of love;
each hand in a hand, a circle of friends.
A circle of love that is open to all;
we open the circle and welcome
  each one of you in.

Each person has something to bring:
a song, a story, a smile, a teardrop,
a dream, and loving to share. (Chorus)

 Who are some of the people you love? How do you show your love for them?

219

PREPARING TO PRAY

For this gathering prayer, the children will listen to a Scripture reading and respond in song.

• Play "A Circle of Love," #26 on the Grade 2 CD. Have the children practice singing.

• Choose volunteers to be the prayer leader and reader. Have them prepare what they will read.

The Prayer Space

• If possible, plan to pray outdoors. If this is not possible, display pictures of families enjoying and caring for each other and creation.

📖 **This Week's Liturgy**
Visit **www.webelieveweb.com** for this week's liturgical readings and other seasonal material.

Lesson Plan

WE GATHER

___ minutes

✝ **Pray**

• If you are praying outdoors, ask the children to sit as they listen to the reading from Scripture.

• Ask the children to stand, join hands to form a circle, and to sing "A Circle of Love," #26 on the Grade 2 CD.

☀ **Focus on Life**

Discuss the responses to the questions. Help the children to see that sometimes we give gifts to express our love. Tell the children that in this chapter they will learn about God's gifts of faith, hope, and love.

Family Connection Update

Ask volunteers to tell what art work of Mary their families discovered.

Catechist Goal

• To describe and care for the many gifts that God has given us in creation and to explain the gifts of faith, hope, and love

Our Faith Response

• To express gratitude for God's gifts and love and respect for others

 new commandment

Lesson Materials

• Grade 2 CD

• copies of Reproducible Master 26

• Scripture and Family reproducible masters (back of book)

Teaching Note

Nurturing Self-Respect

Your own ability and the ability of your second graders to respect others must be founded on a healthy sense of self-respect. Evaluate how you are doing in nurturing your own self-respect by tending to your spiritual, emotional, and intellectual needs. By doing this, you will be better able to help the children develop self-respect.

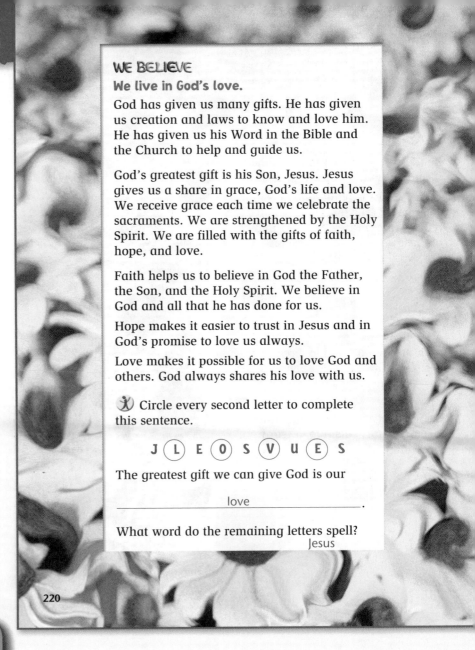

WE BELIEVE
We live in God's love.

God has given us many gifts. He has given us creation and laws to know and love him. He has given us his Word in the Bible and the Church to help and guide us.

God's greatest gift is his Son, Jesus. Jesus gives us a share in grace, God's life and love. We receive grace each time we celebrate the sacraments. We are strengthened by the Holy Spirit. We are filled with the gifts of faith, hope, and love.

Faith helps us to believe in God the Father, the Son, and the Holy Spirit. We believe in God and all that he has done for us.

Hope makes it easier to trust in Jesus and in God's promise to love us always.

Love makes it possible for us to love God and others. God always shares his love with us.

Circle every second letter to complete this sentence.

J (L) E (O) S (V) U (E) S

The greatest gift we can give God is our

_____ love _____.

What word do the remaining letters spell?

Jesus

220

Lesson Plan

WE BELIEVE ___ minutes

Read the *We Believe* statement at the top of page 220. Then have a volunteer read the first two paragraphs. Draw a large circle on chart paper. Write Jesus in the center of the circle. Then ask: *What are the other gifts of God mentioned in the text?* (the world, creation, God's laws, God's Word in the Bible, the Church, faith, hope, and love) Write each gift in the circle surrounding Jesus' name. Then ask: *Why do you think we wrote Jesus' name in the center of the circle?* (because Jesus is God's greatest gift)

Invite volunteers to read the description of the gifts of faith, hope, and love. Then stress: *Love is the greatest gift we can give to God.*

Help the children complete the activity by circling every other letter in the word scramble. When they have finished, invite a volunteer to read the completed sentence. Explain that the remaining letters spell *Jesus.*

Ask a volunteer to read the *We Believe* statement on page 221. Then invite volunteers to read aloud the three paragraphs. On the board print: *Jesus showed us the way to ____.* Leave space for the listed copy. As a volunteer reads each way, write it on the board. Encourage the children to discuss each statement and provide examples of what each means.

Jesus taught us to love others.

God loves us so much that he sent his Son to share his love with us. Jesus shared God's love with all people. He asked his followers to do the same.

Jesus taught his followers to love God and one another. He showed us the way to:

- pray to the Father
- live as a family
- be a friend and neighbor
- love and respect those who are poor, sick, and lonely.

Jesus loved his followers very much. He asked them to follow his example of love.

📖 John 13:34-35

Jesus said, "I give you a new commandment: love one another. As I have loved you, so you also should love one another. This is how all will know that you are my disciples, if you have love for one another." (John 13:34-35)

Jesus' **new commandment** is to love one another as he has loved us.

🧒 For each picture on this page tell how Jesus is showing love. How can you follow his example?

new commandment Jesus' commandment to love one another as he has loved us

221

ACTIVITY BANK

Multiple Intelligences
Verbal-Linguistic

Have the children prepare a good news program that includes eye-witness reports about ways people showed that they were disciples of Jesus during the day. For example:

• One of Jesus' disciples, a second grader, was seen today helping his neighbor pick up groceries that had fallen all over the sidewalk.

Have the children pretend that they are presenting these reports on a television news show.

Read aloud the Scripture passage. Ask: *What do you think it means to be a disciple of Jesus?* Emphasize the importance of loving one another as a way to follow Jesus' new commandment.

🧒 **Direct** the children's attention to the pictures of Jesus on these pages. For each picture discuss how Jesus is showing love and how people can follow his example. Have the children work in pairs. Give each pair a large sheet of drawing paper. Ask the partners to illustrate ways we show that we are disciples of Jesus. When finished ask the pairs to share their drawings with the entire group.

Quick Check

✔ *What is the greatest gift we can give God?* (It is our love.)

✔ *What new commandment did Jesus give us?* (Jesus said to love one another as he has loved us.)

We love and respect others.

Loving as Jesus did brings us closer to God and one another. We show our belief in God by loving and respecting him. We honor God's name as a sign of our love. Together we worship God. We thank God for all he has done for us.

Following Jesus' new commandment helps us to follow all of God's commandments. We try to love our family, friends, and all people as Jesus did. We respect and obey all those who take care of us. We also try to be kind, fair, and truthful. We share the things we have. We respect the belongings of other people.

Underline the sentence that tells how you will follow Jesus' new commandment today.

222

Lesson Plan

WE BELIEVE (continued)

Allow a few minutes of quiet time for the children to read silently the first two paragraphs on page 222. When they have finished, ask: *What does following Jesus' new commandment help us to do?*

Invite volunteers to stage short skits that show people following Jesus' new commandment. You might want to suggest some situations. (for example: The child sitting next to you dropped his pencil case and everything spilled out; or mom had to work late.) After each skit, have the group explain how the people showed love for God and for one another.

Read the directions. Have the children use a highlighter or crayon to indicate their decision.

Ask a volunteer to read aloud the first paragraph on page 223. Have the children highlight or underline the last sentence in their texts.

Invite volunteers to read the last two paragraphs. Explain: *Because we have a special place in God's creation, we have the responsibility to care for the world.*

We respect God's creation.

God asks us to respect his gift of creation. God created the land and the sea, the sun, moon, and stars. God created all the animals and plants. He created us, too! All that God created is good.

People have a special place in God's creation. God has asked us to take care of his gifts of creation. The gifts of God's creation are everywhere!

We care for the world. We protect all that God created. We work together to share the goodness of creation.

WE RESPOND

✘ Put a check ✔ in front of the ways you will take care of God's creation.

☐ Feed and care for my pet.

☐ Put trash in a can.

☐ Recycle cans, bottles, and papers.

☐ Turn off the water.

☐ Plant new trees.

Now add one more way you will help care for creation.

_____

_____

_____

As Catholics...

The gifts of creation belong to all people everywhere. However, there are many parts of the world where people are hungry and thirsty. So we share what we have. We also help them to grow food and find water. This is part of what it means to care for God's creation. Find out what your neighborhood is doing to take care of God's creation.

223

ACTIVITY BANK

Community

Guest Speakers

Invite guest speakers to speak to the children about ways they can care for God's creation. Some speaker possibilities: reservoir workers, recycling-center workers, farmers, fish wardens, oceanographers, park and forest rangers, wildlife preserve workers. Help the children compose questions they would like to ask the speaker. Encourage the children to ask the guests these questions.

✘ **Distribute** copies of Reproducible Master 26. Help the children to make song booklets. Encourage them to share the song and pictures with their families and friends. Play the song "God Made the World," #27, Grade 2 CD. Have the children read the words. Then ask the children to sing the song with you. Have them circle the names of God's gifts in the song.

WE RESPOND   ___ minutes

Connect to Life Ask the children to complete the *We Respond* activity by putting a check mark beside the ways we can care for God's creation this week. Allow a few quiet moments for the children to print one more way that they will help care for creation.

Invite the children to write an ending for the *Chapter Story* on guide page 219E.

Pray Sing "God Made the World."

Catechist Goal

- To review the chapter ideas that are key to growing as disciples of Jesus Christ

Our Faith Response

- To decide on ways to grow as disciples by living out what we have learned

Show What *you* Know

Read aloud the directions. Ask a volunteer to tell what is happening in each photograph. Then have children complete the activity.

Picture This

As the children are drawing, you may want to play "God Made the World," #27 on the Grade 2 CD.

Make *it* Happen

Have a volunteer read aloud the directions. Help the children complete the chart.

What's *the* Word?

Read aloud Saint Paul's words. Discuss the reading.

Take Home

Encourage the children to share with their families ways of discipleship.

Discuss and send home copies of *Sharing Faith with My Family* reproducible master for this chapter (back of book).

Grade 2 Chapter 26

Pray Learn Celebrate Share Choose Live

PROJECT

Show What *you* Know

Circle the picture of the children following Jesus' new commandment.

Picture This

Draw a picture showing a way that you respect God's creation.

> Possible responses: drawings of situations in checklist on page 223.

224   www.webelieveweb.com

DISCIPLE

Pray Learn Celebrate Share Choose Live

Make *it* Happen

Tell your family what the gifts of faith, hope, and love help us to do. To help you prepare, complete this organizer.

The gift of faith	helps us to	believe in God.
The gift of hope	helps us to	trust in God.
The gift of ____ love	helps us to	love God and others.

What's *the* Word?

Read these words from one of Saint Paul's letters.

> "Love is patient,
> love is kind.
> It is not jealous . . .
> it is not rude." (1 Corinthians 13:4–5)

Tell how this is true. **Now, pass it on!**

Take Home

As a family share ways you have learned to be disciples of Jesus this year!

225

CHAPTER TEST

Fill in the circle beside the correct answer.

1. Jesus shared God's love with _____ people.
   - ● all
   - ○ a few
   - ○ some

2. Jesus' new commandment is to love one another as _____ loved us.
   - ○ his followers
   - ○ his neighbors
   - ● he

3. _____ have a special place in God's creation.
   - ○ Plants
   - ● People
   - ○ Animals

4. God's greatest gift to us is his _____.
   - ● Son
   - ○ creation
   - ○ law

5. God's gift of _____ helps us to believe in God and all that he has done for us.
   - ● faith
   - ○ hope
   - ○ love

6. God's gift of _____ helps us to trust in Jesus and in God's promise to love us always.
   - ○ faith
   - ● hope
   - ○ love

7–8. Write two ways Jesus showed us how to love God and others.

Possible responses: pray to the Father; live as a family; be a friend and neighbor; love and respect those who are sick, poor, and lonely

9–10. Write two ways we can follow Jesus' new commandment.

See page 222.

226

CHAPTER TEST

Provide ten to fifteen minutes for the students to complete the test. After all have finished, check the answers. Clarify any misconceptions.

Alternative Assessment

You may want the students to complete the following alternative-assessment activity.

Use pictures or words to show ways people can follow Jesus' new commandment.

Additional Testing

• Chapter 26 Test in *Assessment Book*, pages 51–52

• CD-ROM *Test Generator and Resource*: Use Chapter 26 Test or customize your own.

Review

Review the definition as it is presented in the chapter's *Key Word* box:

• new commandment (page 221).

We Believe Statements

Review the four statements.

• We live in God's love.

• Jesus taught us to love others.

• We love and respect others.

• We respect God's creation.

To use the Chapter 26 Study Guide, visit

www.webelieveweb.com

Easter

The fifty days from Easter Sunday to Pentecost are celebrated in joyful exultation as one feast day…These above all others are the days for the singing of the Alleluia.

(Norms Governing Liturgical Calendars, 22)

Overview

In this chapter the children will learn that Easter is a season to celebrate the Resurrection of Jesus Christ.

For Adult Reading and Reflection
You may want to refer to paragraph 641 of the *Catechism of the Catholic Church*.

Catechist Background

Go to **www.webelieveweb.com**, Catechist/Teacher, We Believe Correlations for this chapter's correlation to the Six Tasks of Catechesis.

What are some of the ways in which you celebrate Easter?

The Church celebrates the fifty days from Easter Sunday to Pentecost as one continuous feast day. They have been called "the Great Sunday" by Saint Athanasius because what Sundays are to the week, the Easter season is to the entire year. "Christ's Resurrection is the fulfillment of the promises of the Old Testament and of Jesus himself during his earthly life" (CCC 652). Jesus' divinity is confirmed by his Resurrection. When he died on the cross, Jesus Christ freed us from the shackles of sin. At his rising, he opened for us the path to new life.

The Resurrection was an historical event attested to by witnesses to the empty tomb and the disciples' encounters with the risen Lord. This transcendent event lies at the heart of our faith; it is the primary truth to which all Christ's followers testify. "If Christ has not been raised, then empty [too] is our preaching; empty, too, your faith" (1 Corinthians 15:14).

Our celebration of the Easter season encompasses the Ascension, the return of Jesus Christ to his Father in heaven, and Pentecost itself. Ascension is celebrated on either the Thursday of the Sixth Week of Easter, or, in many dioceses, on the following Sunday. The Church rejoices that Jesus' post-Resurrection appearances culminate "with the irreversible entry of his humanity into divine glory" (CCC 659).

At Pentecost the Easter season concludes with the outpouring of the Holy Spirit, signaling the fulfillment of Christ's Passover. The promised Advocate has come to strengthen and unify the Church which was made manifest to the world at the first Pentecost.

How will you help others to experience Easter as a season of new life and joy?

Lesson Planning Guide

Lesson Steps	Presentation	Materials
① WE GATHER		
page 227 **Introduce the Season**	• Read the *Chapter Story*. • Introduce the Easter season. • Proclaim words on a banner.	
page 228	Act out ways of showing happiness.	
② WE BELIEVE		
pages 228–229 *Easter is a season to celebrate the Resurrection of Jesus.*	• Present the text about celebrating the Easter season. Act out the Easter story.	• costumes and props • colored chalk
③ WE RESPOND		
page 230	Write an Easter message about Jesus to share. • Discuss ways to share the joyful messages.	
Text page 231 **Guide page 231–232** **We Respond in Prayer**	• Celebrate Easter in prayer. 🎵 Rejoice in song.	🎵 "This Is the Day," #28, Grade 2 CD • prayer space items: white tablecloth, Bible, vase, Easter flowers
Text page 232 **Guide pages 231–232, 232A** **Project Disciple**	• Complete the **Project Disciple** activities. Discuss the *Take Home* activity. • Complete the Reproducible Master 27 activity. See guide pages 232A and 227C. • Discuss/send home **Sharing Faith with My Family**, guide page 232B.	• poster paint (brown and pink) • paint brushes, scissors, glue, cotton balls • sheets of poster board (one for each child) • copies of Reproducible Master 27, guide page 232A • copies of **Sharing Faith with My Family**, guide page 232B

For additional ideas, activities, and opportunities: Visit Sadlier's **www.WeBelieveweb.com**

Chapter Story

Andrew Watanabe's family lived near Washington, D.C. They had moved there in January. Andrew's mother traveled to Washington every day for work.

Andrew wanted to visit Washington. Every Saturday he asked his mother if the family could go. Mrs. Watanabe told Andrew, "We'll go in the spring when the cherry blossoms start to bloom."

One day during the first week of April, Andrew's mom was smiling during dinner. Finally, before everyone left the table, she said, "I noticed today that the cherry blossoms are starting to bloom. I think we can go to Washington on Saturday."

Andrew was so excited he got up from the table. He spun around and then hugged his mother. Andrew's sister clapped her hands and smiled.

How did Andrew and his sister show they were excited about their mother's good news?

PROJECT DISCIPLE
Additional Activities

Take Home

Set up a few work stations for the children. At each station put a container of brown poster paint, a container of pink poster paint, and a bucket or bowl of water. Also place at each station paint brushes, cotton balls, scissors, glue sticks, and an 8 ½ in. x 11 in. sheet of poster board for each child.

Ask the children to cut out their signs from the reproducible master and glue the sign to the poster board. Then have the children paint their branches brown. To make the cherry blossoms, have the children dip small pieces of the cotton balls in pink poster paint. Then let the branches and the blossoms dry.

When the branches and blossoms are dry, tell the children to glue the blossoms on different spots on their branches. Encourage the children to display the signs at home, sharing the Easter message with family and friends.

Make it Happen

Have copies of the reproducible master available. Have the children make extra Easter message signs. Deliver the signs to nursing homes, hospitals, and shelters. Ask volunteers to write notes to include with the signs. Ask the writers to tell people that the children are praying for them.

Christ has risen, Alleluia!

This chapter celebrates the entire Easter season.

SEASONAL · CHAPTER 27

227

Chapter 27 • Easter

Catechist Goal

- To explain that Easter is the season in which we celebrate the Resurrection of Jesus

Our Faith Response

- To share the Good News of Easter

Gather In My Name

Whole Community Catechesis

An Online Resource

Celebrate **Easter** *as a class, school, and/or a parish community. The event comes complete with detailed leader's guides, preparation charts, handouts, promotional ideas, organizational materials, and much more. Go to:*

www.webelieveweb.com

Lesson Plan

Introduce the Season ___ minutes

- **Pray** Sing a familiar Alleluia.

- **Read** the *Chapter Story* on guide page 227C. Ask the children if they have ever seen a cherry blossom tree. Explain: *The cherry blossom trees in Washington, D.C. were a gift from the people of Japan in the year 1912. Today there are more than 3,700 trees that grow near the monuments along the Potomac River. The flowers blossom in the early spring.*

- **Ask** the children to read aloud the chapter title. Explain: *Easter is a season of great joy.* Ask: *What symbols of Easter and spring do you see on the page?* (flowers, butterflies)

- **Invite** the children to look at the photograph as they proclaim the words on the banner.

227

Lesson Materials

- copies of Reproducible Master 27
- costumes and props for dramatization
- poster paint (brown and pink)
- paint brushes, scissors, glue, and cotton balls
- sheets of $8\frac{1}{2}$ in. x 11 in. poster board (one for each child)
- Grade 2 CD

Teaching Note

When to Present the Lesson

To help the children understand that Easter is a season, present this chapter after Easter Sunday.

Easter is a season to celebrate the Resurrection of Jesus.

WE GATHER

How do you show you are happy? Act out some things you do.

WE BELIEVE

The Three Days lead us to the Easter season. The Easter season is a time of rejoicing. This season lasts fifty days.

During the Easter season, we celebrate that Jesus rose from the dead. We give thanks for the new life he brings us.

Take part in the Easter celebration.

Leader: All during the season of Easter, the Church sings the song of "Alleluia." Alleluia means "Praise God!" Let us praise God now.

Leader (singing): Alleluia, alleluia, alleluia!

All (repeat): Alleluia, alleluia, alleluia!

228

Lesson Plan

WE GATHER _____ minutes

- **Focus on Life** Read the *We Gather* question. Refer to the *Chapter Story*. Ask: *What did Andrew and his sister do to show they were happy?* Invite volunteers to act out things they do to show their happiness.

WE BELIEVE _____ minutes

- **Ask** a volunteer to read aloud the first two *We Believe* paragraphs. Have the children highlight or underline the second paragraph.

- **Prepare** for the children to enact the Easter play. Choose a leader, three readers, and two angels. Have the other children pretend they are the women and other disciples. Practice singing a familiar Alleluia response. Also give those who will read time to practice their parts. Have the children who are the women and disciples practice pantomiming appropriate gestures.

- **Invite** the children to gather in the prayer space. Have them act out the Easter play.

📖 Luke 24:1–9

Reader 1: On the first day of the week, at dawn, the women went to the tomb. They were bringing spices to bless Jesus' body. They found the stone rolled away. The body of Jesus was gone!

Reader 2: While they stood there, two angels appeared beside them. The women were frightened.

Angel 1: Are you looking for Jesus? He is not here. He has been raised up.

Angel 2: Remember what Jesus told you. He said that he would give his life for us. He would be crucified. He said that on the third day he would rise again.

Reader 3: Then the women were filled with joy. They ran back to tell the other disciples what they had seen and heard.

All (singing): Alleluia, alleluia, alleluia!

EASTER

229

ACTIVITY BANK

Multiple Intelligences
Spatial, Linguistic
Activity Materials: drawing paper, crayons, colored pencils

Have the children work in pairs. Ask the sets of partners to make a story board of the Scripture account of Easter morning. Explain that they can do this by drawing pictures and writing dialogue in speech balloons. When the children are finished working, ask them to show their Easter story boards to the entire group.

• **Ask:** *What Good News did the angels share with the women?* (Jesus had risen.) **Also ask:** *How do you think the women and the disciples felt when they heard this Good News?* (Possible responses: happy, excited.)

Quick Check

✔ *What do we celebrate during the Easter season?* (We celebrate the Resurrection of Jesus Christ.)

✔ *How long is the Easter season?* (The Easter season lasts for fifty days.)

CONNECTION

Multicultural Connection
Decorating Eggs

Explain to the children: *Eggs are symbols of new life. That is why we decorate them on Easter.* Show the children pictures of Easter eggs decorated by people of different countries.

Tell the children: *People in Greece dye eggs red to remember that Jesus shed his blood for us. In Austria people fasten ferns and tiny plants to eggs. Then they boil the eggs. When the plants are removed from the eggs, a lovely pattern remains on the shells.*

Also explain that people in the Ukraine, the southeastern part of Central Europe, call their decorated eggs *pysanki.* The Ukranian people use a wax-resist method to decorate the eggs. In the past, families would take the pysanki to church to be blessed at Easter.

Like the women at the tomb, we go and tell others about Jesus' Resurrection. We want them to know the Good News that Jesus died and rose for all people. We want to share the joy that comes from believing in Jesus.

WE RESPOND

What joyful Easter message about Jesus would you like to share? Write it here.

<u>Possible responses should include that Jesus died and rose</u>

<u>for all people.</u>

How will you share this Good News?

230

Lesson Plan

WE BELIEVE (continued)

• **Have** a volunteer read the *We Believe* paragraph at the top of page 230. Ask: *What is the Good News of Easter?* Have a volunteer use colored chalk to write on the board "Jesus died and rose for all people."

WE RESPOND
_____ minutes

Connect to Life Read the *We Respond* question. Pause for a minute of quiet time. Then ask the children to write the Easter message in the space provided.

• **Invite** the children to gather in the prayer space. Then pray aloud the following words.

Gracious God,
Through the announcement of the holy women
you bring the good news of your love
to all the peoples of the earth.
Strengthen us to carry that good news
in our lives, in our hearts, and in our words.
We ask this through Christ our Lord.

(Children's Daily Prayer, 2001-2002, Elizabeth McMahon Jeep. Liturgy Training Publications, page 261)

Then sprinkle holy water over the children and say: *Go share the Good News of Jesus.*

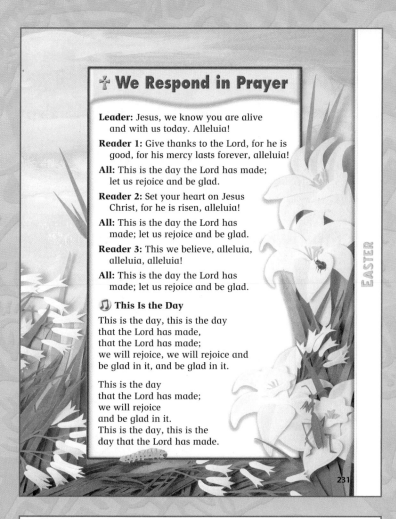

✝ We Respond in Prayer

Leader: Jesus, we know you are alive and with us today. Alleluia!

Reader 1: Give thanks to the Lord, for he is good, for his mercy lasts forever, alleluia!

All: This is the day the Lord has made; let us rejoice and be glad.

Reader 2: Set your heart on Jesus Christ, for he is risen, alleluia!

All: This is the day the Lord has made; let us rejoice and be glad.

Reader 3: This we believe, alleluia, alleluia, alleluia!

All: This is the day the Lord has made; let us rejoice and be glad.

🎵 **This Is the Day**

This is the day, this is the day
that the Lord has made,
that the Lord has made;
we will rejoice, we will rejoice and
be glad in it, and be glad in it.

This is the day
that the Lord has made;
we will rejoice
and be glad in it.
This is the day, this is the
day that the Lord has made.

EASTER

231

We Respond in Prayer (p. 231)

Get ready by placing flowers in the prayer space. Choose three readers and provide time for them to practice their readings. Have the children gather in the prayer space. Lead them in prayer and singing "This Is the Day," #28 on the Grade 2 CD.

📖 **This Week's Liturgy**
Visit **www.webelieveweb.com** for this week's liturgical readings and other seasonal material.

Project Disciple (p. 232)

Show What *you* Know

Read aloud the directions. Help the children to find the message by unscrambling the words.

Celebrate!

While the children are working, play "This Is the Day," #28 on the Grade 2 CD. When they have finished their bumper stickers, ask the children to show the stickers to the group.

Take Home

Read the suggestion. Pray three alleluias now.

Discuss and send home copies of *Sharing Faith with My Family*, guide page 232B.

Project Disciple Additional Activities
See the activities suggested on page 227C of the guide.

Pray Learn Celebrate Share Choose Live

Grade 2 Easter

PROJECT DISCIPLE

Show What *you* Know

Unscramble the words to find an important hidden message.

season of to celebrate is a Easter
Resurrection the Jesus.

Easter is a season to celebrate the Resurrection of Jesus.

_____

Celebrate!

Announce the Good News. Jesus is risen! Decorate this bumper sticker to share the joy of Easter with others.

Take Home

During the Easter season, the Church often prays three alleluias in a row, instead of just one. Add Easter joy to meal prayers or evening prayers. Try praying three alleluias after the Amen. Practice now. Say, "alleluia, alleluia, alleluia!"

Name _____

Cut along the dotted lines.
Paste the sign on a piece of poster board.
Paint the branch brown.
Add cherry blossoms.
Share the Easter message with your family and friends.

Jesus is risen! Alleluia!

SHARING FAITH
with My Family

Sharing What I Learned

Look at the pictures below. Use each picture to tell your family what you learned in this chapter.

Family Prayer

During the Easter season, the Church often prays three Alleluias in a row, instead of just one. Add Easter joy to meal prayers or evening prayers. Try praying three Alleluias after the Amen. Alleluia, alleluia, alleluia!

For All to See and Pray

Share the joy that comes from believing in Jesus. Draw signs of new life on the Alleluia banner. Put the banner in a place where you will see it often.

Alleluia!

Visit Sadlier's

www.WEBELIEVEweb.com

 Connect to the Catechism
For adult background and reflection, see paragraph 641.

ASSESSMENT

Unit 4 Test

Read aloud each set of test directions. Also you may choose to read aloud each test item. Wait for a minute for the children to indicate their responses in writing.

Alternative Assessment

You may want the children to complete the following alternative-assessment activity.

Imagine yourself as a grown-up. Describe how you are living your faith.

Additional Testing

• Unit 4 Test in Grade 2 *Assessment Book*, pages 53–54

• Unit 4 Alternative Assessment in Grade 2 *Assessment Book*, page 56

• Final Test (Units 1–4) in Grade 2 *Assessment Book*, pages 57–59

• CD-ROM *Test Generator and Resource*: Use Unit 4 Test or customize your own.

233 and **234**

Grade 2 Unit 4

UNIT TEST

Fill in the circle beside the correct answer.

1. A _____ is an area of the Church led by a bishop.
   ● diocese   ○ parish   ○ neighborhood

2. _____ is talking and listening to God.
   ○ Penance   ● Prayer   ○ Temple

3. The greatest saint is _____.
   ● Mary   ○ Elizabeth   ○ Joseph

4. The _____ is the leader of the whole Church.
   ● pope   ○ bishop   ○ pastor

Circle the correct answer.

5. Did Jesus teach his Apostles the Hail Mary?   Yes   (No)

6. Did Jesus choose Peter to lead the Apostles?   (Yes)   No

7. Do Catholics throughout the world believe in the Blessed Trinity?   (Yes)   No

8. Is God's greatest gift to us the gift of creation?   Yes   (No)

continued on next page   233

Grade 2 Unit 4

Write your answers.

9. Why do we pray?

   Possible responses: to ask God for help; to tell God how beautiful the world is; to ask for God's forgiveness; to pray for someone who is sick or needs help; to thank God for his love; to ask for God's blessing

10. Why do we honor Mary?

   Possible responses: Mary is the Mother of God's own Son. She always did what God wanted. She is our mother, too. She is the greatest saint.

234

PROJECT DISCIPLE

Pray
Learn
Celebrate
Share
Choose
Live

RESOURCES

Family Survey

Your child brought home three different kinds of family pages this year. Through these pages you shared faith together!

What was your favorite *Dear Family* activity?

_____

_____

_____

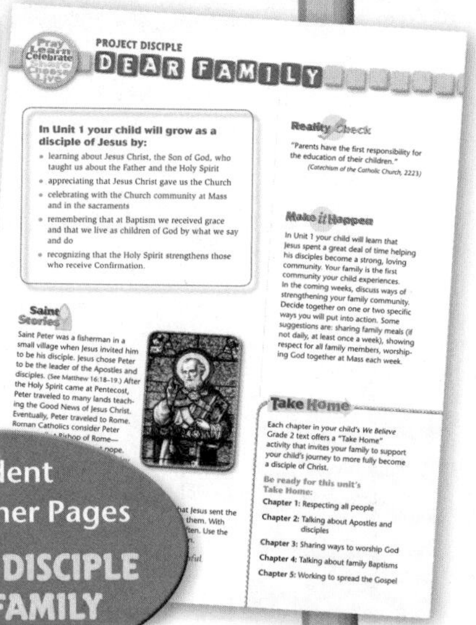

What *Project Disciple Take Home* activity did your family enjoy the most?

_____

_____

_____

What *Sharing Faith with My Family* activity was your favorite? Why?

_____

_____

_____

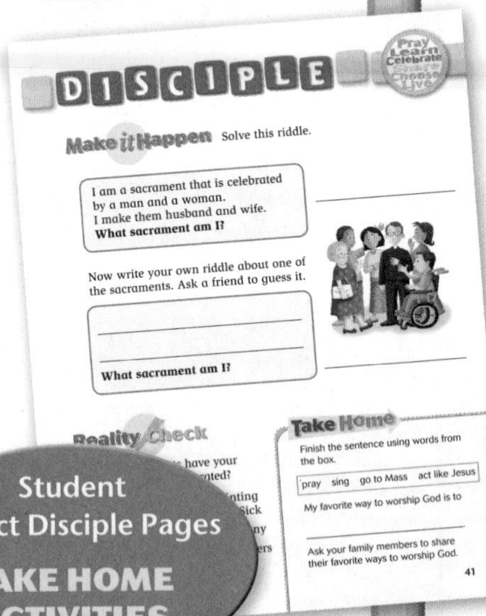

Does your family have any special prayers or activities that you would like to share with other *We Believe* families? If so, tell us about them.

_____

_____

_____

Is there anything else you'd like to share?

_____

_____

_____

We'd like to hear from you!

Send us this survey at: *We Believe* Family Survey
C/O Sadlier, 9 Pine Street, New York, NY 10005
or at:

www.WeBelieveweb.com

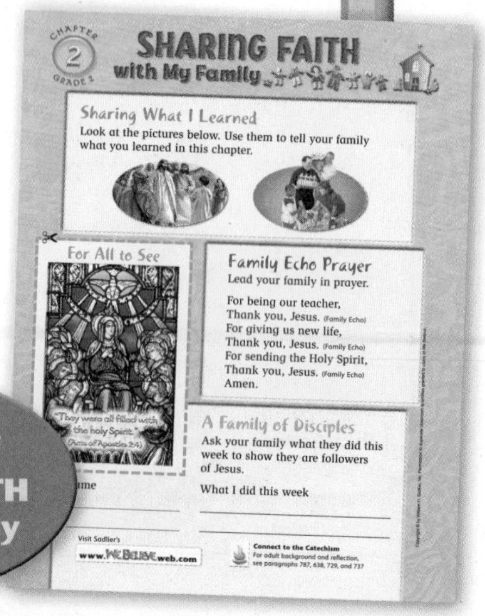

Student
Unit Opener Pages
**PROJECT DISCIPLE
DEAR FAMILY**

Student
Project Disciple Pages
**TAKE HOME
ACTIVITIES**

Catechist Guide
**SHARING FAITH
with My Family**

CONGRATULATIONS ON COMPLETING YOUR YEAR AS A GRADE 2 DISCIPLE!

Fold on this line.

PROJECT DISCIPLE LOG

Pray
Learn
Celebrate
Share
Choose
Live

A RECORD OF MY JOURNEY AS A GRADE 2 DISCIPLE

_____
Name

✂ Cut on this line.

Disciples of Jesus make loving choices.

This year, I made a loving choice

• in my family when I

_____.

• in my school when I

_____.

I can show love for others this summer by

_____.

Disciples of Jesus pray every day.

A prayer I like to pray

• by myself is

_____.

• with others is

_____.

My prayer for summer is

_____.

Disciples of Jesus learn about their faith.

One thing I learned this year

- about following Jesus is

_____.

- about sharing my faith with others is

_____.

2

✂ Cut on this line.

Disciples of Jesus share their faith with family.

My picture of a family member who helps me share my faith

6

Disciples of Jesus live out their faith.

This summer I will

❑ obey my parents

❑ take care of my pet

❑ play fairly with my friends

❑ help with family chores

❑ pray each day

❑ be kind to a neighbor

❑ _____.

7

Disciples of Jesus gather to celebrate.

This year,

I celebrated the Sacrament of

_____.

I celebrated the sacrament with

_____.

I celebrated the sacrament by

_____.

3

Pray
Learn
Celebrate
Share
Choose
Live

PROJECT DISCIPLE

End-of-Year Prayer Service

✝ We Gather in Prayer

Leader: We have learned many things about Jesus this year.

Group 1: Jesus is always with us.

Group 2: Jesus invites us to forgive.

Group 1: Jesus shares God's life with us.

Group 2: Jesus asks us to care for each other.

Leader: We ask Jesus to help us remember all of these good things.

All: Jesus, thank you for loving us.
Be with us this summer.
We want to share your Good News with everyone!

🎵 Take the Word of God with You

Take the peace of God with you
   as you go.
Take the seeds of God's peace
   and make them grow.

Go in peace to serve the world,
   in peace to serve the world.
Take the love of God, the love of God
   with you as you go.

CONNECTION

Multicultural Connection

To Parish

Help the children to realize that the parish church building is like a home to parishioners. Explain that everything in the church has significance for them—from the holy water fonts to the altar.

If possible, make arrangements for the class to tour the parish church and make a visit to the Most Blessed Sacrament. Point out the sanctuary lamp and the tabernacle. Invite a parish priest or deacon to talk to the children about the presence of Jesus in the Most Blessed Sacrament. Ask this person to show the children the inside of the tabernacle and explain that the priests and deacons take the Holy Communion Hosts to the parishioners who are sick or homebound.

Help the children locate the numbered items in the illustration of a parish church. Read the brief description for each item.

238

1. **sanctuary**—area in the church where the Mass is celebrated

2. **altar**—the table of the Lord where we celebrate the Sacrament of the Eucharist

3. **crucifix**—a cross with a figure of Christ crucified

4. **tabernacle**—the special place in the church in which the Blessed Sacrament is kept

5. **sanctuary lamp**—light or candle that is always lit near the tabernacle. It helps us to remember that Jesus is really present in the Blessed Sacrament.

6. **ambo (pulpit)**—place in the sanctuary where the Word of God is proclaimed

7. **chalice**—the special cup that holds the wine that will become the Blood of Christ

8. **paten**—a special plate that holds the bread that will become the Body of Christ

CONNECTION

Multicultural Connection
To Prayer

Remind the children that when we visit Jesus in the Most Blessed Sacrament, we can speak to Jesus quietly. We can tell him of our love, our needs, our hopes, and our thanks.

Pause to allow the children to pray quietly. Then pray aloud the following prayer.

Jesus, thank you for the gift of yourself in the Eucharist. Thank you for strengthening me to be your disciple and to serve others. Help me to give thanks each day and to stay close to you always. Amen.

Find these things in your parish church:

1. sanctuary
2. altar
3. crucifix
4. tabernacle
5. sanctuary lamp
6. ambo (pulpit)
7. chalice
8. paten
9. cruets
10. presider's chair
11. processional cross
12. baptismal font or pool
13. Stations of the Cross
14. Reconciliation room or confessional

9 cruets—glass containers that hold the water and wine

10 presider's chair—chair on which the priest who is celebrating Mass sits

11 processional cross—cross with a figure of Christ crucified that is carried in the entrance procession, may also be carried during the presentation of the gifts, and during the recessional

12 baptismal font or pool—contains the water that is blessed and used during the Sacrament of Baptism

13 Stations of the Cross—fourteen pictures that help us to follow the footsteps of Jesus during his suffering and Death on the cross

14 Reconciliation room or confessional—a separate space for celebrating the Sacrament of Penance. This is a special space where you meet the priest for individual confession and absolution. You may sit and talk to him face-to-face or kneel behind a screen.

PROJECT DISCIPLE

You are learning and living out ways to be a disciple of Jesus Christ.

Look what awaits you in:

We Believe **Grade 3: We Are the Church.**

You will learn about and live out that

- Jesus gives us the Church.
- We are members of the Church.
- The Church leads us in worship.
- We are called to discipleship.

Until next year, pay attention each time you go to Mass. Look around you. Listen.

Here is one thing that I know about the Church.

_____

_____

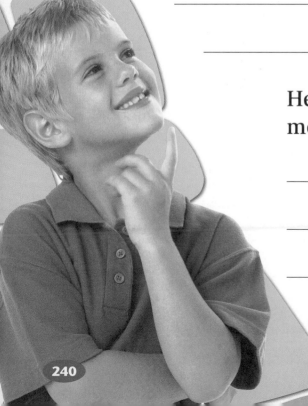

Here is one thing that I want to learn more about next year.

_____

_____

_____

We are blessed to be members of the Church!

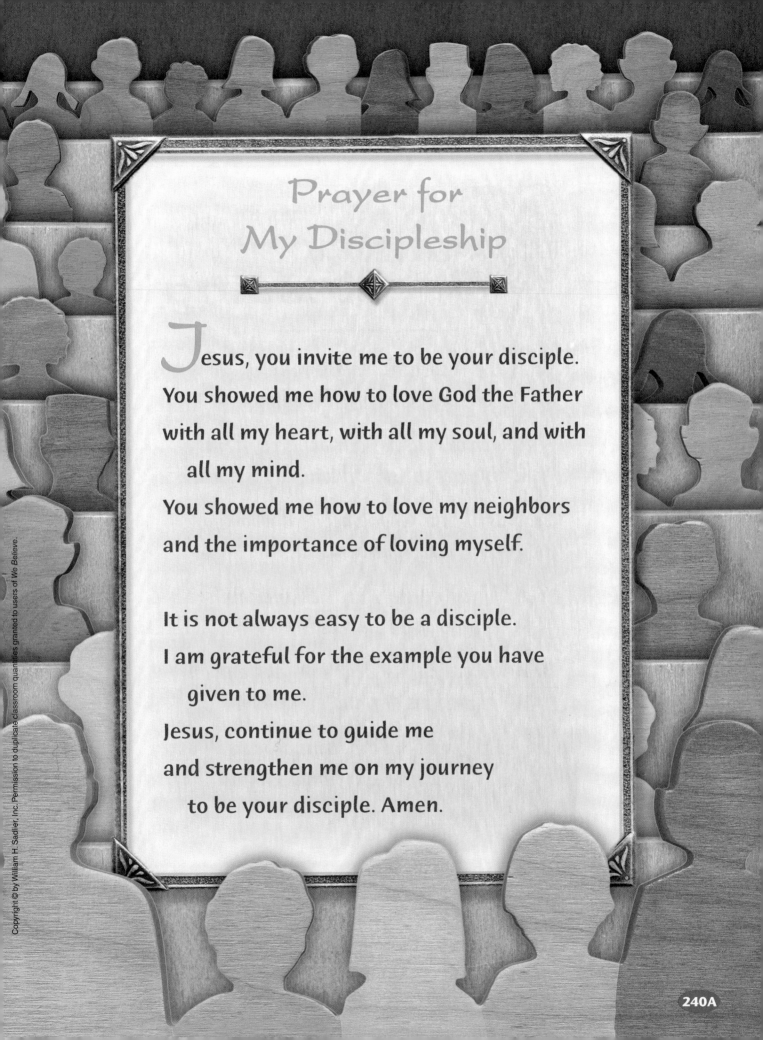

Prayer for My Discipleship

Jesus, you invite me to be your disciple.
You showed me how to love God the Father
with all my heart, with all my soul, and with
all my mind.
You showed me how to love my neighbors
and the importance of loving myself.

It is not always easy to be a disciple.
I am grateful for the example you have
given to me.
Jesus, continue to guide me
and strengthen me on my journey
to be your disciple. Amen.

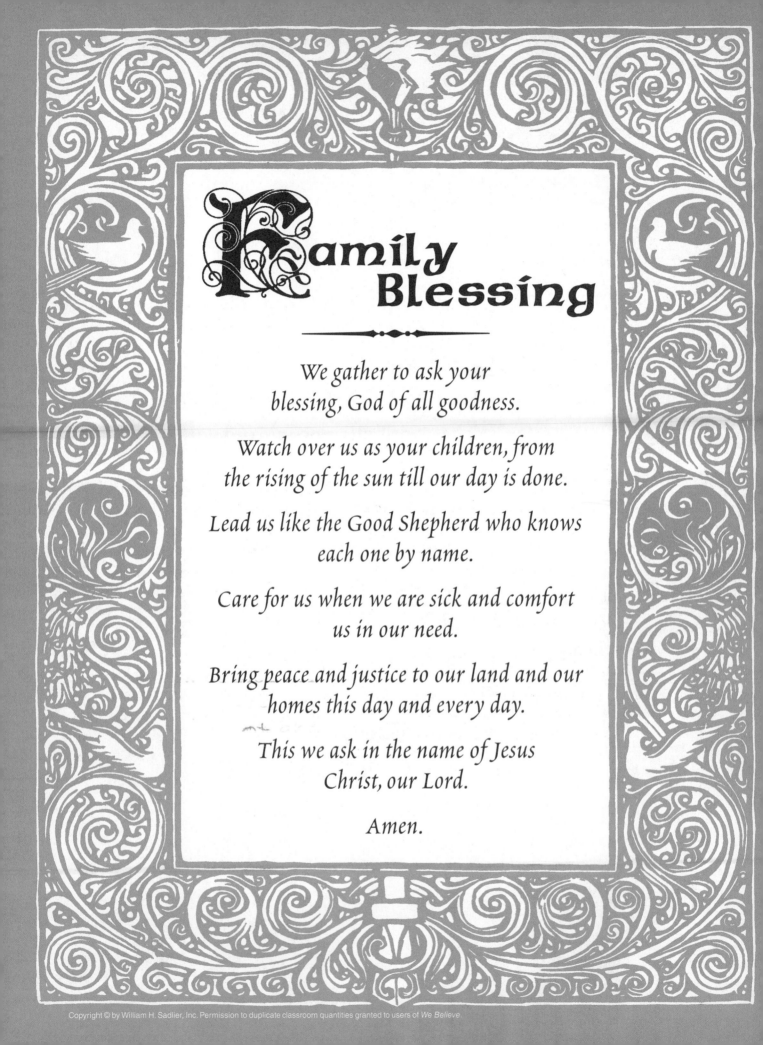

Family Blessing

We gather to ask your
blessing, God of all goodness.

Watch over us as your children, from
the rising of the sun till our day is done.

Lead us like the Good Shepherd who knows
each one by name.

Care for us when we are sick and comfort
us in our need.

Bring peace and justice to our land and our
homes this day and every day.

This we ask in the name of Jesus
Christ, our Lord.

Amen.

My Mass Book

The priest blesses us.
The priest or deacon ~~says~~ *may* say,
"Go in peace ~~to love and serve the Lord~~."
We say,
"Thanks be to God."
We go out to live as
Jesus' followers.

We welcome one another.
We stand and sing.
We pray the Sign of the Cross.
The priest says,
"The Lord be with you."
We answer,
"And ~~also~~ with your *spirit.*

We gather with our parish.
We remember and celebrate
what Jesus said and did at the
Last Supper.

We ask God and one another
for forgiveness.
We praise God as we sing,

**"Glory to God in the highest,
    and ~~peace to his people~~**
        on earth." peace to people
                of good
                    will.

Then the priest invites us to
share in the Eucharist.
As people receive the Body
and Blood of Christ, they
answer,

"Amen."

While this is happening, we
sing a song of thanks.

We get ready to receive Jesus. Together we pray or sing the Our Father. Then we share a sign of peace.
We say,
"Peace be with you."

✂ Cut on this line.

The Liturgy of the Word

We listen to two readings from the Bible.
After each one, the reader says,
"The word of the Lord."
We answer,
"Thanks be to God."

Then the priest takes the cup of wine.
He says,
"Take this, all of you, and drink from it: *for* this is the ~~cup~~ *chalice* of my Blood. . . ."

We stand to say aloud what we believe as Catholics.
Then we pray for the Church and all people.
After each prayer we say,
"Lord, hear our prayer."

Fold on this line.

We stand and sing **Alleluia.**
The priest or deacon reads the Gospel.
Then he says,
"The Gospel of the Lord."
We answer,
**"Praise to you,
Lord Jesus Christ."**

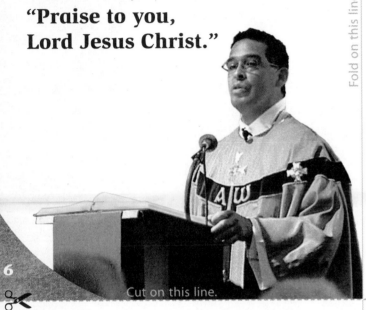

Cut on this line.

We sing or pray,
"Amen."
We believe Jesus Christ is really present in the Eucharist.

Fold on this line.

The Liturgy of the Eucharist

The priest prepares the altar.
People bring gifts of bread and wine to the priest.
The priest prepares these gifts.
We pray,
"Blessed be God for ever."

Then we remember what Jesus said and did at the Last Supper.
The priest takes the bread.
He says,
"Take this, all of you, and eat it: For this is my Body which will be given up for you."

Angel of God

Angel of God,
my guardian dear,
to whom God's love
    commits me here,
ever this day be at my side,
to light and guard,
    to rule and guide.

Amen.

Find other versions of some of these prayers at www.webelieveweb.com

Fold on this line.

Cut on this line.

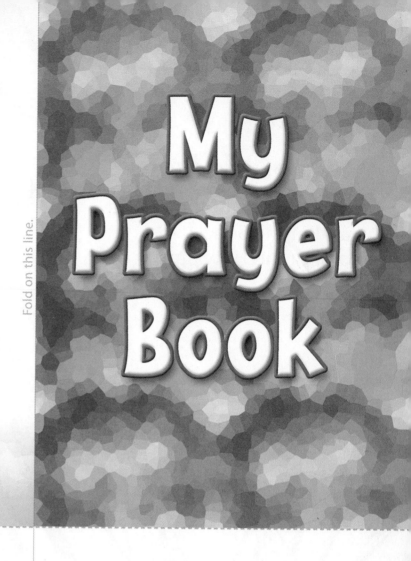

My Prayer Book

The Apostles' Creed

I believe in God the
    Father almighty,
    Creator of heaven and earth.
and ~~I believe~~ in Jesus Christ,
    his only Son, our Lord.
who ~~He~~ was conceived by the power
    of the Holy Spirit
    and born of the Virgin Mary.
~~He~~ suffered under Pontius Pilate,
    was crucified, died and
    was buried,
He descended ~~to the dead.~~ into Hell;
On the third day he rose again.
from the dead;

Glory Be to the Father

Glory be to the Father
and to the Son
and to the Holy Spirit,
as it was in the beginning
is now, and ever shall be
world without end. Amen.

Sign of the Cross

In the name of the Father,
and of the Son,
and of the Holy Spirit.

Amen.

He ascended into heaven,
  and is seated at the right hand of
God ~~of~~ the Father. almighty; from
~~there~~ He will come again to judge
  the living and the dead.

I believe in the Holy Spirit,
  the holy catholic Church,
  the communion of saints,
  the forgiveness of sins,
  the resurrection of the body,
  and ▄▄ life everlasting.

Amen.

Fold on this line.

Cut on this line.

Our Father

Our Father, who art in heaven,
hallowed be thy name;
thy kingdom come;
thy will be done on earth as
  it is in heaven.
Give us this day our daily bread;
and forgive us our trespasses
as we forgive those who
  trespass against us;
and lead us not into temptation,
but deliver us from evil.

Amen.

Grace After Meals

We give you thanks
  almighty God
for these and all your gifts,
which we have received through
Christ our Lord.

Amen.

Grace Before Meals

Bless us, O Lord, and these
    your gifts
which we are about to receive
from your goodness.
Through Christ our Lord.

Amen.

Hail Mary

Hail Mary, full of grace,
the Lord is with you!
Blessed are you among women,
and blessed is the fruit of your
    womb, Jesus.
Holy Mary, Mother of God,
pray for us sinners,
now and at the hour of
    our death.

Amen.

Fold on this line.

Cut on this line.

Morning Offering

My God, I offer you today
all that I think and do and say,
uniting it with what was done
on earth, by Jesus Christ,
your Son.

I firmly intend, with your help,
to do penance,
to sin no more,
and to avoid whatever
    leads me to sin.
Our Savior Jesus Christ
suffered and died for us.
In his name, my God,
    have mercy.

Act of Contrition

My God,
I am sorry for my sins with
    all my heart.
In choosing to do wrong
and failing to do good,
I have sinned against you
whom I should love above
    all things.

Fold on this line.

Evening Prayer

Dear God, before I sleep
I want to thank you for this day
so full of your kindness
and your joy.
I close my eyes to rest
safe in your loving care.

Cut on this line.

Prayer Before the Blessed Sacrament

Jesus,
You are God-with-us,
especially in this Sacrament
of the Eucharist.
You love me as I am
and help me grow.

Come and be with me
in all my joys and sorrows.
Help me share your peace
and love
with everyone I meet.
I ask in your name.

Amen.

The Seven Sacraments

The Sacraments of Christian Initiation

    Baptism

    Confirmation

    Eucharist

The Sacraments of Healing

    Penance and Reconciliation

    Anointing of the Sick

The Sacraments at the Service of Communion

    Holy Orders

    Matrimony

The Ten Commandments

1. I am the LORD your God: you shall not have strange gods before me.
2. You shall not take the name of the LORD your God in vain.
3. Remember to keep holy the LORD's Day.
4. Honor your father and your mother.
5. You shall not kill.
6. You shall not commit adultery.
7. You shall not steal.
8. You shall not bear false witness against your neighbor.
9. You shall not covet your neighbor's wife.
10. You shall not covet your neighbor's goods.

Glossary

absolution (page 109)
God's forgiveness of our sins by the priest in the Sacrament of Penance

Apostles (page 29)
the twelve men chosen by Jesus to be the leaders of his disciples

assembly (page 142)
the community of people who join together for the celebration of the Mass

Baptism (page 45)
the sacrament in which we are freed from sin and given grace

Bible (page 77)
the book in which God's Word is written

bishops (page 197)
leaders of the Church who carry on the work of the Apostles

Blessed Sacrament (page 165)
another name for the Eucharist

Blessed Trinity (page 23)
the Three Persons in One God

called by God (page 188)
invited by God to love and serve him

Catholics (page 37)
baptized members of the Church, led and guided by the pope and bishops

Church (page 31)
all the people who are baptized in Jesus Christ and follow his teachings

commandments (page 85)
God's laws

confession (page 109)
telling our sins to the priest in the Sacrament of Penance

Confirmation (page 53)
the sacrament that seals us with the Gift of the Holy Spirit and strengthens us

conscience (page 102)
God's gift that helps us to know right from wrong

contrition (page 109)
being sorry for our sins and promising not to sin again

diocese (page 197)
an area of the Church led by a bishop

disciples (page 29)
those who follow Jesus

divine (page 23)
a word used to describe God

Eucharist (page 135)
the sacrament of the Body and Blood of Jesus Christ

Eucharistic Prayer (page 157)
the most important prayer of the Mass

faith (page 37)
a gift from God that helps us to trust God and believe in him

free will (page 93)
God's gift to us that allows us to make choices

Gospels (page 79)
four of the books in the New Testament that are about Jesus' teachings and his life on earth

grace (page 45)
God's life in us

Great Commandment (page 85)
Jesus' teaching to love God and others

Holy Communion (page 135)
receiving the Body and Blood of Christ

Holy Family (page 20)
the family of Jesus, Mary, and Joseph

homily (page 150)
the talk given by the priest or deacon at Mass that helps us understand the readings and how we are to live

Last Supper (page 133)
the meal Jesus shared with the disciples on the night before he died

Liturgy of the Eucharist (page 157)
the second main part of the Mass in which the gifts of bread and wine become the Body and Blood of Christ

New Testament (page 79)
the second part of the Bible

Old Testament (page 77)
the first part of the Bible

Original Sin (page 45)
the first man and woman disobeyed God; the first sin

parishes (page 37)
communities that worship and work together

pastor (page 197)
the priest who leads and serves the parish

a penance (page 109)
a prayer or kind act we do to make up for our sins

Penance and Reconciliation (page 101)
the sacrament in which we receive and celebrate God's forgiveness of our sins

pope (page 199)
the leader of the Church who continues the work of Saint Peter

Liturgy of the Word (page 149)
the first main part of the Mass when we listen to God's Word

Mass (page 135)
the celebration of the Eucharist

mercy (page 95)
God's love and forgiveness

mortal sins (page 95)
sins that break our friendship with God

new commandment (page 221)
Jesus' commandment to love one another as he has loved us

prayer (page 205)
talking and listening to God

procession (page 215)
a prayer walk

psalm (page 149)
a song of praise from the Bible

Resurrection (page 29)
Jesus' rising from the dead

sacrament (page 39)
a special sign given to us by Jesus

saints (page 212)
all the members of the Church who have died and are happy with God forever in Heaven

sin (page 95)
a thought, word, or act that we freely choose to commit even though we know that it is wrong

tabernacle (page 165)
the special place in the church in which the Blessed Sacrament is kept

Temple (page 205)
the holy place in Jerusalem where the Jewish People worshiped God

Ten Commandments (page 85)
ten special laws God gave to his people

venial sins (page 95)
sins that hurt our friendship with God

worship (page 37)
to give God thanks and praise

Index

The following is a list of topics that appear in the pupil's text.
Boldface indicates an entire chapter.

Additional Reproducible Masters

Family and Scripture reproducible masters (core chapters) are found in this section.

SHARING FAITH
with My Family

Sharing What I Learned

Look at the pictures below. Use each picture to tell your family what you learned in this chapter.

For All to See

And Jesus advanced [in] wisdom and age and favor before God and man.
Luke 2:52

A Thank-You Prayer

(Begin and end this prayer with the sign of the cross.)

God, our Father, we thank you for all of the blessings that our family shares.

Jesus, Son of God, thank you for showing us what God is really like.

Holy Spirit, thank you for being with us and guiding us to do the right thing.

Jesus with Us

In the Bible we can read about what Jesus did. Ask each member of your family to share his or her favorite story about Jesus.

Name

_____

_____

Visit Sadlier's

www.WeBelieveweb.com

Connect to the Catechism
For adult background and reflection, see paragraphs 422, 470, 548, and 243.

PROJECT DISCIPLE

Pray Learn Celebrate Share Choose Live

Name ____________________

What's the Word?

Reader 1: Everywhere Jesus went, he told people about God's love.

Reader 2: One day Jesus had been teaching, and he was tired. His followers wanted to give him time to rest.

Reader 3: But a group of parents with their children were walking to where Jesus was.

Reader 1: Jesus' followers wanted to turn the people away.

Reader 2: But Jesus said, "Let the children come to me and do not prevent them." (Matthew 19:14)

Reader 3: Then Jesus blessed the children.

Imagine you were in the group that day. Write here what you would have said to Jesus.

____

____

____

SHARING FAITH
with My Family

Sharing What I Learned

Look at the pictures below. Use them to tell your family what you learned in this chapter.

For All to See

"They were all filled with the holy Spirit."
(Acts of Apostles 2:4)

Family Echo Prayer

Lead your family in prayer.

For being our teacher,
Thank you, Jesus. (Family Echo)
For giving us new life,
Thank you, Jesus. (Family Echo)
For sending the Holy Spirit,
Thank you, Jesus. (Family Echo)
Amen.

A Family of Disciples

Ask your family what they did this week to show they are followers of Jesus.

Name   What I did this week

_____   _____

_____   _____

Visit Sadlier's

www.WeBelieveweb.com

Connect to the Catechism
For adult background and reflection, see paragraphs 787, 638, 729, and 737

PROJECT DISCIPLE

Pray
Learn
Celebrate
Share
Choose
Live

Name _____

What's *the* Word?

Reader 1: One day Jesus had a large crowd following him.

Reader 2: Two blind men were sitting by the side of the road. When they heard that Jesus was near to them, they cried out to him.

Two men: Jesus, help us.

Crowd: Be quiet!

Reader 1: But the blind men called out again. Jesus stopped and asked them, "What do you want me to do for you?" (Matthew 20:31)

Two men: "Lord, let our eyes be opened." (Matthew 20:33)

Reader 2: Jesus healed the men. They could see. Then these two men became followers, or disciples of Jesus.

Imagine you are a reporter in Jesus' time. Write what you would say in your report.

_____

_____

_____

Grade 2, Chapter 2

SHARING FAITH
with My Family

Sharing What I Learned

Look at the pictures below. Use each picture to tell your family what you learned in this chapter.

For All to See

"I will sing praise to my God while I live."
(Psalm 104:33)

Gifts from God

Thank God together.

- For our parish community. . . .
- For our parish church where we celebrate the sacraments. . . .
- For sharing with us signs of your love. . . .
- For the gift of meeting Jesus in the Seven Sacraments. . . .
- For giving us a share in the life of grace. . . .

Signs of Love

Ask the family to tell how each family member is a sign of God's love for that person.

Visit Sadlier's

www.WEBELIEVEweb.com

Connect to the Catechism
For adult background and reflection, see paragraphs 1267, 1119, 1123, and 1127.

PROJECT DISCIPLE

Pray
Learn
Celebrate
Share
Choose
Live

Name _____

What's *the* Word?

Reader 1: It was the Sunday before Jesus' Death and Resurrection. Many people were gathered in Jerusalem. They were there to celebrate an important Jewish feast.

Reader 2: When people heard that Jesus was coming, many went out to meet him.

Reader 3: Some people spread out their coats on the road.

Reader 4: Some people cut branches from nearby palm trees. They waved the branches or put them down on the road. Then the people called out to Jesus.

Crowd: "Hosanna!
　　　　Blessed is he who comes in the name
　　　　　of the Lord!
　　Hosanna in the highest!" (Mark 11:9–10)

Imagine you were in the crowd that day. Write a few sentences to tell what you would have told your friends about that day.

_____

_____

_____

SHARING FAITH
with My Family

Sharing What I Learned

Look at the pictures below. Use each picture to tell your family what you learned in this chapter.

For All to See

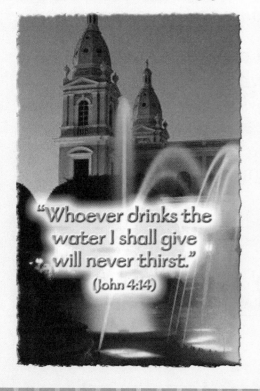

"Whoever drinks the water I shall give will never thirst."
(John 4:14)

We Say "I Do"

(Place a bowl of water in the middle of the table.)

Child: Do you believe in God the Father, Jesus Christ, his Son, and the Holy Spirit, Giver of Life?

All: I do. (Trace the sign of the cross on the forehead of the person next to you.)

Child: Do you believe that Jesus Christ saves us?

All: I do. (Dip your fingers in the bowl of water.)

Child: O God, we thank you for the gift of Baptism. We are members of your Church. We believe in you and we praise you.

All: Amen.

Let's Talk
Ask the members of the family to share what they know about their Baptism celebrations.

Visit Sadlier's
www.WeBelieveweb.com

 Connect to the Catechism
For adult background and reflection, see paragraphs 1213, 1250, 1234, and 1265.

PROJECT DISCIPLE

Pray
Learn
Celebrate
Share
Choose
Live

Name _____

What's *the* Word?

Reader 1: John the Baptist was preparing people for Jesus. He was preparing them by baptizing them in the Jordan River.

Reader 2: One day after Jesus first left his hometown of Nazareth, he went to the place where John was baptizing the people.

Reader 3: "It happened that in those days that Jesus came from Nazareth of Galilee and was baptized in the Jordan by John." (Mark 1: 9)

Reader 1: When Jesus came up out of the water, he saw the sky opening. The Holy Spirit, in the form of a dove, was above Jesus.

Reader 2: Then Jesus heard a voice coming from the heavens. It was the voice of God the Father.

Reader 3: The voice said, "You are my beloved Son; with you I am well pleased." (Mark 1:11)

Grade 2, Chapter 4

SHARING FAITH with My Family

Sharing What I Learned

Look at the pictures below. Use each picture to tell your family what you learned in this chapter.

For All to See

(Place a photo of your family here.)

"... you are in the spirit, if only the Spirit of God dwells in you."
(Romans 8:9)

Calling on the Holy Spirit

(Each member of the family completes one of the following petitions.)

Holy Spirit, give us the courage to

_____ .

Holy Spirit, help us to love

_____ .

Child: Peace be with you.

All: And also with you.

Spirit Alive

Ask each member of the family to share how the Holy Spirit is helping them each day. How can you remind each other that this is true?

Visit Sadlier's

www.WeBelieveweb.com

 Connect to the Catechism
For adult background and reflection, see paragraphs 1285, 1295, 1299, and 1303.

PROJECT DISCIPLE

Name _____

What's *the* Word?

Reader 1: Jesus kept his promise to send the Holy Spirit.

Reader 2: Early one morning the disciples were together in one room. They had been there waiting for the Holy Spirit.

Reader 3: All of a sudden the disciples heard a noise. It was the sound of a strong wind.

All: (Make the sound of the wind.)

Reader 1: Then they saw what looked like flames of fire over each of them.

Reader 2: "And they were all filled with the holy Spirit."
(Acts of the Apostles 2:4)

Reader 3: The disciples of Jesus wanted to tell everyone about Jesus and the Holy Spirit.

Reader 1: The disciples left the house where they had been staying. They spoke to a large crowd.

All: (Make the sound of a crowd talking.)

Reader 2: Peter told the people to be baptized and receive the Holy Spirit.

Reader 3: "Those who accepted his message were baptized, and about three thousand persons were added that day."
(Acts of the Apostles 2:41)

SHARING FAITH
with My Family

Sharing What I Learned

Look at the pictures below. Use each picture to tell your family what you learned in this chapter.

For All to See

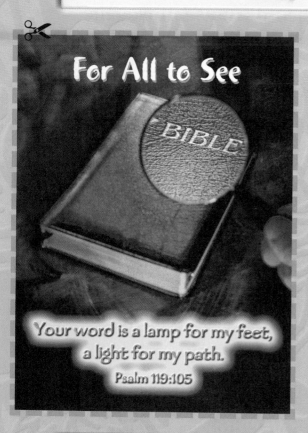

Your word is a lamp for my feet, a light for my path.
Psalm 119:105

Family Prayer

Together look through the family Bible. After you have located each section, pray together the words on the *For All to See* card.

- Find the beginning of the Old Testament.
- Find the last book of the Old Testament.
- Find the beginning of the New Testament.
- Find the beginning of each of the four gospels.

Bible Charades Have each family member act out his or her favorite Bible story. After someone guesses the story, let someone else take a turn.

Visit Sadlier's
www.WeBelieveweb.com

 Connect to the Catechism
For adult background and reflection, see paragraphs 104, 121, 124, and 127.

PROJECT DISCIPLE

Pray
Learn
Celebrate
Share
Choose
Live

Name _____

What's *the* Word?

Reader 1: One day, early in the morning, Jesus went outside a town. He had been there teaching and healing people. Jesus went to pray by himself.

Reader 2: The people of the town went looking for Jesus. They knew he was planning on leaving that day. When the people found Jesus, they tried to talk him into staying with them.

Townspeople: "Jesus, _____

_____

_____

(Write your own words.)

Reader 1: Jesus told the people, "To the other towns also I must proclaim the good news of the kingdom of God because for this purpose I have been sent." (Luke 4:43)

Reader 2: Then Jesus left the people to travel to other towns. He wanted to share God's Word with many others.

SHARING FAITH
with My Family

Sharing What I Learned

Look at the pictures below. Use each picture to tell your family what you learned in this chapter.

For All to See

"The earth, LORD, is filled with your love; teach me your laws."
(Psalm 119:64)

Family Respect

Together make a large sign to put near the *For All to See* card. Print the word *respect* on a large sheet of paper. During the coming week, talk about specific ways your family can show respect for God, yourselves, and your neighbor. Write these ways on the sign.

Family Prayer Pledge

Pray together:

We shall love you, God,
with our whole selves.
We shall love our neighbors
as ourselves.

Visit Sadlier's
www.WeBelieveweb.com

Connect to the Catechism
For adult background and reflection, see paragraphs 2055, 2059, 2067, and 2069.

PROJECT DISCIPLE

Pray
Learn
Celebrate
Share
Choose
Live

Name _____

What's *the* Word?

Reader 1: In the Old Testament we can read about Moses leading God's People through the desert.

Reader 2: One day God told Moses to come to a mountain. God told Moses, "Come up to the mountain," and "I will give you the stone tablets on which I have written the commandments."
(Exodus 24:12)

Reader 3: Moses went to the top of the mountain where God gave him the Ten Commandments. Moses stayed on the mountain for forty days and forty nights.

Reader 1: When Moses didn't return during this time, the people made a golden calf to worship.

Reader 2: When Moses saw the people worshiping the golden calf, he was angry. He smashed the tablets.

Reader 3: But God called Moses to the mountain again. God told Moses to write the commandments on other tablets of stone.

Reader 1: Moses did as God asked. Moses presented the commandments to the people. The Ten Commandments were important to God's People. And they still are important to us today.

SHARING FAITH
with My Family

Sharing What I Learned

Look at the pictures below. Use each picture to tell your family what you learned in this chapter.

For All to See

"If you choose you can keep the commandments; it is loyalty to do his will."
(Sirach 15:15)

What's Your Choice?

Think about and discuss these choices.

• You have just won two hundred dollars. Will you keep all the money or will you share it?

• Everybody in your family is home tonight. Will you join the family in doing something together?

Family Scripture Meditation

Share the story of the father and his son (Luke 15:11–24). Put yourselves in the father or son's place. Then talk about the choices you made. Pray together, "God, thank you for your love and forgiveness."

Visit Sadlier's
www.WeBelieveweb.com

 Connect to the Catechism
For adult background and reflection, see paragraphs 2074, 1730, 1850, and 981.

PROJECT DISCIPLE

Pray
Learn
Celebrate
Share
Choose
Live

Name _____

What's *the* Word?

Read the story of the forgiving father and son.
Then answer the following questions.

1. What was a selfish choice the son made?

_____

_____

2. Were the son's friends good friends? Why or why not?

_____

_____

3. What was a loving choice the son made?

_____

_____

4. What was a loving choice the father made?

_____

_____

5. Write a way you can share this story with others.

_____

SHARING FAITH
with My Family

Sharing What I Learned

Look at the pictures below. Use each picture to tell your family what you learned in this chapter.

For All to See and Pray

Act of Contrition

My God,
I am sorry for my sins with all my heart.
In choosing to do wrong
and failing to do good,
I have sinned against you
whom I should love above all things.
I firmly intend, with your help,
to do penance,
to sin no more,
and to avoid whatever leads me to sin.
Our Savior Jesus Christ
suffered and died for us.
In his name, my God, have mercy.

Visit Sadlier's
www.WeBelieveweb.com

Connect to the Catechism
For adult background and reflection,
see paragraphs 1441, 1446, 1451, and 1454.

Pray
Learn
Celebrate
Share
Choose
Live

Name _____

What's *the* Word?

Reader 1: There was a shepherd who took care of one hundred sheep. One day he saw that one of the sheep was missing.

Shepherd: What should I do? I will leave the ninety-nine sheep. I will go to search for the one that is missing.

Reader 2: The shepherd left the ninety-nine sheep. He went looking for the lost one. He searched in many places. Then he found the sheep. The shepherd was very happy.

Shepherd: _____

_____

_____

(Write your own words.)

Reader 3: The shepherd put the sheep on his shoulders and carried it home. When he reached his home, he called his friends and neighbors together.

Shepherd: "Rejoice with me because I have found my lost sheep." (Luke 15:6)

SHARING FAITH
with My Family

Sharing What I Learned

Look at the pictures below. Use each picture to tell your family what you learned in this chapter.

For All to See

Jesus said, "Peace be with you."
(John 20:21)

Family Examination of Conscience

Each night this week, share these questions for an examination of conscience. Allow a brief time of silence after each question is read. Add questions of your own. Then pray the Our Father.

- Did I make God an important part of my day? How?
- Did I appreciate the many gifts God has given me?
- Was I respectful?
- Did I share with others?
- Did I help other people?
- Did I forgive those who hurt me?
- Did I ask for forgiveness from someone I hurt?
- _____

Visit Sadlier's

www.WeBelieveweb.com

Connect to the Catechism
For adult background and reflection, see paragraphs 1425, 1455, 1468, and 1469.

PROJECT DISCIPLE

Pray
Learn
Celebrate
Share
Choose
Live

Name _____

What's *the* Word?

Reader 1: One day a crowd gathered to see Jesus. Zacchaeus, a rich tax collector, was in the crowd. He wanted to see Jesus but was too short to see over the crowd. So he climbed a tree and waited.

People: Look at Zacchaeus. What is he doing in the tree?

Reader 2: As Jesus walked by the tree, he looked up. He said to the tax collector, "Zacchaeus, come down quickly, for today I must stay at your house." (Luke 19:5)

Reader 3: Zacchaeus climbed down and welcomed Jesus to his house. Some people were upset that Jesus was in the house of Zacchaeus. The rich man had cheated them.

People: Why is Jesus visiting this man?

Reader 4: Then Zacchaeus told Jesus that he would pay back people four times what he owed them. He also promised to give half of what he owned to people in need.

Reader 5: Zacchaeus showed by his words and actions that he was sorry for what he had done. Jesus told Zacchaeus that he was saved.

SHARING FAITH
with My Family

Sharing What I Learned

Look at the pictures below. Use each picture to tell your family what you learned in this chapter.

For All to See

"Do this in memory of me."
(Luke 22:19)

Grace Before Meals

As a family pray before meals. Make up your own prayer or pray the one below.

Bless us, O Lord, and these your gifts which we are about to receive from your goodness, through Christ, our Lord. Amen.

Celebrating a Family Meal

Make one of your family meals this week a special celebration. Together plan the menu and decorations.

Menu   Decorations

_____   _____

_____   _____

Visit Sadlier's

www.WeBelieveweb.com

Connect to the Catechism
For adult background and reflection, see paragraphs 1406, 1339, 1341, and 1382.

PROJECT DISCIPLE

Pray
Learn
Celebrate
Share
Choose
Live

Name _____

What's the Word?

Reread the play about Jesus feeding thousands of people. Then write answers for the following questions.

- Imagine you were the boy who had the bread and fish. What did you say to Jesus when you brought him the food?

_____

_____

_____

- Imagine you were in the crowd. What did you say when Jesus' disciples gave you and your family food?

_____

_____

_____

- Some of your friends were not there that day. When you came home, what did you tell them?

_____

_____

_____

Grade 2, Chapter 15

SHARING FAITH
with My Family

Sharing What I Learned

Look at the pictures below. Use each picture to tell your family what you have learned in this chapter.

For All to See

"I am the vine, you are the branches."
(John 15:5)

Jesus, Help Us

Jesus, help us stay close to you by the words we say and by the things we do.

Jesus, we will keep you close in our hearts when our family is together and when we are apart.

Growing Closer to Jesus

With your family, talk about what each of you has done this week to grow closer to Jesus. Write one thing on each leaf of the vine below.

Visit Sadlier's

www.WeBelieveweb.com

Connect to the Catechism
For adult background and reflection, see paragraphs 1348, 1368, 1389, and 2643.

PROJECT DISCIPLE

Pray
Learn
Celebrate
Share
Choose
Live

Name _____

What's *the* Word?

Group A
"Shout joyfully to the LORD, all you lands;
   worship the LORD with cries of gladness;
   come before him with joyful song."

Group B
"Know that the LORD is God,
   our maker to whom we belong,
   whose people we are. . . ."

Group A
"Enter the temple gates with praise,
   its courts with thanksgiving."

Group B
"Give thanks to God, bless his name;
   good indeed is the LORD,"

Groups A and B
"Whose love endures forever,
   whose faithfulness lasts through every age."

(Psalm 100:1–5)

SHARING FAITH
with My Family

Sharing What I Learned

Look at the pictures below. Use each picture to tell your family what you learned in this chapter.

For All to See

✂

"I wait with longing for the LORD, my soul waits for his word."
(Psalm 130:5)

We Pray for Others

Lead your family in this prayer. Have them say "Lord, hear our prayer" after each part of the prayer.

For the whole Church,
For all the people in our parish,
For those who are sick or in need,

Add your own.

Tips for Good Listeners

- Look at the person who is speaking.
- Pay close attention to what the speaker is saying.
- Picture in your mind what the speaker is talking about.

Discuss how these tips can help your family, especially the next time you listen to the readings at Mass.

Visit Sadlier's

www.WeBelieveweb.com

Connect to the Catechism
For adult background and reflection, see paragraphs 1349 and 197.

PROJECT DISCIPLE

Pray
Learn
Celebrate
Share
Choose
Live

Name _____

What's *the* Word?

Narrator: In the Gospels Jesus points out that it is very important to listen to his teachings. Here is one story about listening. We can find the story in the Gospel of Luke.

Reader 1: One day Jesus and his disciples entered a village. A woman named Martha welcomed Jesus to her family's home.

Reader 2: Martha had a sister Mary. During the visit, Mary sat by Jesus listening to him speak.

Reader 3: Martha was very busy serving her visitors. She was upset that her sister was not helping her. Martha spoke to Jesus.

Martha: "Lord, do you not care that my sister has left me by myself to do the serving? Tell her to help me." (Luke 10:40)

Reader 4: But Jesus told Martha that she should not be so worried about doing so many things. He said that Mary was doing what Jesus wanted her to do. She was listening to his words.

SHARING FAITH with My Family

Sharing What I Learned

Look at the pictures below. Use each picture to tell your family what you learned in this chapter.

Our Prayer to Jesus

Together write a prayer to thank Jesus for the gift of the Eucharist.

_____

_____

_____

_____

_____

For All to See

"This is my body, which will be given for you."
(Luke 22:19)

Our Gift to God

Discuss with your family why it is an honor to bring the gifts to the altar at Mass.

Visit Sadlier's

www.WeBelieveweb.com

 Connect to the Catechism
For adult background and reflection, see paragraphs 1350, 1353, 1355, and 1386.

Name _____

What's *the* Word?

Reader 1: It was the Sunday that Jesus had risen. Two of Jesus' disciples were walking on the road. They were going to a town near Jerusalem.

Reader 2: Suddenly the disciples met a man on the road. The man started walking with them. The disciples did not know that the man was Jesus.

Reader 3: The man asked the disciples, "What are you discussing as you walk along?" (Luke 24:17)

Reader 4: The disciples said they were talking about what had happened during the past three days. They said that Jesus was crucified, had died, and was buried. And now his body was missing from the tomb.

Reader 5: It was getting dark as the three reached town. The disciples asked the man to stay with them. Jesus did stay. "While he was with them at table, he took bread, said the blessing, broke it, and gave it to them." (Luke 24:30)

Reader 6: All of a sudden, the disciples knew the man was the risen Jesus! They knew him "in the breaking of bread." (Luke 24:35)

SHARING FAITH
with My Family

Sharing What I Learned

Look at the pictures below. Use each picture to tell your family what you learned in this chapter.

For All to See

"Peace I leave with you; my peace I give to you."

(John 14:27)

Praying for Peace

Gather together and pray as a family.

Jesus, help us to be peaceful.

Help us to spread your peace and love in our home, in our neighborhood, in our city or town, and throughout the world.

We pray that all families throughout the world may live in peace.

Family Peacemakers

Have a family meeting. Ask each member to discuss what he or she can do to make your home more peaceful. Together write a family peace agreement. Have each member sign it. Then post it for all to see.

Visit Sadlier's
www.WeBelieveweb.com

Connect to the Catechism
For adult background and reflection, see paragraphs 1332, 1397, 1416, and 1418.

PROJECT DISCIPLE

Name _____

What's *the* Word?

Reader 1: The risen Jesus stayed with the Apostles and disciples for forty days after he rose from the dead.

Reader 2: But then it was time for Jesus to return to God the Father. Jesus asked his Apostles to come to a mountain.

Reader 3: When they saw Jesus from afar, they worshiped him. Then Jesus walked closer to them.

Reader 4: Jesus said, "Go, therefore, and make disciples of all nations." (Matthew 28:19)

Reader 5: Jesus told the Apostles that he wanted them to teach people what he had taught them.

Reader 6: Then Jesus said, "And behold, I am with you always." (Matthew 28:20)

Reader 7: Jesus then ascended into Heaven. The Apostles went to Jerusalem to wait for the Holy Spirit to come.

SHARING FAITH
with My Family

Sharing What I Learned

Look at the pictures below. Use each picture to tell your family what you learned in this chapter.

For All to See

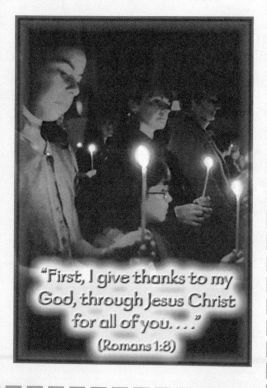

"First, I give thanks to my God, through Jesus Christ for all of you. . . ."
(Romans 1:8)

Read All About It

Many dioceses have weekly newspapers or Web sites. You can read about the ways married and single people, priests, and religious sisters and brothers serve God.

With your family find pictures and stories of people serving God and others. Talk about the ways they are serving.

Our Gift to God

As a family, write a letter to or send an e-mail to the editor of the newspaper. Thank the people you have read about for their love and service.

Visit Sadlier's
www.WeBelieveweb.com

Connect to the Catechism
For adult background and reflection, see paragraphs 30, 1604, 1658, 1578, and 1618.

PROJECT DISCIPLE

Pray
Learn
Celebrate
Share
Choose
Live

Name _____

What's *the* Word?

Narrator: One day there were great crowds on a mountainside listening to Jesus teach. That day Jesus taught them many things about God's love. Imagine the two cousins, written about below, had been in the crowd. Listen as they talk on their way home that evening.

Joseph: What an amazing day! So many people were on the mountain with us. And we could all hear Jesus teaching.

Marah: Jesus taught us so many things! I hope I can remember them all. He taught us how to pray. He told us to do to others as we would want them to do to us.

Joseph: What are you going to tell your friends about Jesus' words?

Marah: Well, the first thing I'm going to tell them is about Jesus explaining that we are light for others. I was so surprised when he said, "You are the light of the world." (Matthew 5:14)

Joseph: I was surprised, too, Marah! Jesus said that our light must shine for others so that people will praise God.

Marah: How can we be lights, Joseph?

SHARING FAITH
with My Family

Sharing What I Learned

Look at the pictures below. Use each picture to tell your family what you learned in this chapter.

For All to See

"Rejoice in the Lord always."
(Philippians 4:4)

Sharing and Showing Our Faith

Gather your family together. Have the family choose a holy day of the Church. Together fill out this chart.

Holy Day	How We Celebrate
_____	_____
_____	_____
_____	_____

Pray the Our Father together. As you pray, picture the people of the Church throughout the whole world. Some are praying the Our Father right now just as you are.

Visit Sadlier's
www.WeBelieveweb.com

Connect to the Catechism
For adult background and reflection, see paragraphs 2179, 886, 882, and 831.

PROJECT DISCIPLE

Pray
Learn
Celebrate
Share
Choose
Live

Name _____

What's *the* Word?

Reader 1: One day an angel spoke to the Apostle Philip.

Angel: "Get up and head south on the road that goes down from Jerusalem to Gaza, the desert route." (Acts 8:26)

Reader 2: So Philip did what the angel asked him to do. Soon Philip saw a man riding in a chariot. The man worked for the queen of a country in Africa.

Reader 3: When Philip was closer to the chariot, he heard the man reading God's Word.

Philip: "Do you understand what you are reading?" (Acts 8:30)

Reader 4: The man said that he did not understand. He asked Philip to get in the chariot and explain the reading. Philip explained the reading and about Jesus' teaching. Then Philip and the man saw water ahead.

Man in chariot: "Look, there is water. What is to prevent my being baptized?" (Acts 8:36)

Reader 5: So the men walked to the water. Philip baptized the man. Then the Apostle left to spread the Good News.

SHARING FAITH
with My Family

Sharing What I Learned

Look at the pictures below. Use each picture to tell your family what you learned in this chapter.

For All to See

"Lord, teach us to pray."
(Luke 11:1)

With Thankful Hearts

At the end of each day this week, have each person in your family share the good things that happened that day. Record the responses in a family journal.

Evening Prayer

Every evening this week, pray the following prayer of thanks together. You can also say your own prayer.

Dear God, before we go to sleep,
we want to thank you
for this day so full of
your kindness and your joy.
We close our eyes to rest
safe in your loving care.

Visit Sadlier's
www.WeBelieveweb.com

Connect to the Catechism
For adult background and reflection,
see paragraphs 2560, 2599, 2759, and 2767.

PROJECT DISCIPLE

Pray
Learn
Celebrate
Share
Choose
Live

Name _____

What's *the* Word?

Leader: God created the world for us and filled it with many gifts. Let us praise God for our wonderful world.

Group A: "Praise the LORD from the heavens,
give praise in the heights."

Group B: "Praise him, sun and moon,
give praise, all shining stars."

Group A: "Praise the LORD from the earth,
you sea monsters and all deep waters;"

Group B: "You mountains and all hills,
fruit trees and all cedars;"

Group A: "You animals wild and tame,
you creatures that crawl and fly;"

Group B: "Young men and women too,
old and young alike." (Psalm 148:1–3, 7, 9–10, 12)

Leader: Let us praise God together.

All: Alleluia, alleluia, alleluia.

SHARING FAITH
with My Family

Sharing What I Learned

Look at the pictures below. Use each picture to tell your family what you learned in this chapter.

For All to See

"Most blessed are you among women."
(Luke 1:42)

Saints' Hall of Fame

Plan together a "Saints' Hall of Fame." Ask each family member to name a favorite saint. Have each person tell why they chose that saint. Talk about the ways you can follow the example of the saints.

A Litany of Saints

Add your favorite saints.

Holy Mary, pray for us.
Saint Joseph, pray for us.
Saint Peter, pray for us.
Saint Elizabeth Ann Seton, pray for us.

Saint _____, pray for us.
All holy men and women, pray for us.

Visit Sadlier's
www.WeBelieveweb.com

Connect to the Catechism
For adult background and reflection, see paragraphs 957, 963, 2676, and 971.

PROJECT DISCIPLE

Name _____

What's *the* Word?

In the New Testament you can read about saints whom
Jesus and Mary knew. Solve each riddle by filling in
one of the saints.

Joseph
Elizabeth
John the Baptist
Peter

I am Jesus' cousin.
I lived in the desert.
I told people to get ready for Jesus.

I am Saint _____.

I was a fisherman.
Jesus invited me to be his disciple.
He asked me to be the leader of the Apostles.

I am Saint _____.

I am Mary's husband.
I am Jesus' foster father.
I worked as a carpenter.

I am Saint _____.

I am Mary's cousin.
Mary visited me and helped me get ready for my baby.
My words to Mary are part of the Hail Mary.

I am Saint _____.

Grade 2, Chapter 25

SHARING FAITH
with My Family

Sharing What I Learned

Look at the pictures below. Use each picture to tell your family what you learned in this chapter.

For All to See and Pray

Paste a photo of your family or draw their picture in the empty space. Gather your family together. Read these words from one of Saint Paul's letters.

> "Love is patient,
> love is kind.
> It is not jealous . . .
> it is not rude . . .
> it does not rejoice over
> wrongdoing but rejoices
> with the truth."
>
> (1 Corinthians 13:4, 5, 6)

Talk about what the words mean for your family.

My Family

Visit Sadlier's

www.WEBELIEVEweb.com

Connect to the Catechism
For adult background and reflection,
see paragraphs 1694, 1823, 1825, and 307.

PROJECT DISCIPLE

Name _____

What's *the* Word?

Read each Scripture passage. Choose one passage.
Design a banner or poster to share with your friends
and family.

Jesus said,

"Where two or three are gathered together in my name, there am I in the midst of them." (Matthew 18:20)

Jesus said,

"And behold, I am with you always, until the end of the age." (Matthew 28:20)

Jesus said,

"Peace I leave with you; my peace I give to you. Do not let your hearts be troubled or afraid." (John 14:27)

Grade 2, Chapter 26

Writing/Development Team

Rosemary K. Calicchio
Vice President, Publications

Blake Bergen
Editorial Director

Melissa D. Gibbons
Director of Research and Development

Dulce M. Jiménez-Abreu
Director of Bilingual Programs

MaryAnn Trevaskiss
Supervising Editor

Maureen Gallo
Senior Editor

Joanne McDonald
Senior Editor

Allison Johnston
Senior Editor

Theresa MacDonald
Editor

Margherita Rotondi
Editorial Assistant

Kathy Hendricks
Contributing Writer

Consulting Team

Michaela Burke Barry
Director of Consultant Services

Judith A. Devine
National Sales Consultant

Kenneth Doran
National Religion Consultant

Saundra Kennedy, Ed.D.
National Religion Consultant

Victor Valenzuela
National Religion Consultant

Media/Technology Consultants

Michael Ferejohn
Director of Electronic Media

Robert T. Carson
Electronic Media Design Director

Erik Bowie
Electronic Media Production Manager

Publishing Operations Team

Deborah Jones
Vice President, Publishing Operations

Vince Gallo
Creative Director

Francesca O'Malley
Associate Art Director

Jim Saylor
Photography Manager

Design/Photo Staff
Andrea Brown, Kevin Butler, Debrah Kaiser, Susan Ligertwood, Cesar Llacuna, Bob Schatz

Production Staff
Diane Ali, Monica Bernier, Barbara Brown, Brent Burket, Robin D'Amato, Stephen Flanagan, Joyce Gaskin, Cheryl Golding, Maria Jimenez, Joe Justus, Vincent McDonough, Yolanda Miley, Maureen Morgan, Jovito Pagkalinawan, Monica Reece, Julie Riley, Martin Smith

Acknowledgments

Excerpts from the English translation of the *Catechism of the Catholic Church* for use in the United States of America, © 1994, United States Catholic Conference, Inc.—Libreria Editrice Vaticana. Used with permission.

Scripture excerpts are taken from the *New American Bible* with *Revised New Testament and Psalms* Copyright © 1991, 1986, 1970, Confraternity of Christian Doctrine, Inc., Washington, DC. Used with permission. All rights reserved. No part of the *New American Bible* may be reproduced by any means without permission in writing from the copyright owner.

Excerpts from the English translation of *Rite of Baptism for Children* © 1969, International Committee on English in the Liturgy, Inc. (ICEL); excerpts from the English translation of *Lectionary for Mass* © 1969, 1981, ICEL; excerpts from the English translation of *The Roman Missal* © 1973, ICEL; excerpts from the English translation of *Rite of Penance* © 1974, ICEL; excerpts from the English translation of *Rite of Confirmation*, Second Edition © 1975, ICEL; excerpts from the English translation of *A Book of Prayers* © 1982, ICEL; excerpts from the English translation of *Book of Blessings* © 1988, International Committee on English in the Liturgy, Inc. All rights reserved.

Excerpts from *Catholic Household Blessings and Prayers* Copyright © 1988, United States Catholic Conference, Inc., Washington, DC. Used with permission. All rights reserved.

English translation of the Glory to the Father, Lord's Prayer, Apostles' Creed by the International Consultation on English Texts. (ICET)

"We Believe, We Believe in God," © 1979, North American Liturgy Resources (NALR), 5536 NE Hassalo, Portland, OR 97213. All rights reserved. Used with permission. "Yes, We Will Do What Jesus Says," © 1993, Daughters of Charity and Christopher Walker. Published by OCP Publications, 5536 NE Hassalo, Portland, OR 97213. All rights reserved. Used with permission. "We Celebrate with Joy," © 2000, Carey Landry. Published by OCP Publications, 5536 NE Hassalo, Portland, OR 97213. All rights reserved. Used with permission. "We Come to Ask Forgiveness," © 1986, Carey Landry and North American Liturgy Resources. All rights reserved. "Stay Awake," © 1988, 1989, 1990, Christopher Walker. Published by OCP Publications, 5536 NE Hassalo, Portland, OR 97213. All rights reserved. Used with permission. "We Remember You," © 1999, Bernadette Farrell. Published by OCP Publications, 5536 NE Hassalo, Portland, OR 97213. Used with permission. "God Is Here," © 1990, Carey Landry and North American Liturgy Resources (NALR), 5536 NE Hassalo, Portland, OR 97213. All rights reserved. Used with permission. "Alleluia, We Will Listen," © 1997, Paul Inwood. Published by OCP Publications, 5536 NE Hassalo, Portland, OR 97213. All rights reserved. Used with permission. "A Gift from Your Children," © 1992, Nancy Bourassa and Carey Landry. All rights reserved. "Jesus, You Are Bread for Us," © 1988, Christopher Walker. Published by OCP Publications, 5536 NE Hassalo, Portland, OR 97213. All rights reserved. Used with permission. "Take the Word of God with You," text © 1991, James Harrison. Music © 1991, Christopher Walker. Text and music published by OCP Publications, 5536 NE Hassalo, Portland, OR 97213. All rights reserved. Used with permission. "We Are Yours, O Lord," © 1996, Janet Vogt. Published by OCP Publications, 5536 NE Hassalo, Portland, OR 97213. All rights reserved. Used with permission. "Alleluia, We Will Listen," © 1997, Paul Inwood. Published by OCP Publications, 5536 NE Hassalo, Portland, OR 97213. All rights reserved. Used with permission. "God Has Made Us a Family," © 1986, Carey Landry and North American Liturgy Resources (NALR), 5536 NE Hassalo, Portland, OR 97213. All rights reserved. Used with permission. "Rejoice in the Lord Always," this arrangement © 1975, North American Liturgy Resources. All rights reserved. "Sing Hosanna," © 1997, Jack Miffleton. Published by OCP Publications, 5536 NE Hassalo, Portland, OR 97213. All rights reserved. Used with permission. "Litany of Saints," © 1992, John Schiavone. Published by OCP Publications, 5536 NE Hassalo, Portland, OR 97213. All rights reserved. Used with permission. "A Circle of Love," © 1991, Felicia Sandler. Published by OCP Publications. All rights reserved. Used with permission. "This Is the Day," Text: Irregular; Based on Psalm 118:24; adapt. by Les Garrett. Text and music © 1967, Scripture in Song (a division of Integrity Music, Inc.). All rights reserved.

Catechesis Tradendae, On Catechesis in Our Time, Apostolic Exhortation, Pope John Paul II, October 16, 1979

Evangelii Nuntiandi, On Evangelization in the Modern World, Apostolic Exhortation, Pope Paul VI, December 8, 1975

Letter of His Holiness Pope John Paul II to Artist, April 4, 1999

Redemptoris Missio, On the Permanent Validity of the Church's Missionary Mandate, Encyclical Letter, Pope John Paul II, December 7, 1990

Ecclesia in America, The Church in America, Post-Synodal Apostolic Exhortation, Pope John Paul II, January 22, 1999

Lumen Gentium, Dogmatic Constitution on the Church, Pope Paul VI, November 21, 1964